WITHDRAWN

This is the first book to focus on the economic and social forces which shaped American theatre throughout its two-hundred-and-fifty-year history. The collection of essays, written by leading theatre historians and critics of the American theatre, represents a variety of methodologies and approaches and reflects the disparity and diversity of the social and economic issues which have molded the cultural heritage of America. Arranged chronologically, the volume explores such topics as anti-theatrical legislation in colonial America; the theatre's response to slavery, prostitution, alcoholism, and women's rights; the significance of black American musical comedy; women managers in nineteenth-century American theatre; economic welfare in the Federal Theatre Project; theatre nostalgia during the Reagan era; and contemporary issues of multiculturalism in today's theatre. Alone or as a collection, the essays will stimulate discussions concerning the traditionally held views of America's theatrical heritage.

The book will be of interest to scholars and students of American theatre and social and cultural history.

# THE AMERICAN STAGE

# THE AMERICAN STAGE

*Social and economic issues from the
colonial period to the present*

EDITED BY

RON ENGLE and TICE L. MILLER

**CAMBRIDGE**
UNIVERSITY PRESS

Published by the Press Syndicate of the University of Cambridge
The Pitt Building, Trumpington Street, Cambridge, CB2 IRP
40 West 20th Street, New York, NY 10011–4211, USA
10 Stamford Road, Oakleigh, Victoria 3166, Australia

First published 1993

Printed in Great Britain at the University Press, Cambridge

*A catalogue record for this book is available from the British Library*

*Library of Congress cataloguing in publication data*

The American stage: social and economic issues from the colonial period to
the present / edited by Ron Engle and Tice L. Miller.
p.   cm.
Includes index.
ISBN 0 521 41238 2 (hardback)
1. Theater and society – United States. 2. Theater – Economic aspects –
United States. 3. Theater – United States – History.
I. Engle, Ron. II. Miller, Tice L.
PN2226.A5 1993
306.4'84'0973–dc20   92–22016 CIP

ISBN 0 521 41238 2 hardback

CE

*Dedicated to the memory of*
*Barnard Hewitt, 1906–1987*

# Contents

# Illustrations

# Contributors

## THE EDITORS

RON ENGLE is the Chester Fritz Distinguished Professor of Theatre Arts at the University of North Dakota at Grand Forks. He is founding editor of *Theatre History Studies*. Engle has published widely in such books as *Shakespeare Around the Globe, American Theatre Companies, Maxwell Anderson and the New York Stage, Foreign Shakespeare*, and has numerous articles in journals including *Theatre Research International, Literature in Performance, Theatre Journal, Studies in American Drama, 1945 to the Present*, among others. He has received grants and fellowships from such agencies as the German Academic Exchange Service, NEH, and the International Research and Exchange Board. In 1989 he was guest Professor in the Institut für Theaterwissenschaft at Munich University in Germany. His forthcoming book *Shakespeare Festivals and Companies: An International Guide*, co-edited with Dan Watermeier and Felicia Londré, is being published by Greenwood Press.

TICE L. MILLER is Professor and Chair of the Department of Theatre Arts and Dance at the University of Nebraska–Lincoln. He is author of *Bohemians and Critics* (1981), Associate Editor of *Shakespeare Around the Globe* (1986), Advisory Editor and contributor to *The Cambridge Guide to World Theatre* (1988), and co-editor with Don B. Wilmeth of the forthcoming *Cambridge Guide to American Theatre*. He has published in *Theatre Journal, Theatre History Studies, Nineteenth-Century Theatre, Theatre Survey* and others. He is a member of the Editorial Board of *Theatre History Studies* and founding Board Member of the Executive Committee of the Mid-America Theatre Conference. He recently organized a cultural exchange program of American drama which toured *A Streetcar Named Desire* to Japan.

THE CONTRIBUTORS

STEPHEN M. ARCHER is Professor of Theatre at the University of Missouri–Columbia. He has recently published articles on American theatre in *Theatre History Studies* and forthcoming is a book *Junius Brutus Booth: Theatrical Promethean* (Southern Illinois Press), and the 3rd edition of his textbook *How Theatre Happens.*

ROSEMARIE K. BANK has published widely in *Theatre Journal, Nineteenth-Century Theatre, Theatre History Studies, Essays in Theatre, Theatre Research International, Journal of Dramatic Theory and Criticism,* among others. She has delivered numerous papers at national and international conferences and is current President of the American Theatre and Drama Society.

OSCAR G. BROCKETT is the Z. T. Scott Professor of Drama at the University of Texas at Austin. He is the author of numerous books including *History of the Theatre,* now in its sixth edition, *The Essential Theatre, The Theatre: An Introduction,* and *Century of Innovation* with Robert Findlay. He is the recipient of numerous fellowships, achievement awards, grants, and honors by professional organizations.

MARVIN CARLSON is the Sidney E. Cohn Professor of Theatre and Comparative Literature and Executive Officer of the Theatre Program at the Graduate Center of the City University of New York. He is the author of a variety of books on theatre history and theory, including *Places of Performance* and *Theatre Semiotics: Signs of Life.*

PETER A. DAVIS is Associate Professor of Theatre History at the University of Illinois at Urbana. He has published on early American theatre in *Theatre Journal, Theatre History Studies, Theatre Survey, Theatre Research International, Nineteenth-Century Theatre,* among others. His book *An Industrious Art: Readings in Early American Theatre History through the Nineteenth Century* is being published by Greenwood Press.

ERROL HILL is Professor of Drama and Oratory, Emeritus, at Dartmouth College, Hanover, New Hampshire. His books include *The Trinidad Carnival* (1972); *The Theatre of Black America* (1980); *Shakespeare in Sable* (1984); and *The Jamaican Stage, 1682–1900* (1992).

MARGARET KNAPP, Associate Professor in Theatre at Arizona State University, has published numerous articles in *Theatre Journal, Theatre History Studies, Journal of American Drama and Theatre, Journal of Popular Culture, Journal of American Culture*, among others. She is co-author with Steve Hart of *The Aunchant and Famous Cittie: David Rogers and the Chester Mystery Plays* and author of the forthcoming *Inventing Times Square*.

STEPHEN LANGLEY, author of *Theatre Management and Production in America* and *Jobs in Arts and Media Management*, is a former managing director of the Falmouth (MA) Playhouse and the Brooklyn College Center for the Performing Arts, where he is now Professor of Theatre and Director of the MFA Performing Arts Management Program. He received his Ph.D. in Theatre from the University of Illinois in 1966.

FELICIA HARDISON LONDRÉ is Curators' Professor of Theatre at the University of Missouri, Kansas City, and Dramaturg for the Missouri Repertory Theatre. Her books include *Tennessee Williams, Tom Stoppard, Federico García Lorca* and her recent *The History of World Theatre: From the English Restoration to the Present* (1991). She is also a playwright and translator of plays from French, Spanish, and Russian.

BRUCE McCONACHIE teaches Theatre and American Studies at the College of William and Mary. His books include *Theatre for Working Class Audiences in the United States, 1830–1980* co-edited with D. Friedman and *Interpreting the Theatrical Past* co-edited with Thomas Postlewait. He has published numerous articles on American theatre and theatre historiography.

DOUGLAS McDERMOTT is Professor of Drama at California State University , Stanislaus. He has published in numerous journals such as *Theatre Survey* and *Modern Drama*, and contributed to *American Theatre Companies*, ed. by W. Durham, and *The Cambridge Guide to World Theatre*. He is also editorial associate for *Theatre West: Image and Impact*.

BROOKS McNAMARA is Professor of Performance Studies in the Tisch School of the Arts at New York University and Director of the Shubert Archive. He has published eight books on theatre, including the recent *The Shuberts of Broadway* (1990). He has been a Fulbright Scholar and a Guggenheim Fellow.

WALTER J. MESERVE, Distinguished Professor of Theatre and English, Graduate School, CUNY, has published fourteen books and is writing a six-volume history of *The Drama of the American People*, including *An Emerging Entertainment* (1977) and *Heralds of Promise* (1986). He is also co-editor of *The Journal of American Drama and Theatre*.

THOMAS POSTLEWAIT, Indiana University, is author of *Prophet of the New Drama: William Archer and the Ibsen Campaign*, co-editor of *Interpreting the Theatrical Past*, and general editor of the series "Studies in Theatre History and Culture" for the University of Iowa Press.

VERA MOWRY ROBERTS is Professor Emeritus of Theatre, Hunter College and the Graduate School, City University of New York. She is author of three books and many articles. Currently she is co-editor of *The Journal of American Drama and Theatre*.

CHARLES SHATTUCK, Professor Emeritus of the University of Illinois at Urbana, was granted the first George Freedley Memorial Award, and is author of eleven books on the theatre, including *The Shakespeare Promptbooks* (1969), *The Hamlet of Edwin Booth* (1969), and most recently two volumes of *Shakespeare on the American Stage* (1976/87).

RONALD H. WAINSCOTT is Associate Professor and Graduate Chair, Department of Theatre and Dance, at the University of Nebraska–Lincoln. He is author of *Staging O'Neill: The Experimental Years: 1920–1934* and various articles on American theatre and drama between the world wars.

DANIEL J. WATERMEIER is Professor of Theatre at the University of Toledo. He is author of the books *Between Actor and Critic* and *Edwin Booth's Performances*. He has published widely on American theatre in *Theatre Journal*, *Theatre History Studies*, *Theatre Studies*, among others. He has been a recipient of a Guggenheim Fellowship and a Folger Shakespeare Library Fellowship

DON B. WILMETH, Professor of Theatre and English at Brown University and Curator of the H. Adrian Smith Collection of Conjuring Books and Magicana. He is author of numerous articles and books, including *George Frederick Cooke*, *Mud Show: American Tent Circus Life*, and *American and English Popular Enter-*

*tainment.* He is co-editor of the forthcoming *Cambridge Guide to American Theatre.*

BARRY B. WITHAM is the executive Director of the University of Washington School of Drama. His publications on American and English theatre have appeared in a variety of books and journals, including *Uncle Sam Presents.* From 1985 to 1989 he served as dramaturg for the Seattle Repertory Theatre.

ALAN WOODS is Director of the Jerome Lawrence and Robert E. Lee Theatre Research Institute at Ohio State University and Director of Graduate Studies in the Department of Theatre. Former editor of *Theatre Journal,* he has published widely, and is active in Audio Description of live theatre for the visually impaired.

# Preface

This collection of essays is an attempt by editors and contributors to shed some light on how economic and social forces have shaped the American theatre in its 250-year history. Written by theatre historians, the essays are arranged chronologically from the colonial theatre to the present day. They represent a variety of methodologies, historiographical approaches, and styles, and reflect the disparity and diversity of social and economic issues which have molded our cultural heritage. The essays are the product of original research, factual in nature and intended for both the scholar and the student of American culture.

In the Introduction, Oscar Brockett provides a brief overview of the field of American theatre scholarship. Doug McDermott argues in the first essay that from its beginnings, the organization of the American theatre was interrelated with that of other social institutions, and reflected the kind of social control people desired. Peter Davis explains that business interests and anti-British sentiments are more important than religious reasons for anti-theatrical legislation in colonial America. Rosemarie Bank, Bruce McConachie and Walter Meserve reflect on how the theatre responded to mid-nineteenth-century social issues such as slavery, prostitution, alcoholism and women's rights, with Bank focused on how such issues are framed for discussion. Vera Roberts considers the success of women managers in the nineteenth-century American theatre.

The following three essays concern the latter 1800s and are more specifically focused. Marvin Carlson considers the American playbill or program as "an important record of changing social and economic forces operative in the theatre." Errol Hill explores the contribution of a sister performance act to Black American musical comedy. Brooks McNamara reviews the publishing history of popular entertainment including minstrel guides, gag books, joke books, sketches and short plays as a reflection of social concerns. Acting as a bridge into the twentieth century, Felicia Londré points up the fact that turn-of-the-century women playwrights could earn large sums of money but were presented in the press within their social roles as mothers and wives.

Moving into the twentieth century, Steve Archer provides a colorful account of the Bernhardt 1905–06 Farewell Tour which made a great amount of money and pitted the Theatrical Syndicate and Shuberts against one another. Ron Wainscott explains how the American theatre treated business and commercialism in the 1920s. Charles Shattuck's essay is a paean to a now forgotten book about the theatre, *Quicksilver* (1942) by Fitzroy Davis, which explores the social workings of the American theatre in the 1930s. Barry Witham explores the "complex system of economic welfare" in relation to the Federal Theatre Project in the 1930s. And Dan Watermeier analyzes the economic failure of the American Repertory Theatre (1946–47).

The final four essays focus on the last forty years of American theatre. Tom Postlewait argues that recent theatre autobiographies are framed with certain progressive values in mind, specifically an attitude towards Hollywood. Alan Woods points to an American theatre of nostalgia and entertainment in the 1980s, a direct reflection of the Reagan Revolution. Peggy Knapp analyzes the "assumptions, methodologies, and rhetorical strategies" utilized in the study of American theatre economics. And Stephen Langley considers how an ethnically diverse and highly technological population will affect the theatre of the twenty-first century. In the bibliography, Don Wilmeth provides a checklist of important books on American theatre.

This collection of essays is also intended to provide the basis for further study and research into the development of American theatre as a reflection of our cultural history. Alone or as a collection, the essays will stimulate discussions concerning the traditionally held views of America's theatrical heritage.

RON ENGLE
TICE L. MILLER

# Acknowledgements

We would like to express our gratitude to our colleagues involved in the planning of this book: Don Wilmeth, Steve Archer, Bob Graves, Felicia Londré, and Dan Watermeier; to others for their encouragement and advice including Marvin Carlson, Alan Andrews, George Glenn, Francis Hodge, Gerald Kahan, Richard Toscan, Richard Moody, Joseph Roach, and Andrew Tsubaki; and to Oscar Brockett for graciously writing the Introduction.

We owe a debt of gratitude to those who handled the correspondence, and helped in the preparation of the manuscript: Pat Douglas and Layne Ehlers at Nebraska, and Barbara Engle in North Dakota. Thanks are also due to our editor at Cambridge University Press, Sarah Stanton, for her encouragement and advice.

On 21 September 1992 Charles Shattuck died before he had a chance to see this work in print. We believe he would have been pleased with the result and are grateful for his inspiration.

And finally we want to express our gratitude to our mentor and teacher, the late Barnard Hewitt, for imparting to us the importance of American theatre history.

# Introduction: American theatre history scholarship

*Oscar G. Brockett*

As a field of scholarly research, American theatre history is primarily a twentieth-century development, having flourished especially during the post-World War II era. This does not mean that no American theatre history was written prior to the twentieth century but rather that the nature of the writing and the circumstances under which it was done differed markedly from those of more recent times.

Little American theatre history published during the nineteenth century was the work of academic scholars. Most was written by actors, managers, or critics, and much of what they had to say was based on memory and personal experience. The earliest work of importance, William Dunlap's *A History of the American Theatre* (New York, 1832), is typical of many nineteenth-century accounts in terms of scope and sources of evidence. Despite its title, the book's primary focus is theatre in New York from the 1780s to 1812 (when Dunlap retired from management), and while much of the account concerning Dunlap's own theatre is accurate, being based primarily on his diaries, the treatment of other topics is often highly inaccurate, depending heavily on memory, hearsay; and anecdote. Writing with limited evidence was perhaps inevitable in the nineteenth century, since there were no major libraries or comprehensive archives; those who wrote about American theatre had little choice but to rely on personal experience, local materials, and the accounts (oral or written) of others. It is probably for this reason that most works about American theatre written during the nineteenth century are local histories or personal memoirs. Among these, some of the best known are William W. Clapp, Jr.'s *A Record of the Boston Stage* (1853); Charles Durang's "The Philadelphia Stage" (a series of articles in the *Philadelphia Sunday Dispatch*, 1854–60); William B.

I

Wood's *Personal Recollections of the Stage* (1855), and Solomon F. Smith's *Theatrical Management in the West and South for Thirty Years* (1868).

Another factor that influenced writing during most of the nineteenth century was the lack of emphasis either by authors or readers on factual accuracy (except in a broad sense). Objectivity and verified fact, major expectations in historical writing through much of the twentieth century, were not prime considerations of most nineteenth-century writers about the theatre. Readers of books or articles about theatre expected to be entertained, and authors sought to meet this expectation through the liberal use of anecdotes, many borrowed from other times or places and reworked to fit the persons or situation at hand. This is not to deny the significance of such writing. It tells much about the personalities and conditions of performance, as well as the assumptions, aspirations, and expectations of the culture within which the theatre existed. But inaccuracies and personal biases in the accounts have made later historians view the works skeptically and seek independent verification of much that is reported in them.

As time went by, the geographic scope of American theatre history continued to grow. It is probably not surprising then that the first comprehensive history of the American theatre, Arthur Hornblow's two-volume *A History of the Theatre in America from Its Beginnings to the Present Time*, did not appear until 1919, just as the American theatre was beginning to gain international stature. By that time, several developments had created conditions that would alter the dominant mode of writing about the American theatre, although works by critics, actors, and other theatrical personnel continued to be the norm until around 1930 (and the most popular strand to the present).

Among the new developments, perhaps the most important were changes in American higher education, ultimately the primary impetus to theatre history's acceptance as a discipline. Prior to the Civil War, American colleges confined themselves almost entirely to undergraduate education and a very limited curriculum emphasizing classical languages and literature. But by 1860 growing interest in scientific and technological concerns had created a demand for training with more pragmatic goals. This demand motivated Congress's passage of the Morrill Act (1862), which provided financial support and official sanction for more comprehensive American institutions (that is, universities), the first of which, Cornell, was founded in 1865. Others followed quickly thereafter. Instruction, however, remained primarily at the undergraduate level until 1876, when Johns Hopkins University was created to provide graduate education (its undergraduate program was added later) based on the German plan and leading to the Ph.D. degree. By the end of the nineteenth century, the assumptions on which twentieth-century research universities have built were in place: higher education should be open to new disciplines; a university of stature must provide advanced, specialized training in a variety of disciplines; undertaking research and making the results known (normally through publication) are both the goals and measures of worth for specialized study; only those persons with advanced degrees and qualifications established through research and publication should be employed to give specialized graduate instruction.

Although many new disciplines soon found their way into the university curriculum, theatre history did so only gradually. It gained its first tentative foothold within literature departments as an adjunct of drama, which itself had won acceptance originally only because of the dominant role of Greek and Latin. During the late nineteenth century such modern "classical" writers as Shakespeare, Molière, and Goethe gained acceptance, and in the 1890s Brander Matthews, at Columbia University, became the first American to hold the title Professor of Dramatic Literature. Not until the early twentieth century, however, was American drama considered a suitable topic for university study. Arthur Hobson Quinn at the University of Pennsylvania probably did most to win admission of American drama into university curricula through his teaching and his *A History of the American Drama from the Beginning to the Civil War* (1923) and *A History of the American Drama from the Civil War to the Present Day* (1927). Acceptance of American drama inevitably led to concern for the theatrical conditions under which the plays were performed, and these concerns eventuated in English departments acknowledging the suitability of dissertations on American theatre history.

The acceleration of interest in American theatre history after World War I was also owing to the establishment of Theatre departments, usually in combination with Speech. Since most of these new departments were not permitted to teach dramatic literature (which remained with English), they often turned to theatre

history for research topics, especially after 1930 when a few universities began to offer doctorates in Theatre (Iowa, Cornell, Wisconsin, Columbia, and Louisiana State University were doing so before
1940). After World War II, the number grew rapidly, and by the
late 1960s some thirty-nine universities were offering doctorates in
Theatre. Subsequently, the number increased, but by 1990 it had
been reduced to thirty-nine once more.

Doctoral programs, both in Theatre and in American Literature,
created the conditions that made American theatre history acceptable as a legitimate scholarly field. They did so in part by increasing
the demand for persons with the specialized knowledge required for
teaching and supervising research in this field and by insisting that
these persons continue to demonstrate their qualifications through
their own research and publication. Writing about American
theatre history was transformed, tentatively after World War I and
aggressively after World War II, from a popular form into an
academic field in which researchers wrote primarily for other
academics, and in which publication became a requisite for employment, tenure, and promotion in universities, which had become the
base for most of those who considered themselves theatre historians.

The nature of these writings differed considerably from those that
dominated pre-World War I years. Standards of scholarship had
become more strenuous as the scientific mode had achieved dominance. Those who wished to be taken seriously were now expected to
provide documentation for all factual information and conclusions.
This, in turn, meant doing much more meticulous research, seeking
out primary evidence wherever it might be located. Newly established theatre collections (among them the Harvard Theatre Collection, which took shape between 1901 and 1917; the Brander
Matthews Dramatic Museum, founded at Columbia in 1911; and
the New York Public Library Theatre Collection, founded in 1931)
facilitated research, as did numerous state and local archives and
historical societies. Among the most favored topics for research
beginning in the 1930s were histories of theatre in restricted
American locales over a limited time span. Such studies accumulated valuable factual information about theatrical history in
virtually every part of the United States. Unfortunately, most did
not connect their findings with what was going on elsewhere, with
events before or after the time period being studied, or with the
cultural forces within which the theatre existed. Anecdotal material,

especially if its purpose was to be entertaining, was usually excluded. Few of these studies could be read for pleasure. Nevertheless, excellent studies of American theatre history, based on impeccable research and providing illuminating interpretations, were written by persons from a variety of fields – theatre, literature, history – in the period between 1930 and 1980 (David Grimsted's *Melodrama Unveiled: American Theatre and Culture, 1800–1850* [1968] comes readily to mind). Professional associations also established journals to encourage publication of scholarly writing. *Educational Theatre Journal* (of which Barnard Hewitt was the first editor) was founded by the American Educational Theatre Association in 1949, and *Theatre Survey* (published by the American Society for Theatre Research) was established in 1960.

Another phase in writing about American theatre history began around 1980 as theoretical issues came to the fore. Semiotics, feminist theory, poststructuralism, new historicism, and variations on these and other critical modes came increasingly to serve as frames within which to view and interpret historical subjects. Some advocates of these approaches denounced historical work of the preceding period as being overtly constrained by a belief in the possibility of objectivity and factuality. The conscious mingling of theory and history became clearly evident in the majority of articles published in *Theatre Journal* (which in 1979 superseded *Educational Theatre Journal*) and in papers presented at meetings of the American Society for Theatre Research. Many of the varied approaches that emerged and were now used in writing about American theatre history are described in *Interpreting the Theatrical Past: Essays in the Historiography of Performance* (1989), edited by Thomas Postlewait and Bruce A. McConachie. Some of those described in that volume are also effectively applied in some of the essays that Ron Engle and Tice L. Miller have assembled here. Perhaps most of all the essays that follow demonstrate how older and newer methodologies now coexist in the academic discipline that American theatre history has become. They also serve as a measure of how far the discipline has developed since its tentative beginnings in the early nineteenth century.

# CHAPTER I

# The theatre and its audience: changing modes of social organization in the American theatre

## Douglas McDermott

Theatre in America serves as an example of the way theatrical organization encodes and communicates social organization to its audience. At certain moments theatrical organization changed in America, and these changes coincided with parallel shifts in the organization of the nation's other social institutions (i.e., church, government). Moreover, such changes seem directly related to changing attitudes about the sort of social control people would accept. Hence, the historical development of American society can be traced in the shifting tides of theatrical fortune, and changes in theatrical operation can be understood as an essential part of the way in which live theatre performs a social function for its audience.

When professional theatre came to America in the eighteenth century, it was organized according to established British custom. Following the model described in John Locke's *Second Treatise of Government*, the basic unit of social organization was an autonomous group of adults who voluntarily entered into an agreement to cooperate for the common good, known variously as a partnership, a colony, or a congregation.[1] Members were accepted because of common qualifications and interest: money and profit in a business venture, health and ambition in a colony, conversion and salvation in a religious congregation. Each was hierarchically organized, the English class structure replicating itself in designating general partners, governors, and elders as responsible for control within their respective types of organization.

This structure contained an inherent tension over the extent to which the governed participated in governance. The conflict Locke resolved theoretically, proved less tractable practically. Matters were most easily managed in business, the partner's influence in the operation of the enterprise being proportionate to his investment. The problem was harder to resolve in other types of organization

6

because the nature of the individual's contribution was less easily measured. In politics a man's worth, and therefore his ability to vote, was initially measured by his wealth, but a growing and mobile population repeatedly compelled governments to lower the amount of wealth necessary to purchase the right to vote, until it was eliminated altogether by the end of the nineteenth century.

Similar population increases and relocations created pressure for democratization within the religious congregations that founded colonies in New England.[2] While the population grew, the number of the elect, from whom and by whom ruling elders were elected, did not. Fewer and fewer in the second generation could prove the experience of salvation necessary for baptism and full congregational membership. Thus the mass of colonists were excluded from the exercise of authority in the colony which they supported with their taxes. Consequently, between 1640 and 1740 Puritan practice was modified to extend a form of franchise to an increasing number. This process culminated in the religious revival known as the Great Awakening in which preachers baptized all who expressed a desire for inclusion.[3]

A similar process occurred in all the colonies, not just those in New England. The search for prosperity and the availability of free land scattered settlements in every case, straining the original hierarchy and creating a demand for greater representation in government. Moreover, the vulnerability of each colony by itself, as demonstrated by the French and Indian Wars, led to widespread toleration and cooperation regardless of differences among the colonies. By the 1760s, they acknowledged a common, if unwritten, belief that those living in the colonies shared certain essential qualities by virtue of living there. The Revolution was the political equivalent of the Great Awakening. Representation was accepted as the principle of governance, and the act of emigration became a profession of faith in a secular covenant in which the republic replaced the congregation and the Constitution replaced the creed.[4]

It is this development from individual experience to corporate acceptance, from hierarchy to representation, from isolated congregation to republic, that constituted a pattern of experience that became the basis of America's myth of origin, and it provides a context for understanding the role of social organization in the theatre's relationship with its audience.

The company of twelve actors Lewis Hallam brought to Virginia in 1752 was similar to earlier congregations. Talent took the place of conversion, lines of acting and shares of receipts functioned as a covenant, and the company, like the congregation, was ruled by its elders, the leading actors. However, the theatrical company did not develop along the same lines as the congregations and colonies. It remained retrograde, an aristocratic hierarchy that only grudgingly accommodated the wishes of its players or its audience.

This is best demonstrated by events of the 1760s. After an initial exploration of audience possibilities in Virginia, Philadelphia, and New York between September 1752 and 1755, the company went to Jamaica where its founder died, and its amalgamation with the Kingston company of David Douglass was confirmed by his marrying Hallam's widow. Under their new proprietor they alternated seasons in North America between the South and the North from 1759 through the spring of 1764, after which they were absent, most likely in Jamaica, for two years.

At one level their peregrinations can be explained as the result of canny management in an attempt to extract maximum profit from the colonial audience. The actors were not skillful enough, their repertory was not varied enough, and the audience was not large or prosperous enough for the players to remain in one place. Thus, movement was the iron law of provincial theatre in America as it was in England. However, the pattern of movement in America was dictated by increasing political resistance to the players. There had always been an economic resistance grounded in the perception that the actors were responsible for a net loss of wealth in the community because they took money away when they left, but a political dimension was added in the 1760s. The actors were all British, and the theatre was organized according to an aristocratic pattern that the Crown wished to sustain in the colonies.

The theatre was not democratizing or changing its way of operating from the pattern of seventeenth-century proprietorship, but religious and political organization in America was changing, and as time passed the theatre seemed increasingly anachronistic. Consequently, in Philadelphia and New York where the agitation for independence was strongest, the theatre met the greatest resistance, while in the South, where the fires of rebellion burned lower, it was more popular; but even there it was most popular in Charleston, the capital of the most conservative colony. Douglass called his company "American" during 1763/64, but the name fooled no one, and the Sons of Liberty burnt the New York theatre during an anti-British riot in 1765.

Douglass was able to bring the players back to North America in 1767 because repeal of the Stamp Act temporarily ameliorated political hostility to British institutions, but after 1770 the company remained in the South; and in spite of elaborate plans for the season of 1774–75 they did not challenge the Continental Congress's resolution discouraging theatrical entertainments for the duration of the coming conflict. Instead, Douglass and his troupe returned to the haven of Jamaica and waited out the Revolution.[5]

While other institutions in the American colonies were changing their mode of organization and operation, becoming increasingly democratic and "American" during the eighteenth century, the theatrical company was not. It remained resolutely British in personnel and aristocratic in government, and the American audience's increasing resistance to it can, in part at least, be attributed to this lack of change. Would-be Americans witheld patronage in spite of the introduction of new faces and new plays because they did not wish to validate the social model and company exemplified, one increasingly inappropriate for the conditions of settlement in North America.

The corollary to this hypothesis would be the return of popularity as the result of a change to an organizational structure perceived as democratic or representative, therefore American; and that, in fact, is what happened between the Revolution and the Civil War. The change was caused by two related developments. First, continuing population growth and territorial expansion created multiple locations which could support theatres without reference to each other. After the Revolution America's population doubled every ten years, and settlement spilled across the Allegheny Mountains and beyond the Mississippi River. In the area of the original colonies between 1792 and 1795, theatres were established in Philadelphia, Richmond, Charleston, Providence, and Boston. After the War of 1812, the new western cities of Pittsburgh, Cleveland, Detroit, Louisville, Nashville, New Orleans, St. Louis, and San Francisco, along with some smaller towns, became homes for resident theatres. At the same time, certain actors became more popular than the companies that employed them. The proliferation of theatres allowed these actors to move from one to another, dictating the choice of plays and division of the profits to the resident managers.

The process was set in motion when Thomas Wignell and Mrs. Morris left the Old American Company in 1791 to found a theatre in Philadelphia. The potential of the star system was first exploited by Thomas Abthorpe Cooper, originally hired by Wignell as leading tragedian in Philadelphia, who found that he could split his time between that theatre and the one in New York to the increased profit of all concerned.[6] The mature pattern of star management was created in 1810 by New York lawyer Stephen Price, a partner in the management of the New York company, who imported George Frederick Cooke, leading tragic actor from London's Covent Garden Theatre, and after his debut in New York franchised his appearances elsewhere.[7]

By 1820 starring actors controlled the operation of the American theatre. In its development the star system represented the shift from independent communities, the members of which depended on each other for mutual support, to pre-industrial entrepreneurship, in which vigorous individuals solicited the attention and loyalty of large numbers of others for personal profit. Like political office holders and revivalist preachers, the stars were representatives of the public's aspirations and values. The advent of the star system in the theatre paralleled the rise in popularity of individual politicians, such as Andrew Jackson and Daniel Webster, and preachers, such as Lyman Beecher and Charles Grandison Finney.[8]

Moreover, just as different political and religious figures appealed to different elements of the population, so did stars. In addition to the stars of tragedy and manners comedy, the American theatre saw the development of a wide variety of stars, each of whom specialized in a particular regional or ethnic type of character, such as the Yankee, the Frontiersman, the Bowery B'hoy, the Tomboy, or the African-American. Perhaps the most striking example of the star actor as representative of audience values was the rivalry between Edwin Forrest, perceived as a Jacksonian democrat, and William Charles Macready, perceived as an urban whig, which resulted in the Astor Place Riot of 1849. It was clear to all in both the press and the street that attendance at a performance by either man was an act of social and political validation.[9] The irony was, however, that the disagreement was over who (person, party, and class) represented the majority interest, and who, consequently, should control the system. There was no disagreement over the desirability of the system itself, and audience attendance validated it in both cases.

The sheer scope of America after the Civil War necessitated a change in the way in which the nation was organized. The previously isolated frontier was integrated into the economic and political geography by the expansion of the railroad and the telegraph. The population tripled between 1865 and 1915 and the Gross National Product increased by 650 percent. Matters became too complex for individuals, however brilliant, to deal with; orderly process required groups of people specializing in particular aspects of society.

In business the individual factory owner specialized his production process as much as possible because the greatest efficiency was achieved by having workers repeat a single task. As workers became specialists they made fewer mistakes and quantity and quality increased. In politics the parallel move was to the specialization of party politics represented by the urban system of wards and bosses.

The only drawback to this system of organization was repeated episodes of boom and bust. People generally agreed that they wanted such fluctuations in the economy eliminated. The obvious answer was to eliminate or control excessive competition, which was accomplished during the 1880s and 1890s by combining competing enterprises into monopolistic syndicates or trusts in manufacture, agriculture, transportation, labor unions, disaster relief organizations, professional associations, and entertainment.[10]

In the theatre the equivalent organizational shift was to the combination company. The gifted individual was given a new context in which to appear. The combinations of the 1860s were comprised of the star and supporting players in a limited repertory with casts completed by actors in the local company. However, the economic depression of the 1870s eliminated almost all resident companies, and combinations were forced to become self-sufficient, requiring nothing but an available stage. These companies normally produced a single play, so the actor played only a single part. Moreover, the distribution of population and the efficiency of the railroads meant that a single play combination could live for years by moving from one place to another. Actors became specialists, not in a single type of character, but in a single character. Competition among these companies was regulated by the creation of theatrical monopolies which were alliances between talent-booking agencies and theatre owners.[11]

Monopoly had remarkable public support in America during the second half of the nineteenth century. Because the cost of living, measured in 1860 dollars, declined every year between 1865 and 1895, Americans identified monopoly with prosperity and believed that laissez faire economics was prerequisite to the system of values popularly expressed in the McGuffy Readers and the novels of Horatio Alger. Consequently, while the mode of social organization changed with the conditions of the nation, shifting from the charismatic individual to the monopolistic organization of specialists, the change was seen as evolutionary, necessary, and beneficial. Change was the product of progress, and all institutions organized in the appropriate way retained their popularity.

Monopoly had its liabilities, however, and in the first decade of the twentieth century people complained and demanded that monopoly be restrained. Immediately prior to World War I, monopoly, present in every aspect of American society, lost its credibility, and that, in turn, was reflected in a loss of theatrical popularity. Thus, American theatre and society went through a crisis similar to the one preceding the Revolution.

Economic monopoly shifted political power. Between the Civil War and World War I, the individual ceased to be the basic political unit. The Jeffersonian ideal had been the literate yeoman farmer, economically self-sufficient and able to enter into social contracts with others for mutual benefit. The problem was that most people in America no longer lived on farms. Because of technological innovation and industrial expansion, the average worker could find a better-paying job in a factory than on a farm, and non-farmers accounted for the larger share of the Gross National Product. Thus, as the farm gave way to the factory, the individual gave way to the group as the basic unit of political organization, and groups of wage-earners could be managed. Economic and political bosses became the power brokers of the majority.

In an attempt to re-enfranchise the individual, reformers established the primary election in place of the party caucus, followed by the Constitutional provision for the direct election of Congress. Referendum and initiative were also introduced at local levels, and political power began passing into the hands of men and women determined to change the system. The presidency was dominated between 1896 and 1915 by Theodore Roosevelt and Woodrow Wilson, both of whom were reforming governors before taking national office. This shift of political power gave the reformers some control over economics. They created legislative and administrative tools, such as the Clayton Act of 1914, which not only strengthened and broadened the Sherman Anti-Trust Act of 1905, but which also established the Federal Trade Commission to supplement the efforts of the Interstate Commerce Commission for controlling the exercise of economic power. At the same time the Supreme Court ordered the break-up of American Tobacco (1910) and of Standard Oil (1911). Thus, the nation was set on a course that would lead to modified market capitalism by World War II.[12]

Theatre had been monopolized in the 1890s, and monopoly eventually produced a crisis of popularity in entertainment parallel to that in politics and economics. The situation can be most clearly illustrated in the case of first-class legitimate theatre, monopolized in 1896 by the Theatrical Syndicate and administered by the booking office of Klaw and Erlanger. In their ruthless suppression of competition, Klaw and Erlanger tried to force the brothers Sam, Lee, and J. J. Shubert, theatre owners and Syndicate clients in upstate New York, to curtail activities. Faced with an ultimatum, the brothers declared their independence and began to compete with the Syndicate in major cities. The resulting war between the two lasted from 1905 to 1913 when a truce was arranged. By then the damage had been done.

Competition caused both managements to reduce expenses as much as possible. The public blamed the resulting decline in production quality on the monopolists. After 1900 the number of combinations on the road no longer increased, as it had each season for the previous decade, and after 1905 it began to decline sharply. By 1915 there were only one-third as many companies on the road as at the beginning of the century. Audiences rejected monopolized theatre, choosing instead to attend productions by independent local stock companies or to patronize neighborhood movie theatres.[13]

By 1915 the American public was rejecting monopoly as a principle of social organization because of the abuses such concentrations of power produced in politics, economics, and entertainment. Monopoly was gradually replaced by the conglomerate – commonly owned but otherwise unrelated businesses, connected only through a corporate structure, and dependent on the technology of communication. In politics, media performance replaced personal appearance, signalled by Franklin Roosevelt's use of radio to sell his New Deal compared to Woodrow Wilson's whistle stop tour to sell the League of Nations. In entertainment, film and radio replaced live dramatic and variety performance for the majority of the audience.

As a consequence, live theatre became the property of a minority audience drawn primarily from the upper-middle class, a group increasingly opposed to the corporate mode of organization. As the century approached mid-point, many people saw the corporation as faceless, autonomous, and unresponsive to the needs of the country. Theoretical calls for change were crystallized by the inroads of foreign companies on America's domestic market. At the same time that American industry seemed to lose its momentum, the nation found itself mired in an unpopular war and unable to fulfill political promises for social reform.[14]

After 1920 theatre became the opposite of what it had been before the Revolution. Then it had been an image of conservatism, struggling against liberalizing, democratizing tendencies. It now became an image of reform, struggling against a conservative corporate society. Its audience rebelled against media as a non-participatory form of entertainment just as many citizens sought an alternative to forms of social organization that, no matter how "representative," seemed equally non-participatory. In this respect theatre emulated the managerial and political alternatives articulated in both theory and practice in the 1960s.[15]

This theatrical reorganization took place apart from Broadway. The Shuberts' control of theatre buildings in New York and other major cities, in conjunction with their participation in production, replicated the controlled corporate organization of post-monopoly business and politics. The persistence of live theatre in community and college theatres between the world wars and the creation of Off-Broadway and regional theatre companies after World War II responded to the desire for a more open, responsive, participatory form of organization as a social norm. Not only was it important that theatre be local in its habitation and control, but, for the first time, as a result of media domination of society, it became important that theatre was live, that the audience was seeing real performers rather than reproduced images of them.

The creation and support of regional theatre since the 1920s, whether amateur or professional, required the expenditure of vast amounts of time and money. Such allocation of resources cannot be explained simply in terms of a desire for entertainment. Movies, radio, and television are more efficient and convenient. At a lower admission charge than live theatre, they deliver uniform images of performers' bodies and voices. Brando and Chaplin are more accessible than Booth or Jefferson ever were. The inference is, then, that live theatre persists because it offers an alternative image of society to an audience that desires one. Apart from the content of the script or even the physical presence of the player, the locally organized, intensely participatory live theatrical performance enacts for its audience an alternative to the corporately organized, centrally controlled social norm represented by media. In Kenneth Burke's terms, the attendance at live performance becomes a symbolic act of revolution. The aesthetic becomes the criterion for social revolution because it dissolves not only the commodity basis of society but also the structure of perception that sees the consumption of commodities as essential to social function.[16] The theatre becomes a participatory ritual of common citizenship in a self-governing local republic represented by the theatre company.

## NOTES

1 The best description of social organization in seventeenth-century England remains R. H. Tawney, *Religion and the Rise of Capitalism* (New York: Harcourt Brace, 1926).

2 Andrew Delbanco gives a good account of the economic pressures the new country exerted on its first settlers in *The Puritan Ordeal* (Cambridge, MA: Harvard University Press, 1972), 1–117.

3 Details of the evolution of Puritan belief and practice in America can be found in Perry Miller, *The New England Mind: The Seventeenth Century* (Cambridge, MA: Harvard University Press, 1949); and in Sacvan Bercovitch, *The Puritan Origins of the American Self* (New Haven, CT: Yale University Press, 1975).

4 For the concept of the development from sacred to secular covenant in America I am indebted to Robert N. Bellah, *The Broken Covenant: American Civil Religion in Time of Trial* (New York: Seabury Press, 1975).

5 Details of early American theatrical history can be found in Hugh F. Rankin, *The Theater in Colonial America* (Chapel Hill, NC: University of North Carolina Press, 1965).

6 The best account of the first stirrings of the star system is William Dunlap, *A History of the American Theatre* (New York: J. & J. Harper, 1832).

7 On the development of the star system see Barnard Hewitt, "'King Stephen' of the Park and Drury Lane" in *The Theatrical Manager in*

*England and America: Player of a Perilous Game*, ed. Joseph W. Donohue
(Princeton, NJ: Princeton University Press, 1971), 87–141; and Philip
H. Highfill, "Edmund Simpson's Talent Raid on England in 1818,"
*Theatre Notebook* 12 (1958), 83–91, 130–40; 13 (1959), 7–14.

8 On the development of star politicians and preachers see Arthur M.
Schlesinger, Jr., *The Age of Jackson* (Boston: Little, Brown, 1945) and
Sydney E. Ahlstrom, *A Religious History of the American People* (New
Haven, CT: Yale University Press, 1972), respectively.

9 The politics of audience behavior prior to the Civil War is dealt with by
both Bruce McConachie, "'The Theatre of the Mob': Apocalyptic
Melodrama and Preindustrial Riots in Antebellum New York" in
*Theatre for Working-Class Audiences in the United States, 1830–1980*, ed.
Bruce McConachie and Daniel Friedman (Westport, CT: Greenwood
Press, 1985), 17–46; and David Grimsted, *Melodrama Unveiled: American
Theatre and Culture, 1800–1850* (Chicago: University of Chicago Press,
1968).

10 Monopoly in America is analyzed by Sydney Fine, *Laissez Faire and the
General-Welfare State: A Study of Conflict in American Thought, 1865–1901*
(Ann Arbor, MI: University of Michigan Press, 1956) and Richard
Hofstadter, *The Age of Reform* (New York: Alfred A. Knopf, 1955).

11 The rise of the theatrical combination company is traced by Alfred
Bernheim, *The Business of the Theatre* (New York: Benjamin Blom,
1964). However, important qualifying information is provided by
Rosemarie K. Bank, "A Reconsideration of the Death of Nineteenth-
Century American Repertory Companies and the Rise of the Combination," *Essays in Theatre* 5:1 (November 1986), 61–75; and Peter A.
Davis, "From Stock to Combination: The Panic of 1873 and Its Effects
on the American Theatre Industry," *Theatre History Studies* 8 (1988),
1–9.

12 The reform movement in America is analyzed in Henry F. May, *The
End of American Innocence: A Study of the First Years of Our Own Time,
1912–1917* (New York: Alfred A. Knopf, 1959); and Robert Wiebe, *The
Search for Order, 1877–1920* (New York; Hill and Wang, 1965).

13 The Theatrical Syndicate is chronicled by Monroe Lippman, "The
History of the Theatrical Syndicate: Its Effect Upon the Theatre in
America," Diss., University of Michigan, 1937; and the story of the
Shuberts' rise to power is told by Jerry Stagg, *The Brothers Shubert* (New
York: Random House, 1968). For an account of local resident stock
theatres see Weldon B. Durham, "The Revival and Decline of the
Stock Company Mode of Organization, 1886–1930," *Theatre History
Studies* 6 (1986), 165–88.

14 Peter Drucker analyzes the shortcomings of traditional corporate
capitalism in *The New Society: The Anatomy of the Industrial Order* (New
York: Harper, 1950). For the negative consequences of this sort of
organization see C. Wright Mills, *White Collar* (New York: Oxford

University Press, 1950); and David Riesman, *The Lonely Crowd* (New Haven, CT: Yale University Press, 1951). The resulting impasse in American society is described by Arthur M. Schlesinger, Jr., *The Bitter Heritage: Vietnam and American Democracy, 1944–1966* (Boston: Houghton Mifflin, 1967).

15 A description of organizational alternatives that have evolved in the last twenty years is provided by Gareth Morgan, *Images of Organization* (Beverly Hills, CA: Sage, 1986).

16 For the concept of symbolic action see Kenneth Burke, *The Philosophy of Literary Form*, rev. ed. (New York: Vintage Books, 1957). The most passionate advocate of aesthetics as revolution is Herbert Marcuse, *An Essay on Liberation* (Boston: Beacon Press, 1969).

CHAPTER 2

# Puritan mercantilism and the politics of anti-theatrical legislation in colonial America

*Peter A. Davis*

When the Continental Congress passed legislation calling for the suppression of "shews, plays and other expensive diversions and entertainments" in the autumn of 1774, it was the culmination of almost a century of anti-theatrical sentiment in the colonies that had seen dozens of similar laws against the stage enacted and repealed.[1] But this statute was not the Puritan moral victory that Taubman reductively argues; nor was it a prudent act of propriety in the face of a coming war, as Quinn, Rankin, and Wilson whiggishly contend.[2] As popular and convenient as these views may be, they are simply not supported by the evidence. The act was the result of a long-standing legal tradition, the product of a Puritan mercantile culture that saw theatre as both an economic threat and a symbol of colonial suppression. As a gesture of mercantile defiance, it was crafted out of a legacy of appeasement towards a London-based council of commerce ultimately responsible for colonial legislation and trade. The 1774 statute and its legislative predecessors were not just products of religious fervor or war-time zeal; instead they reflect the colonies' awkward relationship with the Board of Trade and Americans' increasing desire to break their debt-ridden dependence upon British manufactured goods.

Not surprisingly, histories of American theatre fail to go into much detail about the resolution of 1774 and its legal antecedents, leaving readers to draw their own conclusions about the motivations and purposes of these acts. Considering them in simple sequential order gives the misleading sense that the acts were somehow part of an evolving yet singular discourse of displeasure against theatrical amusements based on Puritanical principles of morality and common decency. Hornblow demonstrates this faulty tendency in *A History of the Theatre in America* (1919), when he urges us to remember that the "great majority of the Northern Colonies were bitterly

18

opposed to the playhouse on religious and moral grounds."[3] Such a generalization presages the equally unacceptable practice of randomly juxtaposing religious fervor with anti-theatrical legislation as illustrated in Wilson's *Three Hundred Years of American Theatre.*[4] Viewed individually, the acts present a different set of problems. Without explication of previous legislative attempts, the resolution of 1774, for example, becomes simply an isolated act, an a priori principle of wartime preparation. Similarly, when theatrical historians such as Meserve, Quinn, and Rankin cite the acts without proper context, it creates the impression that some crucial justifications – particularly those focusing on issues of frugality and unnecessary extravagance – are merely euphemisms for Puritan piety and self-restraint.[5]

There is, nonetheless, a modicum of truth in these perceptions. Political historians, including Bernard Bailyn, Daniel J. Boorstin, and Clinton Rossiter, have shown that much of the legislation reflects the pervasive Puritanism which dominated political and social thought in the northern colonies.[6] Acts were framed in Puritan controlled assemblies with the intention of maintaining their distinctive morality within government. But as Bailyn points out, these same legislative members were also largely from the merchant class and as the colonies moved inevitably toward war with England, the concerns were much less with spiritual morality than with commerce and economic viability.[7] Politically driven economic motivations within their temporal contexts are, thus, central to understanding the anti-theatrical movement and the resultant legislation in the American colonies.

Enacting any colonial legislation, including bills against the stage, was a complex and lengthy process. Even so, most colonies attempted to ban theatre in one form or another at least once during the colonial period.[8] Most significant among these acts were those passed in Massachusetts (1699 and 1750), New York (1709), Pennsylvania (1700, 1705, 1710 and 1759), Rhode Island and New Hampshire (1762).[9] Colonial records on this matter in the United States are surprisingly incomplete and scattered. The only depository containing the complete and authoritative collection of legislative acts, as originally submitted to Whitehall by the colonies, is the Public Record Office in London.[10] Material uncovered there in the Colonial Office papers reveals that the timing of each act was far from haphazard and indicates the direct influence of political events

on theatrical endeavors. Furthermore, the progression of anti-
theatrical legislation, though different in each colony, is clearly
traceable and shows the changing colonial attitudes toward theatre
and the troubled economy.

The multi-level colonial legislative process was purposely cum-
bersome and inevitably corrupt. Its design intensified the rift
between colonist and royalist. The principal legislative body was the
provincial assembly, comprised mostly of colonists sympathetic to
the Puritan mercantile perspective, and often hostile toward the
royal governor. Much of the early eighteenth century is characterized by battles between assemblies and governors over administrative salaries and the royal prerogative.[11] Understandably, it was
in the assemblies where most anti-theatrical legislation originated.
The next rung on the legislative ladder was usually the colonial
council, composed of wealthy merchants and royalists, who despite
their close personal ties to the governor could at times enact oppos-
ing legislation. Usually, however, colonial councils – which by and
large reflected the governors' preferences – rejected bills thought to
be anti-prerogative, including those against the theatre. The final
hurdle before enactment was of course the governor; any bill to get
this far usually had his implicit approval. From here the collected
acts were sent to London for review by the Crown. Not all colonies
were required to do so. The early chartered and proprietary colonies
were under no obligation to have their legislation reviewed, a fact
that caused Whitehall continuous frustration and eventually led to
the revoking of charters and the establishment of crown colonies in
most of the former proprietaries.[12] Although this legislative process
varied somewhat from colony to colony and era to era, the three-tier
hierarchy leading to Whitehall was an established part of colonial
law.

Once in London, colonial legislation was not normally subjected
to parliamentary scrutiny, nor was it simply passed to the monarch
for pro forma approval. All submitted acts were handled by an
advisory commission to the Privy Council known as the Board of
Trade, which was established in 1696 by William III in response to
complaints by the mercantile classes that the existing body responsible for such activity (informally known as the Lords of Trade) was
incompetent. Composed entirely of courtiers, the Lords of Trade
were under the direct control of the monarch as an internal commit-

tee of the Privy Council, bypassing Parliament altogether. The combination of the Glorious Revolution and the Anglo-Dutch Wars left the powerful English merchants financially drained and politically agitated. Seizing the opportunity to wrestle control of trade and plantations from the Crown, Parliament passed a series of acts in 1695 designed to weaken the monarch's authority on matters of colonial commerce by establishing, among other things, a parliamentary council of trade. As a result, King William was forced to compromise, creating the Board of Trade (a hybrid version of the parliamentary council) to prevent further erosion of his prerogative and loss of the lucrative plantations.[13]

Like most committees of the British government, the Board of Trade was composed of two factions, real or paid members – generally eight of London's wealthiest and most powerful merchants – and the nominal or ex officio members, who were the principal secretaries of state. The latter were not required to attend meetings and rarely did, but the paid members who were obligated to attend were only marginally better. Thus the board was sanctioned to operate with a quorum of only three under ordinary circumstances. Its sole purpose was to promote commerce and in this regard was charged with three principal tasks: first "to devise means of fostering manufactures that were useful and profitable and to determine how new and profitable manufactures may be introduced"; second, to find gainful employment for the poor; and third, to oversee the administration and profitability of the plantations.[14] All other considerations were subservient to these tasks and any decisions made were only in support of their primary purpose of supporting colonial commerce. They were given control of governors' instructions, served as the clearing house for all official correspondence and complaints, and most significantly were required to review and approve all colonial legislation as a committee of the Privy Council.[15] Clearly the British view of the colonies' relationship to the home country was quite different from that of the colonists.

The Board of Trade viewed the colonies as a two-fold economic entity; first as suppliers of raw materials and second as purchasers of manufactured goods. The colonists, in contrast, saw themselves as the victims of a politically motivated trade imbalance. While not its original intent, the Board of Trade became more than just the guardian of British commercial interests. With its absolute power to

repeal colonial laws, the Board also bore the responsibility of the
social, political and religious welfare of the colonies. The tendency
to politicize business was inevitable.[16]

Once the power of the Board was established, colonial legislators
realized that the framing of their legislation was as important as the
content. The trick to avoiding eventual revocation, the legislators
soon discovered, was to appeal directly to the Board's primary
responsibilities.[17] As a result acts that assemblies believed might be
perceived as being anti-business were usually preceded by introductions that presented the economic effects and benefits before
moral concerns, as in the 1750 Massachusetts Act which argues in
the opening paragraph that it is

for preventing and avoiding the many and great Mischiefs which arise from
publick stage plays, interludes, and other theatrical entertainments, which
not only occasion great and unnecessary expenses, and discourage industry
and frugality, but likewise tend generally to increase Immorality, impiety,
and contempt of religion.[18]

Even more direct is the 1762 New Hampshire Act which includes
the principal justification that "all young countries have more
occasion to incourage a spirit of industry and application to business
than to countenance schemes of amusements and allurements to
pleasure."[19] Such blatant appeasement to mercantile concerns was
not always successful, but the form and practice nonetheless became
an inherent part of colonial legislation as early as 1700.[20] By the
1750s, however, its significance had changed to become a signal of
anti-British sentiment – an appeal for economic and manufacturing
independence.[21]

This fundamental shift in attitude is initially evident in the
grouping of anti-theatrical acts. The earliest (those written between
1699 and 1710) represent in all cases failed attempts to impose moral
restrictions on what the Board of Trade considered to be commercial
prerogatives.[22] The best example is the series of bills passed by the
Pennsylvania Assembly beginning in 1700, all of which were subsequently rejected by the Board of Trade.[23] Each successive act was
progressively diluted until the final act of 1710 fails to mention
theatre altogether. None contains introductory justifications. It
should also be noted that the final bill is titled "An Act against
Riotous Sports, Plays and Games," indicating that the phrase
"plays and games" or "playing and gaming" found in many early
acts does not always indicate theatre. In this case "plays and games"

signifies gambling, card-playing and conjuring tricks – not theatre.[24] The same is true of the well-known Massachusetts Act of 1699 – long considered the first such legislation – which bans

> all rogues, vagabonds and idle persons going about in any town or county begging, or persons using any subtle craft, juggling or unlawful games or plays, or feigning to have knowledge in physiognomy, palmistry, or pretending that they can tell destinies, fortunes or discover where lost or stolen goods may be found.[25]

At no other point in this lengthy act does it mention stage-plays, interludes, masques, disguisings, mummings or any other key terms used to identify true anti-theatrical bills. The use of the word "play" in this manner can be traced in American legislation as far back as 1646 when Massachusetts passed an act against "Gaming & dancing," ordering that "no Person shall henceforth, use the said Games of shufle-board [sic], or bowling, or any other play or game."[26]

The attitudinal transformation began in earnest with the passage in London of the Molasses Act of 1733 which forced the colonies to purchase molasses, rum, and spirits only from the British West Indies. Followed by the Sugar Act of 1764, the Stamp Act of 1765, and ultimately the Townshend Act of 1767, Parliament unintentionally politicized consumer goods. In response to each act, the colonies progressively learned the effectiveness of boycotting and saw conspicuous consumption as a vital moral issue. In this, I agree with T. H. Breen who points out that

> observances of non-consumption ... forced ordinary men and women to declare where exactly they stood on the great constitutional issues of the day. British manufactures thus took on a new symbolic function, and the boycott became a social metaphor of political resistance.[27]

Out of this increasingly hostile commercial environment arose the second phase of anti-theatrical measures beginning with the Massachusetts Act of 1750.[28] Admittedly, its success in avoiding Whitehall's veto, in addition to its appeal for frugality and industry, may also be the result of an especially lax and ineffective period for the Board of Trade in which most power was temporarily transferred to the Secretary of State. During this time colonial acts received only cursory readings and scant legal attention.[29] Nonetheless, the act became a model for at least one other colony. In 1762, Rhode Island, responding to a petition from angry citizens, banned theatre

in a law that is a verbatim copy of the Massachusetts legislation.[30]
That same year, New Hampshire (reeling from the effects of the
French and Indian Wars), passed a similar law in response to a
petition to begin theatrical entertainments in Portsmouth. This law
was distinct from earlier examples in that it not only appealed to the
usual issues of economy, but also asserted

that it would be more especially Improper & Extraordinary that such
entertainments should be first introduced when the people are laboring
under the calamities of a famine, the effects of which will be felt for years to
come, and though there is at present some relief, yet as that is only by
Importation and on which we must depend[,] ... the distress is far from
being removed; Add to this that we are still deeply ingaged in an expensive
war from which there is no present prospect of deliverance and that
curiosity will tempt the youth in the remotest parts of this Province to take
a journey to Portsmouth.[31]

Citing natural disasters and war as a justification for preventing
theatre is singular in the colonies. But note its initial concern,
nonetheless, is with "importation on which we must depend."

With Parliament's passage of the Townshend Act, the colonial
non-importation movement moved into high gear. In December of
1767, the town of Boston drafted a letter to its representatives in the
colonial assembly expressing its concerns over

the distressed circumstances of the town, by means of the amazing growth
of luxury and the Embarrassments of our trade; and having also the
strongest apprehensions that our invaluable rights and liberties as men and
British subjects, are greatly affected by a late act of the British Parliament,
[they were therefore resolved] to encourage a spirit of industry and frugality among the people.[32]

By February the Assembly approved the Massachusetts Circular
Letter urging all the colonies to suppress idle and extravagant
activities. This was followed in the summer of 1768 by a one-year
non-importation pact among Boston merchants and supported by
every colony except New Hampshire.[33]

The effect on theatre is evident. By the 1760s Puritan merchants,
increasingly sensitive to the lack of specie as a result of the trade
imbalance, focused hostility on anything perceived as emanating
from Britain.[34] The significance of the non-importation movement
was apparently not lost on David Douglass, who changed his
troupe's name in 1763 from the London Company of Players to the
more politically acceptable American Company.[35] Five years later,

William Verling must have acted under similar influences when he adopted the New American Company as the name for his players.[36] Aware of a new morality in commerce, colonists began to attack the theatre as a waste of financial resources and human effort. "The money thrown away in one night at a play," complains one irate New Yorker in a January 1768 edition of the *New-York Journal*, "would purchase wood, provisions and other necessities, sufficient for a number of poor."[37] Another writer in the same publication asserts that

while some actuated with a truly benevolent spirit, have industriously concerted measures for employing not only our necessitous poor, but also many of our tradesmen, who are out of employment, it must give them serious concern to hear that many of those are so thoughtless as to frequent the Play-house with their families; some who are obliged to run in debt for mere necessaries; some who are indebted to others as needy as themselves; ... For such persons to throw away their money on Play-tickets! What compassion! What mercy can they expect?[38]

The sentiments expressed reflect the manner in which the earlier convergence of religious morality and commercial ethics that helped define Puritan mercantilism was now merging, out of economic necessity, with the growing political concerns. Theatre, like all other British commodities, had become politicized.[39]

Whereas much of the non-importation fervor subsided after Parliament rescinded the Townshend Act in 1770, it was renewed with even greater conviction upon the passage of the Tea Act of 1773, and once again theatre was caught up in the movement. Within a year the Continental Congress passed its anti-theatre act. Using the Massachusetts Circular Letter as a model, the delegates resolved to

encourage frugality, economy, and industry, and promote agriculture, art and the manufactures of this country, especially that of wool; and will discountenance and discourage every species of extravagance and dissipation, especially all horse-racing, and all kinds of gaming, cock-fighting, exhibition of shews, plays and other expensive diversions and entertainments.[40]

It must be emphasized, of course, that the act did not stand alone. It was an integral part of a larger package of legislation passed by the Continental Congress in the fall of 1774 specifically intended to further the non-importation movement and to encourage colonial manufacturing. While the act was unenforceable, since the Continental Congress was operating illicitly, it served as a foundation for subsequent theatrical opposition in the United States.[41]

When Douglass and the American Company left the northern colonies for Jamaica in February 1775, it was a tacit acknowledgement of the hopelessness of theatre's commercial prospects as a British commodity rather than a retreat from potential prosecution under the Act of 1774. Theatre had come to represent all that the rebellious colonists despised. Apart from the antiquated moral objections, theatre was now seen as a British manufactured product, expressly suited to royalist tastes. More importantly, it competed with local merchants for the attention of customers and invaluable specie. In this way theatre became much more than just an undesirable amusement; it was a political and social symbol of English oppression.

The development of anti-theatrical legislation during the colonial period (culminating in the Act of 1774) must be contextualized beyond the simplistic explanations of Puritanical sentiment or war-time preparation. The acts document the attempt by colonial assemblies to appease a Board of Trade generally insensitive to the realities of American society and politics. As the Board of Trade became more determined to perpetuate the colonies' subordination to British industrial development and as negative sentiment increased toward British manufactured goods, the colonists looked upon everything originating in Great Britain as politically and socially suspect – including the theatre. Therefore the acts also demonstrate the essential change in the Puritan mercantile perception of theatre, from something religiously objectionable to a commercially immoral undertaking.

## NOTES

(An earlier draft of this paper was read at the 1989 conference of the American Society for Theatre Research in Williamsburg, Virginia.)

1  The resolution was passed on 20 October 1774, one of fourteen articles designed to further commercial autonomy within the colonies. *Journals of the Continental Congress, 1744–1789. Edited from the Original Records in the Library of Congress*, 34 vols. (1774) (Washington: United States Government Printing Office, 1904–37), I, 78.

2  Howard Taubman, *The Making of the American Theatre* (New York: Coward McCann, 1965), 41; Arthur Hobson Quinn, *A History of the American Drama From the Beginning to the Civil War* (New York: Appleton-

Century-Crofts, 1943), 32; Hugh F. Rankin, *Theater in Colonial America* (Chapel Hill: University of North Carolina Press, 1965), 187–88. Garff B. Wilson, *Three Hundred Years of American Drama and Theatre* (Englewood Cliffs: Prentice-Hall, 1982), 11–12. See also Abe Laufe, *The Wicked Stage: A History of Theatre Censorship and Harassment in the United States* (New York: Frederick Ungar, 1978), 3–12 and Harrold C. Shiffler, "Religious Opposition to the Eighteenth Century Philadelphia Stage," *Educational Theatre Journal* 14 (October 1962) 215–23. Other examples could be cited to illustrate the point, but these are among the best known.

3 Arthur Hornblow, *A History of the Theatre in America, From the Beginnings to the Present Time*, 2 vols. (Philadelphia: J. B. Lippincott, 1919), I, 25–26. William S. Dye, in his article "Pennsylvania Versus the Theatre," tries to show that William Penn's religious opposition to theatrical entertainments, articulated in *No Cross, No Crown*, influenced subsequent legislation. Indeed anti-theatrical provisions in the earliest documents support this contention, but Dye is unable to explain why the provisions were soon dropped. Clearly the Pennsylvania Assembly was not as concerned about theatre as Penn. *Pennsylvania Magazine of History and Biography* 55 (1931) 333–72.

4 Wilson, *Three Hundred Years*, 11. Taubman, *Making of the American Theatre*, 27–30. For more comprehensive studies of the foundations of Puritan theatrical opposition see: Jonas Barish, *The Antitheatrical Prejudice* (Berkeley: University of California Press, 1981); Margot Heinemann, *Puritanism & Theatre: Thomas Middleton and Opposition Drama under the Early Stuarts* (Cambridge: Cambridge University Press, 1982); E. N. S. Thompson, *The Controversy Between the Puritans and the Stage* (1903; New York: H. Holt; New York: AMS Press, 1972).

5 Walter J. Meserve, *An Emerging Entertainment. The Drama of the American People to 1828* (Bloomington: Indiana University Press, 1977), 28–30, 61. Quinn, *History of American Drama*, 32. Rankin, *Theatre in Colonial America*, 4, 6, 31, 81, 92, 100–1, 187.

6 Bernard Bailyn, *The Ideological Origins of the American Revolution* (Cambridge: Harvard University Press, 1967), 32–34. Daniel Boorstin, *The Americans: The Colonial Experience*, (New York: Vintage, 1958), 24. Clinton Rossiter, *The Political Thought of the American Revolution*, (New York: Harcourt, Brace & World, 1963), 8–9.

7 Bernard Bailyn, *The New England Merchants in the Seventeenth Century* (New York: Harper & Row, 1955), 174–78.

8 Maryland and Virginia were the only colonies that did not pass anti-theatrical bills. With their largely royalist populations, the southern colonies were traditionally more tolerant of theatrical amusements. Few acts became law and those that did were rarely enforced. David Hackett Fischer, *Albion's Seed: Four British Folkways in America* (New York: Oxford University Press, 1989), 207–32; Meserve, *Emerging Enter-*

*tainment*, 30; Kenneth Silverman, *A Cultural History of the American Revolution* (New York: Thomas Y. Cromwell, 1976), 107–10, 134–40, 142, 250–51.

9 Public Record Office (London), C.O. 5, 275, part 2, p. 65 (overleaf); PRO, C.O. 5, 275, part 1, p. 55 (overleaf); PRO C.O. 5, 273 p. 96 (overleaf); PRO C.O. 5, 273, p. 3 (overleaf), p. 7 (overleaf), p. 9; PRO C.O. 5, 278, p. 129; John Russell Bartlett, ed., *Records of the Colony of Rhode Island Providence Plantations, 1757 to 1769* (Providence: Knowles, Anthony, 1861), VI, 342–46; PRO C.O. 5, 280, p. 15 and overleaf.

10 The only exception is the colony of Rhode Island. As one of the original proprietary colonies it was not obligated to forward its legislation to London for approval. Although it often complied with London's requests for legislative documents, the records at the PRO are incomplete.

11 Oscar Theodore Barck, Jr. and Hugh Talmage Lefler, *Colonial America* (New York: Macmillan, 1961), 255–58. See also Leonard Woods Labaree, *Royal Government in America: A Study of the British Colonial System before 1783* (New York: Frederick Ungar, 1958); Richard Brandon Morriss, *Studies in the History of American Law: with Special Reference to the Seventeenth and Eighteenth Centuries*, 2nd ed. (New York: Octagon, 1974).

12 Barck and Lefler, *Colonial America*, 225–26; William R. Shepherd, *History of Proprietary Government in Pennsylvania* (New York: Columbia University Press, 1896); Clayton Colman Hall, ed., *Narratives of Early Maryland, 1633–1684*), (New York: Charles Scribner's Sons, 1910).

13 Charles McLean Andrews, *Guide to the Materials for American History, to 1793, in the Public Record Office of Great Britain*, 2 vols. (Washington: Carnegie Institution of Washington, 1912–14), I, 85–90; Oliver Morton Dickerman, *American Colonial Government, 1695–1765: A Study of the British Board of Trade in its Relation to the American Colonies* (New York: Russell & Russell, 1962), 17–22; Edward Raymond Turner, *The Privy Council of England in the Seventeenth and Eighteenth Centuries, 1603–1784*, 2 vols. (Baltimore: Johns Hopkins, 1927–28), II, 330–35.

14 Dickerson, *American Colonial Government*, 24. See also Barck and Lefler, *Colonial America*, 243–45; Burner 330.

15 Barck and Lefler, *Colonial America*, 244.

16 Ibid; Dickerson, *American Colonial Government*. For an excellent evaluation of the politicizing of business in the American colonies see T. H. Breen, "'Baubles of Britain': The American and Consumer Revolutions of the Eighteenth Century," *Past and Present*, 119 (May 1988), 73–104.

17 Dickerson, *American Colonial Government*, 225–83; Labaree, *Royal Government in America*, 218–47.

18 PRO C.O. 5, 275, part 1, p. 55 (overleaf).

19 PRO C.O. 5, 280, p. 15 and overleaf.

20 See for example the Massachusetts act of 1699, PRO C.O. 5, 275, part 2, p. 65 (overleaf).
21 Breen, "'Baubles of Britain,'" 90–94.
22 Dickerson, *American Colonial Government*, 228–42.
23 PRO C.O. 5, 1237, pp. 1, 10, 124; PRO C.O. 5, p. 39.
24 *OED*, 7, 976.
25 PRO C.O. 5, 275, part 2, p. 65.
26 *The Colonial Laws of Massachusetts. Reprinted from the Edition of 1660* (Boston: [City Council of Boston], 1889), 153.
27 Breen, "'Baubles of Britain,'" 90.
28 PRO C.O. 5, 275, part 1, p. 55 (overleaf).
29 Andrews, *Materials for American History*, 96–99; Dickerson, *American Colonial Government*, 67.
30 Bartlett, *Records*, 325.
31 PRO C.O. 5, 280, p. 15 and overleaf.
32 *A Report of the Record Commissioners of the City of Boston Containing the Boston Town Records, 1758 to 1769* (Boston: [City Council of Boston], 1886), 227–28.
33 Barck and Lefler, *Colonial America*, 536–38.
34 Breen, "'Baubles of Britain,'" 91–93.
35 Rankin, *Theatre in Colonial America*, 101.
36 *Maryland Gazette*, 16 February 1769, 3.
37 *New-York Journal*, 28 January 1768, 2.
38 *New-York Journal*, 28 January 1768, 2.
39 The social and economic perceptions of theatre surrounding the American Revolution are presented in Kenneth Silverman, "The Economic Debate over the Theater in Revolutionary America" in *The American Revolution and Eighteenth-Century Culture: Essays from the 1976 Bicentennial Conference of the American Society for Eighteenth-Century Studies*, ed. Paul J. Korshin (New York: AMS Press, 1986), 219–39.
40 *Journals of the Continental Congress.*
41 A more stringent ban on theatre was passed by the Continental Congress on 16 October 1778; *Journals of the Continental Congress* vol. XII–XIII (1778), 1001, 1018. The following year the Pennsylvania legislature passed its own anti-theatrical act, imposing a five-hundred-pound fine on violators; *Pennsylvania Archives* Series 1 (Harrisburg: J. Severns, 1874), 10, 141–43.

CHAPTER 3

# "Lady-managers" in nineteenth-century American theatre

*Vera Mowry Roberts*

Almost everyone interested in American theatre history recognizes the name of Mrs. John Drew. That recognition is based usually on the fact that she was the "Mum-mum" (or grandmother) of Lionel, Ethel and John Barrymore, hence matriarch of a fabulous theatrical dynasty. The mystique and the glamor have been perpetuated by her own published "reminiscences,"[1] the memoirs of Lionel[2] and Ethel,[3] and the biographies of John.[4] The devotee will also know that she was the manager of record at the Arch Street Theatre in Philadelphia from August 1861 to May 1892 for what seems one of the longest managerial careers at a single house in the history of American theatre. Her active, day-to-day management of the Arch Street Theatre and its resident company ceased, however, in 1876, when the company was disbanded. Subsequently, as "lessee" of the theatre, she hired managers to oversee the visiting companies, she herself going out on starring tours. Even so, her fifteen-year stint of active management is deservedly famous.

Nonetheless, Louisa Lane Drew would not have been at "The Arch" in the first place had it not been for the successful managerial career of Laura Keene in New York, begun in 1855. It was that example brought to the attention of the Arch's Board of Agents by Adam Everly, son of the board's president, and deliberated over at some length, that finally persuaded the board to commit to Drew.[5] There had been some reluctance at turning over their investment to a woman.

But the brilliant managing career of Laura Keene was not the first example of the actress-manager in the United States. She had been preceded in this endeavor by Anne Brunton Merry and Charlotte Cushman; she was contemporaneous with Catherine Sinclair, and was immediately followed by Mrs. John Wood (Matilda Vining Wood). These six constitute the roster of women who managed major theatres in nineteenth-century America. All six were actresses in the long-standing tradition of actor-managers, and all acted in their own productions throughout their managerial careers.

Throughout most of the nineteenth century, the word "manager" encompassed a great deal more than it has in modern times. The nineteenth-century manager was almost invariably an actor, whose duties included play selection, casting, directing, designing, and looking after finances – all functions which in modern theatre have become specialized and individualized. So it is little wonder that, with the prevailing social climate of the nineteenth century, so few women became theatre managers. The duties attached to such posts meant that a *woman* would be telling men what to do, handling money (sometimes in large sums), hiring and firing employees, and making business deals. All these activities to the nineteenth-century mind were clearly *male* activities, not proper for women to engage in. How did these six come to be managers? How did they carry out their assignments? How successful were they? These are questions worth examining.

Anne Brunton Merry (1769–1808) fell heir to the co-managership of the Chestnut Street Theatre in Philadelphia upon the untimely death of her second husband, Thomas Wignell, on 21 February 1803. She had enjoyed a measure of success in England before accepting Wignell's invitation, in 1796, to join the company at the Chestnut Street Theatre, which had opened in 1794, built in an approximate likeness to the Theatre Royal at Bath, where Merry had enjoyed considerable success as an actress. By 1790 her career had come to a temporary halt because she had, in the face of his family's "opposition," married Robert Merry, a well-born activist and writer who espoused the French Revolution. They embarked on 19 September 1796 and "significantly," as Gresdna Ann Doty points out, "shared their voyage with Thomas Wignell and William Warren, both of whom subsequently became husbands to Anne Brunton Merry."[6]

Her English reputation having preceded her, Merry was soon known as the leading actress in the United States. When Robert Merry died of a stroke on 28 December 1798, Anne stayed on at the Chestnut, occasionally also appearing with William Dunlap's company at the Park Theatre in New York. She married Wignell at a private ceremony on 1 January 1803. He died the following month.

Her initial assumption of co-management with Alexander Reinagle seems to have been mostly in name only. She was pregnant,
and was delivered of a daughter, Elizabeth, in the fall of that year,
the affairs of actual company management being delegated to
William Warren. But by the end of May 1803 she had signed a
contract along with Reinagle to manage the Chestnut for four years.
Doty suggests that Merry (now Wignell) "probably did not initiate
any new policies and most likely attempted to maintain the
company in much the same fashion as had her husband."[7] This
"fashion" entailed spring and fall seasons in Baltimore with occasional forays to Annapolis, and the winter months (usually November through March) in Philadelphia. That she had no easy time of it
is evident in a statement by John Durang that "I was sorry to see her
in this situation, harass'd by some of the performers as she was."[8]
Nevertheless, as Charles Durang attests in his writings on "The
Philadelphia Stage," Mrs. Merry was observant and demanding of
costume propriety, insisted that rehearsals be conducted (usually by
her protégé, William Wood) under performance conditions, and
saw to it that the green room functioned as a proper drawing room,
with polite conversation and elegant manners. She was astute
enough to bolster her seasons with guest appearances by James
Fennell and Thomas Cooper. During her first year of management,
Merry also acted twenty-seven roles in fifty-one performances in
Philadelphia, with an additional sixteen roles in seventeen performances in the spring season in Baltimore.[9]

But despite the brilliance of that season, Philadelphia's inclement
winter weather kept the box office receipts to an average of $750.[10]
At the close of her second Philadelphia season – on 3 April 1805 –
Mrs. Merry Wignell offered her share of the lease of the Chestnut
Street Theatre to William Warren; he accepted and the transfer was
effected with the Board of Agents.[11] So ended Anne Brunton
Merry's brief managership of two years. Charles Durang explains
that transfer by indicating that she "had been a good deal annoyed
in the business of the theatre; some of the actors pressed their affairs
with ungentleness" and Mrs. Wignell, "a sensitive, generous and
confiding woman," lacked sufficient firmness to conduct a company
"where a variety of dispositions are to be met, jealousies are to be
soothed, and intrigues are to be counteracted."[12] She went on to
marry Warren later that year, and to continue acting until she died
in childbirth at the age of thirty-nine on 28 June 1808.

The next lady-manager to appear on the scene was another famous actress, Charlotte Cushman (1816–76), and her reign as manager was even shorter. It also transpired in Philadelphia, from 22 September 1842 to 10 July 1843 and, in the light of her long and brilliant career as an actress on both sides of the Atlantic, is but a footnote to the chronicle. Nevertheless, the circumstances and the outcome are interesting.

Born in Boston and musically gifted, by age fourteen she was singing in the choir of Second Church, where Ralph Waldo Emerson was assistant pastor. Boston voice coach John Paddon offered her an apprenticeship (on a three-year contract) and she worked with him for nine months. A planned two-week visit to New York relatives stretched to three months; when she returned to Boston, Paddon cancelled the contract. But James G. Maeder, recently arrived in Boston, was impressed with her voice and took on her training. That led to her debut on the opera stage in Boston, and her going to New Orleans with Maeder and his wife to inaugurate James H. Caldwell's new St. Charles Theatre where fifteen-year-old Louisa Lane and her mother were also members of the company. Her debut in the soprano role of the Countess Almaviva in *The Marriage of Figaro* on 1 December 1835 in that 4,000-seat house was a disaster. The part was beyond her range, and her professional skills were at a minimum. During the course of that difficult year, she performed in several dramatic pieces as well as operas, and by the end of the season – with Caldwell's sympathetic advice and the tragedian John Barton's able coaching – redeemed herself by appearing triumphantly as Lady Macbeth on 23 April 1836 at age nineteen. At the end of the season, through Barton's recommendation, she secured a contract at Hamblin's Bowery Theater in New York. Her Bowery debut as Lady Macbeth occurred on 12 September 1836 and was enthusiastically hailed. By 1841 her reputation was such that a number of her New York friends including James Gordon Bennett, publisher of the *Herald*, mounted a campaign to get her a theatre of her own. That plan was interrupted when she was offered the managership of the Walnut Street Theatre in Philadelphia by lessee E. A. Marshall, probably to offset and challenge the "lady-manager" just appointed at the Chestnut Street Theatre, Mrs. Elizabeth Maywood, whose tenure was mercifully brief and totally obscure.[13]

Cushman, now twenty-six, did her best. She walked into a

company that included a large contingent of seasoned actors including E. L. Davenport, Clara Fisher, J. M. Field, and W. R. Blake.
The season opened on 22 September 1842 with Cushman playing
Mrs. Racket in *The Belle's Stratagem*. A few nights later she appeared
before the curtain, pledging to the Philadelphia audience that she
would give them plays with "healthy morality and generous sentiments" and would ring down the Saturday night curtain at eleven
in order not to violate the Sabbath.[14] During the season she brought
as guest artists Edwin Forrest, George Vandenhoff, Junius Brutus
Booth, John Brougham, Dan Marble, James Hackett and Josephine
Clifton. She offered *Road to Ruin, King O'Neal, Jack Cade, Romeo and
Juliet, Macbeth* and a host of other plays.

But times were bad and the box office receipts disappointing. A
few of the men in the company resisted being told what to do by a
woman – and such a young one. She became the butt of jokes from
the comedian of the company, W. R. Blake. And the staid Philadelphia audience, unlike its New York counterpart, was shocked to
see her play Romeo in tights, exposing her legs. Her last day as
manager was 10 July 1843. To ease her departure, Marshall
announced that Blake would become her "assistant" and take over
the management. Cushman's career as a manager was finished. Her
comparative youth, a bad economy, and the hostility of some parts
of both her company and her audience had defeated her best efforts.
She never again tried managing. That fall, at his request, she played
opposite the visiting William Charles Macready. At his suggestion,
she went the next year to England to perfect her craft, returning five
years later an acknowledged star. She was called "the first lady of
the American theatre" for many years to come.

It took ten more years for another "lady-manager" to appear on
the American theatre scene, and then there were two. Both made
their debut on 24 December 1853 – Mrs. Catherine Sinclair
(1817–91) as manager of the Metropolitan Theatre in San Francisco, and Laura Keene (1826–73) as manager of Howard's Athen-
aeum and Gallery of the Arts (or, more familiarly, the Charles Street
Theatre) in Baltimore. For a short time, in San Francisco, their
careers intertwined.

Sinclair always billed herself as *Mrs.* Catherine Sinclair, although
everyone knew that she was the recently divorced wife of the famous
Edwin Forrest. The acrimonious divorce proceedings, with accusations of infidelity on both sides, had been settled in Sinclair's favor

in January 1852, although Forrest kept it in appeal for the next sixteen years. The whole affair assumed the dimensions of a national scandal, and remained headline news for years. Sinclair was not a trained actress, although she had some facility for singing. A month after her divorce, and billing herself as "Mrs. C. N. Sinclair, the late Mrs. Forrest," she appeared at Brougham's Lyceum in New York as Lady Teazle in *School for Scandal*. She had persuaded George Vandenhoff to coach her for her debut, and, as might have been expected, this and subsequent appearances drew curious crowds of spectators and the disdain of critics. She left New York in the fall of that year to tour the provinces, ending up in San Francisco at Maguire's Opera House and then at the American.

In that gold-inflated town in 1853, "culture" was on the rise. There were already five theatres operating.[15] Nevertheless, Joseph French built the Metropolitan at a cost of $250,000, and it opened under Sinclair's management on 24 December 1853 with *School for Scandal*, featuring Sinclair as Lady Teazle and James Murdoch as Charles Surface. By 9 April 1854, Sinclair was featuring the newly arrived Laura Keene who, shortly thereafter and briefly, became her rival in management.

In an attempt to bolster her repertoire and her audiences, Sinclair introduced Mme. Anne Thillon "in an operatic season" in the spring of 1854[16] and announced for the fall season Meyerbeer's *Robert the Devil*. For these operas she used visiting artists in the principal roles and augmented them with talented local amateurs. Business, however, was not good. She tried operetta, ballet, pantomime, skits – even reduced ticket prices for the third tier. The San Francisco *Herald* of 8 May 1855[17] quotes Mrs. Sinclair as saying that her first series of sixteen operas lost $3,908 and her second series of sixteen $9,977. She took her benefit 9 June 1855 in her signature piece, *School for Scandal*, this time with Edwin Booth, who had just returned from Australia, as Charles Surface. The Metropolitan was thenceforth a vaudeville house, and offered no more plays or operas.[18] Sinclair had been in San Francisco for a little over two years, and had managed the Metropolitan for about eighteen months. She went on to a brief winter season in Sacramento, then to Australia from whence she arrived in London in September 1857. She played the Haymarket Theatre, then toured the provinces and made her final appearance on the stage at New York's Academy of Music on 18 December 1859. Her theatrical career lasted eight years, a year and a half of which had been as manager. Born on a wave of notoriety, that brief career ended as the wave receded; her last thirty years were spent in complete privacy.

Laura Keene, on the other hand, spent her entire life in the theatre, ten years of it as a resident actress-manager. Only Mrs. John Drew would later retain the title of "lady-manager" for a longer period of time. Keene's first recorded stage appearance was as Juliet in Surrey, England, on 26 August 1851. Two months later she made her London debut at Henry Farren's Olympic Theatre. By 12 May 1852 she was a member of the Lyceum Company, then managed by Madame Vestris and her husband, Charles Matthews. Keene had been married some years before to one Henry Taylor, tavern-keeper, and by the time of her first recorded performance had given birth to two daughters and had seen her husband transported as a felon to Australia. The influence of Madame Vestris was definitive. Her biographer, John Creahan, deplores Keene's association with Vestris as "not, perhaps, the best mentor for a young and very pretty debutante."[19] But Keene herself thought otherwise, for one of her cherished possessions was an ivory miniature of Vestris which she gave to Joseph Jefferson shortly before her death on 11 November 1873.[20]

Recruited by James W. Wallack as leading lady for his company when he took over Brougham's Lyceum (renamed Wallack's Theatre) in 1852, Keene sailed for America that summer, taking along her two daughters (henceforth to be known as her "nieces") and her mother. She never returned to England. During that first season, which opened on 2 September, she played a variety of Shakespearean roles as well as leads in a number of other classical and contemporary plays. She was heralded widely as "a leading woman of personality and distinction."[21] Critics credited her with contributing significantly to the success of Wallack's venture, the *Albion* declaring, "She will spoil the critics' trade, if she continues adding laurels upon laurels to her brow."[22]

In his *Memories of Fifty Years*,[23] Lester Wallack tells the harrowing story of Keene's failure to appear for a scheduled performance as Lydia Languish in Sheridan's *The Rivals* on 25 November 1853 well into Wallack's second season. Creahan remarks that "under the persuasion of well-meaning but injudicious friends, she quitted Mr. Wallack's friendly patronage and went to Baltimore and opened a theatre."[24] Odell later remarks that although "she was badly advised ... after all, she had the delight of managing her own playhouse."[25] Her two daughters were in a convent school in Washington, DC, and she had met John Lutz, the son of a well-to-do mercantile family in the nation's capital. He seems to have committed himself to Keene, was her business manager in later ventures, and her husband from 1860 until his death in 1869. It is likely that Lutz was involved in the Baltimore scheme, which had refurbished the theatre there in Charles Street.

The season opened Christmas Eve and ended on 2 March 1854. An excellent company of actors had been gathered, and more than fifteen plays were successfully presented, starring Keene in light comedy, farce, melodrama, and Shakespeare. By April 1854 Keene was in San Francisco. After appearing for Sinclair, she spent the months of June and July as "sole lessee and manager" of the Union Square Theatre, having a brilliant success with the elaborate *The Sea of Ice: or, The Orphan of the Frozen Seas* before setting off for Australia, with the young but talented Edwin Booth as a member of her company. Had Lutz proposed marriage? Was Keene on her way to Australia to find or verify the death of her legal husband? Whether she found Henry Taylor is not known, but she did not marry Lutz until 1860 when Taylor might be presumed dead.

By April 1855 Keene was back in San Francisco as manager of the American Theatre. She reorganized its company and presented a season through July of melodramas, comedy, tragedy and Shakespeare. The American was a gilt and plush house highly admired as a major theatre[26] with a generous supply of stock sets. Keene's company was composed largely of San Francisco-based performers: Mrs. Judah, Caroline Chapman, John McCabe, and "Doc" Robinson. In addition to some memorable productions of Shakespeare she presented some interesting burlesques: *School for Scheming, Anthony and Cleo Married and Settled.* For many of these productions the stock sets must have been used, but at least for *Midsummer Night's Dream,* in which Keene played Oberon, a spectacular set was concocted. MacMinn quotes the San Francisco *Pioneer*: "The rising moon, the flowing water, which seemed to stretch far back among and under the trees, the flowers opening up on the stage to let Puck out and to display the fairies, the green banks, woodland glade, sprites – all were admirable."[27] This production would become a staple of future seasons. The success of Keene's management at the American may have persuaded Catherine Sinclair to take her final benefit at the Metropolitan on 9 June 1855. As for Keene, she was on her way back to New York by August, headed for the big time. No other "lady-manager" had challenged the New York theatrical scene; she was ready, but it was not easy.

Keene secured a lease on the Metropolitan Theatre (formerly Tripler's Hall) at Broadway near Bond Street. She refurbished the house, calling it Laura Keene's Varieties, announced an opening for 24 December 1855, the anniversary of her Baltimore opening, and hired her company, three of which had defected from Burton's Chambers Street Theatre. Her opening bill was to be *Prince Charming* and *Two Can Play At That Game*. Marshall's Broadway Theatre was offering a piece called *King Charming* at that time.[28] The day before her announced opening, Keene arrived at the theatre to find her scenery irreparably slashed. Was it Burton? Was it Marshall? Or was it someone else giving New York's new "lady-manager" her comeuppance? The opening was delayed to 27 December, when *Old Heads and Young Hearts* and a fantasy-ballet *Valley of Flowers* were presented. The season continued until 21 June 1856 and included four premieres of new works and at least eighteen other productions, including plays of Shakespeare, Sheridan, Brougham and an expressly designed series of ten tableaux in honor of George Washington, on his birthday. Laura Keene's Varieties was an established success, both artistically and financially.

But her old enemy, Burton, acquired the Metropolitan for the next season. Creahan writes that "by some flaw in the lease, or breach of contract on the part of the owner, the theatre passed from Miss Keene's hands" to Burton's.[29] Undaunted, she made a public appeal for a theatre, acquired the property at 622–624 Broadway, engaged John Trimple to build her a new theatre, and opened the Laura Keene Theatre on 18 November 1856, assuming a debt of $74,000 plus interest, to be paid off at the rate of $12,000 annually for seven years. She had completely discharged this debt by May 1863, when she gave up managing for reasons that included failing health (she died of tuberculosis ten years later). But she had given a run for their money to the established New York managers – Wallack, Burton, Marshall. She survived the panic of 1857, to which Burton succumbed, and initiated a number of new managerial practices.

Since her new theatre was not ready for occupancy when members of her company assembled in September 1856, they played in Philadelphia and Baltimore through October.[30] One of her early offerings in the new house was a comedy, *Young New York*, written by Edward G. P. Wilkins, drama critic for the *Herald*.[31] Keene interspersed "literary" drama like *The Marble Heart, Camille*, and *David Copperfield* with lighter fare, even a burlesque called *Young Bacchus*.

The September 1857 season began badly even though the young and brash Joseph Jefferson III had joined the company. Actors went on half-salary, and expenditures for advertising were reduced. But then Keene produced her San Francisco hit, *The Sea of Ice*, and recouped the fortunes of the house by running it consecutively until mid-December. This was followed by the failure of *The Corsican Brothers*, in turn redeemed by a Christmas pantomime, *Harlequin and Bluebeard*. The season also included her first production of a Tom Taylor play, *Unequal Match* and ended successfully.

So she produced season after season, usually beginning about mid-September and continuing until early June, running alternating repertory with an occasional "long-run." *Our American Cousin*, in its first presentation, ran consecutively from 19 October 1858 to the third week of March 1859 and made Jefferson and E. A. Sothern famous.

In January 1860 after a quarrel with Mrs. John Wood at the Winter Garden Theatre, Dion Boucicault and his wife, Agnes Robertson, joined Keene's company, thus beginning a fruitful and profitable association. Boucicault's *Colleen Bawn* ran from 29 March to 18 May that year.[32] The latter half of the 1860–61 season was marked by the 177-night run of *The Seven Sisters*, an extravaganza. Keeping her eyes on both audience and box office, Keene seems to have ended every season "in the black" and still presented splendid productions of the classics and new plays. Quinn credits her with making New York theatre "more hospitable to native plays that had merit as literature as well as possibilities of stage success."[33] Her eight-year record in New York would seem to refute Jefferson's accusation that "Laura Keene's judgment in selecting plays was singularly bad."[34] But even Jefferson admitted that "nothing but the best ever entered her theatre."[35] The *New York Times*' critic in 1862 noted that her work had "a wealth of fancy and artistic finish that has never been equalled or even approached by any other New York theatre."[36] A demon for details and a strict disciplinarian, she drew up and posted a set of "Rules and Regulations" for behavior in the green room, during rehearsals and performance. Her company called her "The Duchess."

Her last attempt at managing a theatre occurred in mid-1869, after the trauma of Lincoln's assassination and widespread touring, and after the death of her husband, John Lutz. She took the lease on the Chestnut Street Theatre in Philadelphia, running a season from 20 September 1869 to 25 March 1870. It was an indifferent success, surprisingly marked by another innovation – a series of children's matinees in November of *Bold Jack, The Giant Killer*, and the December production of Dickens's *A Christmas Carol*. The Philadelphia *Press* had greeted her enthusiastically in October 1869 noting "Refinement and genius, discipline and completeness in detail are conspicuous in all she does."[37] There ought to be an interesting Philadelphia story in that theatrical season with Keene at the Chestnut and Mrs. John Drew at the Arch.

When Keene ended her management in New York, she relinquished her house to Mrs. John Wood (1821–1915), another aspiring actress-manager. Born Matilda Vining to an English theatrical family, she was a child-actress in the English provinces, and developed into a comedienne. After marrying John Wood in 1854, she and her husband emigrated to the Boston Theatre, where they remained for three seasons. For the first few months of that third season they played a special engagement at Wallack's Theatre in New York, during which Mrs. Wood's reputation began to eclipse that of her husband. They played Wallack's again in the summer of 1857, then headed for San Francisco, opening at Maguire's Opera House on 18 January 1858. One of Matilda's early triumphs at Maguire's was Minnehaha in the burlesque, *Hi-a-wa-tha; or, Ardent Spirits and Laughing Waters*; later that year she made a sensation in the breeches role of Amadis in *Love's Disguises*. She also played in *Whittington and His Cat* during the Christmas season.[38] There is evidence she "managed" the Forrest Theatre in Sacramento for a few weeks in 1858, and from March 1859 to the beginning of that summer, the American Theatre. Leaving husband, daughter and mother in California, she returned to New York in mid-1859 to join Dion Boucicault's company at the Winter Garden Theatre. Whatever the quarrel between Mrs. Wood and the Boucicaults, it sent the Boucicaults to Laura Keene and Mrs. Wood to three years of touring including the summer season of 1860 in Keene's house.

When Matilda Vining Wood opened the management of Laura

Keene's Theatre in 1863, she changed its name to the Olympic but retained the majority of Keene's company, including James H. Stoddart, who wrote in his *Recollections* that "Mrs. Wood's career at the Olympic was a brilliant one, and many clever people were engaged for her company."[39] This included Stoddart, of course, E. L. Davenport, Mrs. W. G. Gilbert, and John H. Selwyn as stage manager. Mrs. Wood managed the theatre until 30 June 1866 – not quite three years – after which she sailed for England. She never managed again in America, although she returned as an actress for the 1872–73 season.

During her tenure at the Olympic, Mrs. Wood presented a varied bill with the stress on comedies since that was her acting forte. The nineteenth-century penchant for dramatized novels was satisfied in such productions as *Monte Cristo, Martin Chuzzlewit, Our Mutual Friend,* and *The Three Guardsmen.* Stoddart summed up her tenure: "While she managed her theatre it was conducted in a thoroughly artistic way; she was a power in herself, liberal in her views, and she spared no expense that she deemed necessary to the proper conduct of her theatre."[40]

After her return to England, she managed the St. James Theatre in London from 1869 to mid-1872, improving its ambience and its clientele.[41] After her return to London from New York in 1873 until her retirement in 1893, she acted for and managed several theatres, most notably the Court. She was eighty-three years old when she died in 1915.

Before settling in Philadelphia in the fall of 1852, Louisa Lane had been constantly on the road. She had married the much older actor, Henry Blaine Hunt, in New Orleans, divorced him in 1847, married George Mossop in Albany in 1848 (he died the following year), and, on 27 July 1850 also in Albany, married her third and last husband, John Drew. He, at twenty-two, had expressed to Louisa an interest in her eighteen-year-old half-sister, Georgiana Kinlock. The thirty-year-old Louisa decided to have him for herself, and from that point to the end of her life she was determinedly Mrs. John Drew.[42] An offer from the Chestnut Street Theatre in Philadelphia brought the acting couple to that city which Mrs. Drew would thereafter call home, where she would raise, in a series of houses, two generations of Drew/Barrymores and become a pillar of the community as well as a theatrical legend.

During the following year (1853) William Wheatley of the Arch

Street Theatre asked the popular John Drew to join his company as co-manager. With one child already born in Philadelphia, and another on the way, Mrs. Drew urged her husband to accept the offer and moved to the Arch with him as a member of the company. After two successful years with Wheatley, John Drew left for a tour of Europe and Ireland, leaving behind his pregnant wife and two children. When he returned in 1857, he took over the lease of the National for an unsuccessful three months of managing, after which both Drews joined the Walnut Street Theatre. In the winter of 1858, Drew set off for an extended tour to San Francisco, Australia, England and Ireland. Mrs. Drew rejoined Wheatley's Arch Street company, notably playing Queen Catherine to Charlotte Cushman's Wolsey in *Henry VIII*. Early in 1861, Wheatley told Arch Street's Board of Agents that he would leave at the end of the season to manage Niblo's Garden Theatre in New York and the Board offered the position to Mrs. John Drew. Before accepting, she wrote to her husband in Ireland, seeking his permission. That granted, on 21 August 1861 she became "manager and sole lessee" for the Arch, extending her control for the next three decades not only over that establishment, but also over a widespread, expanding and peripatetic family. While she balanced professional and personal demands, everyone understood that the theatre came first.

During her first season at the Arch – a difficult one in which she had to borrow money to pay the company's salaries – she astutely added to her seasoned players, amateurs from some of the dramatic societies of the city, a move which endeared her to a wide audience. Sinclair had taken the same action earlier in San Francisco. Meanwhile, John Drew had returned covered with foreign laurels to begin a starring engagement early in 1862 at his wife's theatre. The engagement was eminently successful, ending on 27 May 1862. Two weeks later he died as the result of head injuries sustained in a fall down the stairs at his home. Although Mrs. John Drew wore the conventional widow's weeds for the requisite period, she did not waver in her management of the Arch, even moving her family to a house nearer the theatre. How could she waver? She was now the sole support of her mother and her children. The whole family attended St. Stephen's Episcopal Church every Sunday morning, and the children were afforded all the advantages of an upper-middle-class upbringing, a pattern that continued with her grandchildren, the Barrymores.

By the end of her third year at the Arch, she had renovated the theatre, raised the price of the orchestra seats from seventy-five cents to one dollar, and paid off the $20,000 indebtedness which she had inherited.[43] An often-quoted figure is the rise in the value of Arch Street Theatre stock from $500 a share to $750. Whatever the financial records, it is obvious that over a long period of time the stockholders were pleased with their investment and her handling of it, for there is never a suggestion of displeasure on their part. It became legend that she never missed a payroll, distributing salaries personally every Saturday morning. She was able to maximize the income from her 1,400-seat house, and at the end of each season generally showed an entry on the plus side of the ledger. She was astute in balancing expensive star appearances with her regular stock company, so that public interest was maintained while the books still balanced. Her own appearance on stage constituted money in the bank, for she was a popular player. She generally had a business manager and a complement of what we today would call technicians. And in addition to supervising the work of all these, she decided on the repertoire, did the casting and conducted rehearsals. Every day (except Sunday) was full from morning until almost midnight.

Deciding on the plays to be given each season was, of course, the most important thing she did, for on those choices hung financial solvency. She knew her audience, for she had become one of the "first citizens" of her adopted city. And she had to get the most value out of her resident stock company and keep them happy and productive, while at the same time planning ahead for a judicious number of guest stars. Her seasonal offerings over the years show what one might expect: a preponderance of melodramas, a sprinkling of classics and Shakespeare, a healthy dose of comedies, usually one or two "spectaculars" and none of what Olive Logan called "the leg business." It was refined, it was elegant, it was fun. But then she had been all her life in the resident stock company business; it was as familiar to her as morning coffee. When stars began bringing with them groups of supporting players for their visiting engagements (a system called the "combination"), she held out against it as long as she could, and longer than most. But by 1876 she had sent her son Jack and her daughter Georgiana to New York at the invitation of Augustin Daly, and there was no longer a resident company at the Arch. She remained the manager of record, but the

Arch became a booking house for touring attractions while she toured widely in her own productions. She finally retired in 1892, was given a massive ovation at the Arch, and went to New York to live out her days in the household of John Drew, Jr., who had become one of Daly's major stars.

She has been described in the autobiographies, memoirs and reminiscences of many actors and actresses. Besides the books written by her grandchildren, and one by her son, John Drew, Jr., she appeared in the writings of Clara Morris, Joseph Jefferson, Rose Eytinge, Frank Stull, Otis Skinner, Mrs. Gilbert, J. H. Stoddart and Lester Wallack. Some of these extol her keen eye for young talent (cheap and effective – she needed them), her ability to bring out the best in each member of her company, her strict eye for detail and for good housekeeping at the Arch, her kindness, her objectivity, her rehearsal discipline – all details adding confirmation to what one suspects from the beginning she possessed – a very special aptitude for theatre management as it was known in her day. The appellation of "Duchess" was given to her, as it had been to Laura Keene, as a sign of respect, awe and recognition of a kind of imperiousness and supreme self-confidence. She had no doubt in her abilities, and she proved that she was right.

So there they are: six women, spanning the century from 1803 to 1893. One of them was American-born (Cushman); five had been born in England; all but one of these (Wood) made America her permanent home after arrival. All were actresses before they became managers; their theatrical training was accomplished in the long-standing practice of stock company and rotating repertory. All (except Cushman and Keene) married inside the profession, and took their husband's name for professional use, Sinclair calling herself "the late Mrs. Forrest." Two of them (Keene and Wood) succeeded in New York City, three in Philadelphia (Merry, Cushman and Drew), and for a short period of time, three in San Francisco (Sinclair, Keene, Wood). Their paths crossed during their lifetimes. Drew and Cushman were on the stage together, early in New Orleans and much later in Philadelphia. Keene and Drew, for one year, managed rival theatres in Philadelphia. Wood followed Keene in New York. One wonders what mutual influences there were among them.

The achievement of these women is all the more remarkable because they were living in a patriarchal society where civil law and social custom made women second-class citizens. Mrs. Drew asked her husband's permission to sign a contract with the Arch because she was legally bound to do so. Women could not hold title to property; they could not vote nor hold public office nor serve as jurors. During the span of these women's lives, a hard-fought battle was waged for equal rights for women, and all of them were long dead before women got the vote. In the world they inhabited, it was considered "unfeminine" for a woman to occupy a position of authority. All of them, in one way or another (and Mrs. Drew most conspicuously), were obliged to cultivate acquaintances in the accepted social strata in order to demonstrate their respectability – and their acceptability. With all the cards that were stacked against them, it is a wonder that any of them won the game, and at least two of them did so brilliantly – Laura Keene and Mrs. John Drew.

## NOTES

1 Mrs. John Drew, *Autobiographical Sketch of Mrs. John Drew* (New York: Charles Scribner, 1899).
2 Lionel Barrymore, *We Barrymores* (New York: Appleton-Century-Crofts, 1951).
3 Ethel Barrymore, *Memories* (New York: Harper Bros., 1955).
4 Gene Fowler, *Good Night, Sweet Prince,* (New York: Viking Press, 1944).
5 James Kotsilibas-Davis, *Great Times, Good Times: The Odyssey of Maurice Barrymore* (New York: Doubleday, 1977), 97.
6 Gresdna Ann Doty, *The Career of Anne Brunton Merry in the American Theatre* (Baton Rouge, LA: Louisiana State University Press, 1971), 48. This authoritative study is invaluable.
7 Ibid., 111.
8 Ibid., 111.
9 Ibid., 114, 115.
10 Ibid., 118.
11 Ibid., 119.
12 Charles Durang, "The Philadelphia Stage, from the Year 1740 to the Year 1855. Partly compiled from the papers of his father, the late John Durang, with notes by the Editors of the Philadelphia *Sunday Dispatch*" 7 May 1854 to 8 July 1869, *passim* (Microfilm copy in the Research Library of Performing Arts, Lincoln Center, NYC).
13 Joseph Leach, *Bright Particular Star: The Life and Times of Charlotte Cushman* (New Haven: Yale University Press, 1970), 107.
14 Ibid., 109.

15  Edmond H. Gagey, *The San Francisco Stage: Its History* (New York: Columbia University Press, 1950), 27, 38.
16  Ibid., 60.
17  Ibid., 52.
18  Ibid., 63.
19  John Creahan, *The Life of Laura Keene* (Philadelphia: Rogers Publishing Company, 1887), 7.
20  Joseph Jefferson, *The Autobiography of Joseph Jefferson* (New York: Century, 1889), 205.
21  George C. D. Odell, *Annals of the New York Stage*, 15 vols. (New York: Columbia University Press, 1927–1945), VI, 215.
22  Ibid., VI, 218.
23  New York: Charles Scribner's Sons, 1888.
24  Creahan, *Life*, 18.
25  Odell, *Annals*, VI, 298.
26  Gagey, *San Francisco Stage*, 61.
27  George R. MacMinn, *The Theatre of the Golden Era in California* (Caldwell, ID: Caxton Printers, 1941), 91.
28  Odell, *Annals*, VI, 450.
29  Creahan, *Life*, 18.
30  James H. Stoddart, *Recollections of a Player* (New York: Century, 1902), 90.
31  Ibid., 100.
32  Creahan, *Life*, 22.
33  Arthur Hobson Quinn, *A History of the American Drama from the Beginnings to the Civil War* (New York: F. S. Crofts & Co., 1946), 367.
34  Jefferson, *Autobiography*, 184.
35  Ibid., 142.
36  Quoted in Creahan, *Life*, 86.
37  Ibid., 34.
38  MacMinn, *Golden Era*, 186, 419.
39  Stoddart, *Recollections*, 139.
40  Ibid., 143.
41  Jane T. Peterson, "Mrs. John Wood" in *Notable Women in the American Theatre: A Biographical Dictionary*, ed. Alice M. Robinson, Vera Mowry Roberts, Milly S. Barranger (New York: Greenwood Press, 1989).
42  Kotsilibas-Davis, *Great Times*, 92.
43  C. Lee Jenner, "The Duchess of Arch Street: An Overview of the Managerial Career of Mrs. John Drew," *Performing Arts Resources*, vol. XIII (New York: Theatre Library Association, 1988).

# CHAPTER 4

# Hustlers in the house: the Bowery Theatre as a mode of historical information

## Rosemarie K. Bank

In *The Order of Things*, the late French philosopher-historian Michel Foucault alerts us to moments in history when transformation is evident, to "the suddenness and thoroughness with which ... at the same time similar changes occurred in apparently very different disciplines."[1] Such a moment of shifting (at different levels and paces and for varied reasons) in concepts of social organization, history, economics, politics, culture, and in other streams of thought, is evident in antebellum America (1830–60); indeed these decades are often characterized as "extraordinary," "revolutionary," or "explosive" in the degree to and rapidity with which they manifest change in all realms of interest to historians.[2] Many of these changes have been explored by scholars in binary terms – middle vs. working class, Whig vs. Jacksonian politics, popular vs. elite culture, and so on. Such dualistic analytical strategies can be provisionally useful in historical investigation "to change the perspective from time to time and move [us] from *pro* to *contra*." They must themselves eventually be displaced, however, in order to dissolve the idea that there are only two, opposed, sides.[3]

Notably, binary views color the discussions of sex during the Jacksonian era, a subject which itself marks "the point of intersection of the discipline of the body and the control of the population."[4] Sex becomes a matter of political significance, a "problem," to ministers previously content not to discuss it, to politicians previously indifferent to regulating it, to social commentators previously silent about it, to newspapers and journals previously uninterested in exploiting it: hence, sex in the Jacksonian era becomes a "problem" for historical discourse. Discussions of it in antebellum America were often polarized and overdefined insofar as sex was linked to volatile matters of intense concern – to religion, to social status, to political power, or to commercial advantage.[5] As a topic of

47

abiding interest in our own century, historians have read back into binarized Jacksonian discourses additional dualisms concerning such sexual subjects as population control, pleasure, prostitution, the economic oppression of women, and the uses of sex in cultural forms.

This essay asks why the morality of audiences attending the theatre in antebellum America becomes an historical discourse. It focuses upon theatres in New York (Manhattan) and even more specifically upon the Bowery Theatre; and it focuses upon sex, even more specifically on prostitution. Commodified sex within the context of antebellum social and political configurations as they operated in New York will first be considered, followed by an examination of the theatre's positioning within this discourse, by antebellumites and by subsequent commentators.

I

Contrary to twentieth-century impressions, sex in America has not always been a matter for public regulation, for though we appropriate the word puritan as a synonym for controlling discourses about sexual practice, the years prior to 1830 are nearly void of any laws or printed matter about cautionary sex and populated with "a substantial body of *noncautionary* literature about sexuality."[6] The onset of the Jacksonian era is marked by the publication of a range of works concerning sexuality, broadly conceived, in scientific as well as ethical terms, ranging in topic from birth control (Robert Owen's *Moral Physiology* [1829] and Charles Knowlton's *Fruits of Philosophy* [1832]), to masturbation (J. N. Bolles's *The Solitary Vice Considered* [1831]), to abstinence (Sylvester Graham's *Lecture to Young Men on Chastity* [1834]). Articles on these and other aspects of sex appear in medical and educational journals in the 1830s, a decade marking a significant increase of regulatory literature concerning women and sexuality.[7]

An increase in sex literature need not be construed as against sexual practice (though such views were then articulated and applied even within the confines of marriage);[8] yet, that is often how these writings have been read. Similarly, the creation between 1832 and 1846 of such organizations as the New York Female Benevolent Society, the New York Society of Public Morals, the New York Female Moral Reform Society, and the American Female Guardian Society[9] suggest to some scholars a binary opposition, between anti-sex, repressed and repressive middle-class "Puritans" and those who favor natural, unregulated sexuality.

A multitude of socio-cultural differences between that time and our own have helped displace such a two-sided view of the complex issue of prostitution in Jacksonian America. First, there was no statutory definition of prostitution in New York until the early twentieth century. Prior to that time, "when prosecuted, prostitutes were usually treated as disorderly persons or vagrants, and if convicted, it was a misdemeanor not a felony. Prostitution was only a crime in a public street. No law prohibited soliciting in a saloon, dance hall or furnished room[ing] house"[10] – nor, presumably, in a theatre. Second, existing records suggest that prostitution was most typically casual or occasional, rather than habitual or occupational; that is, sex could be exchanged for cash as well as companionship by working women without risk of committing a statutory offense,[11] presuming the act was not consummated in the public street. Indeed, the deplorable and uncertain wages for working women in antebellum America[12] and the poverty which resulted were cited as the cause of occupational prostitution by William W. Sanger in his landmark 1859 survey.[13]

If prostitution lacked statutory definition and prostitutes a clear occupational signature, the locus of the activity in antebellum New York was similarly fluid. Accounts from the era suggest large numbers of streetwalkers, a potential prostitute population whose numbers, lacking a fixable abode, cannot with security be statistically determined. The figures that come down to us were often grossly overdetermined by such publications as the *Journal of Public Morals*, which set the number of prostitutes in New York City in 1833 at 10,000, against an 1830 census population of 101,871 women (37,000 between fifteen and twenty-nine), or 10 percent of all females (27 percent of the prime age group).[14] Even reformers agreed that this figure (sometimes inflated to include estimates of "free" pre- or extra-marital sex) was too high, though they continued to use it throughout the era. Reconstructions of municipal records giving numbers of brothels coupled with estimates of non-brothel activity suggest the following ratios:

1830–39:   1,850 to 3,700 prostitutes
1840–49:   3,500 to 7,000 prostitutes
1850–59:   6,100 to 12,000 prostitutes[15]

The architecture of prostitution (its brothels) assumes a distinct but fluid distribution in Jacksonian New York. Unlike many European cities where prostitution had been geographically segregated for centuries into clearly marked districts, such an erogenous zone did not exist in New York until the 1850s. In 1830, most residents were a ten-minute walk away from a brothel, for they were found in every neighborhood, including the most exclusive. In the West Wards, for example, the elegant mansions of John Jacob Astor, William Aspinwall, John Cox Stevens, Moses Grinnell, John R. Livingston, and Philip Hone stood within one-to-four blocks of brothels, though there were far more, of course, in rough neighborhoods like Five Points.[16] Accordingly, when prostitution became a historical discourse in Jacksonian America, it did so with a certain geographic equality.

Finally, while displacing our views of sex in the earlier nineteenth century, it is useful to remember that the age of consent during the period was ten and there were no statutory rape laws.[17] Moreover, according to general estimates, nineteenth-century working-class women did not reach menarche until about fifteen,[18] confounding further current definitions of adulthood and morality. If this information is accurate, we will expect to find prostitutes at a young age. It is the corruption of youth – both the Bowery B'hoy and G'hal, since iconized in history[19] – that fueled reform movements and the appropriation of sex as a discourse in Jacksonian America.

II

Many historical accounts make a general association between prostitution and theatre in antebellum New York. Unlike earlier characterizations, wherein critics of theatre assume corruption of audiences by plays or by actors, anti-theatre arguments in the Jacksonian decades focus upon corruption through contact of audience members with other audience members.[20] On the face of it, there was cause for concern, for though brothels were scattered over the city, they tended to concentrate close to ferry landings, hotels, and theatres, centers of transient population. In addition, the favorite promenades of *femmes du pavé*, such as the Bowery and Broadway, were avenues adjacent to theatres. The danger moralists saw, then, was threefold: one had to walk through prostitutes to get to the theatre; one encountered them inside the theatre; and they used the theatre as a place to contact clients. We will consider these three arguments spatially: the brothel, the theatre auditorium, and its third tier.

Scholars have observed that between 1830 and 1839, of New York's ninety-three houses of prostitution, 34 percent were within 2.5 blocks of a theatre; between 1840 and 1849, the number of brothels dropped to eighty-seven, but the number near theatres rose to 42 percent; between 1850 and 1859, 53 percent of New York's brothels were within 2.5 blocks of a theatre.[21] "Sarah Brady's establishment on Church Street and Mrs. Brown's on Leonard Street advertised their proximity to the National Theatre." When the National burned in 1841 one of its walls fell on a newly opened "temple of Venus."[22] The Chatham, Bowery, Broadway, and Lafayette Theatres all shared their blocks with brothels and the Park's association with houses, detailed in "Butt Ender's" *Prostitution Exposed, or a Moral Reform, Directory* (1839), was long if not distinguished:

In addition to the dressing rooms for performers [behind the Park in Theatre Alley], Rebecca Fraser ran a brothel in the early 1820's before moving around the corner at Ann Street in 1825. For nearly a decade, from 1831 to 1839, [Sarah McGindy and] Mrs. Newman ran a house with at least eight girls only a few doors behind the Park Theatre [that specifically catered to performers and patrons alike].[23]

If rubbing shoulders with prostitutes and living near them were unavoidable facts of daily life in antebellum New York, any citizen with the price of admission could elect whether to attend the theatre and risk further contamination or stay away. Opinion at the time held that some audience members were prostitutes. Throughout this account, it will be evident that the creation of theatre audiences as a "problem" in antebellum New York leaves us strongly dependent upon contemporary perceptions as to which women attending the theatre were prostitutes, since then, as now, prostitutes wore no identifying tokens. Observers at the time could note that "nob and snob, Fifth Avenue and Chatham Street sit side by side fraternally on the hard benches" of a popular theatre like the Castle Garden,[24] for the only way to avoid contact with "strangers" was to buy out a box. Since this was an expense beyond the means of most youths, critics of theatre like abolitionist merchant Arthur Tappan might forbid their clerks to attend the theatre or to associate with members of the theatrical profession.[25] Similarly, in an 1838 report to the

Society for the Reformation of Juvenile Delinquents, Stephen Allen indicted small, minor theatres as "more injurious to the morals of the city than the older establishments," where prostitution was regulated.[26] Cautionary statements to women concerning the possibility of contact at the theatre with prostitutes or roughs (mainly rowdies, but also mashers) were published in ladies' magazines and newspapers.[27]

"Regulation" was the issue but how should regulation be understood? John J. Jennings's description of a theatre audience in St. Louis speaks to the complexity of identifying the players. From his seat in the parquette, Jennings spies upon two well-dressed women in front of him, one the wife of a traveling man, the other "a *nymphe du pavé* – a street walker – who scoured the principal thoroughfares at night for victims to carry to her 'furnished room,' and who had been educated up to the 'personal' racket by the lonely and wayward young wife of the commercial drummer." Having answered an ad in the paper, the women meet two men from a hotel for a preliminary lookover, ending in a "meal" at one of the local private dining rooms. Jennings found well-appointed women in the dress circles and boxes (presumably not prostitutes) who came to the theatre to flirt; and on matinee occasions, "women of questionable repute who unblushingly advertise their calling." This, he considered "an annoyance that refined and elegant people cannot tolerate." He describes how "fast women" use the theatre to meet old and make new acquaintances; that men frequent the theatre to snare innocent girls; and that managers "know very little if anything" about the assignations made in their theatres by working prostitutes.[28] More delicately, New Yorker Charles Haswell coyly notes in his memoirs, "I saw but two gloved women in the audience; they, by force of their attire, I suppose, felt a certain application of the saying *noblesse oblige*, since they went much out of their way to be agreeable to us, and were very courteous and hospitality minded indeed."[29] If Haswell is offering his readers a coy description of prostitutes rather than of two flirtatious women in gloves, the editor of the *New York Morning Herald* was neither coy nor reticent in his description of an audience at the Park Theatre in 1838:

On Friday night the Park Theatre contained 83 of the most profligate and abandoned women that ever disgraced humanity; they entered in the same door, and for a time mixed indiscriminately with 63 virtuous and respectable ladies ... Men of New York, take not your wives and daughters to the

Park Theatre, until Mr. Simpson pays some respect to them by construct-
ing a separate entrance for the abandoned of the sex.[30]

Did regulation mean the prevention of solicitation in theatres,
behavior not statutorily prohibited, though reducible by vigilant
policing; or segregation of prostitutes (however they were classified)
to parts of the theatre where "refined" persons could avoid them –
such as the upper tiers, where "respectable" working women and
men of modest means sat; or the barring of presumed prostitutes
from the theatre altogether, an action difficult to execute and
without legal authority. Theatre managers seem to have had little
recourse except the low road of discouraging solicitation on the
premises, a course advocated by William Sanger in his 1859 study of
prostitution: "[M]any of the managers of our best theatres have
abolished the third tier, so called, and if any improper woman visits
them she must do so under the assumed garb of respectability and
conduct herself accordingly."[31] Such a response to prostitutes was
consistent with low regulatory interference between theatres and
their audiences, a tradition not without socio-political import and
worth detailing here.

Power/ideology in Jacksonian theatre research offers up, as Clifford Geertz suggests, not "a single system of signification," but
multiple readings of theatre culture.[32] One reading delineates the
operation of nineteenth-century American theatre as a private contract between audience and management. In such a relationship,
noisemaking, even physical protest, was an audience's right. To call
the watch into the house to quell a disturbance would violate the
"contract" and escalate the disturbance, as it did in the Joshua
Anderson affair at the Park Theatre in 1831, for which the press
blamed the Park manager, not the audience.[33] In a similar incident
involving the actor Farren in 1834, Bowery manager Hamblin
contained the damage to the theatre without calling the watch, and
it is important here to note, various presses were accused of being
responsible for the disturbance and the abolitionist attacks with
which it coincided.[34]

The significance of such privatized arrangements between theatre
management and audience increases when we remember that a
police force as we know it did not exist in New York City until
1845.[35] Prior to that, a constabulary or watch kept the peace,
supplemented by various militia in times of great disturbance.
Militia were volunteer units affiliated with regiments, but often

connected to gangs, political groups, fire companies, bars, and gentlemen's clubs.[36] Indeed, the Bowery area had its own militia – the Hamblin guards – led by stage manager John Stevens, that used the theatre orchestra as its band for parades.[37] Law and order, inside theatres and out, assume a very different relationship to behavior when functioning as "unofficial" rather than "official." The resonances of this on micro and macroscopic scales are suggested in the following two instances: Haswell's recollection of how the Park audience – following the publication of *Domestic Manners of the Americans* in 1832 – cried "Trollope! Trollope!" to an habitué of the pit who turned his back on the stage;[38] and in this framing of the Astor Place Riot of 1849:

> The public and magistrates have been accustomed to look upon theatrical disturbances, rows, and riots, as different in their character from all others. The stage is presumed to be a correction of the manners and the morals of the public, and on the other hand the public has been left to correct, in its own energetic way, the manners and the morals of the stage; and magistrates, looking upon it as a matter between the actors and the audience, have generally refused to interfere, unless there was a prospect of a violent breach of the peace, when they have usually ordered the house to be closed.[39]

The morality of audiences becomes a subject for historical discourse both in antebellum America and in current scholarship because it emerges as a "problem" requiring "regulation" of prostitutes. Theatre managers electing to discourage solicitation rather than to segregate or bar prostitutes, recognized the usefulness of basing judgment upon conduct rather than appearance. This is consistent with a lassez faire approach to audience behavior on the whole, and also an acknowledgment of a changing audience profile. As theatre seating capacity between 1830 and 1850 in New York City surpassed population growth by 100 percent,[40] the creation and appropriation of forms and spaces of representation erased any sustainable concept of a stable antebellum cultural center. What emerges instead is a picture of social rupture, captured in 1851 by George G. Foster in his study of Gotham, for our purposes most appropriately titled *New York Naked*:

> [The upper galleries of the Bowery] are filled with rowdies, fancy men, working girls of doubtful reputation, and, least of all, the lower species of public prostitutes, accompanied by their "lovyers" or such victims as they have been able to pick up. The central point of this stratum is the punch

room, where a continual flood of poisoned brandy, rum, and whiskey is poured down the reeking throats of these desperate wretches, until steam being up to the proper point, they take their departure one by one, to the haunts of crime, debauchery and robbery, whence they issue at nightfall like broods of dark ill-omened birds.[41]

Nor was this Stygian portrait restricted to the Bowery, for in 1857, an *Harper's Weekly* editorial complained that the mere construction of a theatre ushered gambling, prostitution, and drunkenness into a neighborhood, ruining "that quarter for any decency of life."[42] To the social ills earlier cited in our consideration of prostitution may be added [class] tensions, a dramatic increase in riots during the antebellum decades, unprecedented immigration, and political shifts that empowered those who had previously been effaced. A major battleground for power was cultural appropriation, fueled by attempts to control modes of information.

The "penny" press radically increased newspaper circulation in the 1830s. Between 1828 and 1840 the population in New York City increased 40 percent while newspaper circulation rose 117 percent.[43] The press redefined news: it printed gossip, lurid details of crimes, and established what constituted a social event or a political scandal. Reflecting or creating public opinion, the press chose sides not only in political but in theatrical affairs.[44] Sometimes, support was bought and paid for by theatre managers;[45] sometimes it was generated by house press agents;[46] sometimes support came reciprocally from the literary gentlemen of the press (who wrote plays) to the artistic gentlemen of the stage (who produced them);[47] and sometimes not even similar political beliefs could prevent vituperation or horsewhipping.[48] At any time and for a variety of reasons, a newspaper editor hungry for respectability or influence might take up the "let there be order and decency in our theatres" cause, shifting our reading of prostitutes and audiences in the direction of the moral.

Both theatre managers and the press in Jacksonian America understood quite well that cultural tastes and arbiters were changing. By 1842, when the Park Theatre reduced its prices, the margin between the cost of "higher" and "lower" entertainment had shrunk; similarly, "box books and subscription plans gave way to cash taken at the door or at hotel lobbies."[49] Sometimes entertainment forms were appropriated and the "refined," driven from the pit to the boxes by undesired contact with those they found socially inferior, abandoned some or all of New York's theatres; more often in America, audiences remained cross-cultural and new forms and stagings appropriated *them*.[50] Yet, even the patrons of cultural diversity sought a redirection of their cultural power by arguing for social control, and clearly the argument for regulation of the theatre's "infamous third tier" was slanted against the people who could but afford to sit there.

Regulation of theatre audiences has been problemized by the issue of respectability. Those Jacksonians who advocated the high road of either excluding prostitutes from theatres or of segregating them in the third tier, equally evoke respectability. Respectability was in part based on conduct, in part on appearance, though the two were often conflated.[51] Dress, as we've seen in the observations of Jennings, Haswell, and Sanger, signaled commodified availability to at least some "respectable" observers. Woe, then, to the working woman whose dress offended or who flirted, for fun or profit, with men, particularly the refined men who alternately judged and exploited her.[52] Whether prostitute or worker, women in the third tier were associated with roughs whose conduct in Jacksonian theatre is legendary and noteworthy here.

Confined by tradition to the uppermost gallery of American theatres, the Bowery B'hoy drank and rained peanut shells and pork-chop bones down upon the habitués of the pit – often depicted in contemporary records as but a more affluent and better-educated form of rough. Above all, the rough was noisy, trading remarks and insults with the pittites and the actors, who played to the "gallery gods." The interjections from on high appear to have been continual, and while accounts from those days often speak of the third-tier roughs – and the Bowery B'hoy in general – with affection for his spirit and humor, they all reflect the genteel bias that noise, drink, and rowdiness without bespoke the Satanic spirit within.

Clambering to the mephitic fourth tier, we watched, as long as untrained lungs could last in that atmosphere, the crowd of rough youth there compacted. Plenty of native sharpness was noticeable in speech and looks among those skyward seats, which doubtless contained also much native good, some of which would work itself clear in time and do something of account in the world; but the main expression of the crowd was of nursing vulgarity and vice with an indescribable air of sordid ignorance and brutal, fierce impatience of all lovely, graceful, delicate things.[53]

Even a tolerant observer decried "the low, unsatisfactory, and demoralizing character of popular amusements" that served as a "sensual stimulus and fierce excitement" to "every little vagabond of this city."[54]

Voices were raised throughout the Jacksonian era encouraging anyone with aspirations toward respectability to defend the theatre against charges of immorality by indicting the rowdy pit and especially that guilty third tier.[55] Accounts from that time are taken by historians to definitely establish both the historical "problem" and its interpretation, as in the following summary:

Of all the accusations hurled at the theatre by its enemies, the charge relating to the third tier was their strongest, least refuted argument. In its influence on American culture the third tier was much more than just a pivotal subject of discussion in the continual war between moralists and artists; it was a theatrical fact of life which probably shaped the American stage much more decidedly than historians have recognized. The assignment of prostitutes to one part of the theatrical house had a profound impact on theater design, on theatrical economics, and on the extent to which theater was accepted and supported in the nineteenth century.[56]

Such summaries are often colored by unexamined biases, as when an eighteenth-century French traveler's observation that "there are women also [with blacks] in the gallery" is read as evidence that the women must have been prostitutes.[57] A reading of the third-tier issue in solely moral terms has been repeated often by social as well as theatre historians. For example:

In even the best conducted theatres, respectable women with escorts could patronize only the dress circle tier, for the floor of the house was for men – and occasionally a certain kind of woman – while the upper boxes and the gallery were the acknowledged haunts of either street rowdies or whores and men seeking temptation.[58]

More dramatically, "The third tier [of the Bowery Theatre] was reserved for prostitutes, bringing workingmen patrons an amenity long available at respectable theatres."[59] The process by which the moral "problem" has become authorized in historical scholarship about the Jacksonian theatre reflects moves as diverse as reading distinctions between reserved and general admissions in 1759[60] to accepting a 1957 account, innocent of documentation, asserting that "prostitutes were among the [antebellum Bowery Theatre's] most ardent habitués. They swarmed the galleries, using them not only for purposes of pickup, but also as places where their relations with unfinicky customers could be consumated."[61]

A univocal and unquestioning reading of the third tier contributes to the perception that the "problem" of audiences attending the theatre in antebellum America is a moral rather than a social issue. Indeed, accounts by theatre figures such as William Dunlap, Noah Ludlow, and Olive Logan, who all had much to lose in the association of theatre with prostitution, are among the many persuasive accounts linking the two.[62] Rather than viewing the presence of prostitutes in Jacksonian theatre as a moral "problem," however, we will profit by seeing the moral as a cloaked reading of social transformations taking place in these decades. When we do so, as Foucault notes, received ideas "jump aside" and the previously hidden is revealed.[63] In the present case, prostitutes in the Jacksonian theatre are displaced from sole ownership of the "whispering third tier"[64] to which the standard bearers of antebellum respectability in New York would have liked to confine them, representative, perhaps, of all those audience members who represented change and the diffusion of power. Instead, we see other occupants, the working men depicted as sordid and brutal and the respectable poorer women of New York dismissed as if they were prostitutes. We begin to consider the impact of taste (in dress, demeanor, and amusements) in these readings.

As we abandon the idea of "that guilty third tier" as the reserve of vice in Jacksonian theatre, we refuse to give the moral "problem" a historical legitimacy it was unable to secure in its own day. Instead we turn to the theatre auditorium as a locus for the free circulation of culture and of vice, the resort of wealthy and respectable brothel owners like John R. Livingston, occasional prostitutes and mistresses, and the majority of their clients. We begin to consider the scientizing of sex as a social concern; the tension between "private contracts" by theatre managers and their audiences, and growing calls for external control of behavior, proximity, and culture; and the impact of these upon theatre people and the work they do. In these displacements, we make evident specific changes in our view of antebellum theatre, not as "a matter of emancipating truth from every system of power (which would be a chimera, for truth is already power), but of detaching the power of truth from the forms

of hegemony, social, economic and cultural, within which it operates at the present time."[65]

## NOTES

1 Michel Foucault, *The Order of Things* (New York: Vintage Books, 1970), xii. See also his "Truth and Power," tr. Colin Gordon, in *Power/Knowledge* (New York: Pantheon, 1980), 109–33.

2 Sean Wilentz's *Chants Democratic: New York City and the Rise of the American Working Class, 1783–1850* (Oxford: Oxford University Press, 1984) is one example among very many viewing Jacksonian America as historically transformative.

3 Michel Foucault, "Power and Sex" in *Politics, Philosophy and Culture*, ed. Lawrence D. Kritzman (New York: Routledge, 1988), 120–21.

4 Foucault, "Truth and Power," 125.

5 An example of bipolar opposition where one would not expect to find it has been located in the "free love" views of Thomas Low Nichols, wherein sex is both extolled and regimented. See Stephen Nissenbaum, *Sex, Diet, and Debility in Jacksonian America: Sylvester Graham and Health Reform* (Westport, CT: Greenwood Press, 1980), 158–73.

6 Nissenbaum, *Sex, Diet and Debility*, 26. Cautionary sex literature would include and is nearly limited to Cotton Mather's 1723 essay against masturbation and the anonymous *Onania* of 1724 on the same subject, and Parson Wadsworth's sermon against adultery in 1716.

7 See, for example, Barbara Ehrenreich and Deirdre English, *For Her Own Good: 150 Years of the Experts' Advice to Women* (Garden City, NY: Doubleday, 1978); John S. Haller and Robin M. Haller, *The Physician and Sexuality in Victorian America* (Urbana: University of Illinois Press, 1974); and John D'Emilio and Estelle Freedman, *Intimate Matters: A History of Sexuality in America* (New York: Harper and Row, 1988).

8 See Graham's *Lecture* and essays by Thomas Low Nichols.

9 These followed the 1820 founding of the New York Society for the Suppression of Vice. See Timothy J. Gilfoyle, "City of Eros: New York City, Prostitution, and the Commercialization of Sex, 1790–1920," Ph.D. dissertation (Columbia, 1987), 18.

10 Ibid., 22–23.

11 See Christine Stansell, *City of Women: Sex and Class in New York, 1789–1860* (New York: Knopf, 1986), 180–92; Marybeth Hamilton Arnold, " 'The Life of A Citizen in the Hands of a Woman': Sexual Assault in New York City, 1790 to 1820" in *Passion and Power: Sexuality In History*, ed. Kathy Peiss and Christina Simmons (Philadelphia: Temple University Press, 1989), 42; Marcia Carlisle, "Prostitutes and Their Reformers in Nineteenth-Century Philadelphia," Ph.D. dissertation (Rutgers, 1982), 89–100, and Gilfoyle, "City of Eros," 25, 189.

12 See both Gerda Lerner, "The Lady and the Mill Girl: Changes in the

status of Women in the Age of Jackson," and Christine Stansell, "The Origins of the Sweatshop: Women and Early Industrialization in New York City" in *Our American Sisters*, 4th ed., ed. Jane E. Friedman et al. (Lexington, MA: D.C. Heath, 1987).

13  William W. Sanger, *The History of Prostitution* (New York: Medical Pub. Co., 1921).

14  *Journal of Public Morals*, 7 March and 8 July 1833, and see note 20 on page 35 in Gilfoyle, "City of Eros."

15  Gilfoyle, "City of Eros," 30.

16  See Gilfoyle's chapter "Sexual Geography of New York, 1790–1860," 37–96. The West Wards had no theatres.

17  See Arnold, "'The Life of a Woman,'" 42, Stansell, *City of Women*, 257–78, and Gilfoyle, "City of Eros," 181. Based upon a shift in language in indictments, Arnold assumes a rise in consent age to fourteen in 1813, but cannot confirm this interpretation in the New York legal code (see her note 29, 54–55).

18  Peter Laslett, *The World We Have Lost: England Before the Industrial Age*, (New York: Scribner, 1984), 84.

19  See Wilentz, *Chants Democratic*, 300–1, and Elliott J. Gorn, "'Good-Bye Boys; I Die a True American': Homicide, Nativism, and Working-Class Culture in Antebellum New York City," *Journal of American History* 74: 2 (September 1987), 408–10.

20  One argument, of course, does not wholly displace the other. The morality of performers both on the stage (see Olive Logan and "the leg business," below) and off (the Hamblin and Forrest divorces) recurs in criticism during the century, as do concerns about the moral values taught by plays (frequently the ground for rebuttals by theatre managers).

21  Gilfoyle, "City of Eros," 84. See note 5, page 85 (misnumbered) for his sources, though the compilation and interpretation – as well as the scholarly labor – are his, and, he thinks, underestimate the number of houses.

22  Ibid., 105.

23  Ibid., 82, 107. Other guidebooks include "Free Lovyer's" *Director of the Seraglios in New York, Philadelphia, Boston, and All The Principal Cities of the Union* (1857–59); and "Charles DeKock's" *Guide to the Harems, or Director to the Ladies of Fashion in New York and Various Other Cities* (1855), both in the NYHS. *Prostitution Exposed* is held by Prof. Leo Hershkowitz of Queens College, CUNY, who, with Dr. Gilfoyle, made many helpful suggestions and kindly offered support to the present project, for which I am grateful to both of them. The extent of my indebtedness to Dr. Gilfoyle's research will be evident.

24  Allan Nevins and Milton H. Thomas, eds., *The Diary of George Templeton Strong* (New York: Macmillan, 1952), II, 455–56.

25  Allen S. Horlick, *Merchant Princes and Country Boys: The Social Control of*

*Young Men in New York* (Lewisburg, PA: Bucknell University Press, 1975), 172. Tappan's attempt at social manipulation of his young workers is relevant to the destruction of his home in 1834 in the aftermath of a disturbance which started at the Bowery Theatre over the actor Farren.

26 Society for the Reformation of Juvenile Delinquents, *Thirteenth Annual Report* (New York, 1838), 14–16, see Gilfoyle, "City of Eros," 103.

27 See *The Ladies Companion and Literary Expositor* and *The New York Mirror* for 1836 and 1837, and my entries for the Bowery and Wallack's in *American Theatre Companies*, vol. 1, ed. Weldon Durham.

28 John J. Jennings, *Theatrical and Circus Life, or Secrets of the Stage, Green Room and Sawdust Arena* (St. Louis: Historical Pub. Co., 1882), 66–67. Of course the account is probably a conflation of several experiences, perhaps even that of the hotel John. Lavishly illustrated with pictures of female performers at work and play, the obvious appeal of Jennings's book to nineteenth-century male readers likely gave it a life not only as a reminiscence, but, despite its occasional high moral tone, as a sample of soft porn and a guide to misbehavior.

29 Charles H. Haswell, *Reminiscences of an Octogenarian of the City of New York, 1816–1860* (New York: Harper and Bros., 1897), 362.

30 "Ladies of New York Look Well to This Thing," *New York Morning Herald*, 19 September 1838, 2.

31 Sanger, *History of Prostitution*, 557. It is not altogether clear how "abolish the third tier" is intended, but likely a change in behavior there rather than architecture is meant. Sanger subsequently cites (page 558) theatres where prostitutes were admitted to this tier, presumably meaning working prostitutes actively soliciting.

32 Clifford Geertz, *The Interpretation of Cultures* (New York: Basic Books, 1973), 89.

33 See Peter G. Buckley, "To the Opera House: Culture and Society in New York City, 1820–1860," Ph.D. dissertation (SUNY–Stony Brook, 1984), 162–80, for a listing of sources and a general discussion of the "contract."

34 Ibid., 181–90, for a discussion of the Farren riot and the attack on abolitionist Lewis Tappan. See also Bruce McConachie, "'Theater of the Mob': Apocalyptic Melodrama and Preindustrial Riots in Antebellum New York" in *Theatre for Working-Class Audiences in the United States, 1830–1980*, ed. Bruce McConachie and Daniel Friedman (Westport, CT: Greenwood, 1985), 17–46.

35 Junius Henri Browne, *The Great Metropolis: A Mirror of New York* (Hartford, CT: American Publishing Co., 1869), 562, cites 1857, but Wilentz (p. 322) and others confirm 1845 as the date when the common constabulary was abolished and a plan for 800 professional police was enacted.

36 Buckley, "To the Opera House," 342.

37 *Clarion*, 19 November 1849.

38 Haswell, *Reminiscences*, 276.

39 H. M. Ranney, *Account of the Terrific and Fatal Riot at the New York Opera House, on the Night of May 10th, 1849* (New York: June 1849, pamphlet at the New York Public Library), 15.

40 Mary Henderson, *The City and The Theatre* (Clifton, NJ: James T. White & Co., 1973), 83.

41 George G. Foster, *New York Naked* (New York: n.p., 1851), 145.

42 *Harper's Weekly*, 1 (1857), 65–66.

43 Buckley, "To the Opera House," 360. See also Frank Luther Mott, *American Journalism: A History of Newspapers in the United States through 250 Years, 1690 to 1940* (New York: Macmillan Co., 1941), 194–205.

44 See my "Theatre and Democracy: Critical Bias in the Jacksonian Era," a paper presented at the American Culture Assn. Annual Meeting, Atlanta, 2 April 1986.

45 *Mirror*, 10 October 1833. The club movement, born in the 1830s, played its role in the influence circuit. See Browne, *Great Metropolis*, 445–54.

46 See my entry for the Bowery Theatre in *American Theatre Companies*, I, 114–21.

47 *Mirror*, 1 May 1830.

48 Editor Bennett of the *Herald* was vituperative, for which Hamblin of the Bowery horsewhipped him. See Mott, *American Journalism* 237.

49 Buckley, "To the Opera House," 146.

50 The often decried entertainments of the 1830–60 decades – melodrama and other popular modes – reflect these "new" non-elite forms.

51 As in rape cases. See Arnold, "'The Life of a Woman'."

52 See the sources cited in note 12. Although "refined" women were frequently drawn into the respectability "problem," it's pertinent here to note (D'Emilio and Freedman, *Intimate Matters*, 59–60, and 84) that contemporary research concerning sexuality and gender is steadily drawing Jacksonian leisure and working women closer together in defiance of nineteenth-century patriarchal accounts that separate them.

53 Haswell, *Reminiscences*, 262–363. Haswell cites actors' remarks like "Is that so boys?" and "Don't you boys?" eliciting roars of appreciation from the gallery. See also Buckley, "To the Opera House," 137. Examples of moral objections to the theatre are cited in many works, including Claudia Johnson, *American Actress: Perspective on the Nineteenth Century* (Chicago: Nelson-Hall, 1984), 3–35.

54 L. Maria Child, *Letters from New York*, 2nd series (New York: C. S. Francis & Co., 1846), 175. Again, the appeal of amusements to youth, perhaps seen here as a scientific issue (overstimulation) is raised, yet Child was not unsympathetic to the theatre. Earlier (page 171), she observes that though by 1846 the Bowery "is out of the walk of

fashionables, who probably ignore its existence, as they do most places for the entertainment of the people at large," she did not "think exclusive gentility worth the fetters it imposes."

55 See, among many examples, William Dunlap, *History of the American Theatre*, 1 (New York: Burt Franklin, 1963, rpt. of 1832 original), 407–12; Noah M. Ludlow, *Dramatic Life As I Found It* (New York: Benjamin Blom, 1966; rpt. of 1880 original), 478–79; Olive Logan, *Before the Footlights and Behind the Scenes* (Philadelphia: Parmalee and Co., 1870), 537–43; *New York Herald*, 1–2 November 1843, and *Spirit of the Times*, 18 July 1846, 2; and Philip Hone, *The Diary of Philip Hone, 1828–1851* (New York: Dodd, Mead and Co., 1927), 347–48.

56 Claudia D. Johnson, "That Guilty Third Tier: Prostitution in Nineteenth-Century American Theatre,'" *American Quarterly* 27:5 (December 1975) 575, and the same article in *Victorian America*, ed. Daniel W. Howe (Philadelphia: University of Pennsylvania Press, 1876), 111, from which the notes for this essay have been taken. These views have extended into several social histories (see next note).

57 Johnson invokes the eighteenth-century French traveler Moreau de Saint-Méry, via Barnard Hewitt's *Theatre USA* (New York: McGraw-Hill, 1959), 39–40 and note page 489. Her reading ("That Guilty Third Tier," 113) asserts: "Whether this meant that the women in the gallery (the cheapest part of the house) were prostitutes is left unsaid, but the fact that they were segregated on a tier with blacks suggests that the writer is speaking of the same women whom Dunlap describes as prostitutes. Hewitt also cites Washington Irving's Jonathan Oldstyle letters which note that the gallery is kept 'in *excellent* order by the constables,' but later recommends that the upper tier have 'less grog and better constables.' Again, there is no clear mention of the gallery's being given over to prostitutes and their customers, but, obviously, it was sufficiently rowdy to demand policing, which suggests that Irving left unsaid what Dunlap knew to be true, that the third tier was the domain of prostitutes." For de Saint-Méry's own words, see Kenneth and Anna M. Roberts, eds. and trans., *Moreau de Saint Méry's American Journey, 1793–98* (Garden City, NY: Doubleday, 1947).

58 J. C. Furness, *The Americans: A Social History of the United States, 1587–1914* (New York: G. P. Putnam's Sons, 1969), 565.

59 Wilentz, *Chants Democratic*, 258.

60 See Joseph N. Ireland, *Records of the New York Stage from 1750 to 1860*, 1 (New York: Benjamin Blom, 1968; rpt. of 1866 original), 29 and Johnson, "That Guilty Third Tier," 117 and note 19.

61 John M. Murtagh and Sara Harris, *Cast the First Stone* (New York: McGraw-Hill, 1957), 204–5. This unverified account of contemporary prostitution is often cited by historians. See also Meade Minnigerode, *The Fabulous Forties (1840–1850): A Presentation of Private Life* (New York: G. P. Putnam's Sons, 1924), 155. This book presents similar

problems to researchers, since it lists sources at its front and refers to them intertextually, but has no notes. It, too, is often cited.

62 See the sources cited in note 55. Ante-Jacksonian Park Theatre manager Dunlap indicted the separate entrance for unescorted women, prefering instead to deny them admission. Whether such a plan would have made that "portion of the boxes'" reserved for women more respectable seems unlikely, since it was the mixing of men with women that encouraged solicitation. Segregating women, on the other hand, invoked no requirements for respectability.

63 Foucault, *The Order of Things*, 326–27.

64 D'Emilio and Freedman, *Intimate Matters*, 59–60, 84.

65 Foucault, "Truth and Power," 133.

# CHAPTER 5

# Museum theatre and the problem of respectability for mid-century urban Americans

*Bruce A. McConachie*

In 1865, following the destruction of his American Museum by fire, P. T. Barnum wrote a stinging response to a letter in the *Nation* charging that his lecture room theatre had presented immoral plays to pander to degraded spectators. "No vulgar word or gesture and not a profane expression was *ever* allowed on my stage," he insisted. "Even in Shakespeare's plays, I unflinchingly and invariably cut out vulgarity and profanity." To the accusation that "it had been many years since a citizen could take his wife or daughter to see a play on that stage," Barnum countered that his productions had educated and uplifted many families in New York City. Admitting that the taste of his audience "was not elevated," that "millions of persons were only induced to see [his educational plays and curiosities] because, at the same time, they could see whales, giants, dwarfs, Albinos, dog shows, et cetera," Barnum nonetheless defended the respectability of his establishment. He had even hired detectives, he pointed out, to keep his museum above reproach:

I would not even allow my visitors to "go out to drink" and return again without paying the second time, and this reconciled them to the "icewater" which was always profuse and free on each floor of the Museum. I could not personally or by proxy examine into the character of every visitor, but I continually had half a score of detectives dressed in plain clothes, who incontinently turned into the street every person of either sex whose actions indicated loose habits. My interest ever depended upon my keeping a good reputation for my Museum ...[1]

Barnum was right to be concerned. During the middle decades of the century, arbiters of the dominant culture advocated distinctive modes of fashion, etiquette, and morality to separate respectable folks from the "dangerous classes" of immigrants and native-born wage earners. By the 1850s, many urbanites saw two different societies when they looked at their cities: a world of comfortable

parlors, restrained behavior, and sentimental affection, and a world
of crowded slums, gang fights, and moral depravity. By mid-
century, several social barricades segregated the genteel from the
unwashed in northeastern cities: housing patterns kept the poor in
their own districts, public schools were established to train workers'
children out of "all the vicious habits of low bred idleness," and new
metropolitan police forces maintained order on city streets. Those
with the economic means could demonstrate their gentility through
the trappings of sentimentality. But the families of many shop-
keepers, artisans, clerks, and others near the class margin unable to
afford the costumes and rituals of the emergent culture had to look
elsewhere to convince themselves and others of their respectability.[2]

The proprietary museums that flourished from the mid-1840s
through the '50s in the urban centers of the northeast served this
compelling need. At a time when nearly all forms of urban entertainment fell on one side or the other of the class line, museums drew
their audiences from both groups; opera-goers and Bowery theatre
spectators who would never meet at a concert or at a race between
fire companies rubbed shoulders at the American Museum. Because
mixed-class patronage was vital to their success, Moses Kimball at
the Boston Museum and Barnum at the American developed entertainments respectable enough to preserve the reputations of their
establishments, yet affordable enough to attract "the millions."
These museum exhibits and performances produced a variety of
effects and won a place in the hearts and minds of antebellum
spectators. Several of these effects, however, – especially those
inducing sentimental or, less often, gothic responses – helped to fold
thousands of status-anxious urbanites into the embrace of business-
class culture. At the same time, the meanings generated by these
experiences contained contradictions that would help to undermine
even as, in the short run, they helped to support the emerging
dominance of the bourgeoisie.[3]

While there is little direct evidence concerning the class, gender,
and cultural orientation of most museum-goers in Boston and New
York in the 1840s and '50s, it's likely that the popularity of museums
cut across most lines distinguishing social groups. William W. Clapp
noted in his history of theatre in Boston [1853] that

[Kimball's] museum attracted all classes, and it was the resort not only of
the middling and lower classes, but of the more wealthy residents, for the
pieces were well put upon the stage and the actors above mediocrity. The

museum was then and is now patronized by a large class who do not frequent theatres.

Given the low admission prices at both museums – twenty-five cents for adults and twelve-and-a-half cents for children – plus the preponderance of low- and moderate-income people in both cities before the Civil War, it's probable that most of their patrons came from moderate-income groups, citizens especially vulnerable to status anxiety.[4]

Regarding working-class patronage, Barnum regularly featured Bowery stars who were already popular with working-class theatregoers; he hired J. R. Scott, the king of Bowery bombast, for a season in the mid-1850s, for instance. Similarly, Kimball paid J. S. Jones, the resident playwright at Boston's working-class theatre, to construct plays for his museum. To reach the several communities of these artisans living on the outskirts of Boston, Kimball arranged special omnibuses and, later, trains so that respectable workers and their families living in Roxbury or Cambridge could be sure of a ride home after the show. During the 1850s when New York managers were moving their elite and middle-class theatres uptown beyond Astor Place, Barnum remained at Broadway and Ann Street, a reputable neighborhood below City Hall but within easy walking distance of the lower east side and nearby moderate-income districts.[5]

Barnum and Kimball also encouraged the patronage of women and children. Noting the numerous women spectators at New York museums, one contemporary commented, "Thousands who, from motives of delicacy, cannot bring themselves to attend theatrical representations in a *theatre* find it easy enough to reconcile a *museum*, and its vaudevilles and plays, to their consciences." The museum impresarios encouraged this distinction to attract female customers. In a printed letter widely circulated before the opening of his much enlarged lecture room in 1850, Barnum stated:

My whole aim and effort is to make my museums [he owned a smaller museum uptown] totally unobjectionable to the religious and moral community, and at the same time combine sufficient amusement with instruction to please all proper tastes and to train the mind of youth to reject as repugnant anything inconsistent with moral and refined taste.

Kimball, who operated his lecture room as a complete theatre six years before Barnum, began scheduling matinee performances to increase female attendance. Other managers had tried matinees before, but as long as the theatre was a predominately male ritual few afternoon performances had been profitable. By the 1850s, with Barnum offering five matinees a week, afternoon performances for women had become a theatregoing convention.[6]

Further, these men and women of moderate means were predominately Protestant in cultural orientation, if not in religious practice. Neither manager featured the kinds of entertainment popular primarily with Irish- and German-American Catholic working-class audiences. Rather, they produced many moral reform melodramas like *The Drunkard* and *The Six Degrees of Crime* which derived from the traditions of Calvinism and appealed mostly to native-born workers and lower-strata members of the business class. Both managers also trumpeted their endorsement of temperance, a cause offensive to most Catholic immigrants, and prohibited drinking at their establishments. Museum audiences, then, were predominately native-born family members of moderate income, oriented toward Protestantism, and probably included as many women as men.

Concern for their position in mid-century urban society led to a variety of responses among these city dwellers. During the depression years of the early 1840s, many artisans turned away from union activity and toward movements, such as temperance and health reform, which promised independence and social status through a regimen of self-control. As soon as they could afford to do so, many married women of moderate means stopped working for wages and practiced domesticity; the emergent culture defined respectable women as wives and mothers, not workers. Hoping to train their children in habits of discipline and morality which might aid their later success, parents near the class margin enrolled them in the new public and Sunday schools. Rather than turning to social co-operation or political action in order to alter the norms of respectability, most mid-century urbanites fearful of their status looked to their families and themselves for security and success.[7]

Families of moderate income also turned to the culture of domesticity to enhance their status. Though generally sentimental in orientation, domesticity limited the objects and goals of sentimental compassion to those approved by the emerging culture of business-class respectability. According to the moralists of domestic culture in the pulpit, the government, and the publishing industry, men should control the institutions of worldly power while women exercised their more spiritual expertise in home and family matters. Genteel propriety mandated that self-control and spirituality restrain and purify the tensions of home life. Family members, led by the mother, should treat one another with sincerity and "sensibility," a term which mid-century Americans took to mean sensitivity to and concern for the feelings and morals of others. Thus if her home were a place where "heart meets heart, in all the fondness of a full affection," the sentimental wife might believe she was performing her duty to her husband and children. The central values of domesticity – self-control, spirituality, sincerity, and sensibility – turned the problems of social order and economic justice back onto the family and the individual. Neither led status-anxious urbanites to question the emerging culture of respectability.[8]

Kimball and Barnum built their businesses partly on the impeccable reputations, but poor profitability, of earlier institutions dedicated to educating the public in the arts and sciences. Charles Willson Peale had established a museum in Philadelphia in 1786 where, as he observed, "every art and every science should be taught by plans, pictures, real subjects, and lectures." By 1840, proprietary museums in several cities of the northeast featured scientific displays, waxwork figures, small menageries, landscape and portrait paintings, and magic lantern shows in lecture rooms. When Kimball and Barnum began their museums in 1841, however, interest in these leftovers from the American Enlightenment had waned. Although Peale had exhibited few "human curiosities," the new museum impresarios made most of their profits from their highly-touted dwarfs, albinos, Siamese twins, and giants.[9]

For the most part, they set these attractions within a framework of sentimentality. *Tom Pop's First Visit to the Boston Museum, Giving an Account of What he Saw There and What he Thought*, a pamphlet distributed by Kimball evidentally intended to be read to children, demonstrates the impresario's appeal to the conservative values of domesticity. The pamphlet centers the reader's attention on Tom, his sister, and their grandfather:

And when they found themselves inside – my! – didn't they catch their breath and hold on tight by grandfather's coattail, and stare at the beautiful ceiling and the huge pillars and the long high galleries and the pictures and the marble women and the dear little children running about and peeping into the great glass windows and giggling and chirping like fun.

Having established this tone of breathless, innocent delight, the anonymous writer has grandfather instruct the children on the specifics of the stuffed birds and fossils, not neglecting to correct the children's minor (and lovable) mistakes in grammar and etiquette. At an exhibit of monkeys, grandfather ties the superiority of Christian culture to the value of a dollar. These monkeys, he tells Tom, "are worshipped in some parts of India; and when the Portuguese [sic] pillaged Ceylon, they found a poor monkey's tooth in a temple there which the poor simpletons offered 700,000 ducats for! – more than $1,500,000 dollars. What d'ye think o' that, my lad?"[10]

In the course of their sentimental education, Tom and his sister discover that nature, like human society, has its villains and victims. Grandfather points to a stuffed anaconda crushing a "poor little antelope." The children see an orangutan that "refuse[d] to eat after his wife died" and a female polar bear that "kept pawing her cub and moaning over him after he was shot." Grandfather frequently links such scenes of domestic pathos to a religious sensibility. Indeed, he says, the entire museum is "a kind of Noah's ark ...., bigger than the biggest church you ever saw." The pamphlet presents the museum as a series of object lessons in a domestic culture which has colonized religion, society, and nature. The exhibits have only to be interpreted by a sincere teacher like grandfather to reveal homey truths and induce a sensible reaction.[11]

Barnum and Kimball provided domestic environments for their exhibits to encourage and enhance such sentimental effects. Both impresarios surrounded their rows of artifacts, stuffed animals, and mechanical marvels with many of the attributes of a well-to-do parlor. Kimball placed his exhibits in alcoves off "a spacious and lofty hall of Grecian design," positioning several chairs where his visitors might relax in the midst of their moral education. Adorning the walls of this hall were pictures of "a chasteness and propriety ... that cannot but please the most fastidious taste," including Sully's painting of Washington crossing the Delaware.[12]

Barnum eschewed Greek revival for the ornamental style then coming into vogue. Writing to Kimball in the summer of 1844 about refurbishing his museum, Barnum stated his desire for "plenty of gold leaf, rich chandaliers [sic], looking glasses, etc. to make it look novel ...." The showman even added a domestic touch to his housing for part of his menagerie. No doubt Tom Pop and his grandfather would have applauded Barnum's "Happy Family":

natural enemies – owls and mice, eagles and rabbits, cats and rats, etc. – caged together and trained to tolerate each other. In 1872, looking back over thirty years of enjoyment at the Boston Museum, a reporter for the *Boston Journal* remarked, "Indeed, the place has seemed to many more like a cozy home, abounding in pleasant conversation and lively humor, than as a temple of public amusement ..." In the Boston and American museums, working-class families could experience the environment of business-class domesticity – surroundings they might emulate but could never afford.[13]

This cozy environment no doubt influenced spectator response to the displays mounted by Barnum and Kimball which miniaturized and domesticated mechanization and industrialization. Signor Vivaldi's "wonderful mechanical figures," robot-like dancing dolls, appeared frequently at the Boston and American museums. Barnum exhibited a sewing-machine, "Barnum's Self-Sewer," powered by a dog on a treadmill. For two weeks during the summer of 1849, Kimball displayed "The Beauties of Mechanism, or Lowell in Boston" which featured "the manufacture of cloth from raw material using miniature machines." Such exhibits anticipated the celebration of technological progress in the world's fairs later in the century. Most museum technological wonders, however, were right at home in the parlor-like environment of their exhibit halls. Moderate-income customers could see that progress enhanced domestic bliss, but they may have wondered when their own or their neighbor's experience of mechanization would be as beautiful.[14]

Museum-goers' fascination with miniatures carried over into their adoration of Barnum's most profitable attraction during the antebellum era, General Tom Thumb. By endowing Charles Stratton, the dwarf's real name, with "status-enhancing characteristics," notes sociologist Robert Bogdan, Barnum exhibited his freak to the public in the "aggrandized mode." This included advertising the four-year-old as eleven, changing his place of birth from Bridgeport, Connecticut, to London, and re-christening him Tom Thumb. Audiences usually laughed with Tom Thumb, rarely at him. In the vehicle crafted for his public performance, Charles played the role of an upper-class gentleman, jocular with the men and decorously flirtatious with the women in the audience. Taking his spectators into his confidence, he dressed up as different characters – a Fellow at Oxford, Napoleon Bonaparte, and other high-status roles – sang popular songs, and danced with animation. His "levees," as Barnum advertised them, ended with the General assuming the poses of several familiar statues.[15]

Audiences were enchanted. One critic who had little good to say about the American Museum conceded, nonetheless, that General Tom Thumb "was really worth seeing, not only for the remarkable minuteness and perfection of his physical composition, but for the precocity and brightness of his mental attributes." Barnum toured his prime attraction around the country, eventually assenting to Kimball's letters entreating the showman to allow him to exhibit the General in Boston. "My receipts in New York were over $16,000 – so help me God – in four weeks," bragged Barnum to his friend. Were he managing Tom Thumb's royal entry into Boston, P.T. continued, "Our miniature equipage would be in Boston perambulating the streets daily." Barnum had puffed Charles Stratton's introductions to the elite of New York to increase his status with the American public; after the showman took him to England and France and advertised his audiences with Queen Victoria and King Louis Philippe, the dwarf's popularity skyrocketed.[16]

For the thousands of museum-goers anxious about their own status, "aggrandized" freaks like Tom Thumb offered reassurance as well as amusement. The giants, living skeletons, bearded ladies, and other human curiosities that Barnum exhibited in the aggrandized mode demonstrated the apparent democracy of the norms of respectability. If such freaks of nature commanded the respect and attention of the elite, surely all Americans who could afford to enter a museum could count themselves among the genteel. The presentation of these antebellum freaks in the "aggrandized" mode projected the aesthetics of sentimentality into the display of human oddities. By extending their compassionate concern to these freaks rather than laughing at them, spectators could celebrate their own sincerity and their sensitivity to the wonders of God's Nature.[17]

Barnum and Kimball exhibited other freaks designed primarily to induce gothic horror. The "exotic" mode of freak presentation which, states Bogdan, "cast the exhibit as a strange creature from a little known part of the world," probably thrilled and revulsed most antebellum spectators. Typically, these were non-western people with physical differences whom the showmen presented as bizarre by costuming them appropriately, emphasizing the strangeness of their place of origin, producing pseudo-scientific explanations for their deformities, and occasionally staging them behind bars. Their exotic freaks included Hervey Leach, a "monkey man" presented as a "missing link"; the original Siamese twins, Chang and Eng; a Negro with vitiligo, cast as a "leopard-spotted slave"; and the "Aztec children," two microcephalics or "pinheads," supposedly "captured" from the wilds of Central America.

These freaks joined other gothic horrors at both museums. Chief among them was the "feejee mermaid," apparently the upper torso of a monkey joined to the lower half of a large fish, a "black, shrivelled thing," according to Barnum, which both impresarios exhibited in a jar. Some of the waxwork tableaux also induced gothic responses from museum visitors. The actor Otis Skinner remembered his "horror" as a boy when viewing "Three Scenes in a Drunkard's Life." Many adults, too, probably experienced a secret thrill at the sight of the drunkard killing his wife with a gin bottle while their "moron son" looked on.[18]

By presenting an image of "otherness" that was primitive, erotic, or bestial, these gothic exhibits probably recalled fears of Calvinistic sin and damnation for their mostly northeastern Protestant spectators. According to critic Joel Porte, gothic fiction was often a form of "religious terror" which represented "for its producers and consumers alike a genuine expression of profound religious malaise." Likewise, especially for viewers who attended temperance meetings and read *Pilgrim's Progress* (next to the Bible, the most popular book among antebellum readers), gothic exhibits at museums may have induced a kind of liminal experience: viewers were both relieved to discover their own normality through the contrast to "pinheads" and drunkards, and appalled to see nightmarish images of what they might become if they gave way to temptation. Struck by the physical oddity, strange customs, and indecorous behaviour of "exotic" freaks, museum spectators could congratulate themselves on their own ordinariness, civilization, and decorum. The same exhibits, on the other hand, were also radically unsettling because they suggested the mutability of human forms; ordinary Dr. Jekylls might become fiendish Mr. Hydes. Although both responses probably worked to reaffirm the dictates of respectable domesticity for most spectators most of the time – inducing the belief that they were already normal or the fear that they had better become more so – the liminality of the experience opened up the possibility of responses that could not be easily contained by the emerging culture. In this regard, sentimental exhibits were less problematic than gothic ones.[19]

In their modes of exhibit presentation, Kimball and Barnum mostly continued previous traditions; their primary innovations were in centralizing and marketing their displays. They broke with tradition, however, in attempting to convince the public that their moral lecture rooms differed substantially from immoral playhouses. From the mid-eighteenth century, liquor and prostitution had been a part of playgoing in America. Since the 1820s, theatre architects had been designing semi-private saloons and separate entrances for "unescorted ladies," with the consequence that respectable women rarely attended the theatre unless accompanied by a father or husband. As the New York and Boston elite gradually withdrew from regular theatregoing to attend opera in the 1830s, young male workers populated theatre pits and galleries in greater numbers than ever before. By the early 1840s, most theatres had a reputation as sinkholes of degradation and riot.

Despite the clear risk to his own and his museum's respectability, Kimball opened his lecture room as a theatre in 1843. Soon named "the deacon's theatre" because Kimball gave free tickets to all the clergymen in Boston, the first museum playhouse seated twelve hundred in rows of plain, hard chairs. As one reporter later recalled, "The 'lecture room' was in another building similar in shape and size to the first, standing parallel to it, separated from it by a wide court, and connected with it by a few bridges and corridors, so that they who had conscientious scruples about the propriety of theatrical shows need not even set foot within the four walls that contained them." Following the phenomenal success of *The Drunkard*, written by Kimball's stage manager, the impresario expanded his lecture room in 1846 to seat 2,500. The new theatre featured an "orchestra" with rows of padded chairs, a "parquette circle" around it of more chairs in short rows divided by aisles, and a first and second balcony above the parquette. Gone was the hierarchical box, pit, and gallery division and in its place a seating arrangement that assured his public that all audience members were equally respectable. Kimball also abandoned the usual hierarchy of ticket prices. In fact, Kimball sold no theatre tickets at all; spectators were charged nothing extra to walk from his exhibit halls into his lecture room.[20]

Barnum initially used his lecture room to exhibit Tom Thumb and other freaks, but did not open it for fully-staged productions until 1840. Soon after opening his enlarged lecture room with *The Drunkard*, Barnum expanded the house again to seat 3,000 spectators. Although no architectural plan of the theatre remains, it is likely that Barnum followed Kimball's lead in abolishing the pit; a contemporary illustration of the interior suggests this conclusion. Barnum's theatre, however, may have been more richly appointed than Kimball's. Sensing the public's desire for mixing morality and luxury, Barnum puffed on his *Drunkard* program that his "new and gorgeous lecture room [was] fitted up in the most voluptuously luxurious style and is really surpassed in its elegance, taste, refinement, delicacy, and superb finish by no royal saloon in the world." Like his friend Kimball, Barnum allowed his museum-goers to enter the lecture room for free. Although both men were soon charging an extra twenty-five cents for reserved seats, they retained the appearance of non-hierarchical pricing, evidently an important consideration for their status-conscious patrons.[21]

The showmen's theatrical success hinged on their reputation as producers of moral drama. Although their repertoires did not differ substantially from those of conventional playhouses during the same period, both museum theatres were well known for their long runs of moral-reform plays like *Uncle Tom's Cabin* and the lack of smut and innuendo in all of their productions. And the frequency of minstrel troupes on both stages complimented the reassuring (though not the threatening) impression made by "exotic" freaks. Audiences experienced a similar feeling of superiority while enjoying the uncivilized buffoonery of whites in blackface.[22]

Museum theatre, however, used mostly sentimental strategies to assure spectators of their gentility. The hallmark of all genres of mid-century theatre was their implicit sincerity. Theatrical signs communicated idealized types of action – the villain, the shrewd Yankee, the minstrel fool – easily read at a glance by audiences; like the ideal of sentimental domestic behavior, stage images assured their spectators that truth and appearance were one. In addition to the transparency of these theatrical conventions, many performances spoke directly to the religious needs of their spectators. Watching Little Eva ascend to Heaven on a canvas cloud or the drunkard achieve regeneration and respectability through spiritual conversion reaffirmed for many mothers the central role religion must play in their own and their children's lives. Finally, if sensibility were the emotional response, as one critic put it, to "the least twitch on the spiderfine filaments of memory and pity," what better way to confirm one's "sensibile" emotions than to weep at a melodrama. Far from undercutting one's social image as sincere, self-controlled, spiritual, and sensible, attending a museum theatre enhanced one's social acceptability.[23]

Most theatre critics smiled at such sentimental strategies, including museum impresarios' refusal to call their lecture rooms playhouses. A few, however, pointed with contempt at their hypocrisy. "If the stage be distasteful, in [Barnum's] judgement, to the habits and morals of the audience who visit his establishment," demanded theatre critic W. K. Northall, "why not eschew them altogether, not wheedle the public into his trap and thus oblige them to patch up their damaged consciences with the paltry excuse that it was the museum and not the play they came to see." Northall's dislike of the showman's unconventional success apparently blinded him to the truth that by paying money to enter a museum, Barnum's public washed clean the sin of going to the theatre inside.[24]

Indeed, many museum-goers did have "damaged consciences" and needed just the "excuse" Barnum provided to "patch them up." As historian Robert Wiebe points out, conventional mid-century morality left "men and women with no place to hide their flaws. The human formed a simple whole [from their point of view], with body, mind, and soul merged into a single expression of character, and a weakness anywhere permeated the entire person." The exhibits and plays at the American and Boston museums underlined this unitary notion of human character and provided their customers with strategies for preventing their slip from upright and moral to bestial and degraded. Thus, Barnum and Kimball made it easy for their conscience-stricken customers to rationalize their enjoyment of museum exhibits and performances as domestic lessons in self-improvement. After such edification, how could museum-goers doubt that they had a greater claim to respectability than the exotic freaks, minstrel blacks, and melodramatic villains they saw on stage? On the other hand, Northall was right: museum entertainment was based on hypocrisy. In the name of propriety, the showmen helped their customers to believe that lecture rooms were not playhouses, that natural enemies like cats and rats could learn to love one another, and that the realities of Lowell cotton mills fitted comfortably within domestic parlors.[25]

Perhaps the museums' largest hypocritical claim was their implicit assurance that temporary respectability meant social equality. Barnum and Kimball did all they could to erase the traditional markers of class distinction within their museums: all paid the same admission price, all sat in the same lecture hall seats (except for some, later on, who paid an extra twenty-five cents for reserve seating), and all saw the same curiosities and shows. While inside the Boston and American museums, customers could believe that they were just as respectable as the wealthier patrons among them and much more genteel than the "dangerous classes" of Catholic immigrants, free blacks, and urban poor who either could not afford the twenty-five cents admission or preferred less "moral" entertainment. But this involvement in what might be called lowest-common-denominator respectability masked an important reality. Most museum spectators had played no role in establishing the ideology and respectability that limited and channelled the kinds of entertainment and edification they enjoyed. Nor could these members of moderate-income families effectively challenge or change the cognitive and normative boundaries of respectability as they were being shaped by the arbiters of the emergent culture. Perhaps this contradiction between the promise of social equality and the reality of increasingly hegemonic subjection led some museum-goers to reject the bourgeois discourse of respectability. But for the majority of spectators, the mostly sentimental and occasionally gothic inducements of museum exhibits and performances probably helped to enroll them in a culture that was shifting from emergent to dominant. Indeed, in retrospect, museum entertainment partly served to effect this transition.

## NOTES

1 The *Nation* published the original letter on 27 July 1865. Barnum's reply appeared in the 10 August issue. Both recent biographers of Barnum underline his concern with propriety and decorum at his museum. See Neil Harris, *Humbug: The Art of P. T. Barnum* (Boston: Little, Brown, 1973), and A. H. Saxon, *P. T. Barnum: The Legend and The Man* (New York: Columbia University Press, 1989).
2 School reformer Henry Barnard quoted in Robert H. Wiebe, *The Opening of American Society: From the Adoption of the Constitution to the Eve of Disunion* (New York: Knopf, 1984), 332. On class division in antebellum northern cities, see Paul Boyer, *Urban Masses and Moral Order* (Cambridge, MA: Harvard University Press, 1978); Wiebe chapter 16;

and Sean Wilentz, *Chants Democratic: New York City and the Rise of the American Working-Class, 1788–1850*, (New York: Oxford University Press, 1984). Although Stuart Blumin makes a case for a distinct antebellum middle class in "The Hypothesis of Middle-Class Formation in Nineteenth-Century America: A Critique and Some Proposals," *American Historical Review* 90 (April 1985), 299–338, I find that Wiebe's two-class division, respectable and unrespectable, accords more closely with the social realities of the period. This Victorian bourgeoisie was emergent, but not yet fully hegemonic in the 1840s and early 1850s, in the sense of Raymond Williams's notion of emergent culture as "active and pressing, but not yet fully articulated," *Marxism and Literature* (Oxford: Oxford University Press, 1977), 126.

3 Regarding class divisions in mid-century urban entertainment, see my articles on opera-going and Bowery theatre: "New York Operagoing, 1825–1850: Creating an Elite Social Ritual," *American Music* 6 (Summer 1988), 181–93, and "'The Theatre of the Mob': Apocalyptic Melodrama and Preindustrial Riots in Antebellum New York" in *Theatre for Working-Class Audiences in the United States, 1830–1980*, ed. Bruce A. McConachie and Daniel Friedman (Westport, CT: Greenwood Press, 1985), 1–46. Also useful is Lawrence W. Levine, *Highbrow/Lowbrow: The Emergence of Cultural Hierarchy in America* (Cambridge, MA: Harvard University Press, 1988).

4 In later editions of his autobiography, Barnum reported that he sold 38 million admission tickets between 1841 and 1865. See, for instance, *Struggles and Triumphs* (1889), 314. Since the total population of the US in 1865 was only about 35 million (and allowing for Barnumesque exaggeration of his ticket sales), it's clear that he drew in the lowest common denominator of theatre patron. Further, Barnum's and Kimball's admission prices in the 1850s were as low as any in either city. William W. Clapp, *A Record of the Boston Stage* (Boston: James Munroe, 1853), 471.

5 Clapp, *Record*, 471. On the respectability of the neighborhoods near Barnum's museum, see Mary C. Henderson, *The City and the Theatre: New York Playhouses from Bowling Green to Times Square* (Clifton, NJ: James T. White, 1973).

6 Critic quoted in Henderson, *City and Theatre*, 80; Circular Letter (c. June 1850) reprinted in *Selected Letters of P. T. Barnum*, ed. A. H. Saxon (New York: Columbia University Press, 1983), 43.

7 See Boyer, *Urban Masses*, Wiebe, *Opening*, Wilentz *Chants Democratic*; also, Herbert Gutman, "Protestantism and the American Labor Movement: The Christian Spirit in the Gilded Age," *American Historical Review* (October 1966), 71–101; and Ian R. Tyrrel, *Sobering Up: From Temperance to Prohibition in Antebellum America, 1800–1860* (Westport, CT: Greenwood Press, 1979).

8 *The Mother's Assistant* (July 1845) quoted by Karen Halttunen, *Con-*

*fidence Men and Painted Women: A Study of Middle-Class Culture in America, 1830–1870* (New Haven, CT: Yale University Press, 1982), 59. Sentimentalism did not necessarily support domesticity; see, for example, Blanche G. Hersh, *The Slavery of Sex: Feminist-Abolitionists in America* (Champaign–Urbana, IL: University of Illinois Press, 1978). On sentimental culture, see Nancy Cott, *The Bonds of Womanhood: "Woman's Sphere" in New England, 1780–1835* (New Haven, CT: Yale University Press, 1977); Halttunen, *Confidence Men*; Mary P. Ryan, *Cradle of the Middle Class: The Family in Oneida County, New York, 1790–1865* (Cambridge: Cambridge University Press, 1981); and Barbara Welter, "The Cult of True Womanhood: 1820–1860," *American Quarterly* 17 (Summer 1966), 151–74. In her *The Empire of the Mother: American Writing About Domesticity* (New York: Institute for Research in History and Haworth Press, 1982), 142, Mary P. Ryan notes that the doctrine of domesticity undermined the possibility of fundamental social change.

9 Peale quoted in Harris, p. 56. On Peale's museum, see Charles C. Sellers, *Mr. Peale's Museum: Charles Willson Peale and the First Popular Museum in Natural Science and Art* (New York: W. W. Norton, 1980).

10 *Tom Pop's First Visit to the Boston Museum with his Grandfather, Giving an Account of What he Saw There and What he Thought*, (Boston: [n.p.], 1848), 6, 14.

11 Ibid. 15, 1.

12 Howard M. Ticknor, "The Passing of the Boston Museum," *New England Magazine* 28 (June 1903), 384.

13 The illustration is in *Gleason's Pictorial Drawing-Room Companion*, 29 January 1853; Barnum to Kimball, 17 June 1844, Barnum–Kimball Letters, Boston Atheneum; "Boston Museum, An Interesting Retrospect," reprinted in *The Golden Jubilee of William Warren: His Life and Reminiscences* ([Boston]: James Daly, 1918), 27, at the Boston Public Library.

14 Vivaldi noted in Boston Museum program for 26 December 1845 (Boston Public Library Collection); Lowell in Boston noted by Claire McGlinchee, *First Decade of the Boston Museum* (Boston: B. Humphries, 1940), 314.

15 Robert Bogdan, *Freak Show: Presenting Human Oddities for Amusement and Profit* (Chicago: University of Chicago Press, 1988), 97. Saxon, *Barnum*, 126–28, presents excerpts from Barnum's script for Stratton. 16. William K. Northall, *Before and Behind the Curtain, or Fifteen Years' Observations among the Theatres of New York* (New York: W. F. Burgess, 1851), 20; and Barnum to Kimball, 38, in *Letters*.

17 On the aesthetics of sentimentality, see Gregg Camfield, "The Moral Aesthetics of Sentimentality: A Missing Key to *Uncle Tom's Cabin*," *Nineteenth-Century Literature* 43 (December 1988) 319–45 and Philip Fisher, *Hard Facts: Setting and Form in the American Novel* (New York: Oxford University Press, 1985).

18 Bogdan, *Freak Show*, 97. Regarding Barnum's exotic freaks, see Saxon,

80

*Barnum*, 97–103. Skinner in *Documents of American Theatre History: Famous American Playhouses. 1716–1899*, ed. William C. Young (Chicago: American Library Assn., 1973), 105.

19 Porte, "In the Hands of an Angry God: Religious Terror in Gothic Fiction" in *The Gothic Imagination: Essays in Dark Romanticism*, ed. G. R. Thompson (Pullman, WA: Washington University Press, 1974), 42–64. On liminal experiences and rituals involving human mutability, see Mary Douglas, *Purity and Danger: An Analysis of the Concepts of Pollution and Taboo* (New York: Routledge, and Kegan Paul 1966).

20 Ticknor, "The Passing of the Boston Museum," 385; architectural plan for the 1846 theatre in "The History of the Boston Museum" by Ticknor included in the *Golden Jubilee of William Warren*, 10. The success of Kimball's democratic seating and ticketing policies effected a minor revolution in theatrical architecture and managerial practice. By the mid-1850s, most theatre managers had banned liquor and prostitutes, replaced the pit with an orchestra of cushioned chairs, and changed the illicit third tier into a "family circle" to encourage the attendance of women and children.

21 *Gleason's Pictorial Drawing-Room Companion*, 29 January 1853; *Drunkard* program in Joseph N. Ireland, *Extra-Illustrated Records of the New York Stage*, 1867, MS, Harvard Theatre Collection, II: Pt. 13, 163.

22 For Kimball's repertoire, see McGlinchee, *First Decade*; for Barnum's see George C. D. Odell, *Annals of the New York Stage*, 15 vols. (New York: Columbia University Press, 1929–49), vols. v and vi. Also useful is *American Theatre Companies, 1749–1887*, ed. Weldon Durham (Westport, CT: Greenwood Press, 1986), 38–44, 68–75. On the reassuring qualities of minstrelsy for antebellum audiences, see Robert C. Toll, *Blacking Up: The Minstrel Show in Nineteenth-Century America* (New York: Oxford University Press, 1974).

23 J. M. S. Tomkins, *The Popular Novel in England* quoted by Halttunen, *Confidence Men*, 57.

24 Northall, *Before and Behind the Curtain*, 166.

25 Wiebe, *Opening*, 276.

# CHAPTER 6

# Social awareness on stage: tensions mounting, 1850–1859

## Walter J. Meserve

In his essay on "The Eighteenth Presidency," 1856, Walt Whitman wrote: "No man knows what will happen next, but all know that some such things are to happen as mark the greatest moral convulsions of the earth." The decade of the 1850s was surely a period in which the various strands of American society, both entangled and stretched taut by fanatic individualism, experienced a turmoil of ever-increasing intensity. The fermenting search for personal freedom that stimulated the imaginations of many individuals also pushed boundaries westward and encouraged idealism and dreams. In the rapidly developing nation of immigrants, however, conflicts arose from a persistent jealousy and greed fed by opportunities which not all wanted to share. Anti-foreignism grew in politics and society, as the "root hog or die" concept warred with the attitude of humanists concerned with issues of slavery, temperance, suffrage, and religion. Eastern cities, particularly New York, bore the brunt of the "moral convulsions" that would engulf a society fragmented by that idealism insisted upon by men and women of good conscience and by the grosser nature of mankind that chased a Midas rainbow and exploited the dreams of others. But the conditions of social and political upheaval only continued to increase until the inevitable violence erupted from the one issue that could seriously divide that nation.

Crime-ridden, dirty, poverty-stricken lower New York, a spectacle in itself, was an irresistible attraction for America's journeymen dramatists, sensationalists by nature. Those with higher aspirations for American drama might comment with a modicum of originality on the social conditions that surrounded them, but their objective was usually the exploitation of social events for the effect of novelty, spectacle, and sensation based on the popular fears and fascinations of big city life. Muckraking for the sake of amusement

became a lucrative theatrical venture during the last years of the
decade. As the variations of Dion Boucicault's *The Poor of New York*,
1857, show, the scene was universal, and the "poor" could easily be
transferred to London or Liverpool; it was the poverty that people
wanted to see and the injustice of villainy overcome, as only the
melodramatic stage could rescue lives in a society bent on creating
tragedy.

Fascination with crime and the ugliness of certain parts of society
was not new in the theatre, but localizing the incidents produced
fresh horror. *Life in Brooklyn, Its Lights and Shades – Virtues and Vices*,
1857, introduced scenes in and about the City Hall, City Hotel,
Montague, the Engine House, Station Houses and Churches. Thad-
deus Mehan's *Modern Insanity; or, Fashion and Forgery*, 1857, was
described in *The Spirit of the Times*[1] as "a thing of the time, abounding in sharp and telling hits and illustrative of some of the dark
phases of city life" (*ST*, 21 March 1857, 72). There was evil in the
new world, so the message went, jeopardizing that vaunted "opportunity," and J. Burdette Howe, that cosmopolitan English actor-
playwright who lived in America at this time and contributed
markedly to amusements, wrote of *The Mysteries and Crimes of New
York and Brooklyn*, 1858, in which an Italian villain (anti-foreign
influence) and his quadroon mistress almost annihilate all of the
virtuous characters in the play. Repeated event for event in dozens
of plays, this activity represented life in New York and Brooklyn, not
always exaggerated according to the reformers of the day but greatly
trivialized for the theatre.

Not all of the plays concerned with New York society were
obviously sentimental and exploitive, although the theatre of this
period tended to emphasize such features. The decade opened, in
fact, with the production of three plays that deserve some comment
as more serious reflections of dramatists of the period. The comedy of
*Extremes* by J. Austin Sperry centered upon the activities of a
wealthy merchant, a young widow, and a hopelessly romantic
woman. Although written in haste, according to the *Spirit* (*ST*, 2
March 1850, 24), the play appealed to audiences and by the following year became a repeated attraction at the Broadway Theatre. In
November 1858 Burton opened his new theatre with "Mr. Sperry's
celebrated, fashionable, satirical and political American comedy,"
which was described as having "been played throughout the
country with general approbation" (*ST*, 27 November 1858, 516).

Edward Sherman Gould (1805–85), a Connecticut Yankee with strong opinions, made his living in New York as a merchant and as a writer of novels, sketches, anecdotes, and translations. His comedy of *The Very Age*, 1850, provides an excellent picture of mid-century America and is better written than many that were successful on stage at this time. Reviewing the published play, *The Knickerbocker* called it "a satire upon the fashionable apes of foreign follies and vices" with "biting and incessant" insights into "upper tendom" and the advantage of stirring situations and spirited dialogue.[2] The scene is New York, 1850, and the characters include a New York millionaire, a fake count, a physician, a dandy just returned from the grand tour, an old maid from the country, and various fashionable ladies. The essence of "the very age," however, is revealed more in the dialogue than in the plot, which is darkly comic. The mother of Charles Rodney attempts revenge upon the millionaire Erskine, who abandoned her and their infant son years past, by forcing Charles to pretend that he is a count and by promoting his marriage with Erskine's daughter by a later marriage. Gould exposes New York as a place where a "man may play the rogue with impunity so long as he carries a full purse, covers his wife with diamonds, and lives up to the fashionable standard of extravagance" (I, ii). Society in New York is described by one of the fashionable ladies as consisting of receptions, balls four times a year, opera three times a week, church if the weather is good: "We go to the theatre whenever a dancer is announced who can swing her foot the top of her head" (IV, iii). Had Gould not flirted too closely to an incestuous relationship in his plot, his play might have been staged, although it lacks a distinctive and dominating major character, a fact which was demanded in a theatre controlled by starring actors and actresses.

Beginning with the 1850s, an increasing number of American playwrights began to comment – humorously and seriously, with a light touch or a heavy hand – on various aspects of American society. The phenomenon occurred in theatres across the country, but the concept of "peeping" or "looking" at life in America obviously began in New York. Plays such as the *New York Directory for 1856* (and others of comparable titles) which opened on New Year's Day at Burton's Theatre and featured Burton as Picadilly, fresh from London, suggest the opportunities for looking at New York. Another view would be presented that same year at the Chamber's Street Theatre entitled *New York by Day and Night; or,*

*The Soap Fat Man.* A sign of the times in New York was Thomas De Walden's *Wall Street,* 1857, featuring Knickerbocker Van Dorn, Alfred Highbred, Mrs. Uptown, and Quicksnap. De Walden presented Wall Street in the current view as "a gaming table where men play with marked cards and loaded dice, a battle-field, a dark alley, where you are grabbed and robbed; a chess board and many other things. All parties are bitten with the mania of speculation" (*ST,* 28 March 1857, 84).

Playwrights were quick to understand that money was important to people in New York. At Brougham's Lyceum in 1851 the *Spirit* noted (15 November 1851, 468) the owner's adaptation of Balzac's *Mercadet* as a two-act comedy entitled *Money Market; or, A Romance of Wall Street:* "It is a subject of the time" (*ST,* 15 November 1851, 488). Henry Morford (1823–81), a New York journalist and writer, tried to capitalize on the popularity of "local plays" and contemporary issues with *A Struggle for Gold,* 1858. More ambitious and less talented than Brougham, with whom he later wrote a romantic play on the Revolution, *The Spur of Monmouth,* 1876, Morford touches upon issues of drunkenness, filial obligation, gambling, and the worship of money. The plot follows a young man who returns from college to discover that his father, faced with financial ruin, has committed suicide and that in order to marry his sweetheart, who has now been forbidden by her father to see him, he must regain the family fortune. In one sense this is a modern version of the classical theme in which the returned son must avenge his father's death or ruin before he can marry his intended, i.e. duty before love. Eventually, the young man accomplishes his task through gambling at western card tables, and all turns out well. The *Spirit,* however, was quick to point out that "the author has committed a grievous error in giving the public to understand that gambling is a more easy and certain mode of accumulating a fortune than legitimate business" (*ST,* 13 March 1858, 60). The point may be well taken because the Puritan critics sometimes drew a solid line between the real tables of the western casino and the speculative business ventures of Wall Street, although the plot of the play was a true indication of the spirit of the times.

The singular success of Anna Cora Mowatt Ritchie's *Fashion* in 1845 and her popularity as an actress over the next several years undoubtedly stimulated playwrights to look at and make fun of the life they saw down the street and across town. One of the more memorable plays on city life in the 1850s was *Self*, 1856, by Sidney Cowell Bateman (1823–81), daughter of the actor Joe Cowell, mother of the sensational child actresses Kate and Ellen Bateman, and herself a fair actress and manager of the Lyceum Theatre in London. The plot of *Self* is relatively simple. An extremely wealthy New York merchant, Mr. Apex, is facing bankruptcy. Mrs. Apex, an ambitious and extravagant society matron, needs money for her own enormous debts as well as the gambling losses of her profligate son, Charles, by a former marriage. Therefore, she importunes Mary, Mr. Apex's daughter from a previous marriage, who has her dead mother's legacy of $15,000. An astute Mary refuses Mrs. Apex but gladly writes a check for $5,000 to help her father, only to discover that Charles has forged her name and depleted the account. It is left to John Unit, a shrewd and soft-spoken Yankee, to solve the problems of the family, berate everyone for their extravagance, and declare that "after all, our labors are prompted by that great motive power of human nature – self!"

Comparisons with Mrs. Mowatt's *Fashion* are immediately apparent – among the characters and within the plot: extravagant wife, a savior in the form of a moralizing Yankee, a good woman rejected, forgery, and the major crisis brought about by a misunderstanding. *Fashion*, with all of its problems, is the better-written play. *Self*, on the other hand, in tune with life in the 1850s, emphasizes local topics and allusions, and satirizes many more particular aspects of society. Patent medicines are lampooned; slavery is mentioned as a contemporary problem; daguerrotypes are a new invention; women's rights is a topic of controversy. Produced by H. L. Bateman at his St. Louis Theatre before being brought to New York, the play was praised as a step toward a national drama – a play that drags "our errors out of their hiding places for the just condemnation of the world, yet never forgetting, in the desire to amend an evil that we visit the theatre for amusement, and not for a sermon" (*ST*, 5 July 1856, 252).

*Young New York*, by Edward G. P. Wilkins (1829–61), the drama critic for the New York *Herald*, clearly reflected the topics of the day when it opened at Laura Keene's Theatre in the late fall of 1856. Critics found it both well written and morally respectable. "The piece was a complete success, and if the good people of Gotham would only profit from this lesson Mr. Wilkins lays before them in this interesting comedy, they may yet hope for better government"

(*ST*, 29 November 1856, 504). In contrast to *Self*, *Young New York*
dramatizes the strength and determination of a young woman, Rose
Ten-per-cent. Addicted to the writings of Ralph Waldo Emerson,
she rejects the life style of her merchant father and marries her
singing teacher, Signor Skibberini. She also recites the moral at the
final curtain: We must not "be censured by the poor for being rich,"
she says, nor vice versa, "But every man and woman is to be tried by
the standard of their own acts alone, and upon them is to stand or
fall. How do you like Young New York?"

Many did, because *Young New York* showed a very positive attitude for a country approaching serious trouble, although the many
topical observations suggested existing problems. There were bitter
comments on congressional elections, journalistic practices, "money
campaigns," current prices, and health cures such as "Dare-'em-
all's" syrup for bronchitis, a dollar a bottle. Perhaps most interesting is the comment on a train wreck in which twenty-eight immigrants were killed. Being only second-class passengers, however,
there would be no fuss over them. The attitude is a clear forerunner
of Mark Twain's comment about a steamboat blowing up –
"nobody hurt, killed a nigger" – and surely reflects local humor.
Although burdened with a conventional plot and weak dialogue,
*Young New York* is a revealing play by a shrewd observer.

Thomas Blayden De Walden (1811–73), born in London, made
his acting debut in America in 1844 and, with exception of a single
year's sojourn in London, enjoyed a successful, if minor, career in
the American theatre. Among De Walden's numerous plays *The
Upper Ten and the Lower Twenty*, 1854, was immediately successful
and frequently performed. Acknowledging the popular work as an
"excellent expose of New York life and a play of startling merit," the
*Spirit* quickly stated, however, that "we consider it a gross libel upon
New York and unmeritorious as a dramatic composition" (*ST*, 25
November 1854, 492). The plot encompasses a period of fourteen
years during which the main character, Christopher Crookpath,
leads a life of moral degradation as part of his successful attempt to
avenge himself upon a Mr. Simper, the seducer of his wife. The
means of his revenge and his constant companion during these years
is a child, "the issue of the adulterous intercourse," stolen by
Crookpath, made a beggar and ultimately killed by want and
exposure. The critic for the *Spirit*, although revolted by these details,
was incensed by the manner in which New York was presented. "We

feel a pride in this city, and in its people, and we rest assured that character is appreciated and sustained as fully and as particularly here as in any place in the world, all the dramas to the contrary notwithstanding."

*'Tis Ill Playing With Edged Tools* opened in Boston early in April, 1856 advertised as a "new American comedy" whose author preferred to remain anonymous. On 16 April the play opened at Burton's Theatre in New York. "The scene is laid in New York in 1854," wrote "Acorn," and is intended to illustrate fashionable life, with some of its vices, as it is said to exist in that goodly city" (*ST*, 12 April 1856, 103). Mrs. Goldie, young wife of an older man absorbed in his business affairs, reacts to this neglect first by showing some interest in a young visitor from her past and then by flinging herself into society where she becomes fascinated with cards and gambling. She wins heavily, invests in stocks, and then falls dangerously in debt before she regains the money she needs, partly through gambling and partly through the efforts of her old lover who has married her sister. The lesson of her acts is somewhat clouded both by her reversion to gambling and by the subsequently revealed joy of old Colonel Goldie who manipulated the market to his own advantage, never realizing that "his wife's money was in the sinking boat." It is a clear indication of the morality of the times that speculation and gambling were accepted aspects of the American character as portrayed by the hero or by the heroine in drama. In earlier and later plays such qualities would mark the villain, but at this time several plays show clearly that such was accepted behavior, rather than a weakness, the basis of a fascination from which comedy as well as pathos would be extracted.

Henry Clay Preuss published his play on the *Fashion and Follies of Washington Life* in 1857, an attempt, he explained, "to exhibit a panoramic view of character and events" in social and political Washington with the true objective to advance reform. The plot centers on two governmental clerks: Colonel Delaney, an upright gentleman with a lovely daughter, Emma, and John Sharker, the villain, who feels abused because Delaney will not encourage his interest in Emma nor assist him in his loose pursuits. Sharker's objective is to destroy Delaney and possess Emma. Within the five acts of this melodramatic conflict Preuss manages to say a great deal about Washington society, with politics the major issue – old arguments and new problems. Delaney and his friend, Captain John

Smith, argue Federalism vs. Jefferson as well as Henry Clay, "one of nature's noblemen," vs. Andrew Jackson, who "dodged his foe behind cotton bales" (I ii). Arguments center on the treatment of office seekers and the tenuous position of government clerks who are victims of the doctrine of rotation politically sanctioned by General Jackson. "Why, sir, the most menial occupation in life requires some kind of apprenticeship – but any man who has party influence to back him can assume the most responsible public trusts, altho' he hasn't an ounce of brains in his head" (II, iii). Although Preuss worked out his plot in an amateurish manner, venting his spleen on political issues, he hoped that his play would be remembered as reflecting "the Fashions and Follies of Washington Life" (v, ii).

A moving society always has its pressures and corresponding tensions, and mid-nineteenth-century American society had more than its share. With a population marked by individuality, stimulated by a philosophy of self-reliance, and harboring certain innate propensities for achievement, the country seemed burdened with problems – social, legal, political, general humanitarian – for which an increasing number of its citizenry were eager to provide solutions. Just as playwrights took sentimental advantage of the deplorable conditions in the cities, they were also likely to exploit the occasionally spectacular efforts of the reformers, those crusaders who found ready issues as they marched along America's streets. Most significant for the playwrights during these mission-burdened years were temperance, slavery, and women's suffrage in addition to the ever-present religious, social, and political reform movements.

Within a few years after the American Temperance Society was founded at Boston in 1826, a thousand-odd local groups sprang up along with temperance crusades featuring pictures, pamphlets, and reformed drunkards as lecturers. By mid-century the movement gained political force with passage of the "Maine Law" of 1851, at the instigation of Neal S. Dow, "the Father of Prohibition." Before the decade was over eight states and the Nebraska Territory followed Maine's example. The best-known temperance lecturer of the 1850s was John B. Gough (1817–86), a hopeless drunkard at the age of twenty-six who had spent several years as a comedian in stock companies in Boston and New York. Gough clearly found his proper stage when he signed the pledge in 1842 and spent the rest of his life writing and lecturing on temperance. Doubtless his acting experience was an advantage to his greater career, and he was known to dramatize his appeal by seating examples of the more disreputable local drunkards on the edge of his platform stage. Many writers capitalized on the commercial value of the temperance novel, but the most popular temperance novel of the decade was T. S. Arthur's *Ten Nights in a Bar-Room and What I Saw There*, 1854, second only to *Uncle Tom's Cabin* as a best seller.

Alcohol was a natural ingredient of many melodramas and farces that entertained nineteenth-century Americans audiences. Good people might celebrate with it; the unwary and the weak would make fools of themselves with it; villains were expected to abuse it or to use it to bring ruin or embarrassment to others. The temperance appeal simply allowed playwrights to concentrate upon an established spectacle in the theatre and enhance it with an acceptably popular moral. If the theatre served the temperance issue, that issue also served the theatre. As *The Drunkard*, 1844, continued its sensational popularity into the 1850s, the *Spirit* commented on its success as "the principal item in the entertainment of the evening" at the Bowery: "We know of nothing more conducive to the cause of Temperance than the spectacle at the Bowery" (*ST*, 13 July 1859, 252).

There was a general formula for temperance plays comparable to that presented in the temperance tracts, the "Demon Rum" fiction, and the appeal of the urgent lecturers. It was also blatantly obvious, as playwrights destroyed a happy situation only to have the fallen saved at the final curtain. C. W. Taylor's *Adrian Grey; or, the Redemption*, 1852, is a good example of formula playwriting. A prize temperance play, it featured an "apotheosis" with the Genius of Temperance plus Drunkenness, Famine, Theft, Murder, Virtue, Faith, Hope, Charity, and Mirth. Its three acts were titled The Tempted, The Deserted, The Redeemed. Taylor's *The Drunkard's Warning*, 1856, dramatized the horrible results of intemperance in the life of Edward Mordaunt, the son-in-law of a wealthy merchant, whose moral resurrection is the result of the efforts of an ardent temperance worker and a number of speeches by zealous women. His curtain speech is typical: "May Temperance be cherished in our midst as an unerring beacon of our future joys, the star of our prosperity, the foundation of our happiness, and the connecting link between our welfare here and our hopes of blissful peace hereafter" (III, v).

T. S. Arthur's *Ten Nights in a Bar-Room*, adapted by William W.

Pratt, opened at the National Theatre in New York on 23 August 1858 with Yankee Locke as Sample Switchel, drawing "thunders of applause and roars of laughter." The critic for the *Spirit* advised "all to witness it; a more profitable and interesting evening's entertainment can seldom be had." Not fully aware of the significance of the play but accepting its reality, the critic wrote: "The drama depicts a series of truthful scenes in the course of a Drunkard's life. Some of them are touching in the extreme, and some are dark and terrible. Step by step is portrayed the downward course of the tempting vendor and his infatuated victims, until both are indeed in hopeless ruin" (*ST*, 28 August 1858, 348).

As a melodrama *Ten Nights in a Bar-Room* does not match the theatrical effectiveness of William Smith's *The Drunkard*, 1844. Episodic and poorly structured, no part of the plot is well dramatized; the dialogue is highly artificial and buttressed by obvious expository soliloquies; characters, with the exception of Sample Switchel, are bland illustrations; and the action is mainly left to the actor's discretion. But the message was very clear: drinking leads to disaster! When Mr. Romaine, "temperance philanthropist" and former alcoholic, visits "the quiet village of Cedarville," he finds Sample Switchel, a Yankee who likes to drink; Slade, a former mill owner who has just purchased the tavern and is beginning to drink; Slade's son, Frank, who is open to temptation; Willie Hammond, a rich young man who enjoys a little gaming, a little drinking, and the company of questionable companions; and Joe Morgan, a pathetic alcoholic whose habits bring great sorrow to his wife and daughter. Ten years later (Act v) Willie has been killed in a fight with a corrupt companion; the death of Morgan's daughter has made him a teetotaler; Switchel has sworn off liquor; and Simon Slade, dissolute and filthy in appearance, has been killed by his own son Frank in an argument over a bottle of brandy. At the Morgan home where all is happiness, Romaine gives the temperance pitch: "you must cut off the fountain if you would dry up the stream ... A large majority of the people, I am convinced, will vote in favor of such a measure" (v, iv).

A good number of plays written during the 1850s, both directly and indirectly, through the dramatis personae or by the action represented, commented on Negroes as a part of American society or the slavery issue. Like the problems of alcohol, slavery would remain to plague America and no play was more popular than the dramatization of Harriet Beecher Stowe's *Uncle Tom's Cabin*, truly the world's greatest hit! A powerful novel, *Uncle Tom's Cabin* became a powerful play – or rather a powerful and entertaining theatrical tradition, because its innumerable staged interpretations make it impossible to discuss as a single work. Very soon after its first appearance in the theatre, people became aware of its extraordinary effect upon audiences.

Charles W. Taylor's adaptation opened at the National Theatre in New York, 23 August 1852, and ran for two weeks. Using his imagination and a cheerful disregard for his model, Taylor omitted St. Clair, Eva, and Topsy and changed George Harris to Edmund Wilmot. Act I included Negro celebrations, choruses of "Nigga 'n de cornfield," a Kentucky Breakdown Dance and episodes picturing slave dealers, a midnight escape, a search, Tom driven from his cabin, and the Negro's hope. The frozen Ohio River, a snow storm, and a chase in which Edmund shoots his pursuers were features in Act II, while the climax in Act III brought the return of Uncle Tom, freedom for the Wilmots with the help of Crazy Mag of the Glen and a good amount of repentance and remorse from the sinful. A more memorable *Uncle Tom's Cabin*, however, opened at the National the following summer, 18 July 1853, and featured N. B. Clarke as Simon Legree in six acts, eight tableaux and thirty scenes. A separate part of the theatre was provided for "respectable colored persons."

The real tradition of *Uncle Tom's Cabin* began with the adaptation by George Aiken, a young actor in the company of George C. Howard, manager of the Troy Museum in Troy, New York. Aiken's three-act version, opening on 27 September 1852, ended with the Death of Eva, but as interest in the issue of slavery increased with the national election, Aiken wrote a four-act sequel entitled *The Death of Uncle Tom; or, The Religion of the Lowly*. This play attracted some attention with the creation of Gumption Cute but made little sense to anyone not familiar with the first three-act Aiken version that ran for 100 performances in Troy. Music in the form of plantation melodies and minstrel tunes was added to create an effect. It was this version that played at the National Theatre for 325 consecutive performances – the first play in New York to become the entertainment for the entire evening.

Four other versions of *Uncle Tom's Cabin* appeared in New York that fall. The Bowery employed Thomas Dartmouth Rice as Uncle

Tom and advertised new roles as the days passed. Competition became cut-throat as the Franklyn Museum mounted its version, and Christy's Minstrels provided a burlesque. Henry J. Conway adapted the novel for Barnum's American Museum and added a Yankee character named Penetrate Partyside who, together with additional black characters, created a benign picture of southern slavery in general.

The English were particularly fascinated by *Uncle Tom's Cabin*. Before the end of 1852 there were at least eight versions of the play at different theatres in London, including an equestrian version at the Adelphi and a pantomime at Drury Lane. The adaptation by Tom Taylor and Mark Lemon was entitled *Slave Life* and pointedly subtitled "Negro Life in America" rather than "Life Among the Lowly." Edward Fitzball explained his part in the sensationalism and, consistent with English desires, provided a happy ending to the play by concentrating all of the villainy in Legree and by allowing Shelby to repurchase Tom and Harry and manumit them with the rest of the slaves:

The publication of *Uncle Tom's Cabin* set all the managers mad to produce it on the stage. Every theatre nearly produced its version. I don't know whose was the best. I was engaged by three managers to write three distinct pieces, which I did to the best of my ability; indeed, it did not require any remarkable ability as it was only to select scenes and join them together.[3]

Modern critics have dismissed Mrs. Stowe's second abolition novel, *Dred: A Tale of the Great Dismal Swamp*, 1856, as a well-forgotten failure, marred by excessive theological discussion and the mistake of doing away with the heroine halfway through the book. At least three playwrights accepted the challenge to adapt *Dred* to the stage, but none was successful. C. W. Taylor's version opened at the National on 22 September 1856, underwent a rewriting after the first week but lasted only five weeks, even with Cordelia Howard, the celebrated star of *Uncle Tom's Cabin* and *Hot Corn*, as the careless, good-for-nothing Tom Tit. John Brougham opened his adaptation at his own Bowery Theatre on 29 September 1856 and closed two weeks later. H. J. Conway opened his *Dred* at Barnum's American Museum on 6 October 1856 and altered the role of Tom Tit to accommodate the acting abilities of General Tom Thumb. It closed 15 November 1856. Only in London where H. Young dramatized *Dred* for the Victoria Theatre in late September 1856 were there claims of sustained success. In America the critic for the *New*

*York Daily Tribune*, 10 November 1856, begged managers not to produce another *Dred*.

The slavery issue was touched upon in a number of plays during the 1850s, sometimes seriously, sometimes for humor. Like temperance or the topical interest in spiritualism and local politics, slavery and Negroes were part of the journeyman dramatist's arsenal of devices. On 16 December 1859, for example, Laura Keene brought out a "new American play" entitled *Distant Relations; or, a Southerner in New York* which advertised "No North, no South, but Justice and Fraternity" with characters such as a rich southern planter and Paddy Murphy, a Central Parkite. But the approaching conflict was on everyone's mind. *Ossawattomie Brown; or, The Insurrection at Harper's Ferry* by Mrs. J. C. Swayze, a young actress, is a biographical melodrama and a plea for sympathy for the hero. Sentimental scenes dramatize the death of each of Brown's sons, and Brown, presented as a martyr for the abolitionist cause, makes a sentimental farewell to his daughter-in-law: "We look upon ourselves as workers in a great and good cause, to which we have sacrificed our lives" (III, vi).

William Wells Brown (1816?–84) is the first-known American Negro to write abolitionist plays which, although not produced during his lifetime, were typical melodramas of the period. *Experience; or, How to Give a Northern Man a Backbone*, 1856, was a satire on a northern clergyman with southern sympathies. Early in April 1856 Brown read this play in Brinley Hall, Worcester, Massachusetts, and continued to present it to audiences across New England through the summer of 1857.[4]

Brown's better-known play, *The Escape; or, A Leap for Freedom*, 1858, was eventually produced in 1971. As a former slave, Brown dramatized his own experiences. Basically, his play is a bitter protest against the American system and is more blatant propaganda and debate than a produceable play. Its most theatrical point is the leap onto the deck of a Canadian ferry, but it is the message of the play that overwhelms any action: "the worst act that a man can commit upon his fellow man is to make him a slave" (v, i).

*Neighbor Jackwood* is a five-act drama by J. T. Trowbridge (who also wrote the novel), produced first on 16 March 1857 at the Boston Museum under the direction of William H. Smith. As the very successful author of *The Drunkard* and co-author with H. J. Conway of a popular version of *Uncle Tom's Cabin*, Smith also had something to do with this dramatization. It was, at any rate, very successful, continuing on the Boston stage for the next eight years after opening in New York at Barnum's American Museum on 4 May 1857.

Set in Vermont, *Neighbor Jackwood* tells the story of a runaway slave girl, Camile, but with a sufficient number of flourishes to create the typical complicated melodrama of the period involving spectacle, comedy, mystery, and propaganda. An honest and upright farmer, Jackwood befriends Camile and at the play's climax, a courtroom scene in which Camile is discovered to be free, is thanked for his efforts: "We shall never forget who was neighbor unto her who fell among thieves" (v, vi). For her part, Camile refuses the villain in one of those memorable lines in nineteenth-century American melodrama: "Come a thousand evils! Come slavery! Come death! I can die, but I cannot sin!" (iii, i). The thesis of the play, however, is revealed best in Jackwood's reaction to the authority he had to fight: "a human critter's of more account than all the laws in Christendom" (iv, ii).

Not many plays during the 1850s effectively concentrated their power upon the slavery issue. It was used more frequently as a device for the greater end of amusement and entertainment, and no dramatist used slavery more effectively than Dion Boucicault in *The Octoroon*. Throughout the decade, however, and for decades to come, *Uncle Tom's Cabin* served propaganda interests in the slavery issue and expanded into excellent entertainment. Perhaps that single play was enough.

From the concern of critics and editors to the eagerness of novelists, and to the arrogance, real or pretended, of actors and theatre managers, it is difficult to misunderstand the growing force of plays on the American stage as an opportunity to influence while entertaining the public, either as a reflection of social issues or as clear and persuasive propaganda. Free to promote, ridicule, or reflect any imaginable position on the issues of the day, playwrights, because they felt bound by an unwritten law to amuse their audiences first and foremost, were somewhat tentative in their brashness. A few recognized and took advantage of their editorial privileges. John Brougham and Charles Walcot made definite appeals; E. P. Wilkins and Mrs. Bateman presented clear positions. Mainly, they stopped short of such obvious partisan fervor as Augustin Daly's pronouncement through the lips of his patriotic hero, Snorkey, at the climax of Act iii in *Under the Gaslight*, 1867, as Laura "leans exhausted against the [railroad] switch" "Victory! Saved! Hoorah! And these are the women who ain't to have the vote!" The effect of *Uncle Tom's Cabin* on stage, however, must have given playwrights courage. Comments on society in America, direct or indirect, permeate the decade, echoing the public concern for its various trials and tribulations.

The writer, D. K. Lee, who introduced the publication of J. J. Austin's *The Golden Age to Come; or, The Victory of Faith, and Hope, and Love*, 1854, stated his view clearly: "There is, perhaps, no kind of literature which has more power to strengthen the intellect, and stir the heart, than that which takes the style of drama." After confronting an atheist with the views of the Deist, the Calvinist, the Armenian, and the Universalist, Austin presented a "mysterious" preacher who explained the "promised Golden Age" ruled by the "pure religion of the Gospel – the Religion of Love." Most of the plays promoting, questioning, or discussing religion during the 1850s were written for a reading rather than a viewing public. Sylvester Judd's (1813–53) *Philo: An Evangeliad*, 1850, is a long (244 pages) play, written in scenes but without act divisions. In essence it is an optimistic Christian sermon in blank verse. Charles James Cannon wrote mainly for the closet and in blank verse. *Poems, Dramatic and Miscellaneous*[5] includes *The Compact* in which a disappointed hero, although warned by his Guardian Angel, sells his soul for "accursed gold/ To buy a wanton's love" and is cast into the flames of the Infernal region before a miraculous escape inspired by true love redeems him. James B. Congdon (1802–80) wrote a dialogue in blank verse entitled *Quaker Quiddities; or, Friends in Council*[6] in which he shows his dissatisfaction with a religion that is isolated and declining because it does not grapple with the problems of the world.

More relevant to the demands of theatre audiences, Charles M. Barras's *The Modern Saint*, 1857 (copyright 1856) was, according to the printed preface "a satire upon the loud-mouthed professional humanitarians of the present day." Barras, a well-known critic from Cincinnati who wrote under the pseudonym of "Muggins" and would become the author of *The Black Crook*, is openly antagonistic toward the church which, in his play, has its own evils such as the habitually intoxicated bishop. With Gangrene Canker, Suction Leech, Killjoy Croaker and Unction Potter, all "gentlemen interested in the amelioration of the moral and physical conditions of humanity at large," Barras creates a predictable plot in which the greed and lechery of the do-gooders is justly revealed. At a time when social ferment seemed everywhere, irritating even the distant Ralph Waldo Emerson, a reasonably popular lecturer during the 1850s who once felt himself besieged by every crack pot with a system, such blatantly expressed views well blended with comic relief were acceptable on the stage.

Among the less accepted experimenters in religious individuality, the Mormons undertook their trek to Utah in 1846 after flagrant persecution in Illinois. One play which commented on their activities, *The Mormons; or, Life at Salt Lake City* by Thomas Dunn English, was first performed at Burton's Theatre on 16 March 1858. According to theatre bills quoted in Odell's *Annals of the New York Stage*, vol. VIII, it was

written to exhibit a practical view of the actual and exciting doings of the Mormons in their own homes – the Policy of their Rulers, their connection with the Indians, Hostility to the Federal Government – the Workings of their peculiar domestic institutions – Sufferings of the numerous wives and children – Public ceremonies and private habits and manners, with an interesting story of American emigrants, and the assassinations by the Danites.

Any reading of the play, however, shows that English exercised a strong bias against the Mormons. The *Spirit* assessed the play as "an ephemeral production, intended only to hold the popular attention for a brief period" (*ST*, 20 March 1858, 72). When the play proved to be more permanently popular, James Wallack was challenged to mount *Deseret Deserted or, The Last Days of Brigham Young* in May. An extravaganza, presumably written by the OOO Club, it included among its characters a fireman, an Irishman, a Flower of the Prairie, dancers and a man called Lucifer Sparks, described in the program as a "deliver of persecuted young ladies and champion of oppressed but virtuous crinoline." The *Spirit* (*ST*, 12 June 1858, 214) described the plot as "a most facetious view ... taken of recent events and coming shadows in the territory of Utah." It was not soon forgotten, however, and was noted in *The American Cyclopedia* as "still occasionally represented."[7]

Dr. English (1819–1902) took a medical degree in 1839 and "was called to the bar" in 1842. By 1844 he moved freely in New York political and journalistic circles where he was considered a crusty gentleman who took offense easily and readily gave it back. In modern times he is remembered, if at all, as the author of the popular song "Ben Bolt," 1842, and for his literary altercation with Edgar Allan Poe. *The Mormons; or, Life at Salt Lake City*, a melodrama in three acts, features such characters as Eagle Eye, alias Walter Markham, searching for the murderer of his sister; Dahcomah, a friendly Kiowa chief; Mary, an orphan; Pratt, a Mormon elder; Mr. and Mrs. Woodville, new and eager converts to Mormonism; Noggs, played by Burton, a crooked New York civil official who has turned Mormon to escape the law; Whiskey Jake, Sargeant M'Fadin and units of the U.S. Army. The plot, which is pure melodrama and scenic spectacle, concentrates on the revelations of "true" Mormonism to the Woodvilles, the rescue of Mary from the rapacious Mormons, and Eagle Eye's discovery of his sister's murderer who conveniently and guiltily kills himself as the Army rescue party reaches Mary in the final scene of the play.

The women's rights movement made a spectacular beginning at Seneca Falls, New York, with its Women's Rights Convention of 1848 at which Mrs. Elizabeth Cady Stanton read her "Declaration of Sentiments." The press and the pulpit immediately reacted, and the stage was not far behind. Although there were no major plays performed in the commercial theatres that either extolled or condemned the erupting feminism, it was an issue that frequently appeared in comedies of the period, if almost entirely in a fashion that belittled the seriousness of the movement. There was, for example, a new comic piece at Burton's Theatre on 13 December 1856, entitled *The Rights and Wrongs of Women:* "Though there is nothing peculiar in the farce, yet those who miss seeing it lose a half-hour's entertainment of the happiest kind" (*ST*, 13 December 1856, 528). Consistent with the popular comedies, it was male-oriented and concerned with women as property.

One of the better places in which to understand the issues that bothered people, or to realize the sources for comedy that sophisticated people enjoyed, was in the private theatricals or the parlor theatricals, which became exceedingly popular during the decade of the 1850s. The large number of books explaining, collecting, and advocating these theatricals clearly reflects the growing popularity of this phenomenon during the 1850s and its continued acceptance throughout the last half of the nineteenth century. Although suffragists were apparently reluctant to use the parlor theatrical as a serious means of achieving political power, the feminist issue occasionally entered the parlor or living room by this device. *Women's*

*Rights*, 1856, for example, by William Beatley Foule (1795–1865) published in *Parlour Dramas; or, Dramatic Scenes for Home Amusement*[8] suggests a common theme. The opening curtain reveals the parlor in the home of Mr. Manly, a merchant, who lives with his wife and his sister Myrtilla. Excited by the second (1855) refusal of Lucy Stone to include the phrase "to obey" in her marriage to Henry Blackwell and her own lack of a household budget as well as the accepted inferior position of women in society, Mrs. Manly states her position: "I am resolved, Myrtilla! This last outrage has determined me, and I henceforth revoke the promise, that in my folly I once made, to serve, honor and obey. Out on me for a traitor to my sex!" Failing to dissuade Myrtilla from getting married – "Since the world began, woman has been a slave" – she plots to change the duties of husband and wife. Eventually, she fails, and Myrtilla is "not surprised at the result of the experiment. The hen was never made to swim." Mr. and Mrs. Manly laugh and accept the old status quo.[9] Written by a man with a sense of superior humor rather than a commitment to a cause, *Women's Rights* suggests adverse propaganda showing the male bias.

The sensitivity or insensitivity of playwrights to issues of the day was doubtless a major reason why many plays were produced at all, even for brief runs. Certain plays by Oliver S. Leland (1834–70), dramatic critic, playwright, and essayist for Boston and New York periodicals, illustrate this point. A clever writer of some wit and skill who borrowed from the French and generally set his plays in England, Leland concerned himself with the usual domestic and comic situations but managed to touch the developing issue of the feminist movement. In *Caprice; or, Lover and Husband*, which opened at Wallack's Theatre in November 1857, after playing at Boston as *Caprice; or, A Woman's Heart*, Leland named his heroine Lucy in a plot that attempted to relate love to marriage and concluded without much reason that "Woman makes man the slave of some caprice." Another play of similar devices and concepts was called *Beatrice; or, The False and the True*, 1858.

Leland's *The Rights of Man*, 1857, a comedy in two acts, exploits a romantic plot and an untypical heroine, raised to love liberty, who has difficulty reconciling herself to "play the part of the silly slave which nature seems to have given to my sex" (i, i) and accenting her father's statement that "the beard is the symbol of power." Consequently, her friend, a widow, must explain to her that happiness comes in two editions: one, marriage, is large, heavy and difficult to move; the other, love, the small pocket edition, women take wherever they go. On the other hand, there are those who think that a "wife should have no thoughts; it is her husband's duty to think for her" (I, i). Hating the word marriage, the heroine finds the "rights of man" revolting until she is led to question whether or not men have any rights at all and, if they do, what value these rights assume in society. The curtain line to the play, spoken by a man, that "Women will rule, despite the 'Rights of Man'" was the frivolous and condescending male reaction to the endeavors of contemporary feminists, whether or not it was written for that purpose. Nor would it have appeased the "Lucy Stoners" of 1857 that the critic for the *Spirit* was "hugeously tickled with this bagatelle" (*ST*, 30 May 1957, 192).

No one during the 1850s knew what America's future would be, but many had ideas – dreams of a society that boasted almost unlimited opportunity, fears lest man fall victim to ever-present evils. Few imagined or were concerned with the "greatest moral convulsions of the earth" that shadowed the thoughts of Walt Whitman. As tensions mounted in the social and political worlds, the theatre reacted, generally with caution and, in its own way, always aware that audiences must be amused. In a number of instances playwrights struck a serious note; sometimes they stimulated controversy. In one way or another, they reflected the principal issues and tensions of the period. In general, however, they trivialized the public voice, while the major convulsions in which they were interested would be the appetite for laughter in a theatre audience.

## NOTES

1 Hereafter cited as *ST* in references.
2 "Literary Notices," *The Knickerbocker* 36 (August 1850), 186.
3 Edward Fitzball, Esq., *Thirty-five Years of a Dramatic Author's Life*, 2 vols. (London: T. C. Newby, 1859), II, 260–1.
4 W. E. Farrison, "Brown's First Drama," *College Language Association Journal* 2 (December 1958), 4–10.
5 (New York: Edward Dunigan and Brother, 1851).
6 (Boston: Crisby, Nichols, Lee and Co., 1860).
7 *The American Cyclopedia*, 16 vols. (New York: D. Appleton, 1883), VI, 647–48.

8 (Boston: Chase and Nichols, 1865), 7–17.

9 See also "Introduction," *On to Victory, Propaganda Plays of the Woman Suffrage Movement*, ed. Bettina Friedl (Boston: Northeastern University Press, 1987).

# CHAPTER 7

# The development of the American theatre program

## Marvin Carlson

The theatre program or playbill has long been utilized by theatre historians as a privileged primary document in their research, and many an acting career or theatrical repertoire has been reconstructed largely on the basis of the information contained in such documents. Somewhat surprisingly, the program itself, though it has been a standard part of the theatregoing experience now for at least two and a half centuries and an important record of changing social and economic forces operative in the theatre, has received only the most modest attention from these same historians. A somewhat whimsical account of the English playbill, with a number of important examples and details, was published in *The Gentleman's Magazine* in 1900 by Percy Fitzgerald. Fitzgerald remarks that his subject, though fascinating, is "little known or inquired into" and that these essential items in the history of the stage were not even seen as worthy of notice by such collectors as the British Museum.[1]

The collection of playbills is of course now an accepted practice at the British Museum and at countless other archives around the world, but the subject of the playbill itself has been scarcely further "inquired into" than it had been when Fitzgerald's article appeared. The only other subsequent attempt to pursue this matter in any serious fashion that has come to my attention was an entry by Gabrielle Enthoven that appeared in the early editions of the *Oxford Companion to the Theatre*. Unfortunately, it cannot be found in the most recent edition. Enthoven says much less than Fitzgerald about the actual contents of playbills at different times but is also much more specific about the actual evolution of the playbill, especially in the latter part of the nineteenth century. These two accounts, although very limited in size and scope, provide at least a starting point for study of the use of the playbill in the British theatre. For the American theatre, I have been unable to find even this much.[2]

The purpose of this article, then, is to provide at least a preliminary study in this area, focusing upon the pivotal years between
1850 and 1900, during which time the American playbill departed
from the British model to develop in its own way and by the end of
which time the modern program, essentially in the form we still use
today, had come into general use in America, to be introduced in
turn into England following the First World War. One sometimes
finds in modern historical writing on the theatre a distinction
attempted between a playbill, taken to mean the long and narrow
theatrical announcements almost universally employed in England
and America in the eighteenth and early nineteenth centuries and a
program, containing perhaps identical information but composed of
one or more folded sheets printed on both sides. Connected with this
distinction is the assumption that the function of playbills is for
public posting, and that of programs for distribution or sale within
the theatre. This distinction confuses at least as much as it clarifies.
There is no question that about the middle of the nineteenth century
the traditional "playbill" format, in use in England and America for
more than a century, began to be replaced by a variety of alternative forms, the ancestors of the modern "program," but it is also
true that the old style "playbills" were not simply posted but were
often distributed and sold by the orange girls in theatres, thus
making them essentially "programs" rather than bills. The terms
program, playbill, and bill of the play were all used more or less
interchangeably throughout the late nineteenth century. My own
discussion will deal with printed material, whatever it was called,
designed to be available to the audience member during the actual
production, whether brought into the theatre from outside or, more
commonly, obtained there.

To provide a certain perspective on this development, I should
like to begin by summarizing Enthoven's very helpful discussion of
the British playbill during this same period. Enthoven places the
beginning of the modern program about 1850 when the Olympic
began to distribute small playbills, about 9 inches by 12 inches,
printed on one side, probably only to the occupants of the more
expensive boxes. Drury Lane next took up this practice, and other
theatres followed. A major change occurred in the 1860s when the
perfume concern of Rimmel began supplying four-page notepaper-
size programs to a number of London theatres, perfumed and with
paper lace borders, a practice continued in some theatres until the

1880s. The fourth page of these programs was an advertisement for Rimmel, suggesting a commercial development for the theatre program that was central in America, but much more marginal in England until after the First World War.

A new style of program, called by Enthoven a "magazine-program," was introduced by the St. James Theatre in 1869. This was called the *Bill of the Play*, with the actual playbill on the first page, then two pages of literary material, with a final page devoted to omnibus routes, cab fares to the theatre and charges of the Spiers and Ponds Refreshment Department. Similar transport details appear in a few other theatre programs of the 1870s, but the only other "magazine" was *The Firefly*, printed by the Criterion Theatre, a program that in the later 1870s began to add sketches of the play and actors for embellishment. About 1880, thin cardboard programs appeared, often in color. Each theatre offered its own programs, and formats varied greatly. The commercial messages so typical of American programs of the same period were almost unknown, though business concerns that provide items for use in the production received a kind of advertising in program acknowledgements. Only the Gaiety Theatre in the late 1880s offered an eight-page program in which the majority of the space was devoted to advertisements.

The practice of each London theatre providing its own programs of differing colors, formats, and sizes continued until around 1910, when refreshment contractors began taking over this business and imposing a uniformity on the programs. After the 1914–18 war, magazine-programs of up to twenty pages in the American style began to appear, some twenty years after these had become standard in America.[3]

When we turn to the American theatre of these same years, we find a very different pattern of program development and usage. Before 1850 American programs are almost indistinguishable from British, almost universally following the traditional playbill style of long sheets printed on one side. In early November of 1856 a new sort of playbill appeared in New York, establishing a pattern that would be often imitated during the next thirty years. This was *The Programme*, a daily announcement of New York dramatic activity that continued through the early 1860s. *The Programme* was essentially a small four-page newspaper laid out in what would become a familiar format in New York. Across the top of the first page was the paper's logo, and a large center column offered information about a play being offered that day – the name of the theatre, author and title, cast list, scene list, and usually additional information, for example, a listing of musical numbers played during the evening.

The second page provided some modest publishing information about the paper itself, but was primarily devoted to brief news items about other New York theatres and their current offerings. The third page offered a collection of short general columns on such subjects as "Theatrical Gossip," "Musical Gossip," and "Music and Drama on the Continent," along with a few advertisements. The final page was given over entirely to advertising. The format was, in short, essentially the same as the "magazine-program" described by Enthoven as appearing in London thirteen years later.

The in-theatre use of this magazine-program as well as its commercial orientation was stressed by a notice that often appeared on its second page: "As you glance over the contents of this sheet, look around you and observe that almost every person in the house is reading it. During the intermissions every line is read and each advertisement is scanned. Business men can at once perceive its value as an advertising medium."[4] *The Programme* was distributed without charge. In 1856 it claimed a circulation of 30,000, which had grown to 45,000 by 1863. It then claimed to be "furnished as House-Bill to every theatre in the city, and to Mechanics' Hall, Wood's Minstrel Hall, Stuyvesant Institute, Irving Hall, the Brooklyn Academy of Music, etc."[5]

*The Programme* does not seem to have inspired any serious rivals for a number of years, and only one imitator, *Burton's Daily Bulletin and Broadway Advertiser*, launched in January of 1857. The New York Correspondent of the *Boston Saturday Evening Gazette* remarked that the sheet, despite its imposing title "seems to have been started for the purpose of presenting glowing eulogiums of the performers and performances" at Burton's Theatre. The *Bulletin* stoutly denied the charge that it had been founded "for the sole purpose of puffing Burton's theatre and actors. It was started with the determination to give a fair exposition of public sentiment, and to refute by the publication of the truth, the continued petty, paltry, spiteful, and mendacious statements of some of the small fry of would be theatrical critics, prose-run-mad scribblers who are 'down on Burton.'"[6]

This response is not very reassuring, but in fact in the three issues of this ephemeral journal I have been able to locate, there is indeed little "puffery." Aside from the fact that only one theatre's offerings are chronicled, the format is very similar to that of *The Programme* – a center program with side ads on the first page, a second page devoted to theatre gossip, jokes and filler, and two pages of advertisements. The major concern of the two papers seems to have been much the same – to offer information on the play being presented, to gain some income from advertising, and to provide enough interesting "filler" to encourage reading of the advertising as well. The wedding of commercial advertising and entertainment so central to American culture in general was clearly indicated.

As the Civil War drew to an end and America entered the "Gilded Age," the revival of theatre activity and commerce made the advertising potential offered by *The Programme* much more attractive, and the period between 1863 and 1870 saw a flourishing of this style of theatrical newspaper. A few theatres, such as Niblo's Garden and Wallack's, followed the example of Burton's in publishing theatrical newspapers for their own establishments (after a few months, the Wallack's paper was re-named *The Lorgnette* and it began including other theatres as well), but these seem to have been few and short-lived.[7] Much more successful were new ventures on the model of *The Programme* (which I have been unable to trace past 1865). The first of these was the *Brooklyn Daily Program*, established in 1863 and lasting, under various titles, until 1891. Then in 1864 came *The Play Bill* and also *The Theatre* (according to its subsequent issues, although I have in fact discovered no issues of it from any year but 1867). Like the older *Programme*, *The Play Bill* emphasized its commercial potential, claiming to be "printed daily for circulation in hotels, restaurants, theatres, news agencies, etc. Business people advertising in the Play Bill can now feel assured that their notices will get into the hands of the people they want to reach. Unlike the old programmes, there is not a copy to be found in the theatre after the audiences leave. They are all carried home."[8]

Doubtless theatregoers, then as now, in fact left many of these programs in the theatre, but the editors of *The Play Bill* attempted to make their product more likely to be kept by adding interesting and attractive new material within the usual four-page format. The two center pages, though including some advertisements, were largely devoted to theatrical gossip, musical items and news of foreign theatres, especially those in England, Germany, Italy, and Spain.

A rival theatrical paper, *The Stage*, established in 1865, was unquestionably the most successful of the many early newspaper-programs in New York. It seems to have driven most of its competitors from the scene by mid-1867, and easily held its own against a series of younger would-be rivals. It last appeared in something close to its original form in 1881, though after that time it seems to have become the official house program for Wallack's Theatre, and in that more modest form lasted at least until 1888, still called *The Stage* and still proudly bearing the claim "founded in 1865."

The general format of *The Stage* was anything but innovative. Like its predecessors, it consisted of four pages. On the first, beneath the logo and the date and volume number, was the program of a current production in the center of the page. In a column on either side were advertisements. The second page contained information on other New York theatres, and general theatrical gossip. The third page would contain more theatrical filler, but would be primarily advertisements, as would the entire back page. A comparison of the goods and services featured in such advertising with those in theatre programs today provides interesting evidence of a changing social and economic composition of the audience, or at least of the audience seen by theatre managers and commercial entrepreneurs as their likely public. The transient theatregoer has of course remained a major part of the theatre audience, witnessed in the programs of 1870 and 1970 alike by ads for hotels, restaurants, and travel. For both tourists and local population, there is a clear assumption of an interest in luxury items. The piano, an essential element of the middle- and upper-class household in the mid-nineteenth century, was the dominant item of interest in theatre advertisements of this period. Full-page piano advertisements were as ubiquitous in these programs as full-page cigarette ads (an item still unknown in the 1860s) were in the 1920s. Equally predictable, if less extensive, were advertisements for other luxury items, such as perfumes, pipes, opera glasses, gloves, fans, and similar luxury items. The assumption of a correlation between theatregoing and a taste for luxury goods has of course not changed in the intervening century, indeed it has obviously been reinforced by the continual upward trend in ticket prices. Looking at a Broadway program picked up in a theatre the night before I write these words (late October 1990) I find, of course, no ads for such dated items as fans, pipes, or gloves, but the opera glasses and perfumes are still there, along with jewelry, luxury handbags, and Rolex watches. What has

1 Program of *The Stage*, 31 May 1880

most clearly disappeared from such advertising, and indeed had essentially disappeared before the end of the nineteenth century, were notices of less elegant goods and services, such as bedding, patent medicines, dress and dry goods, and insurance.

Clearly one of the major reasons for the success of *The Stage* was its ability to gain the endorsement of an important segment of the major professional theatres in New York, an important argument in gaining advertisers, who were naturally interested in the widest possible circulation of their publicity. Almost every issue carries the notice on the second page "The only authorized programme for ... " followed by some twelve to eighteen of the leading New York theatres, such as the Academy of Music, the Olympic, Irving Hall, Wallack's, Niblo's Garden, and the Fifth Avenue Theatre. The longevity of *The Stage* and the many greater numbers of it preserved gives this claim some credence, but there was clearly no mechanism in operation to protect such a monopoly. *The Theatre* in 1867 claimed itself as the authorized program for nine theatres, every one of them also claimed by *The Stage* that same year, and the younger *The Season*, founded in 1867, called itself in 1869 "the only authorized housebill" for eleven theatres, all but one of them also claimed by *The Stage* in its list of eighteen "exclusive" patrons presented the same month.[9]

At least four other program-papers apparently competed for the public of the late 1860s and early 1870s. *The Evening Amusement* in 1865 called itself the house-bill for the Olympic, Niblo's and Barnum's.[10] *The Pleasure Season* claimed an originating date of 1866, but I have found no example of it before 1877 (when it seems associated only with the Grand Opera House), so I have been unable to determine what theatres it may have represented during its first decade.[11] *The Figaro* covered a number of theatres, though provided no listing of them, and claimed at least in its third volume (1870) to be "devoted to music, the drama, and Freemasonery." The issue of 16 February 1870 offers a cast and music list on the first page and Masonic news on the second,[12] but the earlier issues I have found are more conventional in format. *The Ladies' Theatrical Bouquet* claimed in an issue of 4 June 1870 to be "distributed to Ladies" at nine listed places of amusement including such standard theatres as Booth's, Wallack's, the Grand Opera, and the Olympic, all claimed at this same time as "exclusive" distribution points for both *The Stage* and *The Season*. The *Journal of the Day*, which styled itself "A Morning

Record of Society, Music, Art, and Literature" and claimed a circulation of 20,000 in 1872, seems to have overlapped these other programs only in such theatres as the Academy of Music, but it did supply programs there even for regular dramatic productions.[13]

Between 1868 and 1872 a major transition took place in the theatre programs in New York, from newspaper-programs like *The Stage* or *The Season*, provided by a single publisher to a group of theatres, to programs with a similar format produced for a single theatre. Clearly this change was inspired, at least in part, by British practice, and a few of the new-style American programs of the late 1860s even followed the recently established English practice of offering scented programs provided by perfumers as advertising. I have located programs from the spring of 1868 supplied and perfumed by Phalon and Son for the Newark Opera and Niblo's Garden,[14] and 1869 and early 1870 Booth offered programs scented by Rimmel, the same firm who provided programs of this sort for London theatres.[15]

Few new newspaper-programs in the old style appeared after 1870, and those that did apparently survived only by becoming associated with one or two theatres. Booth's Theatre announced in 1872 that the program *Our Gossip*, having absorbed *The Bill of the Play* and *The Prompter*, was now the "exclusive and official housebill" for that theatre[16] (though subsequent Booth's programs, while claiming the same exclusivity, dropped the *Our Gossip* title and simply called themselves by the name of the theatre). *The Bill of the Play* continued to be used for a time by several theatres (mostly managed by Augustin Daly) during the 1870s, but only the Fifth Avenue Theatre seems to have continued the use of this title into the next decade. By the mid-1870s, the only regularly appearing newspaper-programs in the old style, produced by a single publisher and serving several different theatres, were apparently *The Stage* and the *Brooklyn Daily Program*, which at the end of 1874 was rechristened the *Brooklyn Daily Stage*.[17]

During this decade such notices as "the only official programme for this theatre," "the official and only Paper circulated in this theatre," or Booth's determined "The public are hereby notified that this is the ONLY programme circulated in this theatre" became a standard feature of theatre programs, although the format of these programs for individual theatres did not differ markedly from that of the earlier newspaper-programs utilized by groups of theatres. Some even kept a generic sort of program name, such as *The Drama* (at the Grand Opera House), *The Idle Hour* (at Haverly's), or *The Curtain* (at the Eagle Theatre) although most theatres now simply used their own names as program titles. A typical Booth program for the fall of 1873 consisted of four pages. The first displayed the logo of the theatre at the top, then the bill in a central column, with advertisements along the sides. The second page had an article on Booth, but was primarily more advertising. The third page offered a column of theatrical gossip, and the fourth was entirely advertising. The subjects of these ads were essentially those now well established in the program business. The side ads on the first page featured pianos, clothing, rubber goods, and silver. Those on the second were for dry goods, china, opera glasses, silver, furniture. The third promoted lace, dry goods, jewelry, drugs, a hotel and a restaurant, and the fourth, cameos, chop houses, ice cream, hats, horseblankets, oyster houses, and that favorite of theatre program advertising, pianos.

Some theatres solicited such advertisements themselves and then commissioned a printer to produce the program, often one of the Broadway printers such as Henry Watson or H. A. Thorn (located side by side at 742 and 746), but more commonly, the advertising was organized by a firm which might itself produce the program or in turn arrange for the printing. An early example of such an arrangement was J. W. Morrisey's *Evening Advertising* firm at 860 Broadway, which collected advertising and prepared individual programs for a number of theatres in the mid-1870s, among them the Olympic, the Broadway, the Grand Opera, and Barnum's Hippodrome. These programs were printed by Cushing and Bardun on Centre Street. Certain printers and certain advertising firms, often in combinations like Morrisey, Cushing, and Bardun, came to be particularly associated with the preparation of theatrical programs from the late 1870s onward. Thus gradually certain printing firms began to take on the functions earlier performed by the editors of the first newspaper-programs – preparing standardized formats for which they solicited commercial advertising on the one hand and playbill formats on the other.

The leading publisher of theatre programs at the end of the 1870s, especially in the Union Square area, was A. S. Seer, conveniently located in the square. Among his clients were the Standard, the Olympic, the Fifth Avenue, the Union Square, the Madison Square, and Niblo's Garden, utilizing a variety of advertising agents. During the early 1880s the name most frequently encountered in the publication of theatre programs is J. T. Cowdery, on Barclay Street, who did both publishing and advertising at first for the Fifth Avenue, the Standard, the 14th Street and a decade later, after moving to 42nd Street, for Carnegie Hall, Abbey's, the Broadway, and the Metropolitan Opera. These outlets were usually listed in the Cowdery programs for the early 1890s with the note "The patrons of the foregoing places of amusement are the cultural and refined portion of the city's population. Business houses desiring to reach this class through an advertisement will readily see the advantages these programmes offer them."[18] Clearly potential advertisers agreed with this assessment, for by late 1887 Cowdery was able to move from the four-page format that had been standard, in varying sizes, since the introduction of the modern theatre program in America, to a much more impressive sixteen-page program, almost entirely advertising. A typical format was a theatre logo on the first page, cast listing on a late page (usually 9 or 11) and a listing of scenes and/or music two pages later. The rest was advertising, with as yet very little of the filler that would characterize later "thick" programs. Cowdery was apparently also the first program publisher to insert in each program floor plans of the theatre, with fire exits marked, beginning in the fall of 1882.

As the 1890s passed, Cowdery was gradually pushed from the scene by two more successful publisher and advertisers, first Leo von Raven, and then Frank V. Strauss, who by the end of the century had established a virtual monopoly on the production of theatre programs in New York. Both von Raven and Strauss began as sellers of advertising who gained a particular interest in theatre programs and then moved into producing them for an ever-increasing number of patron theatres. I have first found von Raven listed as organizing the advertising for the Thalia Theatre late in 1884. By 1888 he was providing programs for ten New York theatres, among them the Thalia, the Casino, and the Windsor, and two in Brooklyn. The Amberg, the Eden Musee, and the 23rd Street were added in 1889 and several others in the early 1890s, including the Union Square and the Standard, but by 1895 von Raven was already being overshadowed by the rapidly growing organization of Frank Strauss.

Strauss is reported to have begun his advertising business on

Walker Street about 1884, but the earliest program listing for him
so far discovered is for September of 1885, for a production at the
Madison Square Theatre. During the next several years Strauss
provided some programs on his own and organized advertising for
others, such as the popular program publishing firm of W. J. Mof-
fatt.[19] In 1888 Strauss opened his own press on Walker Street and
gradually began overtaking rival program suppliers. By 1895 he had
a listing of twelve theatre outlets in New York, three in Brooklyn,
and two in New Jersey, about the same number as von Raven, but
Strauss's list on the whole included larger and better-known houses,
such as the Empire, the Lyceum, Herald Square and Union Square.
By 1898 his listing ran to twenty-nine New York theatres and twelve
in Brooklyn. Even more significantly, his additions over these three
years included not only such major houses as Wallack's, but a
number of houses previously serviced by von Raven, such as the
Bijou, Koster and Biak's, the Eden Musee, and the 23rd Street. The
format of a sixteen-page Strauss program of this period did not
greatly differ from a Cowdery program of a decade before. The front
cover displayed the theatre logo, often with an advertisement, and
the back cover was a full-page cigarette ad. Pages 9 and 11 gave the
bill of the play and pages 8 and 10 contained miscellaneous filler –
all four of these pages contained advertisements as well. Page 13 had
maps of the theatre and an announcement of the next attraction,
and page 14 listed all of the Strauss theatres. It was not until the
early years of the new century that the Strauss programs began to
feature regular columns on such subjects as "What the Woman Will
Wear," "What the Man Will Wear," "Beauty Hints," "The
Hostess," "For Book Lovers," and "For the Automobilist," the
ancestors of the articles and features in contemporary playbills. By
the end of the nineteenth century, although many theatres continued to issue individual programs, Strauss had established a
national network for theatre programs. This was of course the era
when consolidation into various forms of trusts and syndicates was
becoming an increasingly common phenomenon in American
economic life, and the Strauss program empire echoed this consolidation on its own modest scale. Indeed Strauss's interests coincided
perfectly with those of the contemporary Theatrical Syndicate, and
it was almost inevitable that Strauss became, as he did, the Syndicate's program supplier. By 1903 Strauss was providing programs
for 250 theatres, including forty in New York, four in Brooklyn, and

eleven in Chicago. When the Syndicate disappeared, however, Strauss survived and continued to flourish. The *Playbill* distributed today in most New York theatres is the direct descendant of his enterprise.

## NOTES

1 Percy Fitzgerald, "The Play-Bill," *The Gentleman's Magazine* 288 (January–June 1900) 529–30.
2 An article by Charles Burnham, "The Bill of the Play," *The Theatre* 26:198 (August 1917), 68, 112, gives a little information on late eighteenth- and early nineteenth-century practice, and almost nothing on anything later. An article in the *New York Times*, "Leafing Through the Playbill" by Bosley Crowther (11 April 1937) discusses the current situation but provides almost no historical information. A short un-signed article in *Broadside* 11:3 (Winter 1983/84) and the histories of *The Play Bill* magazine found in the Centennial issue of that magazine (April and May 1984) and in an unpublished manuscript by Louis Botto at the *Play Bill* offices complete the commentaries I have been able to discover.
3 This brief synopsis of the late nineteenth-century London playbill is summarized from the Enthoven article on that subject in the *Oxford Companion to the Theatre*, ed. Edith Hartnoll (Oxford: Oxford University Press, 1957), 619–20.
4 *The Programme* 1:31 (8 December 1856). The programs used in putting together this study were largely from the Billy Rose Theatre Collection at Lincoln Center, though these were supplemented by collections at the Museum of the City of New York, the Players' Club, and the Special Collections at Cornell University. In references to specific Lincoln Center programs, library call numbers are provided. MWEZ + + + n.c. 6066.
5 *The Programme* 8:2054 (21 July 1863) MWEZ + + + n.c. 6066.
6 *The Programme* 1:32 (19 February 1857) Cornell University.
7 I have found no copies of the original *Lorgnette* later than 1864 (pasted in vol. II of J. S. Hagan, *Records of the New York Stage* in the Cornell University Special Collections). Vols. I and II of a second *Lorgnette* appeared in 1870 (ibid., vol. IV, and NYPL MWEZ + n.c. 5070, 6729, 8155).
8 *The Play Bill* 1:47 (3 February 1865). MWEZ + + + n.c. 6066.
9 *The Season* 4 (27 May 1869); *The Stage* 6 (21 May 1869). MWEZ + n.c. 6729.
10 Niblo's Garden folder, Museum of the City of New York.
11 Grand Opera House folder, Museum of the City of New York.
12 NYPL MWEZ + + + n.c. 6066.

13 Program of 9 July 1872, Cornell Special Collections, "Academy of Music."

14 9 March 1868 in NYPL MWEZ n.c. 6773 and April 1868, *Records of the New York Stage*, vol. III, Cornell Special Collections.

15 NYPL MWEZ n.c. 6770.

16 30 March 1872 NYPL MWEZ + + + n.c. 5071.

17 In 1874 the *Brooklyn Daily Program* changed its name to the *Brooklyn Daily Stage*. Several issues under this title from 1877 and 1888 may be found in the Players' Library in the unsorted box 6. On 21 November 1887 the name changed again to *The Theatre-Goer*, according to an issue of that publication dated 4 April 1891, in the NYPL (MWEZ + n.c. 8148).

18 Abbey's program for 27 November 1893. NYPL MWEZ + n.c. 7583.

19 The history of Strauss and *The Play Bill* is engagingly and thoroughly traced in the unpublished *Playbill: A Century of Playgoing Pleasure* by Louis Botto, available at the *Playbill* offices in New York. In 1972 *The Play Bill* offered $1,000 to anyone who could bring in a copy of an 1884 program with Strauss's name on it, but none was found.

# CHAPTER 8

# The Hyers Sisters: pioneers in black musical comedy

### Errol Hill

Black musical comedy has enlivened the American stage for well over a century. Though it began in the halcyon days of minstrelsy, black musical comedy had a different format. It was based on a scripted story with intermittent music, singing and dancing rather than on the revue-type of performance favored by the minstrels. Students of black musical theatre will be familiar with early contributions to the genre by the teams of Bob Cole and the Johnsons, Bert Williams and George Walker, and other similar ensembles but the Hyers Sisters preceded them all. While references to the Sisters exist from an early date in various biographical and historical writings, the information contained in these sources is for the most part vague, inaccurate, and contradictory. This essay will attempt to set the record straight and give the most complete information at present known about the Sisters and their contributions to the American theatre.

Of the published commentaries the most reliable source appears to be Trotter,[1] a contemporary writer who recounted the Sisters' early concert performances, quoting from newspaper reviews but with few dates which makes it difficult to corroborate him. Trotter published his sketch of the Sisters in 1878, just as they had embarked on their musical theatre productions which he considered beyond the scope of his essay. As a result his usefulness to the present study is limited.

The second important source is T. A. Abajian who tracked down biographical details from city directories and census reports.[2] Because some of this information is misleading, further detective work was necessary to piece together a reasonably accurate record of the Sisters' vital statistics. The third important source is Southern who, in her second edition of *The Music of Black Americans* (1983), gives the most complete listing of the Hyers Sisters' theatre pieces but without citing references.[3] As we shall see, some of her data are open to question.

Let us begin with the name. Is it Hyer, Hyers, Heyer, or Heyers? Newspapers of the period were apparently lax in the spelling of proper nouns and use all four forms. Trotter, Abajian and Southern use Hyers, Toll uses Hyer,[4] Sampson uses both Hyer and Heyer,[5] and Belcher uses Hyer and Hyers.[6] From contemporary programs, captioned photographs and copyright records we have established that the correct spelling is Hyers. Their Christian names were Anna Madah and Emma Louise, but often they reversed the order or dropped one name so that we find, for example, Madah A. Hyers or plain Louise Hyers. There was also a May Hyers who appeared in the records at a later date and will be discussed shortly.

When and where were the Sisters born? Most sources claim that the Hyers came from California. Southern gives their birth-place as Sacramento. Abajian informs us that the family moved from New York to California in 1856 at which time Anna Madah was a year old and that her sister Emma Louise was born in Sacramento in 1857 being two years Anna's junior. Southern gives their birth-dates, with interrogatives, as 1853 and 1855 respectively. The actual dates are 1855 for Anna and 1857 for Emma. As musical prodigies, the Sisters were sometimes billed younger than they in fact were. At the time of their concert debut in 1867, for instance, they were advertised as eight and ten years old when they were really ten and twelve.

Samuel B. Hyers was their father and Annie E. Hyers (nee Cryer) their mother. Sam Hyers came from a family of barbers and owned a barber shop in Sacramento before he abandoned the trade to manage his daughters' concert careers. His wife, Annie Hyers, was skilled in embroidery, leather work and wax work, and at one time offered a class in these crafts to young women. Both parents had some rudimentary musical training and appeared as soloists at their daughters' debut performance. They were in fact the first instructors of the young ladies.

Soon after the children began singing in public, the parents were separated. Mrs. Hyers moved to San Francisco then to Stockton, taking one or both of the children with her for a time. Eventually she remarried and by 1900 was back in Sacramento with her new husband. One should not be misled by a 1900 census entry for Sacramento which shows that a Mrs. Madah A. Stafford, actress, resided with her father William S. Price. Price was actually her stepfather who had married Annie Hyers, her mother, around 1880. In that same census report Anna Madah's date of birth is given as 1869 making her thirty-one years old when she should have been forty-five. Her husband at the time, Harry Stafford, was then forty-two. The fact that he was three years her junior might have prompted his wife to claim that she was fourteen years younger than her actual age.[7]

Apparently Anna Madah was married three times. Her first marriage, reported in the press on 15 September 1883, was to Henderson Smith, a cornet player;[8] her second, around 1891, was to Harry Stafford, stage manager for Isham's *Octoroons*; and her third was to Dr. Robert J. Fletcher, a chiropodist, with whom she spent her retirement years back in Sacramento. It is believed that Anna Madah died sometime in the early 1920s.

Her sister Emma Louise also married a cornet player but in a more unique fashion. She and George Freeman, the company's brass band leader, were publicly united on the stage of the Baldwin Theatre in San Francisco on 8 September 1883 during a performance of Callender's Minstrels. The wedding ceremony was actually advertised as part of the performance.[9] The most that can be said of that unusual exhibition is that it was a benefit evening for the newly-weds, though with a banquet on stage after the show for three hundred invited guests, one fears that the couple might well have ended up in the red. Eleven years later, in August 1894, Emma Louise was again married, this time to Walter Espy who was acting Uncle Tom to her Topsy in the Davis company's production of *Uncle Tom's Cabin* then playing in Cleveland.[10] Emma's last known performance was with Isham's *Octoroons* at the Eighth Avenue Theatre in New York in 1896. Thereafter only her sister, Anna Madah, is mentioned with the touring *Octoroons* and by 1901 Emma is said to have died.

Now about that third Hyers girl, May: her name first surfaces in 1883 as a member of Samuel B. Hyers's newly formed Colored Musical Comedy Company. Initially she was referred to in press notices as *Miss* May Hyers, later as Mrs. May Hyers, leading one waggish critic to write years later: "there was a third Hyers girl – Lucy – but as to whether she was the wife or the daughter of old Sam B. Hyers we are unprepared to say."[11] From Monroe Major's *Noted Negro Women* (1893), it appears that May Hyers was formerly Mary

C. Reynolds of Tioga, Pennsylvania. She was apparently little more than a teenager when she persuaded her father to allow her to join the Hyers Sisters company in 1882. The very next season she was married to Sam Hyers, then fifty-three years old and manager of the company. (Incidentally the name Lucy cited by the critic is not found in the records and may be due to a faulty memory on his part.)

May Hyers was a contralto singer and thus in direct competition with Emma Louise. As the young wife of the company manager, it is possible that her sudden acquisition caused a rift between Sam Hyers and his daughters, for by the spring of 1883 the Sisters had left their father's company which thereafter was called by his name, the S. B. Hyers Company. The Sisters found engagements elsewhere, sometimes with their own combination or in league with other managements, sometimes with the minstrels. It is a curious fact that of some twenty sources consulted, no one seems to have noted that from the year 1883 onwards, there were actually two separate Hyers troupes. One continued to be referred to as the Hyers Sisters Combination and the other as the S. B. Hyers Colored Musical Comedy Company in which May Hyers performed leading roles. As evidence of this bifurcation we have the Hyers Sisters with Callender's Minstrel Festival playing *Uncle Tom's Cabin* in San Francisco in September 1883 while at the same time the S. B. Hyers Company were appearing in *The Blackville Twins* at the Criterion Theatre in Chicago.

Turning now to the professional life of the Hyers Sisters, one may divide their careers into three phases. First is their concertizing which took them across America from the west to the east coast. Second are productions of musical comedies which they presented on several cross-country tours over a period of some fifteen years. Third are their appearances, either together or individually, as featured actors or singers with the minstrels and other *ad hoc* variety troupes. At times these activities overlapped and the Sisters performed their specialities in different formats whenever and wherever there were opportunities to do so. But the general flow of their careers followed the pattern described, that is, from concert singers to musical comedy actors to variety theatre artists, always with a strong emphasis on singing a range of songs from popular to operatic.

Phase 1, the early concert career of the Sisters from 1867 through

1876, has been well documented by Trotter and needs only be summarized here. The Sisters gave their first public concert at the Metropolitan Theatre in Sacramento on Easter Monday, 22 April 1867. It was an unqualified success. For the preceding two years they had been trained, first by their parents, then by the German professor Hugo Sank who taught them vocalization and piano playing, and finally by the opera singer Mme. Josephine D'Ormy from whom they learnt enunciation, intonation, and stage presence.

Anna Madah was a soprano and Emma Louise a contralto. The review of their debut performance referred to Miss Madah's "pure, sweet soprano voice, very true, even and flexible, of remarkable compass and sweetness," while Miss Louise was called "a natural wonder, being a fine alto-singer and the possessor of a pure tenor voice. Her tenor is of wonderful range; and, in listening to her singing, it is difficult to believe that one is not hearing a talented young man instead of the voice of a young girl."[12] Emma Louise was also a gifted comedienne and her character songs made her an immediate favorite with audiences.

After several appearances in the Bay area of Oakland and San Francisco, the Sisters embarked in 1871 on the first of their cross-continental tours under the management of their father. They sang in Salt Lake City, St. Joseph (Missouri), Chicago and Cleveland among other cities, before reaching New York where they appeared at the Steinway Hall and in Brooklyn. To support the young girls in their east coast performances, Mr. Hyers engaged the services of Wallace King, tenor, of Camden, New Jersey, and John Luca, baritone, of the celebrated Luca family from New Haven, Connecticut. A. C. Taylor, pianist, of San Francisco, had traveled with the Sisters as their accompanist and the violinist John T. Douglas joined them for several New York appearances. Their concert program always included operatic selections from composers such as Verdi, Rossini, and Donizetti, along with semi-classical pieces, sentimental ballads, and so-called Negro jubilee songs and spirituals. They sang solos, duets, and quartets. The New York press was as flattering as the provincial. The *Evening Telegram* called Madah's voice "a very pure soprano" and Emma's "an equally excellent contralto ... singly or together their execution is marked by a refinement, culture, and attractiveness that deserve first class audiences and first class appreciation."[13]

Phase II of the Sisters' careers consists of musical theatre pro-

ductions. This is the area where confusion exists over which plays
were done by the Sisters Combination and which by the S. B. Hyers
Company. Moreover, it has so far proved difficult to corroborate
reports that some plays were done at all. Southern, who supplies the
most complete list of titles, mentions eight productions:[14]

1. *Out of the Wilderness* (1876)
2. *Out of Bondage* (1876)
3. *In and Out of Bondage* (1877)
4. *Urlina, the African Princess* (1877)
5. *Colored Aristocracy* (1877)
6. *The Underground Railroad* (1879)
7. *The Blackville Twins* (1883)
8. *Plum Pudding* (1887)

In addition to these eight titles, Tom Fletcher adds one more:

9. *Princess of Orelia* (or *Princess Orelia of Madagascar*) starring Sam
   Lucas;[15]

and we have evidence of yet another production:

10. *Uncle Tom's Cabin* (first presented by them in 1880).

We will look at each of these titles in turn.

On Monday, 26 March 1876 at the Academy of Music in Lynn,
Massachusetts, the Hyers Sisters presented for the first time a
musical drama written expressly for them by Joseph Bradford of
Boston and titled *Out of the Wilderness*. Along with the two Hyers girls
and Messrs. Luca and King, Sam Lucas, formerly of the Georgia
Minstrels, had joined the company. The troupe began touring their
show to New England towns, playing mostly one-night stands. By
June of that year, they had changed the title of their offering to *Out
of Bondage*, which was essentially the same show as *Out of the Wilderness*. In fact, a manuscript copy of the play in the Library of Congress has Act II closing with several voices singing the spiritual:
"Oh, ain't I glad to get out of de wilderness" which must have given
the play its earlier title. Under the new name, *Out of Bondage*, the
musical drama, copyrighted by Bradford in 1876, became the principal stock piece in the Hyers Sisters repertoire.

How does one characterize this play? Its various subtitles give a
clue: "From Slavery to Freedom," "Before and After the War,"
"From the Cotton Field to the Opera." Act I introduces a slave
family and friends at dinner in the south before the Civil War. There
are Uncle Eph and Aunt Naomi, the sisters Narcisse (a proper house
servant played by Anna Madah) and Kaloolah (a mischievous field

hand played by Emma Louise), two male hands Prince and Henry, and Little Jim, referred to as a picaninny. They dine off hoe-cake and 'possum meat, drink whisky, sing camp songs and spirituals. Act II shows the exterior of the cabin as Union troops approach to do battle with the southern rebels. Four younger slaves plan to go north but Eph and Naomi will remain. In Act III the family group are reunited in Boston after an interval of five years. Eph and Naomi learn that the four young people have become professional vocalists who are paid for singing, that in the north they are free and treated as equals, and that they can attend performances sitting among white folks. Little Jim has become a concert pianist. The final act takes the form of a concert during which the Sisters sing selections from their regular repertoire.

Throughout the little drama songs are sung at appropriate junctures. This was the show that was played regularly by the Hyers Sisters in the northeast, the west coast, and on several nationwide tours. The scenario was flexible and could be expanded or compressed depending on available local supporting talent. The show proved to be popular with audiences and it remained in the Sisters' theatrical repertoire for some fifteen years until at least 1891.

I could find no reference to a production of *In and Out of Bondage* (show number 3). It is a musical drama in three acts written by the same Joseph Bradford and was copyrighted by S. B. Hyers in 1877. That an author would have two plays with such similar titles is beyond understanding.[16] Southern does not give production references and I have so far been unable to locate this play on the boards.

*Urlina, the African Princess* (show number 4) written by E. S. Getchell, was presented by the Sisters at the Grand Opera House, Indianapolis, on 13 January 1879 and at other venues in Illinois and Iowa on their return trip to California. Called an "operatic bouffe extravaganza"[17] the musical was introduced to San Francisco audiences in the second half of a four-week season at the Bush Street Theatre following performances of *Out of Bondage*. The plot is laid in Africa where a usurping king has banished the Princess Urlina, rightful successor to the throne. But the usurper's son, Prince Zurleska, sees a picture of the princess, falls in love with her, and sets out with his ally Kekolah to rescue her and her maid. However, as the young people return to the kingdom they are seized by the king's soldiers, imprisoned, and left to starve to death. Kekolah escapes, disguises himself as a traveler, and with the help of friends succeeds in freeing the prisoners and overthrowing the usurper.

In the cast of fourteen, Madah Hyers played the princess while her sister Emma Louise, in the tradition of English pantomime, was the prince. Willie Lyle was a female impersonator as the maid and Billy Kersands, one of the two leading black comedians of the period (the other being Sam Lucas), took several comic roles including an Irish missionary, an African fetish man, a Christian Chinaman, and a pig-tailed Puritan. At the end of the San Francisco run, the production moved to New Market, Oregon, which supplied this critique of the show:

Operatically and dramatically the piece and the performance can not be judged by any of the legitimate or standard rules of criticism. There is much in the performance which pleases, amuses, and even touches the tender sympathies of the audience. *Urlina* combines harmoniously the elements of comedy, burlesque and pathos.[18]

The stage apparel (which I take to mean both sets and costumes) was rich to magnificent and, according to the report, the opera was given with a perfection of detail and spiritedness of singing and acting that fully equaled the finest performances of the best-known opera bouffe troupe. "The real gem of the evening," wrote the critic, "was the Midnight Quartet from *Martha*" sung by the Sisters, John Luca and Wallace King.[19] Even allowing for some puffing in the remarks, the production was obviously a clear success, a view that the San Francisco notice confirmed in calling the troupe "second to none in the United States."[20]

I could find no evidence that show number 5, *Colored Aristocracy*, and number 7, *The Blackville Twins*, were ever presented by the Hyers Sisters. In fact, after the split with their father in the spring of 1883, the Sisters joined Callender's Minstrels in New York and traveled with that troupe to San Francisco. Meanwhile S. B. Hyers formed his Colored Musical Comedy Company, which in September 1883 appeared at the Criterion Theatre in Chicago in *The Blackville Twins*.[21] Hyers also copyrighted the play that year. Then his company took it on tour. In the company were Billy Banks, Billy Cook, the Harper sisters, May Hyers and William Morris. Several years later, in 1891, there is another newspaper entry to the effect that the S. B. Hyers Company were playing *Out of Bondage, Blackville Twins*, and *Colored Aristocracy* in the east.[22] (Sampson shows this entry as the Hyers Sisters Company but he is clearly in error.)

2   Anna Madah Hyers as Urlina in the opera bouffe *Urlina, the African Princess*

As for *The Underground Railroad* (show number 6), written by the black novelist Pauline Hopkins, that was actually the secondary title for a musical drama registered for copyright as *Peculiar Sam, or The Underground Railroad* in 1879. It was also called *The Slave's Escape*, and was advertised in the *Boston Evening Transcript* as *Escape from Slavery* for a one-week production at the Oakland Garden starting on 5 July 1880.[23] Although both Sam Lucas and the Hyers Sisters were

3   Emma Louise Hyers as Prince Zurleska in the opera bouffe
*Urlina, the African Princess*

featured players, the production was offered under the banner of Hopkins's Colored Troubadours, that is, a troupe put together by the author herself. This piece was not in the repertoire of either Hyers company. The Sisters and other members of their troupe merely supported Ms. Hopkins in getting her play staged. Of the production, Lucas wrote many years later: "the piece failed as the time was not propitious for producing such a play."[24]

I have so far found no reference to a production of *Plum Pudding* (show number 8). The Library of Congress has a typescript of this play which is a slight comedy of love and marriage with farcical elements and occasional interspersed songs. The script seems an unlikely vehicle for the Hyers Sisters since it neither deals with black history nor is set in Africa as is the case with their other productions. Until we are able to discover a production of this play, further judgment must be suspended.

Two plays remain: *The Princess of Orelia*, or *Princess Orelia of Madagascar* (show number 9) and *Uncle Tom's Cabin* (show number 10). In his 1954 book, Tom Fletcher recalls a conversation with Sam Lucas who declared that the Hyers Sisters staged *Princess Orelia of Madagascar* in which Lucas was the star.[25] No other source has mentioned this play nor has it surfaced in newspaper accounts. Most probably either Fletcher or Lucas confused Princess Urlina with Orelia, and probably also with *The Princess of Madagascar*, an operetta copyrighted in 1883 by John Haverly of minstrel fame, about the time that the Sisters were in their heyday. For the present we must hold in abeyance further comment on this possible production and proceed to *Uncle Tom's Cabin*.

The Hyers Sisters Combination staged their version of this most popular nineteenth-century drama, based on Harriet Beecher Stowe's novel, at the Gaiety Theatre in Boston in March 1880. Black performers had been incorporated in Tom shows some years earlier, but only as plantation choruses, and Sam Lucas was singular when in 1878 he was picked to play the title role in an otherwise white company. With their production, the Sisters had a truly inter-racial cast with blacks playing black characters and white actors taking white roles. This first fully inter-racial casting of record on the American stage is an indication of the respect accorded the Sisters by members of the theatrical profession.

Sam Lucas again appeared as Tom and recited a new prologue written by Mrs. Stowe. Emma Louise was a natural for Topsy while

Anna Madah played Eliza Harris and sometimes a second Topsy. The Sisters took their production to Rhode Island, Connecticut, Vermont, New Hampshire, and back to Massachusetts. In 1883 they persuaded the two separate Callender's Minstrel Festival Companies (black and white) to combine their members in a spectacular production of the play in San Francisco, and in 1891 the Sisters were still playing a version of it under their own auspices at the Bijou Opera House in Milwaukee, Wisconsin, when they were assisted by the Nashville Students.[26]

Phase III of the Hyers Sisters' career can be quickly surveyed. It began at the time they left their father's company in 1883 and sought a home in other musical combinations and with the minstrels. They performed with Callender's Colored Minstrels and with his combined Festival troupe; they were featured with Donavin's Famous Tennessee Singers and in his Colored Dramatic Company doing a road show of *Out of Bondage* when they met with a train accident outside of Des Moines, Iowa, in 1886. They appeared with McCabe and Young's Genuine Darky Minstrels in 1892 and with Isham's *Octoroons* in 1896 when Emma Louise took part in the skit "The Blackville Derby" and Anna Madah provided "vocal gems." Emma was Topsy in the Davis company's 1894 production of *Uncle Tom's Cabin* and Anna Madah went to Australia with Curtis's Afro-American Minstrels in 1899. She was in the cast of Williams and Walker's musical comedy *In Dahomey*, which she left to return to Sacramento and retirement in 1902.

The Hyers Sisters Combination constituted one of the earliest professional black theatre companies in America. They were not the first such company – that honor belongs to the African Theatre of lower New York City earlier in the century – but in 1876 the Sisters' troupe, under the business management of their father Samuel B. Hyers, embarked on the production of black musical comedies of a scope and scale that had not previously been attempted by any other black company. Three full-scale productions are attributed to them: *Out of Bondage*, *Urlina, the African Princess*, and *Uncle Tom's Cabin*; *The Underground Railroad* in which they appeared briefly having been produced by its author, Pauline Hopkins. Forced to leave their father's management in 1883 when they were still in their twenties, the Sisters continued on their own, traveling extensively across America from coast to coast, bringing their talent and message to audiences black and white, large and small.

What was their message? Making their concert debut just two years after the Declaration of Emancipation, the Hyers Sisters, under the guidance of their father, seem to have had a clear mission in view: to demonstrate to the country at large that black artists – and by extrapolation all black people – would be the equal of whites in any field of endeavor. Their chosen field was lyric theatre and their singing received high praise even from those critics who were less enamoured over their acting ability or with the material they presented. But the Hyers women also had a message for blacks. It was that even with superior talent such as theirs, excellence is not attained without arduous labor and study. When Uncle Eph in *Out of Bondage* says that "freedom's a fraud" because black freedmen have to work just as hard as when they were slaves, Narcisse replies that freedom does not mean idleness but labor. They all have a responsibility to humankind, she says, because "neither man nor woman has any right to live in the world without striving to make it better."[27]

By the seriousness with which they viewed their mission, by their demeanor on and off stage, by their choice of plays and the people with whom they worked, the Hyers Sisters were able to realize their goals. They were models of decorum and this consciousness of being representatives of their race at all times may have affected the sincerity of their characterizations, for as one critic observed in reviewing *Urlina, the African Princess*, "they are an earnest pair, but really dead earnest is not exactly the spirit in which to approach burlesque."[28] In this context, the marriage of Emma Louise on stage at a public performance may be interpreted as an opportunity to demonstrate that blacks too were now entitled to participate in the sacrament of marriage that had been denied them as slaves.

In choosing their supporting players, the Hyers Sisters Combination went for the best among the race. Wallace King was probably the finest young tenor of his time; John Luca, bass, belonged to the already celebrated Luca family of musicians; Sam Lucas was the leading comedian of the day and when he left the Combination, the Sisters replaced him with Billy Kersands, who was equally gifted in mirthmaking. James Bland, the well-known composer, was also a member of the troupe for a time. But in no other area was the Sisters' mission so well fulfilled as in their choice of material. Starting out as classically trained vocalists, they soon extended their repertoire to include black music such as spirituals, camp songs, and sentimental ballads. They were just ahead of the renowned Fisk Jubilee Singers, who made their first tour in 1871, but the Sisters presented a broader range of music than the Fisk group.

In their lyric theatre pieces the Sisters performed dramas that had been written specially for them or that were adapted for their purpose. These works focused on the rapid improvement of the race from slavery to freedom, from the slave cabin to the concert stage. The Hyers Sisters were, I believe, the first black theatre company to stage a musical set in Africa, a trend that was followed by Cole and Johnson, Williams and Walker, and other notable black companies in later years. Long before the Oriental American Company or the Black Patti Troubadours of the 1890s, the Hyers Sisters introduced the singing of operatic selections to round out a performance. They were, in fact, the precursors of black musical theatre in America.

When the Sisters decided to present *Uncle Tom's Cabin*, a dramatization that was beginning to lose its moral thrust because of the caricaturing of black folk by white actors in blackface, the Sisters cast black actors in the black roles and had them perform against authentic whites. The fact that some critics felt their stage characters were unreal, that they developed too rapidly and were too poised or too imitative of classy white folk, did not deter the Hyers women from their clear mission.

In my view, the major criticism that can be leveled at the Sisters is that they overworked themselves. As youthful singers their voices must have been under considerable strain. They performed six nights a week with two matinees while traveling from one town to another almost daily. It was an incredible schedule and explains the comment by one reviewer that the singers were all as hoarse as crows.[29] The frequently reiterated promise by Sam Hyers that he would take his daughters abroad for a period of extended training in Europe never materialized. Such an opportunity would have allowed them to rest their voices from the harrowing performance schedule while cultivating them under the finest tutors. Nevertheless the Sisters persisted and achieved much, with or without the tender loving care and business acumen of their father. What Ira Aldridge did for the black dramatic actor in Britain after the emancipation of slaves in British colonies, the Hyers Sisters accomplished for the black lyric performer after the emancipation of slaves in America. We are in their debt and their contribution deserves our prideful recognition. Little wonder that when Ike Simond wrote his pocket history of the colored profession from 1865 to 1891 he called the Hyers Sisters Combination "the greatest of all colored shows in the country."[30]

## NOTES

1 James M. Trotter, *Music and Some Highly Musical People* (Boston: Lee and Shepard, 1878). A list of secondary sources is appended to this essay.

2 James de T. A. Abajian, "The Hyers Sisters of California," San Francisco Negro Historical and Cultural Society, California History Series, Monograph No. 5, January 1966 (unpublished).

3 Eileen Southern, *The Music of Black Americans: A History*, 2nd ed. (New York: W. W. Norton & Co., 1983).

4 Robert C. Toll, *Blacking Up: The Minstrel Show in Nineteenth-Century America* (New York: Oxford University Press, 1974).

5 Henry T. Sampson, *Blacks in Blackface: A Source Book on Early Black Musical Shows* (Metuchen, NJ: Scarecrow Press, 1980).

6 Fannin S. Belcher, "The Place of the Negro in the Evolution of American Theatre, 1767 to 1940," Ph.D. Thesis, Yale University, 1945.

7 1900 Sacramento county census, reel 98, district no. 82, p. 207B.

8 *Cleveland Gazette*, 15 September 1883.

9 *San Francisco Chronicle*, 8 September 1883, and *New York Clipper*, 15 September 1883.

10 *Cleveland Gazette*, 25 August 1894.

11 *Freeman*, Indianapolis, 22 February 1902.

12 *San Francisco Chronicle* quoted, without dates, by Trotter, *Music*, 162–63.

13 See ibid., 173.

14 Southern, *Music of Black Americans*, 250.

15 Tom Fletcher, *100 Years of the Negro in Show Business* (New York: Burdge & Co., 1954), xix, 53, 71.

16 To add to the confusion, the Library of Congress records a third play, "Out of Bondage, a musical drama by J. B. Williams" which was copyrighted by S. B. Hyers in 1876. These several similar titles may be taken as evidence of the play's popularity with audiences.

17 *Pacific Appeal*, San Francisco, 5 April 1879.

18 *Oregonian*, 22 April 1879, reprinted in *Pacific Appeal*, San Francisco, 8 May 1879.

19 *Ibid.*

20 *Pacific Appeal*, San Francisco, 12 April 1879.

21 *New York Clipper*, 25 August and 8 September 1883.

22 *Freeman*, Indianapolis, 14 November 1891.

23 *Boston Evening Transcript*, 6 July 1880.

24 "Sam Lucas Theatrical Career Written by Himself in 1909," *New York Age*, 13 January 1916.

25 Fletcher, *100 Years*, 53 and 71. Fletcher also refers to this play as *The Princess of Orelia* on p. xix.
26 *Appeal*, St. Paul, MN, 23 May 1891.
27 Manuscript copy of *Out of Bondage* in Library of Congress, Washington, DC.
28 *Argonaut*, San Francisco, 5 April 1879.
29 *Argonaut*, San Francisco, 22 March 1879.
30 Ike Simond, *Old Slack's Reminiscence and Pocket History of the Colored Profession. From 1865 to 1891* [n.d]. Reprint. (Bowling Green, OH: Popular Press, 1974), 7–8.

## SECONDARY SOURCES

Abajian, James de T. A., comp. *Blacks in Selected Newspapers, Censuses and Other Sources*. 3 vols. Boston: G. K. Hall, 1977

Beasley, Delilah. *Negro Trail Blazers of California*. Los Angeles: n.p., 1919

Claghorn, Charles. *Biographical Dictionary of American Music*. West Nyack, NY: Parker Publishing Co., 1973

Cuney-Hare, Maud. *Negro Musicians and Their Music*. Washington, DC: Associated Publishers, 1936

Davis, Marianna W., ed. *Contributions of Black Women to America*. 2 vols. Columbia, SC: Kenday Press, 1982

Hopkins, Pauline E. "Famous Women of the Negro Race," *Colored American Magazine*, November 1901: 45–53

Locke, Alain. *The Negro and His Music*. Washington, DC: Associates in Negro Folk Education, 1936

Majors, Monroe A. *Noted Negro Women: Their Triumphs and Activities*, 1893. Reprint. Freeport, NY: Books for Libraries Press, 1971

Patterson, Lindsay, comp. and ed. *The Afro-American in Music and Art*. Cornwells Heights, PA: The Publishers Agency, 1978

Riis, Thomas. "Black Musical Theatre in New York, 1890–1915." Ph.D. Thesis, University of Michigan, 1981

"Sam Lucas Theatrical Career Written by Himself in 1909," *New York Age*, 13 January 1916: 5

Scruggs, L. A. *Women of Distinction*. Raleigh, NC: L. A. Scruggs, 1893

Southern, Eileen. *Biographical Dictionary of Afro-American and African Musicians*. Westport, CT: Greenwood Press, 1983

# CHAPTER 9

# Money without glory: turn-of-the-century America's women playwrights

### Felicia Hardison Londré

The period from 1890 to 1929 brought a remarkable expansion of women's careers in various aspects of commercial theatre besides acting. Women directors, producers, and company managers appeared with increasing frequency, but all were surpassed by the numbers of women playwrights. Many of them became quite wealthy in those days before the income tax, and in the aggregate they gained a certain visibility as their emergence was played up in numerous magazine articles. However, the press coverage during those decades tended to focus on their success as a social phenomenon more than it celebrated them as individuals. And those feature articles devoted to individual women playwrights tended to make a point of describing them within the context of their domestic settings.

A survey of popular writing about women dramatists during those four decades suggests how consistently journalists relied upon those two basic approaches, often using them in tandem. Stressing the vast sums of money generated by the women's success seemed to justify their extradomestic activities. But at the same time it was important to show how a woman dramatist's essential femininity – her attractive appearance, her social position as a wife, her ability to run a household, her maternal devotion, and so forth – had not been impaired by her writing career. Typical of the latter slant is Walter Prichard Eaton's concluding statement in a 1911 profile of Josephine Preston Peabody, to whom he refers by her married name, Mrs. Lionel Marks:

When you see Mrs. Marks, in her modish gown, rising to speak in a measured and gentle voice at a banquet in her honor, or meet her chatting pleasantly at tea, her large, black eyes snapping with kindly humor, you do not wonder at the seeming lack of any difference between her and the other well-bred well-dressed and charming women about her. Genius does not have to be "queer," nor the women of creative powers unsexed. Mrs. Marks has the imagination of a poet, the sympathetic insight of a dramatist – and the commonsense of a housewife.[1]

The necessity of that approach becomes evident in view of the fact that as late as 1918, in an article on philanthropic women playwrights, Ada Patterson felt constrained to conclude:

Strange as it seems there are husbands who regard the writing talent as an intruder and resent its place in the household. One woman playwright met precisely such an attitude in her family. That a woman should seriously engage in any pursuit besides the time-honored one of housekeeping and family rearing, she says, pained her first spouse. Since our subject wrote as spontaneously and habitually as a bird sings, her husband's view did not harmonize with hers. As she put it, the pen became a sword beneath their roof.[2]

Thus, in the 1920s it was still necessary to insist upon the woman dramatist's domesticity, as exemplified by the caption under a photograph of Mary Roberts Rinehart: "Her life is a beautiful example of how a busy woman can keep busy and also keep her good looks. 'Doing house-work,' she declares, 'isn't any harder than writing several thousand words a day, keeping a large house in working order, and attending to three grown-up sons.'"[3]

In her study of nineteenth-century American women writers of fiction, Susan Coultrap-McQuin shows that despite their statistically increasing visibility (women wrote nearly three-quarters of all published novels by 1872), women writers were often undervalued by their publishers and by the public.[4] She finds that their book royalties appear to have been "comparable to men's,"[5] that – by comparison with their male peers – women were "less disadvantaged" financially than they were in terms of "literary canonization."[6] Marion Fairfax, author of The Talker and other successful comedies, said as much in 1911:

Women can write just as good plays as men can write, and they have proved it, but it's a difficult thing to make the public and the managers believe it. The best thing an aspiring playwright can do is to be born a man, and then he'll be treated like a "business equal" when he hustles out into the market of the world with something to sell.[7]

It could be argued that the preponderance of women authors' names on books did not particularly challenge the prevailing view of women as the center of domestic life, because writing novels and stories was a way of earning money without ever leaving the home. The woman playwright, however, could scarcely sustain a trajectory of success without going to rehearsals and becoming involved in the practical side of theatrical production. Martha Morton summed up the problem in an 1891 interview:

A woman cannot call on an actor or a manager unceremoniously, as a man can. The very fact that she is a woman prevents her meeting people. She cannot go into a bar and talk about a scenario over a cocktail. In a word, a woman, by her sex, is debarred from being "in the swim," as vulgar parlance has it. This is a very serious difficulty a woman has to overcome, and there is no doubt that this explains why so few women have succeeded in writing for the stage.[8]

Morton gained early recognition as "America's pioneer woman playwright," "the first successful woman dramatist," and "the dean of women playwrights." Between 1888 and 1911, fourteen of her plays were professionally produced in New York, and she herself directed many of them. But the media recognition of her work might be exemplified by a newspaper photograph showing Martha Morton pouring tea for her husband while a butler stands behind them; the caption reads: "The first woman to invade the profession is here shown lunching en famille in her beautiful New York home. In private life she is Mrs Herman Conheim, her husband being a successful business man. Her plays are well known and have brought her a fortune."[9] Because of the difficulties she had encountered in launching her own career, she gave zealous aid and encouragement to younger women playwrights. When women were excluded from membership in the American Dramatists Club, Morton rallied a charter membership of thirty women for a Society of Dramatic Authors, which eventually attracted so many men into its ranks that the two organizations were merged, with Morton as vice president.

Another trailblazer, Lottie Blair Parker, reminisced in a 1936 interview: "I was one of the first women playwrights in America. Martha Morton had been writing plays before me, but I was among the first of them ... We were not much relished by the men back in those days." Concerning *Way Down East*, the play upon which her reputation rests, she recalled: "I was considered to have written an immoral play. I was the first playwright to use unashamedly the word 'baby' on the stage, right out in plain language. You don't know what that meant in those days. Babies were referred to as children, not as babies."[10] In 1896 she sold the rights to *Way Down*

MARTHA MORTON.

The first woman to invade the profession of playwright is here shown lunching en famille in her beautiful New York home. In private life she is Mrs. Herman Conheim, her husband being a successful business man. Her plays are well known and have brought her a fortune.

4    Unidentified New York newspaper clipping c. 1910: Martha Morton,
"The first woman to invade the profession of playwright"

*East* for $10,000 to producer William A. Brady, who had been looking for "one of those rural things that were cleaning up everywhere."[11] By 1902 it was heralded as "the best paying play ever credited to a woman."[12] But, having sold the play outright, Parker never earned anything from the half-dozen touring companies, the 1903 and 1905 New York revivals, the play's twenty-seven-year popularity in other cities, or D. W. Griffith's purchase of the screen rights for $175,000 in 1920, which resulted in the screen masterpiece starring Lillian Gish. Although only two other plays by Parker won New York productions, their success on the road brought her considerable wealth. Upon her death in 1937, she left an estate of over $100,000 to friends, charities, and her late husband's relatives.

Of course, there had been successful women dramatists before Morton and Parker – Anna Dickinson, Anna Cora Mowatt, Louisa Medina, and Olive Logan, to name a few – but it was Morton who truly opened the way for the numerous others who flourished in the 1910s and 1920s. A *New York Herald* headline (16 November 1896) proclaimed: "Women Who Write Plays/ They Have Become A Remarkable Factor in New York Professional Life/Recent Pronounced Successes Were by Martha Morton, Madeline Ryley, Ada Bascom, Alice Ives, and Miss Merington/Have Linked Industry and Ambition/Work Not Ephemeral and All Have New Ventures to Launch Upon the Sea of Popular Approval." A 1903 article by A. von Ende in *The Theatre* traced the rise of the woman playwright from Hroswitha of Gandersheim through Aphra Behn and a variety of continental Europeans to arrive at a one-sentence summary of the American contribution: "The work of Mrs. Craigie, Madeleine Lucette Ryley, Martha Morton, Mrs. Haines, Marguerite Merington and others is too well known to receive more than mere mention in this brief review, which was only to show the distance traversed by the woman-drama since its birth in the convent of Gandersheim."[13] In 1905 *The Theatre* published the portraits of thirty-five "American Dramatists Who Supply Our Stage with Plays," of whom six were women. Virginia Frame profiled fifteen contemporary women playwrights for the same magazine in 1906.[14] Two years later, Lucy France Pierce claimed that "among about one hundred recognized playwrights turning out successful work each year, about thirty are women."[15] In a 1910 article, Shirley Burns described Morton's work and that of no fewer than thirty-four other women playwrights, with the observation that "more plays by women have been presented on the American stage in the past two years than ever before in America in a like period."[16] On the other hand, when Montrose J. Moses surveyed "younger American playwrights" in 1914, his tendency to overlook the women was apparent in his attribution of plays by Harriet Ford solely to her male collaborator,[17] and in his failure to name Fanny Hatton, referring instead to plays written by Frederic Hatton "with his wife";[18] nevertheless, the article acknowledges seven emerging women playwrights along with twenty-seven men. By 1917, Alan Dale could review his thirty years of theatregoing and come up with forty-one names of women who had "delivered the goods."[19]

In a 1911 article acknowledging the plethora of women dramatists ("I have cause to know that the woods are full of them!"), producer David Belasco dangled the lure of riches as an incentive for others to try their hand at playwriting:

There is no profession in the world which offers such splendid emolument to a woman when she has made a success of it. Not even the successful actress who has become a money-making star can equal the income of the woman who has succeeded in landing two or three big successes. And there is this difference between them, mark you: the actress, after years of a struggle, study, and achievement, has to repeat her performance day by day. The playwright, once the travail of composition and production is over, can sit back quietly and enjoy her royalties, without lifting another finger until she is ready to sit down and construct her next play! With such a great financial goal in sight it has always been a marvel to me that more women have not gone in for this line of endeavor.[20]

A 1910 article by Shirley Burns corroborates that view: "Many women are now drawing royalties from plays. Managers are as willing to consider their work as that of the men, and if her play is accepted, she receives just as much money for it as if it had been written by a man."[21] Burns went on to describe Martha Morton's gracious home and demeanor, that of "the well accustomed woman of society and the world";[22] the fashion sense and the luxuries earned by Rida Johnson Young;[23] the country house and foreign travels of Margaret Mayo, "another of the women dramatists who has learned the joys of picking money off the royalty bush";[24] and the domesticity of Mary Roberts Rinehart's household, in which her three small sons "had all sorts of fun planning ways to spend the royalties . . . Each one spoke for a pony, and of course he got it."[25] A photo spread of eight magnificent "Houses That Royalties Built" in a 1917 *Theatre Magazine* includes two mansions owned by women, those of Rida Johnson Young and Marion Fairfax.

Among the phenomenally successful plays of the period, *Mary Jane's Pa* by Edith Ellis won raves when it opened in New York in 1908, did excellent business on the road for several years, then was produced by stock companies all over the country, and remained available in print until the 1930s. A form letter, dated 26 September 1914, from Ellis's agents to stock managers vividly extolled the play's merits based upon the balance sheet: "As a medium for bringing in large, 'juicy dollars' in the box office of every stock company for two years past, *Mary Jane's Pa* needs no encomiums from Sanger and Jordan. Its popularity and its ability to extract the nimble coin without pain from the patrons of the stock company is a matter of record."[26]

Another high-income playwright, Lillian Mortimer, also acted in her own plays as well as directing and designing them and managing the company; she cleared about $10,000 a year, and bought homes on Long Island and in Michigan. Fanny Hatton and her husband Frederick co-authored dozens of risqué comedies; they were called "the Happy Hattons," because – it was noted in *Every Week* – "when they open their morning mail, money rolls out on the breakfast cloth."[27] Rida Johnson Young, author of twenty-six plays and musical comedies, including *Naughty Marietta* and *Maytime*, was able to indulge her passion for automobiles and jewels; she was most often photographed tending the flowers at one of her large estates on Long Island or in Connecticut. "I never received more than $18,000 from a play in my life," said the disingenuous Marion Fairfax; "why, when I talk to women like Margaret Mayo, Martha Morton, Rida Johnson Young and authors in their class, and when they tell me about $65,000 from this play, $100,000 for last year's work and such things, I realize what a nobody I am in the theater world."[28]

"There were weeks when I made $180,000 net profit. I bought stocks and bonds and most of Flushing," Anne Nichols recalled in 1962, looking back on a professional playwriting career that had begun in 1916. Her "million dollar hit" *Abie's Irish Rose* opened in 1922 and ran five years, "earning her more money than any single play has ever earned for a writer."[29] Yet, as Doris Abramson and Laurilyn Harris comment, her name is virtually unknown and her achievements "either belittled or pointedly ignored."[30] "After all is said and done," declared Margaret Mayo, "the box-office receipts are the only test of whether or not you have achieved a success."[31] Mayo was virtually penniless when she came to New York from Portland, Oregon, to become an actress. Luckily she discovered her talent for playwriting and made a fortune with *Polly of the Circus* (1907) and *Baby Mine* (1910). By 1911, with several American companies doing *Baby Mine*, she had signed contracts for productions of it in fifteen foreign countries. She noted:

At present the farce is getting a good deal of free advertising, for there are "Baby Mine" dolls and "Baby Mine" hats. The baby elephant at the Hippodrome is named "Baby Mine," and I am told there are "Baby Mine" cocktails. In fact a good many things are called "Baby Mine," but the thing that interests me most, of course, are the "Baby Mine" dollars.[32]

According to Lucy France Pierce, however, money was not the primary motive for the woman dramatist:

A man measures his success by its financial returns. But every keenly intelligent woman is more or less of a gambler – one who loses as gracefully as she wins. Man demands immediate recognition of his work. Action, alone, is in itself gratifying to an ambitious woman ... Merely to test her strength is a joy, merely to be allowed to measure her intellectual power is reward.[33]

A case in point is Marion Fairfax, who declared: "What I have needed all my life, and what other women need, is the necessity to work. It prepares one for a fuller enjoyment of the future."[34] Zelda Sears, a character actress-playwright who worked her way up from long years of poverty to reported royalties of $50,000 a year,[35] attributed her success to "always looking ahead – and looking for something better ... I not only wasn't afraid of work, I wasn't afraid of *extra* work. I always wanted to see what I could do."[36] Her generosity toward other theatre folk earned her the epithet "Lady Great Heart and Loose Purse of the profession." In a similar vein, Lottie Blair Parker told Earl Sparling that she was glad to see her play *Way Down East* make money for others: "I want anything even remotely connected with my work to be a success."

For several socially prominent women playwrights who clearly did not need the income generated by their efforts, the money was not an end in itself, but something that could be directed to a greater purpose. Ethel Watts Mumford, for example, told interviewer Ada Patterson that "a rich woman" should not take a penny less "for the product of her brain than the woman who must write to live"; her earnings could then be distributed to worthy causes, "into such channels that the world will be better for her having lived."[37] Although Margaret Mayo retired after World War I with a fortune estimated at two million dollars, she spent most of it on charitable projects, including building homes for needy theatre people, litigation on behalf of the townspeople of Croton-on-the-Hudson, where she lived, and institutions for animal care. Eleanor Gates, author of *Poor Little Rich Girl* and seven other Broadway plays, worked toward building a hotel for wage-earning women with children.[38] Mary Austin saw one of her plays reach Broadway – *The Arrow-Maker* (1911) – and thereafter devoted herself to causes like women's suffrage, preservation of Native American crafts, and problems of water-diversion in the desert. Playwright-librettist Anne Caldwell adopted an orphaned boy.

Although few plays from the period 1890–1929 by either men or women dramatists are remembered or revived today, the women clearly contributed to the intellectual ferment of their time. They used their money and their voices to make a difference. As an indication that they succeeded in this, an article found in the Anne Caldwell clippings file at the Theatre Collection of the New York Public Library might be cited:

When one comes to think of the needs of the theatre seriously, of how badly it stands in need of simplicity and of that real realism so much missed today, one may say off-hand that only women should write our plays . . . Welcome the hour when the male playwright hands over his sceptre to his sister. From Pinero on (not to go further back), men playwrights have been engaged in teaching us the emptiness of life. A woman's theatre may create a different atmosphere over a world of splendid things.[39]

It is apparent that even if the individual woman dramatist was destined to reap the rewards of money but not glory, the hundred or so women who had marched in Martha Morton's footsteps by 1929 earned a collective glory that must resonate across the decades to our own time.

## NOTES

Research for this essay was made possible by a grant from the National Endowment for the Humanities.

1 "Notes and Pictures: Josephine Preston Peabody," *Metropolitan Magazine* 34 (May 1911), 190–92, p. 192.
2 "Wealth Not a Bar to Playwriting," *Theatre Magazine* (May 1918), 296–97, p. 296.
3 Delight Evans, "The Mother of the Sub-Deb," *Photoplay* (January 1920), 74–75, 104, p. 75.
4 *Doing Literary Business: American Women Writers in the Nineteenth Century* (Chapel Hill: University of North Carolina Press, 1990), 2–5.
5 Ibid., 40.
6 Ibid., 39.
7 Archie Bell, "Marion Fairfax, Winsome Young Author of 'The Talker' Says That It's a Handicap to Be a Woman but She Can't Prove It," *The Plain Dealer*, Cleveland, 23 July 1911.
8 Ali Baba, "Mirror Interview XXI: Martha Morton," *Dramatic Mirror*, 7 November 1891.
9 Undated clipping in the Theatre Collection of the New York Public Library at Lincoln Center.
10 Earl Sparling, "Mrs. Parker, Who Wrote 'Way Down East' in 1887, Likes Cocktails, Cigarets, and Peach Velvet Gowns," *New York World Telegram*, 31 October 1936.
11 William A. Brady, "Drama in Homespun," *The Stage* 14 (January 1937), 98–100, p. 99.

12 "The World's Most Successful Woman Playwright: Lottie Blair Parker Has Three Plays in New York, a Fourth Soon to Open," *The North American*, Philadelphia, 9 February 1902, 6.

13 A. von Ende, "The Rise of the Woman Playwright," *The Theatre* 3 (1903), 115–17, p. 117.

14 "Women Who Have Written Successful Plays," *The Theatre* (October 1906), 264–67, ix–x.

15 "Women Who Write Plays," *World To-Day* (July 1908), 725–31, p. 725.

16 "Women Dramatists," *Green Book Album* (September 1910), 632–39, p. 632.

17 "Younger American Playwrights," *The Bellman*, 14 March 1914, 333–38, p. 334.

18 Ibid., 336.

19 "Women Playwrights: Their Contribution Has Enriched the Stage," *The Delineator* (February 1917), 7, 42–43, p. 43.

20 "The Great Opportunity of the Woman Dramatist," *Good Housekeeping Magazine* 53 (November 1911), 627–32, p. 628.

21 "Women Dramatists," 632.

22 Ibid., 633.

23 Ibid., 634.

24 Ibid., 637.

25 Ibid., 635.

26 Edith Ellis scrapbook 25, 767 New York Public Library Theatre Collection at Lincoln Ceter.

27 "Mrs Shakespeares," *Every Week*, 26 February 1917, 11.

28 Bell, "Marion Fairfax."

29 Arthur Gelb, "Author of *Abie's Irish Rose* Reviews 40 Years," *New York Times*, 21 May 1962, 40.

30 "Anne Nichols: $1,000,000,00 Playwright," *Players* 51 (April–May 1976), 123–25, p. 123.

31 "Margaret Mayo," *McClure's Magazine* (September 1912), 597–99, p. 599.

32 Margaret Mayo, "My Most Successful Play," *Green Book Album* (April 1911), 871–74, p. 873.

33 "Women Who Write Real Successes," *Green Book Album* 7 (May 1912), 1058–64, p. 1064.

34 Bell, "Marion Fairfax."

35 *New York Star*, 6 April 1921.

36 Mary B. Mullet, "She Opened Half a Dozen Doors, Then Found the Lucky Seventh," *American Magazine* 100 (December 1925), 18–19, 157–62, p. 162.

37 "Wealth Not a Bar," 296.

38 *New York Times*, 4 January and 11 February 1914.

39 *New York Sun and Herald*, 14 March 1920.

# CHAPTER 10

# "For laughing purposes only": the literature of American popular entertainment

*Brooks McNamara*

> *Madison's Budget* has among its subscribers performers and managers in every branch of the business the world over, and it is written and edited in a way best calculated to satisfy the average comedy needs of the largest number.
>
> Everything appearing in its columns is "for laughing purposes only" and is intended merely as satire, never ridicule. It is the earnest desire of the publisher to offend no race, creed or color.
>
> James Madison, *Madison's Budget*, 1921

In 1983 I edited an anthology of jokes, songs and comedy routines.[1] The anthology was essentially an attempt to bring together in one place some traditional texts associated with American popular entertainment. Some of the material was based on tapes that I had made of routines presented by old performers. But much of it was taken from written sources, many of them published.

Obviously, there was a strong oral tradition among entertainers, but I found that there was also a considerable literature of American popular entertainment on paper, and that it presented a rich resource on both the structure and the content of such forms as minstrelsy, vaudeville, burlesque, the medicine show, and tent repertory – as well as on related types of amateur performance. In the introduction to the 1983 anthology I discussed the relationship between the literature of popular entertainment and the structure of popular performance forms. In the present essay I would like to explore a little of the publishing history of that literature, as well as something about the nature of its content.

I

Printed collections of jokes, monologues, sketches, recitations, and songs circulated widely among both professionals and amateurs from the middle of the nineteenth century through the 1930s. Among them were the "minstrel guides," anthologies of minstrel routines and songs, frequently published by old entertainers, often with an eye not only to professionals but to the producers of club, and lodge and school shows. As Frank Dumont noted in the introduction to his 1899 publication, *The Witmark Amateur Minstrel Guide and Burnt Cork Encyclopedia*, "every amateur, college student and professional comedian will find it of the greatest value as a book of reference to 'think up' and construct monologues or gags at short notice."[2]

So-called "gag books" like James Madison's *Budget* and William McNally's *Bulletin* were regularly published anthologies of comedy material, aimed at vaudevillians, burlesque entertainers, and early radio performers. On the back cover of his gag books, McNally advertised a whole range of his other stage-oriented publications, including *Mack's Minstrelsy*, *Mack's Recitations*, and *Mack's Vaudeville Guide*, which contained "every detail of the Vaudeville Profession . . . made so clear that anyone can understand just what to do to enter the vaudeville profession." He points out that, in addition, "there are many articles in this book that professionals also could profit by reading, as it is the only book that truthfully gives all the information about vaudeville that is desired."[3]

Madison's volumes carried advertisements for a whole range of products and services aimed at both amateurs and professionals. There were ads for 'BERT MARION, Author of Vaudeville Ideas (Special Songs and Acts) Written to Order," "SAM MORRIS, STAGE DIRECTOR, Staging Minstrel Shows a Specialty," and "LUTHER B. ANTHONY, PLAY FIXING, if you can't put the punch in your skit or play, consult a doctor. I am administering to lame Plot patients right along." "Are You A Member of the ELKS, SHRINERS, AMERICAN LEGION or MASONS?" asks an advertisement for The Joe Bren Production Company of Chicago. "If so, tell your ENTERTAINMENT COMMITTEE to write us at once relative to a big HOME TALENT MINSTREL OR MUSICAL COMEDY."[4]

Serving much the same function on a more personal level were the homemade gag books and file collections assembled by entertainers out of clippings and manuscript material from hundreds of different sources. Jerry Cohan had such a book, as did Lew Fields, and I have seen an extensive personal gag book belonging to an old medicine-show entertainer, "Goober" Buchanan, who is still active. Typically, these books were anthologies tailored to the interests of a particular performer. They tended to be made up of clippings from published gag books and more general joke books, together with manuscripts contributed by other entertainers, and material written by the owner of the book.

A number of show people, however, went beyond a simple homemade gag book, assembling large file collections of published and manuscript material during the course of their careers. Bob Hope, for example, is said to have mammoth joke files, and an old burlesque performer, Chuck Callahan, brought together a collection of nearly three hundred burlesque and vaudeville sketches that is now in the Hampden-Booth Library of The Players. Some old performers, like "Uncle Cal," of Frederick, Maryland, and Mel J. Thompson of Aurora, North Carolina, typed up and duplicated material from their files, selling the manuscripts to other entertainers as crude homemade gag books.[5]

Directed primarily – though not exclusively – at the amateur market were such cheap joke books as the 1902 *The Boys of New York End Men's Joke Book* ("No Amateur Minstrels is Complete Without This Wonderful Little Book'), *Gus Williams' Monologues, Recitations and Joke Book, Original and Otherwise*, and various editions of a kind of generic publication, *New Stage Jokes*, containing – or allegedly containing – popular theatrical material.[6] Books of this sort were available through the mail and at news stands around the country, usually published by the same companies that produced such pamphlets as "A Thousand Ways to Get Rich" and the "Gypsy Witch Dream Book." Whether the jokes in the so-called stage joke books actually originated on stage is probably not of much consequence. Most people who read and used the books undoubtedly believed that the origin of the material was the popular theatre, and in time at least some of it undoubtedly found its way on stage, even if it had not actually originated there.

Somewhat more expensive were the "personality" joke books. Some, like the 1904 *Comical Confessions of Clever Comedians*, and the 1917 *Vaudeville Wit*, were anthologies of material attributed to popular performers.[7] Others were written by – or ghost-written for – such stars as Will Rogers, Eddie Cantor, Harry Lauder, and Joe Cook. Most either contained jokes taken from the comedians' acts or topical material gathered especially for the book, such as Rogers's *The Cowboy Philosopher on the Peace Conference* ("You can't tell *Peace* from *War* without this Book") and Cantor's *Caught Short! A Saga of Wailing Wall Street*, possibly the origin of the hoary "I'm the Kuhn, of Kuhn, Loeb and Company" gag.[8]

If there was not a topical occasion behind such a book, there was often a whimsical gimmick: Lauder's 1932 *Wee Drappies*, for instance, had the silhouette of a whisky bottle cut out of every page, and Cook's 1930 *Why I Will Not Imitate Four Hawaiians* was paginated backwards and issued with a certificate for ten shares of "VERY COMMON STOCK" in "The Joe Cook Amalgamated Anticipated Radium Mines of North America."[9] The famous vaudevillian "Doc" Rockwell published a line of small magazines, *Dr. Rockwell's Mustard Plaster*, that were somewhere between gag books and personality joke books.[10]

Books of recitations, collections of "parlor entertainments," how-to books on such subjects as presenting a magic show or becoming a ventriloquist, and separately published editions of short farces, sketches, and stunts were aimed primarily at the home market in a time when there were few competing home amusements. These books tended to disappear early in the twentieth century, or to begin to shift their emphasis from the home market to schools and Sunday schools, women's clubs and other institutional amateur organizations.[11]

An 1859 volume, *Parlor Theatricals; or, Winter Evenings' Entertainment*, is a typyical mid-nineteenth-century parlor entertainment guide "containing acting proverbs; musical burlesques; parlor farces, etc., etc.," as well as brief instructions about how to construct a stage, make up actors, rehearse a skit, and so on.[12] Like many of the home-oriented books, *Parlor Theatricals* begins with a disclaimer, which advises the reader that the pieces it contains are "innocent, harmless, and easy of attainment ... These PARLOR THEATRICALS serve, indeed, a higher purpose than mere amusement. They stimulate the faculties, arouse the wit, and under the guise of amusement, develop and exercise the mental functions. Nor is this all; they foster harmony and unity of feeling; and, by community of pleasure, cultivate love, sympathy, and good-fellowship in youthful hearts."[13]

The individually published sketch or short play was a staple of parlor and amateur entertainment. Baker, the Dramatic Publishing Company of Chicago, Samuel French, and a host of other smaller companies like the De Witt Publishing House of New York City, offered material for amateurs, such as O. J. Wenlandt's 1901 *The*

*Nigger Store-Keeper* ("A Farcical Nigger Sketch"), and the 1900 *The Spinsters' Convention* ("An Evening's Entertainment in One Scene"). A nineteenth-century Samuel French catalogue advertised "PLAYS! PLAYS! PLAYS! PLAYS! For Reading Clubs, for Amateur Theatricals, Temperance Plays, Drawing Room Plays, Fairy Plays, Ethiopian Plays," along with a whole range of "Guide Books, Speakers Pantomimes, Tableaux Lights, Magnesium Lights, Colored Fire, Burnt Cork, Theatrical Face Preparations, Jarley's Wax Works, Wigs, Beards and Moustaches at reduced prices. Costumes, Scenery, Charades."[14] De Witt, which specialized in plays and other entertainments for amateurs, offered an extensive line of "Ethiopian and Comic Dramas," and "De Witt's Drawing-Room Operettas," along with a group of play anthologies, containing standard works "especially adapted for presentation by amateurs, and for parlor and drawing-room entertainments."[15]

There was considerable overlap among the entertainment source books, but it would be a mistake, of course, merely to lump all of them together indiscriminately. Obviously their various compilers envisioned quite different audiences, and the differences from one book to another – and one type of book to another – are as great as their similarities. For example, although some minstrel guides included a certain number of sentimental songs and poems, for the most part the gag books, joke books and minstrel guides tended to feature comedy material, much of it of a fairly unsubtle sort.

The source-book anthologies aimed specifically at parlor entertainers, on the other hand, clearly tended to be at least somewhat more sedate and refined. And unlike other kinds of source books, they seem to have been conceived primarily as anthologies of nostalgic, sentimental, inspirational and patriotic material, and they ordinarily contain only mild comedy pieces of the kind that editors felt were appropriate for performance in the home, often by children. Acland Boyle was careful to point out in the introduction to his 1883 *Recherché Recitations* that the "Pieces for Parlor and Platform" to be found in his work were carefully selected with reference to "good taste," as well as "variety" and "availability."[16]

Beyond that, of course, there were changes in taste and emphasis over the years that make many of the books published in the thirties, for example, quite different in their emphasis from those that came out half a century earlier. Because the majority of the books relied on topical humor, central events in American culture – wars, Prohibition, the coming of the motion picture and the Flapper, the Depression – led to new material and new perspectives on American life.[17] And yet many of the old jokes and sketches appear in the later volumes, and some of the same books were still in print in their original form half a century after their first appearance. Acland Boyle turns this idea into an advertising device, noting on the title page of his anthology that, "A number of these pieces are entirely new candidates for public favor, – written especially for this book; others make their first appearance as adaptions; some are gleanings from the latest magazines and other literary fields; the rest are standard selections which 'the world will not willingly let die.'"[18]

Finally, however, what ties all of the books together is the fact that they were not created simply to be read, but to serve as resources for performance. Like the musicians' "fake books," they existed primarily to be mined for useful material. And especially in the period before the Depression and the growth of radio and sound film, there was a considerable demand for them. The publishing of source books constituted a small industry; hundreds of thousands – perhaps millions – of them must have appeared by the end of the thirties, when they finally faded away in the wake of new forms of competition in the entertainment world. Minstrelsy and vaudeville were dead, burlesque and the medicine show were dying, and parlor entertainment had gone the way of the dodo and the dinosaur. The traditional source books quietly followed them.[19]

II

As I suggested in the 1983 anthology, the basic components of the source books – and of most American popular entertainments – appear to have been: jokes and other comic material; the monologue, the pitch and the lecture; the dialogue and the bit; and the sketch.[20] Given those divisions, the content of the books may be analyzed in various ways. One approach is to focus on their social content. Some of the jokes and quips and rhymes, of course, are simply plays on words or neutral anecdotes that do not depend on such content. For example, a stage joke book offers: "'I see your sister does a nice two-step.' 'Yes. She learned it off my two step sisters.'" From a gag book: "Of all the sad surprises/There's nothing to compare,/With treading in the darkness/On a step that isn't there." And from a minstrel guide: "Why is a cow half way through a gate like a penny? Because it is head on one side and tail on the other."[21]

But most of what one finds in the source books is concerned to some degree or other with the exploration of social values. And here the issue of content becomes more complex. There is a certain working-class ambiance to some of the books, which almost certainly reflects the working-class origins of so many of the people involved in popular entertainment.[22] But most of the books seem not to have been especially parochial or rigidly class-oriented in the terms of their day. On the contrary, taken together, they obviously presented the views that their compilers and publishers believed would help entertainers communicate most effectively to all classes and ages, to the broadest possible audience across America. Like Madison's *Budget,* most were obviously "written and edited in a way best calculated to satisfy the average comedy needs of the largest number." In their way, the source books, like the first motion pictures, were early documents in the history of American mass entertainment.[23]

Obviously, it is impossible at this distance to say precisely how influential the books were. But they *were* influential; both professionals and amateurs clearly read them, memorized material from them, and relied to some extent on that material in their performances. The jokes and songs and sketches that appeared in the source books made their way to stages all over the nation. And the content of the source books obviously had an impact, not only on performers, but on American audiences, as well. But that was only part of the cycle. The second part lay in the fact that the views of society found in these books seem to have been those already endorsed by the audiences themselves. Popular audiences, as George Jean Nathan wrote in 1918, have always been attracted to material that reflects "their own thoughts and emotions," that repeats "to their ears those things they already know and feel."[24] The source books clearly offered entertainers values that had previously been tested and confirmed by their audiences.

It may be that the bulk of the source books were, as Madison put it, designed "to offend no race, creed or color." But offense is in the eye of the beholder, and in the terms of the late twentieth century, most are, if not offensive, at least unnerving. The source-book material dealing with economics, class, race, and gender seems almost invariably defensive. It is largely pro-white male, anti-professional, anti-higher education, anti-art, anti-black, anti-foreign, anti-female – obviously intended, at some very basic level, not just "For Laughing Purposes Only," but to reinforce certain established views about American society.

The average white male and his point of view seem to be celebrated in virtually all of the source books.[25] The working stiff usually becomes a hero of sorts. He is not highly educated or urbane; he is ordinarily a poor man, often down on his luck, but fundamentally honest and large-spirited. He is manifestly not a bum or a rube – and certainly not a black or an ethnic – all of whom appear only as low-comedy figures. The working stiff is much put upon by his boss, his wife, and his mother-in-law, and by the institutions that control the direction of his life, from the rich man and the politician to taxes and the Model-T Ford.

The frustrations of the ordinary white man's life are always in evidence in the books: "I just met the stage manager outside," says a comedian in a 1926 gag book, "and he told me he had a new mother-in-law gag. I told him I'd buy one, if he thought it would gag mine." A Madison burlesque of "My Country 'Tis of Thee" begins, "My auto, 'tis of thee,/Short road to poverty,/Of thee I chant./I blew a pile of dough/On you three years ago;/Now you refuse to go,/Or won't, or can't." The burden of taxes in the Depression era is addressed in another gag-book parody, this one to the tune of "Roll Out the Barrel." "Cut down the taxes," it begins, "and give the poor man a chance."[26]

The source books invariably take a dim view of the rich, the socially prominent, and the highly educated, all of whom are presented as the "Other" – those in control of the average man's economic and social destiny. Perhaps the quintessential example of this wariness comes from a stage joke book dating from about 1920 in which a millionaire, wrapped in his luxurious fur coat, approaches a beggar on the street and asks him how long he has been there. The beggar explains, with a glimmer of hope in his heart, that he has been out in the cold for hours and that he is freezing. "'Ah,' said the millionaire as he walked on, 'now what you want to do is to move about a bit.'"[27] But occasionally a kind of rough justice prevails and evens the score, as in a Depression-era gag-book parody of "It Ain't Gonna Rain No More':

The crooked bankers took our cash,
To them it was a joke,
But when we tried to get it back
They said "The bank is broke."
CHORUS
But they ain't gonna reign no more, no more,
They ain't gonna reign no more.
We're sending them to Levenworth
Where they ain't gonna reign no more.[28]

Even though it is a commonplace that Americans have always valued knowledge and education, higher education and pretensions to culture are invariably looked on askance in the source books. Professors are hopeless incompetents or ponderous bores, and college men are know-it-alls who, in the final analysis, know little or nothing: "'De noive o' that guy,' complained Jimmy the office boy, 'Offerin' me $6 a week. What's he tink I am – a college graduate?'"[29] Similarly, the books routinely make fun of "high art" and its creators. Such elitist and incomprehensible forms as opera, painting, classical music, ballet, and the work of "serious" authors are seen only as subjects for low comedy, and the painter and "longhair" musician, like the college professor, are generally portrayed as freaks, charlatans or bores. Thus a young woman remarks to her father at the end of a lengthy musical composition: "'Isn't it too bad, Daddy; the man who wrote this piece died two weeks ago.' Father: 'Did they find the murderer?'" A pompous composer confides to a music lover that his new lullaby can't be played in public: "It was tried at a rehearsal by the Philharmonic Orchestra but it is so charmingly sweet and tender, that after the adagio the entire orchestra had fallen asleep."[30]

Likewise, serious authors and their work – especially poetry – came in for considerable derision. *Hamlet* was seen as the epitome of highbrow art ripe for parody.[31] A minstrel guide, for example, offers "Hamlet on the Hash House," which deflates the Prince's famous soliloquy by restating it in banal terms: "To eat or not to eat, that's the question./Whether 'tis better on the whole to suffer/The slurs and slaps of rambustious waiters/Or to take up arms against the set of trollops,/And, by shooting, end them?"[32] And the manuscript of a vaudeville recitation systematically reduces the whole of *Hamlet* – and incidentally the theatrical profession – to patent absurdity when a working stiff is given a theatre ticket:

Last night the boss slips me a ticket
  For one of them opera shows.
An' the name of the show is called "Hamlet,"
  So I digs up my glad rags and goes.
Well, it's gloom from the minute it opens
  'Till the time the theayter shuts.
An' the company's half of them looney
  An' the rest of the cast is plain nuts.[33]

Like the artist and the college professor, the educated professional was always the butt of source-book humor. Lawyers, doctors and dentists, for example, all seem to have been viewed as natural enemies of the ordinary man. The lawyer is a gouger and a crook ("Why should lawyers sleep well? Because it is immaterial on which side they lie"), and the doctor and dentist invariably appear in a highly unflattering light.[34] Physicians of course have always been associated in the popular consciousness with illness and suffering, and the source books invariably balance the account by showing them to be incompetent, vain, greedy, lascivious, sadistic, and/or quite mad. A manuscript from the Callahan Collection, for example, presents Smith and Dale in one of their famous medical routines. In it Dr. Kronkhite hires the cretinous Smith as his assistant, a kind of quack-in-training. "I'll pay you according to what you are worth," says Kronkhite. "I refuse to work that cheap," Smith replies. Dr. Kronkhite retires to his surgery and his nurse enters. She is filling out a form and asks Smith his vocation. "Last two weeks in August," he tells her. She inquires about his age. "I'm twenty-six," he says. "I would have been twenty-eight but I was sick two years."[35]

Thus the sketch creates a kind of reverse angle on the polite view of the physican as healer, authority figure, and pillar of the community. Instead, the doctor has become subhuman, the essence of incompetence. Dr. Rockwell's comedy magazine, *Mustard Plaster*, is devoted largely to exploring this premise. In 1928, for instance, Rockwell ("Still Practicing on the Public") lays out the symptoms of appendicitis, warning readers against the mistake "of thinking you have the disease, because one or two of the symptoms are present, as both the desire for *liquor and distaste for work occur when appendicitis is not present.*" In 1929, the Doc ("Quack. Quack. Quack.") provides professional advice on insomnia, "or the inability to sleep. The word Insomnia is derived from two words – Insulation, meaning covering,

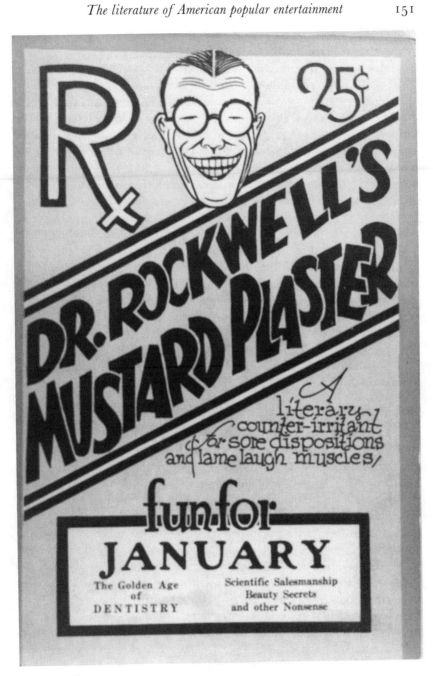

5   Advertisement for *Dr. Rockwell's Mustard Plaster*

and omnia, meaning all, or ALL COVERING, which interpreted means too many bed clothes."[36]

If doctors are quacks and fools, dentists are sadists and crooks. A 1904 collection of sketches by well-known comics includes a dental monologue attributed to Francis Wilson. His dentist's office was a frightening place, Wilson said. "There was a large chair in the center of the room that seemed to be stretching out its big arms for me, eager to grapple with my carcas [sic], while all the sets of teeth lying about the place seemed to be snapping at me, anxious to get a bit of my plump anatomy." The dentist entered, and Wilson asked him not to shave him too close. He responded by jerking back Wilson's head "as though it was a brake handle," and yanking open his mouth. The dentist "held tightly onto my chin and forehead," he said. "Afraid he'd fall in, I suppose. Then he took a tack puller with a mirror attachment at the end and commenced to search my mouth for something. I thought maybe he had dropped his hat in." Before operating, the dentist gave Wilson gas. When he awoke, "my toothache was gone. So was my watch. So was the dentist."[37]

The source books also represented a clearing-house for traditional views of women, ethnics and blacks. Indeed, they must have been, as much as live performance itself, very important popular disseminators of such views. Almost invariably, the source-book material trades on the kind of commonplaces that were at the center of American popular culture of the day: the Irish are drunks, Jews are greedy and devious, blacks are thieves, lazy and ignorant, and women are frigid or harridans or whores. There are tens of thousands of examples of Irish, "Dutch," Italian and "Hebrew" comedy in the source books, and countless jokes and songs and comedy routines about blacks and women. For the most part they are cynical and defensive.

The minstrel guides, of course, are predominately anthologies of black jokes, trading on the usual stereotypes ("TAMBO: Bob, I've got some fine poultry down at my house. BONES: I missed some from my hen roost; that accounts for it."), although characteristically they also contain a certain amount of "Dutch" and Irish comedy.[38] This triune of comedy material carries over to the stage joke books and gag books, along with the addition of "Hebrew" jokes and, to a lesser extent, stereotypical Asian, Italian and Scottish material: "Have you ever seen any races?" asks the Straight. "Many of them," the Comic answers. "What was the closest race you ever saw?" "The

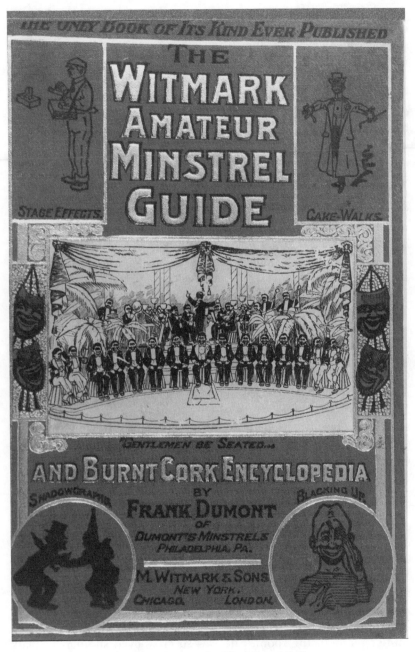

6   Advertisement for *The Minstrel Guide*

Scotch."[39] The "Hebe" two-act was a standard with McNally, who offered such routines as "Levinsky and Son," "Goldberg and Silverstein" and "Levi and Cohn." James Madison – whose material, we recall, is "satire, never ridicule" – dispatches two groups at a blow when he has the Interlocutor of "Madison's Merry Minstrels" inquire of Tambo: "Why is Henry Ford sore at the Jews?" "That's easy," Tambo replies. "Henry is sore at the Jews because they make more money selling secondhand Fords than he makes selling new ones."[40]

Casual ethnic and racial slurs, however, represent only one small corner of the social value system built into the source books. As Jill Dolan has suggested about women and burlesque comedy, "from the famous Henny Youngman line, 'Take my wife – please!' backwards and forwards in the history of American comedy, women have been an easy target for men's jokes."[41] Certainly this was the case with the source books; women, almost more than any other single group, preoccupied the creators of stage comedy material.

Their portraits in the volumes of parlor entertainment material are perhaps less overtly damaging to women than those in the joke books, minstrel guides and gag books. But even in the books designed for the home entertainment market, the portraits of women traded on stereotypes. Thus a 1906 book of tableaux contrasts "The Old Maid and Girl Bachelor." "Old maid," the text of the tableau runs, "wears corkscrew curls at side of face, a queer, much-trimmed bonnet, old-style dress and shawl, cotton gloves and glasses with steel bows. The girl bachelor wears a trim tailor suit, white standing collar and mannish tie, mannish-looking hat, nose glasses with chain. They stand looking at each other, the old maid with hands uplifted and horrified expression on face, the girl bachelor smiling superciliously, head held high."[42]

Gag books, joke books, and minstrel guides seem only to have dealt with the unmarried woman in totally negative terms – generally focusing on the absence of a man in her life. Thus, "'My spinster aunt said if ever a man made love to her she'd call in the authorities.' 'Yes, the justice of the peace and the chief of the marriage license bureau.'" Or: "The trouble with unmarried women is they get peculiar. I knew an old maid who became so bashful she wouldn't take her clothes off at night because there was a rubber plant in the room. She was so cross-eyed she had to walk backwards across a room to keep from bumping into people." Or: "Last week I was in a butcher shop when an old maid came in and said to the butcher, 'Is your steak tender?' He said: 'Madam, it's as tender as a woman's heart.' She said: 'Then give me mutton chops.'"[43]

Indeed, all women are presented negatively in the source books – as blatant sex objects, physical grotesques, shrewish wives, termagant mothers-in-law, and sinister gold diggers. Marriage is viewed as a trap for the male, and women are always incompetent in one way or another. A wife's cooking, for example, gave her husband indigestion "South of the Border, right under my belt." "I have slipped on skins of a banana,/But that never ruined me like her pies,/Each bite I thought I ate a pi-an-a/Or a steam shovel in disguise."[44]

Most wives and girl friends had glaring physical defects. To the tune of "There's a Rainbow 'Round my Shoulder," the groom notes about his bride that, "There's a mole up on her shoulder,/And a wart upon her chin,/Since I wed that girl,/My head's awhirl,/I'm all in." Besides being unattractive, wives and sweethearts were generally unfaithful. Thus, "In the good old summer time," the hero met "a girl built like a truck," who said he "kissed divine." But "when my arm slid round her waist,/I felt a man's hand touch mine,/He was coming round the other way,/In the good old summer time."[45]

But there is always revenge for the gag-book male. He invariably has the last laugh at the female's expense – in one case the very last laugh. The gag-book comedian has decided to marry his girl Sadie as a sure-thing investment. "I love my Sadie," he says, "My Sadie loves me,/She has a good shape,/And plenty mon-ey,/And she is sickly,/She's dying, I know,/So why should I worry!/I'll get lots of dough."[46] There are a thousand more possible examples, but perhaps the main points about the source books are clear enough. The literature of American popular entertainment was widespread and extremely influential. It was frequently trivial and corny – and often offensive. Threatening groups within the society seem always to have been shown in stereotypical terms, and thus presented as somehow less than fully human. Yet, like all popular literature, the books capture an extraordinary sense of the concerns and frustrations of ordinary people. They tell us a great deal about the attitudes of professional showmen and amateur entertainers in the period from the Civil War to World War II – and, by extension, a great deal about what was on the minds of their audiences.

For the most part, the social values that emerge from the guide books are ones that most Americans today, at least in theory, would probably choose to reject. And to a certain extent, perhaps, we have rejected them. Or to put it another way, perhaps our culture no longer asks so clearly for the reinforcement of certain defensive values and traditional stereotypes. And yet one wonders about the material created by such contemporary entertainers as Andrew Dice Clay and 2 Live Crew. Perhaps it will not be surprising if historians half a century from now find the literature of our own popular entertainment – the television and film script, the nightclub routine, the song lyric – as cynical and defensive in its way as anything conceived by showmen a hundred years ago. Certainly it will tell researchers as much about our social attitudes as the old source books can tell us about the values of an earlier day.

## NOTES

1 Brooks McNamara, ed., *American Popular Entertainments* (New York: Performing Arts Journal Publications, 1983).
2 Frank Dumont, ed., *The Witmark Amateur Minstrel Guide and Burnt-Cork Encyclopedia* (Chicago: M. Witmark, 1899), 4. Unless otherwise noted, all popular entertainment source books discussed in this article are from the collection of the writer.
3 William McNally, ed., *McNally's Bulletin* (1934), rear cover.
4 James Madison, ed., *Madison's Budget* (1921) 74, 72, 74, 79.
5 See Llewellyn H. Hedgbeth, "The Chuck Callahan Burlesque Collection" in *Performing Arts Resources*, vol. III, ed. Ted Perry (New York: Theatre Library Associations, 1976), 143–50; "Uncle Cal's Manuscript" no. 7, no pagination, no date; untitled manuscript by Mel J. Thompson, no pagination, no date.
6 Anon., *The Boys of New York End Men's Joke Book* (New York: Frank Tousey, 1902), title page; Gus Williams, ed., *Gus Williams' Monologues, Recitations and Joke Book, Original and Otherwise* (New York: Frank Tousey, 1902); Anon., *New Stage Jokes* (Racine, Wisconsin: Western Printing and Lithographing, n.d.); Anon., *New Stage Jokes No. 2* (New York: Wehman Brothers, n.d.).
7 F. P. Pitzer and De Wolf Hopper, eds., *Comical Confessions of Clever Comedians* (New York: Street and Smith, 1904); Carleton B. Case, ed., *Vaudeville Wit* (Chicago: Shrewesbury Publishing, 1917).
8 Will Rogers, *The Cowboy Philosopher on the Peace Conference* (New York:

Harper and Brothers, 1919); Eddie Cantor, *Caught Short!* (New York: Simon and Schuster, 1929).

9 Sir Harry Lauder, *Wee Drappies* (New York: Robert M. McBride, 1932); Joe Cook, *Why I Will Not Imitate Four Hawaiians* (New York: Simon and Schuster, 1930).

10 George Rockwell, ed., *The Mustard Plaster*, various issues, 1928–29.

11 I have not included discussion of school- and Sunday-school-oriented source books in this article. Although they are clearly related in certain ways to parlor entertainment guides and other amateur source books, they seem to me to constitute a separate area of publishing, with objectives that are often distinctly different.

12 Anon., *Parlor Theatricals; or, Winter Evenings' Entertainment* (New York: Dick and Fitzgerald, 1859), title page.

13 Ibid., unnumbered page.

14 O. J. Wendlandt, *The Nigger Store-Keeper* (Chicago: The Dramatic Publishing Company, 1901); Anon., *The Spinsters' Convention* (Chicago: The Dramatic Publishing Company, 1900); quoted in Anon., *Truly Yours: One Hundred and Fifty Years of Play Publishing and Service to the Theatre* (New York: Samuel French, 1980), 14.

15 Advertisements in Frank Dumont, *Scenes in Front of a Clothing Store* ("De Witt's Ethiopian and Comic Drama," no. 160), (New York: De Witt, 1889), cover pages.

16 Acland Boyle, ed., *Von Boyle's Recherché Recitations* (New York: De Witt, 1883), unnumbered page.

17 Cf. Albert F. McLean, Jr., *American Vaudeville as Ritual* (Lexington: University of Kentucky Press, 1965), 106–37.

18 Boyle, *Recherché Recitations*, title page.

19 Until recently, an old New York City entertainer named Billy Glason continued to publish compilations of comedy material for individuals, as well as a gag magazine. Glason was probably among the few remaining publishers of such material.

20 McNamara, ed., *American Popular Entertainments*, 13–24.

21 *New Stage Jokes No. 2*, xx, William McNally, ed., *McNally's Bulletin* 17 (1931), 52; Anon., *Bones, His Gags and Stump Speeches* (New York: Wehman Brothers, 1879), 21.

22 Cf. Benjamin McArthur, *Actors and American Culture, 1880–1920* (Philadelphia: Temple University Press, 1984), 27–54; Bruce McConachie and Daniel Friedman, eds., *Theatre for Working-Class Audiences in the United States, 1830–1980* (Westport, CT: Greenwood Press, 1985), 3–15.

23 Cf. McConachie and Friedman, eds., *Theatre for Working-Class Audiences*, 5.

24 George Jean Nathan, *The Popular Theatre* (New York: Alfred A. Knopf, 1918), 22.

25 Cf. Robert Toll, *Blacking Up* (New York: Oxford University Press, 1974), 3–23.

26  William McNally, ed., *McNally's Bulletin* 10 (1924), 11; *Madison's Budget*, 24; *McNally's Bulletin* 21 (1940), 91.
27  *New Stage Jokes*, 45–46.
28  Madison, ed., *The Comedian* 6 (1934), 9.
29  *New Stage Jokes*, 57.
30  Ibid., 58; Carl Hauser, *Fun for the Millions* (New York: Carl Hauser, 1915), 151.
31  Cf. Lawrence Levine, *Highbrow/Lowbrow* (Cambridge, MA: Harvard University Press, 1988), 11–81.
32  Dumont, *The Witmark Amateur Minstrel Guide*, 95.
33  Manuscript, no pagination, no date. The full text is reprinted in McNamara, ed., *American Popular Entertainment*, 45–46.
34  *Bones, His Gags and Stump Speeches*, 47.
35  Manuscript, no pagination, no date.
36  George Rockwell, ed., *The Mustard Plaster* (November 1928), 8; (February 1929), 7.
37  Pitzer and Hopper, eds., *Comical Confessions*, 37–45.
38  Anon., *Tambo, His Jokes and Funny Sayings* (New York: Wehman Brothers, 1882), 21.
39  Case, ed., *Vaudeville Wit*, 83.
40  Madison, ed., *The Comedian*, 43. Cf. Paul Antonie Distler, "Ethnic Comedy in Vaudeville and Burlesque" in *American Popular Entertainment*, ed. Myron Matlaw (Westport, CT: Greenwood Press, 1977), 33–42.
41  Jill Dolan, "'What, No Beans?' Images of Women and Sexuality in Burlesque Comedy," *Journal of Popular Culture* 18 (Winter 1984), 37–47.
42  Marie Irish, *Tableaux and Scenic Readings* (Chicago, T. S. Denison, 1906), 120.
43  *McNally's Bulletin* 21 (1940), 45; Madison, ed., *The Comedian*, 4; Case, *Vaudeville Wit*, 61.
44  *McNally's Bulletin* 21 (1940), 93.
45  *McNally's Bulletin* 15 (1929), 109; Madison, *The Comedian*, 8.
46  *McNally's Bulletin* 21 (1940), 94.

# E pluribus unum: *Bernhardt's 1905–1906 farewell tour*

## Stephen M. Archer

In 1925 President Calvin Coolidge correctly identified the chief business of the American people as business, underscoring the radical changes in America between the Spanish-American and First World Wars. The United States had emerged as a world power with new muscles to flex, domestically as well as internationally, and money was to be made by businessmen with organizational acumen. The money tree quickly yielded its fruit; by 1900 318 American organizations enjoyed a capitalization of over seven billion dollars. Six corporations controlled 95 percent of America's railroads, and United States Steel dictated prices as they saw fit. In 1890 the Sherman Antitrust Act prohibited combinations in the form of trusts, and a great "trust-busting" era ensued. By 1902 a Federal commission posited that since prices had risen and the cost of raw materials had lessened, the differential revealed the increased profits for the trusts. As a result the cost of living in the United States rose about 35 percent between 1897 and 1913.

In the relatively ungoverned world of the American theatre, the box office dictated some substantial changes. The long run had replaced repertory for the most part; Augustin Daly had become the first to stand forth clearly as a *régisseur*; playwrights even received royalties. The rise of theatrical realism increased production costs, but competition was free and easy; no holds were barred. This laissez-faire attitude with its inherent inefficiency led first to the formation of booking combinations or wheels and then inevitably to the ominous, infamous Theatre Syndicate.

For two decades the Syndicate (or Theatrical Trust) held sway, opposed by a few wealthy actors and producers at first, but successfully repelling all comers. Then out of western New York State came a trio of brothers, the Shuberts – Sam, Lee, and Jacob – with a borrowed $15,000 and dreams beyond avarice. A few years later they would be worth half a billion and the Syndicate's monopoly would lay in shambles.

At first the brothers cooperated with the Syndicate, managing theatres in the northeastern states. By 1905 the Syndicate grew leery of the Shuberts' increasing influence and ordered them to stop acquiring theatres. The brothers immediately declared independence and formed their own booking circuit. By the close of the 1905–6 season the Shuberts controlled about fifty theatres and their war with the Syndicate was fully joined.[1]

The Shuberts also controlled an impressive roster of talent and shows,[2] but they gained a major strategic advantage that same season when they signed perhaps the most famous actress of all time, Sarah Bernhardt. Foreign stars had been touring North America for almost a century: the elder and younger Kean, William Charles Macready, Henry Irving and Ellen Terry, Constant Coquelin, and dozens of others had found adoring publics and inflated income west of the Atlantic. None, however, matched in drawing power or publicity Sarah Bernhardt who had begun her visits to the United States in 1880 in spite of opposition by ecclesiastics and other supervisors of public morals. She returned in 1886, 1895, and 1900, gathering momentum and receipts with successive visits. In 1905 she announced her farewell tour, to be produced by the Shuberts.

The contract between Bernhardt and Lee Shubert, signed 28 June 1905 in London, stipulated a tour of twenty weeks including at least 140 performances at the rate of seven a week. Bernhardt could appear only in theatres "managed or hired" by Lee Shubert. The star agreed to supply costumes, special accessories, and scenery, while Shubert agreed to "defray" the costs of mounting, dismounting, and repair of these items. All travelling expenses for the company were Shubert's responsibility including providing for Bernhardt a private Pullman car and a carriage in every city visited.

As manager, Bernhardt would receive a minimum of $900 for each performance, regardless of receipts, and 30 percent of anything over $1,800 for any single performance, to be paid at the end of each performance. A Bernhardt representative would personally check the receipts.

In addition, Bernhardt received $200 a week for hotel expenses and a 75,000-franc advance. Since Bernhardt claimed royalties for

*Adrienne Lecouvreur*, she received an additional $50 for each perform-
ance of that script.[3]

Bernhardt and her company arrived in New York after her ship
had been delayed some twenty hours. They departed immediately
for Chicago by special train, averaging about sixty miles an hour
and arriving in the Windy City seventeen hours and forty-five
minutes after leaving New York.[4] Following the Chicago opening,
Bernhardt and her company would play Canada briefly, then tour
the east coast until mid-February. After several one-night stands in
the midwest, the company would then visit the south, the Syndicate
stronghold. Returning through Texas and the Indian Territory
(Oklahoma) Bernhardt would pass through the midwest again,
travel to the northwest through Wisconsin and Montana, then come
down the coast to San Francisco. For the final leg the company
would journey east through the middle of the country – Denver, St.
Joseph, Cleveland – then play a few final dates in the east, closing
the tour in New York in June 1906.

The Syndicate forbade Bernhardt to appear in any of their
theatres; Bernhardt swore she would never set foot in any Syndicate
house, then or ever. The press sided with the Shuberts and against
the Syndicate, specifically Abraham Erlanger. It had been Erlanger
who sent the word to all Syndicate theatres they were not to book
Bernhardt on pain of blacklisting.[5]

This forced Bernhardt, international star or not, to perform in
several miserable venues: convention halls, skating rinks, a combined swimming pool–auditorium in Tampa, a summer theatre five
miles outside Little Rock, a boathouse in St. Joseph, Missouri, and if
she had not cancelled the engagements, an ex-stable in Mont-
gomery, and the dining room of the Poinciana Hotel in Palm Beach.
Advance crews did what they could with portable stages, but the
Shuberts soon realized that an entire auditorium could tour as well,
and the epic of the Bernhardt tent began.

The Baker and Lockwood Company of Kansas City prepared a
special tent capable of seating 6,000.[6] This facility, which provoked
much publicity during the tour and much misinformation afterwards, was 180 feet long by 130 feet wide, known in the trade as "a
130-foot round top with a 50-foot center."

A 40- by 35-foot stage was also contracted, complete with a full
set of lights and a proscenium arch. The Bernhardt train, which

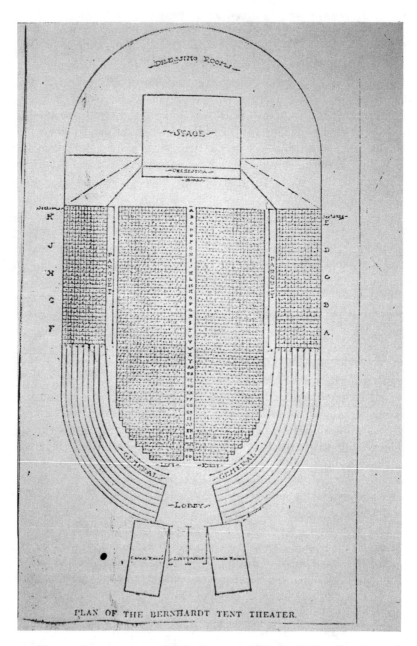

PLAN OF THE BERNHARDT TENT THEATER.

7   The seating arrangement for the 6,000-seat "Bernhardt Tent" constructed
     by the Baker and Lockwood Co. of Kansas City in 1906

began as five cars, now added four more, three to hold the tent and one to contain the thirty men required to erect it. The canvas theatre cost about $3,000; Bernhardt's manager was to pay $500 for its use the first day, then $350 per day until it was paid off.

Some Bernhardt biographers later maintained she played coast to coast in this tent, but reconstruction of the tour reveals only five such appearances: 26 March in Dallas; the next night in Waco; a benefit performance in Chicago on 26 April for the victims of the San Francisco earthquake; in Duluth on 30 April; and in Springfield, Massachusetts, on 8 June.

Although the tent proved an unsatisfactory substitute for a proper theatre, its publicity value was boundless. For the first performance under canvas, Dallas newspapers announced that forty men would spend four hours erecting the tent. The day before Bernhardt arrived, the stage, curtain, seats, and electrics were to be added, all to be ready by the time the actors arrived.[7]

The entrance to the park, which housed a summer theatre, still had painted over it in big, black letters, "Ten, twenty, and thirty cents!" A laconic Texan sauntered up to the box office, dropped down a quarter and a nickel, and requested, "Gimme the best seat you've got in the durned tent." The manager explained the facts of life and three-dollar tickets to him.[8]

A mob – no other word is accurate – began to gather about five in the afternoon, and a nervous management opened the doors early. The rush of people swept away security officers; customers sat anywhere they wanted, some patrons with one-dollar tickets took possession of three-dollar seats, others filled the aisles and stood on extra seats. While some five thousand persons were somewhere near the performance, the entire venture became a disaster for the audience. Reports suggested that after the tent filled no one past the tenth row could hear a word, and those who could hear did not understand French. After a time, patrons in the rear tired of pantomime and began to invent other means of amusement, filling the air with peanuts and paper wads. Some of the audience began to abuse the actors, bedlam broke loose, and police were called in to quiet the audience during a halt in the performance. And all of this, one paper reported, in the name of "divine" art.[9]

But no hint of blame was attached to Bernhardt; she dazzled the local reviewers, although the script of *Camille* was considered "malodorous."[10] By her third night in Texas, Bernhardt's spirits were dampened, partly by the fiasco of the tent, partly because of a downpour which greeted her. Still she took time to travel to the state house to meet the Texas legislature late in the afternoon.[11] When she visited her tent, Bernhardt found it soaked with rain, water running down the aisles and between the seats. In an avalanche of French, the star swore she would never inflict such indignity on her audiences and demanded her driver take her to the principal theatre of the city.

That proved to be the Hancock Opera House, part of the Klaw and Erlanger chain. At first Bernhardt's formidable charm could not convince the managers to turn a Syndicate house over to a Shubert company, but she persisted, recruited a stage crew, played the Hancock, and Austin turned out in force. Bernhardt responded with one of her more memorable performances, and her caravan moved on.[12]

Nor had she wasted her time in the state capital. No less than Governor Lanham received her in the state reception room of the capital building, after which the actress visited the house of representatives to a mighty ovation. No mention was made of any discussion of the Syndicate and its hold in Texas.[13]

Bernhardt's Camille appeared in San Antonio in a combination beer and music hall, but it was at least indoors.[14] Again control of the crowd broke down, people were not always able to occupy the seats they had paid for; and those who arrived fashionably late had to stand against the side walls of the structure. But still the show went on and the reviewers attested to the company's brilliance in the face of adversity.[15]

Critics in almost every case found themselves incapable of evaluating the Bernhardt phenomenon; she was often beyond criticism. *Theatre Magazine* proclaimed her fortnight's engagement in New York the artistic, popular, and financial sensation of the season; her first day's gross had been $20,000.[16]

In Philadelphia the *Inquirer* critic tried to analyze her acting, reporting that she did not "create characters but expresses emotion within a limited range"; also that Bernhardt's characters were all women of the same type, controlled by the same passions. Nevertheless he found her characters drawn with a convincing sincerity few actresses had ever approached, citing the "charm of her Zoraya, the beauty of her Adrienne, the imperiousness of her Phedre, the impressiveness of her Camille, the glow of her Sapho and the majesty of her Fedora."[17]

A few critics dared note that Bernhardt could not play scenes as violently as once she had.[18] And one reviewer pointed out the star was, "well – stout!" In Duluth a matinee performance in the tent while a northeaster chilled the entire endeavor prompted a local commentator to suggest that in a real theatre one might accept a sixty-two-year-old Camille, but in the tent under sunshine he could only wonder how a young and handsome Frenchman could show such passionate love for his grandmother.[19]

Most reviewers exercised more gallantry, one even critiquing her in French, calling her the "reine incontestée du théâtre."[20] Several others later commented on the lavishness of the star's costuming and lack of scenic investiture, noting that the company depended for scenery on the theatres they visited, often with less than satisfactory results.

The Shuberts billed these engagements as Bernhardt's farewell tour. Audiences were willing to pay inflated prices, as much as a five-dollar top, to see her, although three dollars was the more usual top ticket price. The French actress was a mistress of publicity, causing far more ink to be spilled in the newspapers than any other performer of her time.

Bernhardt could turn even a natural disaster to her advantage. While she played Chicago on 18 April, a catastrophic earthquake struck San Francisco, resulting in the destruction of four square miles of the city and half a billion dollars in property damage. But equal to the challenge, on 26 April she "worked up" a benefit for the earthquake victims and held it in her huge tent at noon on the lake front. Several important stars appeared with her: E. H. Sothern, Julia Marlowe, E. S. Willard, Robert Loraine, and Mrs. Leslie Carter, all of whom were appearing locally. She appeared at noon, arriving from Peoria to deliver a speech, helping her American colleagues raise over $15,000 for the relief fund.[21] She then raced back to Peoria on a special locomotive, breaking all speed records and arriving about six in the evening.[22]

Bernhardt's appeal was undeniable. She sold out almost every performance in Montreal, averaging about 2,550 persons per performance and grossing about $30,000.[23] Receipts set records for Montreal, despite the best efforts of local Catholic authorities who requested that the faithful abstain from her performances on the grounds that the theatre, especially the French stage of Montreal, represented the enemy of good morals, the enemy of Christian traditions because of the presentation of scenes of passion and criminal love.[24] After the engagement in Quebec as the company headed for their train to leave, M. Max, an actor, was struck in the back of the head with a rotten egg; at the same time Mayer, Bernhardt's manager, was hit with a stick, described by Bernhardt as "a real big stick, too."[25]

But overall no one can deny that Bernhardt's tour was a popular success, although her appeal was, perhaps, more faddish than theatrical. Audiences usually bought French–English texts of the shows (one woman asked for a "libertto") which they would follow during the performance. "You see," said one customer, "I didn't dare look at the stage. If I did I was sure to lose my place, and then I wouldn't know what was going on."[26]

Another index of her audience's appreciation of French nuances emerged in Youngstown, Ohio, when Bernhardt, angry at a less than full house, scolded the audience during the production. She inserted into a tender love scene with Armand her observations that the Youngstown people were stupid and utterly lacking in appreciation. This interpolation was greeted by wild applause from the Ohioans.[27]

Most auditoriums were full, and some sort of record was set in Kansas City when Bernhardt played the Convention Hall to a house of 6,543 and a gate of just under $10,000. *Theatre Magazine* called this the "largest single night's receipts from a dramatic entertainment ever known in the history of the stage."[28] The local manager trumpeted the crowd as "the largest that ever saw a dramatic performance in this or any other country," and no one reminded him of classical theatre capacities.[29]

The tour had its bad nights, too. Only about a third of a house greeted Bernhardt in Butte, Montana, where she performed in a hastily constructed theatre inside a skating rink. The acoustics were "awful," but the audience couldn't understand the show anyway. Nor did those who converted the space manage to add any heat to the building, so the audience shivered its way through the proceedings.[30]

In Savannah she performed to about 1,500 spectators. Acoustics were again terrible, but since the performance was in French and since "street boys" shouted at the windows and rolled stones across the roof, not much mattered. The racket outside was counterpointed by dull thuds inside as the three-dollar seats (chairs borrowed from a dance hall) collapsed, dropping audience members at regular intervals. The next day the *Morning News* suggested Savannah had probably provided the worst set of circumstances under which Bernhardt had ever tried to perform.[31] The French star's comments remain unrecorded.

The Divine Sarah also came a cropper in northern Kansas, even though she had no engagement there. The makeshift theatre at St. Joseph, Missouri, was a glorified boathouse five miles from town, but that was the least of the problems. Bernhardt's private car broke an axle near Mankato, about half-way across northern Kansas, late in the afternoon of 25 May. The actress frantically demanded another engine, claiming the original one had been "hoodooed."[32] An estimated five thousand citizens turned out in St. Joseph to see Bernhardt, only to learn by telegram of the delay. The show finally began at 11:15 p.m., by which time the crowd had dwindled to a few hundred. Bernhardt decided to present *Camille* without the "special scenery," using instead "one simple house setting, with varying furniture and door backings," very likely the same arrangements so condemned at previous stops. The curtain descended shortly after 1:00 a.m. the next morning, the show having been "cut materially." No financial announcements were made.

Later a one-night engagement in Trenton, New Jersey, may have been the financial nadir of the tour. The company was barred from the other three theatres in Trenton by the Syndicate; only about a third of a house, less than five hundred people, attended *Camille*.[33]

When money was involved, more drama might happen backstage than on. Advised by her manager that the guarantee had not been paid, Bernhardt threatened to stop the show in Toledo, Ohio, after the third act. The house manager maintained it was a question of advertising, a matter of about $500, but the audience waited for half an hour. The house manager then announced the show would not go on, but Bernhardt's manager followed him on stage to announce the actress had relented and would finish the play. The curtain rose on a group of bewildered actors, then Bernhardt appeared and died of consumption in record time.[34] She collected in full.

During the San Francisco engagement Bernhardt appeared in *Phèdre* at the open-air Greek Theatre at Berkeley. Critics waxed rhapsodic; one proclaimed the performance "one of the great events in the world's dramatic history."[35] Some five thousand persons attended; the weather and the acoustics cooperated completely; and *Phèdre* scored a huge success. Bernhardt allowed herself to be photographed by the newsreel cameramen as she was driven through the earthquake-ravaged city, then the company moved on.

June saw the last hurrah of the Bernhardt tent in Springfield, Massachusetts, the company having run afoul of the Syndicate one final time. While two Trust theatres in the heart of the city sat vacant, Bernhardt pitched her circus tent near the North-end Bridge on Coliseum Field and set up for business. Advertisements called the structure the "Anti-Trust Bernhardt Tent." The Springfield *Republican* took umbrage that not once during the past season had any independent attractions been seen in their city, nor did it appear that one would the next year. Neighboring, smaller cities such as Holyoke and Northampton might see Julia Marlowe, Mrs. Fiske, E. H. Sothern, Lena Ashwell, David Warfield, Mrs. Leslie Carter, or Blanche Bates, but not Springfield.[36]

The Shuberts and Bernhardt could not have expected a greater financial success than they received. *Billboard* announced the results of the tour:

The gross receipts week in and week out ... have never fallen below $34,000. And that was when she played in Chicago. The best six nights of one-night stands showed a gross of $42,000. The best single performance was a matinee on Ash Wednesday in Kansas City in the Convention Hall, the receipts for which were an even $10,000. The average gross receipts for each week of the tour ... is between $34,000 and $39,000.[37]

Before Bernhardt sailed for France, she reigned as the guest of honor at a dinner during which the tour's total receipts were announced: 206 performances grossed just over one million dollars. The star received $305,000; the Shuberts $210,000.

The rise of the Syndicate had not been without virtue; it had solidified business practices in the theatre and offered a degree of job security to theatre workers who were willing to do business exclusively with them. The Shuberts shattered this *pax romana*, and their success with the Bernhardt tour contributed to their establishment as worthy Syndicate opponents. Their financial success was considerable, but more important was the publicity the brothers received from the media. By offering an equal choice, the Shuberts, albeit every bit as money-grabbing as Erlanger at his worst, restored something approaching free enterprise to the American theatre. Eventually the government had to break up the Shubert monolith, but that was years in the future; the theatre then as now was a thing of the present.

Bernhardt, arguably the most avaricious of the lot, had had her usual impact upon local theatre scenes; patrons stayed home for weeks before she arrived in their community, saving their money in order to pay her inflated ticket prices. After her departure most had little or no entertainment dollars for the theatre, and some time would pass before theatregoing could return to normal. An anonymous poet in Detroit wryly commented:

> When Sarah leaves, we sigh and say:
> "Artiste divine, oh, stay! oh, stay!
> Nor take thy genius bright away,"
> Our sky grows grim and glummest gray,
>     When Sarah leaves.
> 'Tis not alone her talent's sway,
> Which lightly moves from grave to gay,
> Nor glances that may charm or slay
> That moves us so to sigh and say,
>     When Sarah leaves.
> The saddened thoughts to which we're prey,
> Include the swift and subtle play
> Of vivid vision of the way
> We've had to drag our jeans and pay,
>     When Sarah leaves.[38]

Bernhardt sailed for France on 14 June 1906; when she returned for the second of her farewell tours a few years later she found the Syndicate more amenable; in New York she played the Globe Theatre under the management of Charles B. Dillingham, former partner of Charles Frohman, Marc Klaw, and Abraham Erlanger, Syndicate founders all. Business was, after all, business.

## APPENDIX: THE BERNHARDT ITINERARY

A complete record of the Bernhardt tour follows, divided by city. Following the name of the theatre, each performance is enclosed in parentheses, listing first the date as an Arabic number, the month as a lower case Roman numeral, and the script performed indicated by a two-letter shorthand, thus:

*AD* = *Adrienne Lecouvreur* by Bernhardt based on an earlier script by Gabriel Legouvé and Eugène Scribe. Bernhardt played the title role.

*AN* = *Angelo* by Victor Hugo. Bernhardt played La Tisbé.

*CA* = *La Dame Aux Camélias (Camille)* by Alexandre Dumas *fils*. Bernhardt played Marguerite Gautier.

*CL* = *La Femme de Claude* by Alexandre Dumas *fils*. Bernhardt played Césarine.

*FE* = *Fédora* by Victorien Sardou. Bernhardt played the title role.

*MA* = *Magda (Die Ehre)* by Hermann Sudermann. Bernhardt played the title role.

*PH* = *Phèdre* by Jean Racine. Bernhardt played the title role.

*SA* = *Sapho* by Alphonse Daudet. Bernhardt played Fanny Legrand.

*SO* = *La Sorcière* by Victorien Sardou. Bernhardt played Zoraya.

*TO* = *La Tosca* by Victorien Sardou. Bernhardt played Floria Tosca.

Thus for the first performance in Chicago (20xi*SO*) indicates that on the twentieth day of the eleventh month Bernhardt performed in *La Sorcière*. Asterisks indicate matinee performances; on the twenty-second in Chicago Bernhardt performed *Angelo* at the matinee and *Adrienne Lecouvreur* for the evening performance.

Chicago: Grand Opera House. (20xi*SO*) (21xi*CA*) (22xi*AN*,*AD*) (23xi-*SO*,*SA*) (24xi*FE*) (25xi*CL*,*PH*)

Montreal: Théâtre Française. (27xi*SO*) (28xi*CA*) (29xi*AD*,*AN*) (30xi-*CA*,*TO*) (1xii*FE*) (2xii*CL*,*PH*)

Quebec: Auditorium. (4xii*CA*) (5xii*AN*,*AD*)

Ottawa: Russell Theatre. (6xii*AD*) (7xii*CA*)

Kingston: Grand Theatre. (8xii*AD*)

Hamilton: Grand Theatre. (9xii*AD*)

New York City: Lyric Theatre. (11xii*SO*) (12xii*CA*) (13xii*AD*,*AN*) (14 xii *SA*) (15xii*FE*) (16xii*PH*,*CL*) (18xii*AD*) (19xii*MA*) (20xii*CA*,*TO*) (21xii*SA*) (22xii*PH*) (23xii*FE*,*SO*)

Syracuse, NY: Alhambra. (25xii*CA*)

Rochester, NY: Baker Theatre. (26xii*CA*)

Auburn, NY. (27xii*AD*)

Binghamton, NY: Stone Opera House. (28xii*CA*)

Baltimore, MD: Lyric Theatre. (29xii*SO*) (30xii*CA*,*SA*)

Washington, DC: Belasco Theatre. (1i*SO*) (2i*CA*) (3i*AD*,*AN*) (4i*SA*) (5i*TO*) (6i*PH*,*FE*)

Philadelphia: Lyric Theatre. (8i*SO*) (9i*CA*) (10i*AD*,*AN*) (11i*SA*) (12i*TO*) (13i*PH*,*FE*)

Boston: Boston Theatre. (15i*SO*) (16i*CA*) (17i*AD*,*AN*) (18i*SA*) (19i*FE*) (20i*PH*,*CL*, & *Bohémos*) (22i*AD*) (23i*MA*) (24i*CA*,*TO*) (25i*SA*) (26i*CA*,*PH*) (27i*FE*,*SO*)

Portland, ME: Portland Theatre. (29i*SO*)

Providence, RI: Shubert Theatre. (30i*CA*,*SO*)

Worcester, MA: Franklin Square Theatre. (31i*CA*)
Northampton, MA: Academy of Music. (11ii*PH*)
New Haven, CN. (2ii*CA*)
Newark, NJ: Empire Theatre. (3ii*SO*)
Albany, NY: Harkmanus Bleeker Hall. (5ii*CA*,*SO*)
Utica, NY: Majestic Theatre. (6ii*TO*)
Bradford, PA: Bradford Theatre. (7ii*SO*)
Pittsburgh, PA: Belasco Theatre. (8ii*SO*) (9ii*AD*,*TO*) (10ii*CA*,*SA*)
Buffalo, NY: Lyceum Theatre. (12ii*SO*) (13ii*CA*,*TO*)
Youngstown, OH: Grand Opera House. (14ii*CA*)
Cincinatti, OH: Music Hall. (15ii*SO*) (16ii*CA*) (17ii*PH*,*TO*)
Louisville, KY: Hopkins Theatre. (19ii*CA*,*SO*)
Milwaukee, WI: Pabst Theatre. (20ii*SO*) (21ii*CA*,*TO*)
Minneapolis, MN: Auditorium. (22ii*SO*) (23ii*CA*) (24ii*PH*,*TO*)
Davenport, IA: Grand Theatre. (26ii*CA*)
Omaha, NE: Auditorium. (27ii*CA*)
Kansas City, MO: Convention Hall. (28ii*CA*)
St. Louis, MO: Garrick Theatre. (1iii*SO*) (2iii*PH*,*TO*) (3iii*CA*,*SA*)
Hot Springs, AR: Auditorium. (5iii*CA*)
Little Rock, AR: Forest Park Theatre. (6iii*CA*)
Memphis, TN: Grand Opera House. (7iii*CA*,*SO*)
Nashville, TN: Ryman Auditorium. (8iii*CA*)
Asheville, NC: Auditorium. (9iii*CA*)
Salisbury, NC: Meroney's Theatre (10iii*CA*)
Savannah, SC: Mutual Skating Rink. (12iii*CA*)
Tampa, FL: Tampa Bay Casino. (13iii*CA*)
Jacksonville, FL: Skating Rink. (14iii*CA*)
Augusta, GA: Miller Walker Hall. (15iii*CA*)
Chattanooga, TN: Auditorium. (16iii*CA*)
Atlanta, GA: Peachtree Rink. (17iii*CA*)
New Orleans, LA: Greenwall Theatre. (18iii*SO*) *(19iii*CA*)* (20iii*TO*)
    (21iii*AD*,*SA*) (22iii*FE*) (23iii*CA*) (24iii*PH*,*SO*)
Dallas, TX: Tent. (26iii*CA*)
Waco, TX: Tent in Padgitt Park Enclosure. (27iii*CA*)
Austin, TX: Hancock Opera House. (28iii*CA*)
San Antonio, TX: Beethoven Hall. (29iii*CA*)
Houston, TX: Auditorium. (30iii*SO*) (31iii*CA*,*TO*)
Tyler, TX: Grand Opera House. (2iv*CA*)
Muskogee, Indian Territory: Hinton Theatre. (3iv*CA*)
Oklahoma City, Indian Territory: Overholser Opera House. (4iv*CA*)
Shawnee, Indian Territory: Becker Opera House. (5iv*CA*)
Wichita, KS: Toler Auditorium. (6iv*CA*)
Topeka, KS: Auditorium. (7iv*CA*)
Battle Creek, MI: Post Theatre. (9iv*CA*)
Toledo, OH: Collingwood Theatre. (10iv*CA*)

Canton, OH: Grand Opera House. (11iv*TO*)
Akron, OH: Music Hall. (12iv*CA*)
Columbus, OH: Memorial Hall. (14iv*CA*)
Chicago, IL: Auditorium. (16iv*TO*) (17iv*MA*) (18iv*CA*,*FE*) (19iv*SA*)
    (20iv*CA*) (21 iv*PH*,*SO*)
Grand Rapids, MI: Auditorium. (23iv*CA*)
Ft. Wayne, IN: Princess Rink. (24iv*CA*)
Indianapolis, IN: German House. (25iv*CA*)
Benefit in tent in Chicago, 26iv
Peoria, IL: Coliseum. (26iv*CA*)
Des Moines, IA: Ingersoll Park Theatre. (27iv*CA*)
Madison, WI: Fuller Opera House. (28iv*CA*)
Duluth, MN: Temple Rink in Tent. (30iv*CA*)
Winnipeg: Auditorium Rink. (1v*CA*)
Helena, MT: City Auditorium. (4v*CA*)
Butte, MT: New Holland Rink. (5v*CA*)
Spokane, WA: Natatorium Park. (7v*CA*)
Seattle, WA: Pavilion at Leschi Park. (8v*SO*) (9v*CA*,*SA*)
Tacoma, WA: Savoy Theatre. (10v*CA*)
Portland, OR: Armory. (11v*CA*) (12v*CA*,*no eve. performance)
Oakland, CA: Ye Liberty Playhouse. (14v*TO*) (15v*SO*) (16v*CA*,*SA*)
    (17v*PH* in Greek Theatre, Berkeley)
Venice, CA: Auditorium. (18v*SO*) (19v*CA*,*TO*)
Salt Lake City, UT: Saltair Pavilion. (21v*CA*)
Pueblo, CO: Minnequa Theatre in Park. (23v*CA*)
Denver, CO: Elitch's Garden. (24v*CA*,*SO*)
St. Joseph, MO: Casino at Lake Contrary. (25v*CA*)
Chicago, IL: Auditorium. (26v scenes from *Frou-frou*, *Hamlet*, and *Camille*,
    combined bill)
Detroit, MI: Light Guard Armory. (28v*CA*)
Cleveland, OH: Colonial Theatre. (29v*CA*,*composite)
Lexington, KY: Woodland Park Auditorium. (30v*CA*)
Charleston, WV: Burlew Opera House. (31v*CA*)
Wheeling, WV: Wheeling Park Casino. (1vi*CA*)
Pittsburgh, PA: Belasco Theatre. (2vi Act II of *L'Aiglon*, II of *Camille*, II of
    *Hamlet*, III of *Frou-frou*)
Washington, DC: (5vi Act II of *Hamlet*, III of *Camille*, II of *L'Aiglon*, II of
    *Frou-frou*)
Atlantic, NJ: Young's Pier Theatre. (6vi*CA*)
Philadelphia, PA: Lyric Theatre. (7vi Act II of *L'Aiglon*, III of *Frou-frou*, II of
    *Hamlet*, III of *Camille*)
Springfield, MA: Tent in Outing Park. (8vi*CA*)
Boston, MA: Boston Theatre. (9vi*CA*,*evening was Act II of *L'Aiglon*, III of
    *Frou-frou*, III of *Hamlet*, and IV of *La Sorcière*)

New York, NY: Lyric Theatre. (12vi Act II of *Hamlet*, II of *L'Aiglon*, IV of *La Sorcière*, III of *Frou-frou*) (13viCA,* Act II of *Hamlet*, II of *L'Aiglon*, IV of *La Sorcière*, III of *Frou-frou*)

## NOTES

1 Alfred L. Bernheim, *The Business of the Theatre: An Economic History of the American Theatre, 1750–1932* (New York: Benjamin Blom, 1964), 66f.
2 For the 1905–6 season the Shuberts had engaged Ada Rehan, David Warfield, Mrs. Fiske, Leslie Carter, Blanche Bates, Bertha Kalich, Jefferson De Angelis, De Wolf Hopper, Eddy Foy, Henry Miller, Margaret Anglin, and Charles E. Evans.
3 Bernhardt–Shubert contract, Shubert Archives, New York City.
4 *Chicago Daily Tribune*, 20–21 November 1905.
5 Jerry Stagg, *The Brothers Shubert* (New York: Random House, 1968), 84f.
6 *Kansas City Times*, 22 February 1906.
7 *Dallas Morning News*, 25 March 1906.
8 *Helena Daily Independent*, 3 May 1906.
9 *Houston Chronicle*, 1 April 1906.
10 *Dallas Morning News*, 27 March 1906, and North Bigbee, "Texas Tent-Show Camille," *Texas Parade* 16 (May 1956), 31–34.
11 *Waco Daily Times-Herald*, 29 March 1906.
12 Bigbee, "Texas Tent-Show Camille," 34, and *San Antonio Daily Express*, 1 April 1906.
13 *Tyler Daily Courier*, 30 March 1906.
14 Ibid.
15 *San Antonio Daily Express*, 30 March 1906.
16 *Theatre Magazine* (January 1906), 2.
17 *Philadelphia Inquirer*, 14 January 1906.
18 *Tampa Morning Tribune*, 14 March 1906.
19 *Duluth Evening Herald*, 1 May 1906.
20 *Los Angeles Daily Times*, 19 May 1906.
21 *Chicago Tribune*, 27 April 1906.
22 *Duluth News Tribune*, 23 April 1906.
23 Ibid.
24 *Montreal Gazette*, 27 November 1905.
25 *New York Times*, 11 December 1905.
26 *Binghamton Press & Leader*, 28–29 December 1905.
27 *New York Times*, 15 February 1906.
28 *Theatre Magazine* (May 1906), 115.
29 *Kansas City Star*, 28 February 1906.
30 *Butte Miner*, 6 May 1906.
31 Robert Overstreet, "Sarah Bernhardt in Savannah," *Western Speech* 39 (Winter 1975), 24–25.

32  *St. Joseph Gazette*, 26 May 1906.
33  *Daily State Gazette* and *Daily True American*, 5 June 1906.
34  *Columbus Citizen*, 11 April 1906.
35  Mabel Craft Deering, quoted in *Putnam's Monthly* 1 (November 1906), 214–15.
36  *Springfield Republican*, 3 June 1906.
37  *Billboard*, 23 June 1906, 13.
38  *Detroit Evening News*, 23 March 1901.

# CHAPTER 12

# Commercialism glorified and vilified: 1920s theatre and the business world

## Ronald H. Wainscott

A review of popular American theatre and film reveals that the business world and commercialism held a distinct fascination for the American public and artists of the 1980s. This is by no means a recent phenomenon, however, and can be seen rising periodically in theatrical eras in the United States, especially when the economy is riding high, as it was in the 1920s. Successful attacks on the corruption of the business world also predate the 1920s as we can readily review in Lois C. Gottlieb's article, "The Antibusiness Theme in Late Nineteenth Century American Drama."[1] This theme rises again in the 1920s, addressing subject, character and conflict in all dramatic genres. Predating the resurrection of anti-business sympathies, however, and continuing well into the boom years was an outburst of commercial glorification not unlike 1980s paeans to acquisitive tastes and practice.

From the close of World War I to the disaster of Black Tuesday, American drama and theatre reeled from the shock of new dramatic possibilities in themes focusing on the aftermath of the Great War, the Russian Revolution and Prohibition. After a post-war recession which was well over by 1922, entrepreneurship flourished, the stock market roared and the United States government discovered many new sources for garnering revenues such as taxing personal income and theatre admissions. From 1920 onward the daily newspapers were replete with reports of financial escapades and "easy money." In the mid 1920s Calvin Coolidge was quoted everywhere as saying that "the business of America is business." Warren Harding's Teapot Dome scandal erupted after his death in 1923 and dragged on in the courts for years covering the oil industry and many in government with the taint of corruption. Reckless Wall Street management encouraged naive speculators to buy on margin, thus losing much more than they invested or could afford to invest when the false bottom dropped out of the stock market.

The question arises naturally, how did the drama of the period treat big business and commercialism in this era? If one examines all of the plays produced in commercial Broadway houses during this decade one is struck by an enduring interest in these themes. More than one hundred Broadway plays of this period include the business world in a significant way, but at least thirty-nine have business as the subject or use the business world to affect dynamically the characters' development or the ideas of the play. Although all plays cannot be analyzed here I have selected significant characteristics of the most emblematic.

I have divided these thirty-nine business plays into ten categories which reflect the approaches to the subject as well as suggest a line of development which leads to the more familiar anti-management/pro-labor drama of the 1930s. The ten categories are: (1) entrepreneurs and big business on parade (1919–25); (2) Soviet and socialist threats to capitalism (1919–23); (3) corrupt individuals give a good system a bad name (1920–26); (4) satire on business peeks into serious and comic work (1921–28); (5) gender conflict in business (1922–26); (6) heavy-handed satire attacking the system (1923–28); (7) business versus art (1924–26); (8) serious business corruption goes unpunished (1927); (9) socialism as a positive force (1929); (10) business as a killer (1927–29).

(1) After the armistice of the First World War many plays appeared which measured personal success by the accumulation of wealth. From 1919 to mid-decade entrepreneurship and big business were unequivocally glorified. Benevolence in men at the top of business, for example, was demonstrated in the saccharine *Letty Pepper* (1922), a musical comedy by Oliver Morosco. Success in business and love were designed here to journey hand in hand. In *First Is Last*, a 1919 comedy by Samuel Shipman and Percival Wilde, nine friends meeting three years after college graduation all measure success by how much money they have made. On a more serious if naive note *Made in America* (1925) by Mr. and Mrs. M. H. Gulesian enshrined the economic American dream through a poor Armenian immigrant rising from Ellis Island to social prominence in Boston due to his sharp business acumen.

Plays such as the farce *Barnum Was Right* (1923) by Philip Bartholomae and John Meehan, John Booth's *Like a King* (1921), and *We've Got to Have Money* (1923) by Edward Laska glorified rags to riches schemes, a theme which had recurred at intervals at least since 1910 when George M. Cohan's *Get-Rich-Quick Wallingford* gloried in a young climber's manipulation of other people and their money in order to get something for nothing. In all such plays the protagonist finds a gimmick which successfully dupes others. Invariably, the hero or heroine is rewarded for duplicitous efforts and conniving masquerades.

Perhaps most notable in this category is Guy Bolton's 1923 comedy *Polly Preferred* in which an out-of-work salesman, Bob Cooley, is so taken with Polly Brown, a chorus girl presently at liberty, that he offers to promote her like a commodity. "I think I could sell you ... I want a good sensible girl with nothing on her mind but success."[2] Setting up a business scam, Bob parades Polly at "Fashion Row" in the Biltmore, pretending that Polly is a rich girl who is about to break into the movies backed by wealthy investors. Although Bob's charade is eventually unmasked, a film director is fooled by Polly's impersonation and convinces all the downtown financiers to make a movie with her. Polly is precipitously incorporated as "Polly Pierpont" and the men buy shares in her career. According to Bob's scheme "Miss Pierpont is to be our only asset. She must not only work for us, but live in a way we consider best for the interests of the company ... We invest money to make her a successful screen star, and if that purpose is accomplished she must regard herself as our property."[3] Although incorporating a performer is commonplace today, it was a novelty in 1923.

Of course all ends happily with Polly's career soaring as Bob and Polly head for the marriage altar. What is most significant here is the playwright's positive presentation of a human being as a business commodity and the ultimate success of Bob and Polly who began their business partnership under fraudulent conditions. Also, rewarding the acquisitive, often self-centered hero with romantic satisfaction is typical of business plays of the early 1920s.

(2) While capitalism was boisterously paraded on the stages of Broadway, a number of xenophobic plays began to reflect fear of the stirrings of socialism and the implications of the Russian Revolution. Although many plays, beginning with *The Red Dawn* (1919) by Thomas Dixon, attacked Soviet and socialist ideology and their purported disastrous effects on the United States, some, such as *The Challenge* (1919) by Eugene Walter and *Give and Take* (1923) by Aaron Hoffman, carried the theme into the business world.

Despite its subject matter Hoffman's play is a farce depicting a canning factory in California which is turned over to disgruntled employees led by the owner's crusading son Jack, a recent convert to socialist ideology. Although the factory owner is highly suspicious of organized labor, he nonetheless allows this experiment in "industrial democracy" because the alternative is a labor strike which would cost him the mortgage on his business. The factory is nearly ruined anyway when the employees demand fifty percent of the profits in addition to their wages. The bank tries to foreclose since, as the bank president says, "We ain't going to stand any of that Bolshevickeyism."[4] The day is saved, however, not by industrial democracy but by a capitalist, an eccentric millionaire, who buys up all the products of the factory indefinitely to stock his scheme of nation-wide mobile grocery stores.

(3) Beginning in 1920 plays appeared which demonstrate corrupt individuals who give a good system a bad name. Monatague Glass and Jules Goodman added the comedy *Partners Again* (1922) to their popular series of Potash and Perlmutter plays; *Cheaper to Marry* (1924) by Samuel Shipman, very seriously offered business as a role model; and Samuel Golding's *Open House* (1925) featured a steel industrialist who exploits his wife by making her flirt with and entertain foreign clients until they sign contracts with him. Until 1926 such plays were common, and most, not surprisingly, were melodramas.

In a business competition of their own, producers Al Woods and William Brady rushed similar plays to New York in the summer of 1920: *Crooked Gamblers* by Samuel Shipman and Percival Wilde and *Opportunity* by Owen Davis. Both plays attempt to present fast-paced, authentic Wall Street offices and market practices complete with cacophonous jargon. Both plays also turn on a young protagonist who rises and falls in the world of the stock market, each time brought down by the unethical practices of others.

*Opportunity*, for example, involves the hero Larry Bradford with a siren in the manner of George Barnwell in *The London Merchant*. Bradford rises from office boy to stock market king before being undermined by sexy, wicked Nellie Ross ("the most brazen vampire since Cleopatra's day"),[5] who tempts him away from his long-suffering wife Joyce and temporarily distracts him from his financial world. After losing his fortune, Bradford manages to overturn the forces of evil, repents, and returns to Joyce and a conservative life.

In all these plays the innocent or well-meaning are nearly destroyed by unscrupulous business people who are not content with
mere accumulation of wealth and power, but insist on demolishing
others as they play their treacherous games. It must be noted that
acquisitiveness and greed are not brought into question, but the
lengths to which the villains will go to overturn the good fortune of
others is nearly unlimited.

(4) Early in the decade and continuing to 1926, satire on business
can be found in both comic and serious plays which are also
pursuing a non-business agenda. *The Bronx Express* (1922), a comic
fantasy by Owen Davis, presents a scene in which advertising
placards on a subway train come to life in the dream of an old
button maker. Fantasy figures like Aunt Jemima and Mr. Green
Wrigley convince the old man that advertising is the way of life in
America. In two scenes in Marc Connelly's otherwise gentle comedy
*The Wisdom Tooth* (1926), the playwright satirizes the self-serving
but turgid conversations of businessmen, who demonstrate contempt for anything imaginative or beautiful while trying to impress
each other with their talk of money. In the Fifth Avenue scene of
Eugene O'Neill's *The Hairy Ape* (1922), promenading automatons
represent the business world and wealthy elite, who, despite the
stoker Yank Smith's insults, bravado and extreme physical efforts,
are impervious to him as he bounces off of these mindless, humorless,
uncaring creatures with each attack. Even a musical comedy, *Helen
of Troy, New York* (1923) by Bert Kalmer and Harry Ruby lightly
satirized advertising and big business by evoking a world "where
any man may be captain of industry 'who can hold his job and not
be bored to death.'"[6]

In 1921 Marc Connelly collaborated with George S. Kaufman to
create the very popular *Dulcy*, a portrait of scatterbrained Dulcinea
Smith who interferes with her husband Gordon's business deal.
Several scenes satirize a rich businessman, and a pushy "advertising
engineer."[7] Tom Sterret, the ad man, for example, modestly com-
pares himself to great artists when explaining that his promotional
achievements are not so unusual for a young man. Angela attacks
Sterret who is in love with her but will never win her because his
"idea of romance is to sit in the moonlight and talk about the income
tax."[8]

Philip Barry in *Holiday* (1928) stylishly rejected the business ethic.
While America was at the height of a financial boom, this play

presented youth and individualism versus big business and snob-
bery. Johnny Case, a lawyer afraid of being entombed alive, wants
to retire at thirty to pursue the pleasures of the world while he is
young enough to enjoy them. He invades the Seton family by
engaging himself to Julia but falls for free-spirited Linda who is
Barry's chief mouthpiece for denigrating the greed of her family of
bankers. "The fact is," she quips, "money is our god here."[9] Julia, of
course, epitomizes everything Linda despises: "But you haven't an
idea yet of how exciting *business* can be ... There's no such thrill in
the world as making money."[10] Obviously Barry is satirizing the
spiritual emptiness of avarice. It should be noted, however, that
Johnny has already made a handsome nest egg in the stock market,
and now wishes to flee before wasting his good years on the obsessive
labor typical of the Wall Street mover who can never have enough.

(5) With increasing interest in women's rights, it is not surprising
that the gender conflict in business became evident in a number of
plays from 1922 to 1926. In all of these plays, however, business
success is enshrined. In *Up the Ladder* (1922) by Owen Davis and
Willis Goodhue's *Head First* (1926), working couples are shown in
conflict. In the former the husband John succeeds in business at the
expense of his once independent and self-supporting wife Jane. In
the latter Frank Beckwith, the husband, is fired from his clerk's job
only to find his wife Anne giving up housework to secure his old
position. She quickly climbs the management ladder, however, until
she heads the company's Paris branch. Not surprisingly, the marriage flounders. It was clear that by the 1920s women were making
inroads in the business world and the old patriarchal standards,
according to those who believed in them, were at risk.

In the most successful play in this category, Kaufman and Connelly celebrated the wife as the real power behind the throne of the
businessman. *To the Ladies* (1922) introduces Leonard Beebe, a clerk
rising to administrator, who is confident of success but very short on
intelligence and talent. His wife Elsie makes all important decisions
while convincing Leonard that he is taking care of her. Ultimately
we learn that both Elsie and the boss's wife silently run the business
while their husbands front for their much wiser wives.

Even musical comedy contributed to the subject in *Clinging Vine*
(1922) by Zelda Sears and Harold Levey. The authors created a
successful business heroine, Antoinette, who runs a paint business in
Omaha and shows herself "a marvel of scientific intelligence and

mercantile efficiency,"[11] but a neophyte in love. A similar theme was handled more effectively in *The Advertising of Kate* (1922) by social reformer Annie Nathan Meyer in which a woman is shown as the equal business partner of a man. The *Journal of Commerce* at the time observed that "the idea of the beautiful – but brainy – woman immersing herself in 'trade' to the utter exclusion of all else, including affairs of that heart, is rapidly becoming commonplace."[12]

(6) Beginning in 1923, often aided by the tenets of expressionism, heavy-handed satire began to attack in earnest the capitalist system, and its exploitative methods. *The Adding Machine* (1923) by Elmer Rice remains a classic as it presents depersonalization in an industrial world. Mr. Zero, the unimaginative, bigoted bookkeeper burdened with a repetitious life, is engulfed by numbers, enslaved for twenty-five years by the business world. When Zero is unceremoniously replaced by an adding machine, he loses all self-control and kills the Boss, who never knew Zero's name. After execution Zero finds himself in "another office" working perpetually at an adding machine, the paper tape of which fills the room.[13] Even in afterlife Zero cannot escape the mindless monotony and dehumanization of the labor force.

In 1928 another expressionistic journey play presented the business world as a great deadener. *Machinal*, Sophie Treadwell's dark drama about a nameless Young Woman swamped by mediocrity and loneliness, reveals an office scene with stylized repetition of duties. Utilizing cross talk, the workers think aloud with machine-like personalities, yet all the workers realize that their environment is unnatural. The Young Woman, in the midst of office cacophony, expresses "the confusion of her own inner thoughts, emotions, desires, dreams [which cut] her off from any actual adjustment to the routine of work."[14]

John Howard Lawson's *Roger Bloomer* (1923), *Processional* (1925) and *The International* (1928) were the plays most consistently critical of business and commercialism. The earliest of these centers on a confused young loner who grows up in a business environment in the midwest, rejects it and flees to New York to "chase rainbows."[15] Everywhere Roger turns he is bombarded by greed. Louise, the one person he loves, aptly tells him, "This town makes you think ... Money! ... It's everyone for himself."[16] Since she works for a Wall Street broker, she attempts to get Roger a position there, but even as Louise invites Roger she elucidates the deadly monotony and lifeless conformity of the commercial world: "You must come, get in the crowd, get in the subway, get in the procession ... It's a kind of dance of death."[17] The expressionistic Wall Street setting is a series of offices, in which all workers "move in unison like wax-works."[18] It is not surprising that in a dehumanized environment, the broker dismisses Roger on the basis of his lackluster appearance. As Roger falls, so does Louise who commits suicide. Once Roger is in jail, suspected of killing Louise, he has an expressionistic nightmare which exorcises many of the demons of commercialism, greed, power and corruption. Although the play ends with a new beginning for the protagonist, Lawson presents a depressing, commercial world whose major promise for those of sensitivity and creativity is a bleak one.

*Processional* is a disjointed but poetic play combining elements of vaudeville, expressionism, musical extravaganza and satire. With social reform as his thesis, Lawson depicts a West Virginia coal miners' strike with the explicit purpose of attacking big business exploiting workers. Greedy, insensitive management is represented by the pretentious but cowardly "Man in Silk Hat," who regularly calls for law and order. He attempts unsuccessfully to manipulate the press: "Remember the stock market!" he advises, "Stocks and bonds should be the main concern of a newspaper writer."[19] After many vicissitudes the workers appear to win corporate concessions. Management, however, is only posturing for the press. Thus the celebratory conclusion of a "jazz wedding" in the community is undercut by the knowledge that corrupt management will get its revenge.

Such a cynical conclusion also marks the less well-known *The International*. Combining large choruses with modern music, Lawson opens up his satirical tragedy on a global scale. Filthy rich Wall Street financiers wish to take over newly discovered oil fields in Thibet, at the risk of starting another world war. Nonetheless, because "prosperity must be served,"[20] they pursue and the result is not only warfare, but world-wide rebellion of the working classes. Like Jack in *Give and Take*, but in a much larger arena, David Fitch rebels against his powerful father because he wants to "join" the working class to try to understand the world. This personal family and generational struggle personalizes the world-wide greed, chauvinism, and social struggle which is the true subject of the play. For example, when David asks "how big will this war get?," he is told "that depends on how much there is to be got out of it."[21] Fitch and his business partner Spunk manipulate not only the stock market, but governments. Their economic decisions are political choices; commerce is synonymous with public policy. Once the workers' rebellion begins, martial law is declared, and New York erupts in civil war. The red labor forces, which include David, are ultimately gunned down and crushed by the US military in league with the fascist Italian Air Force. The action ends on the barricades with the triumph of capitalism and the destruction of organized labor and socialist ideology.

Obviously, Lawson risked alienating much of his potential audience with such a volatile subject, especially when the United States was riding high financially. Therefore, rather than a left-wing triumph of socialism which ideologically he would have preferred, he gave victory to forces which much of his audience would have supported but emphasizing the cost to humanity of such a position. Also by focusing so much of his action on a personal story, he was able to humanize the struggle and structure this play as both a personal and societal tragedy.

In a less devastating but more satirical examination of gluttonous babbitts, *Marco Millions* (1928), Eugene O'Neill created a Marco Polo who is a crass, ostentatious capitalist, full of self-importance and insensitive to beauty and the feelings of others. Reacting to Marco's excesses, Kublai Kaan expresses what many playwrights observing the 1920s commercial skyrocket feared: "We have everything to lose by contact with [the West's] greedy hypocrisy ... Let the West devour itself."[22]

(7) Business versus art is emphatically explored in the rollicking *Beggar on Horseback* (1924) by George S. Kaufman and Marc Connelly, and in Eugene O'Neill's esoteric and gravely serious *The Great God Brown* (1926). Kaufman and Connelly satirically and humorously depict American mass production carried to absurdity and runaway commercialism ensnaring the creative artist. Neil McRae, a struggling New York composer, is exhausted from orchestrating popular tunes, which prevents him from writing his own serious music. In desperation to support his creative work he agrees to marry Gladys Cady because her father is a manufacturing millionaire. Mr. Cady, however, spells out his own materialistic values and suggests that Neil could join the Cady business. Due to fatigue, anxiety and the influence of tranquillizers, Neil begins to dream

expressionistically. In his nightmare the bewildered Neil marries Gladys and listens to Cady telling everyone that he purchased Neil for his daughter. After Cady forces Neil into his business, Neil must fill out a host of requisitions at every turn and file through myriad offices, even to procure a pencil. Desperate again because he never has time to create his music, Neil kills the entire Cady family.

At his murder trial Neil is found guilty because his music is too highbrow and he is sentenced to work in "the Cady Consolidated Art Factory"[23] where he must generate popular tunes in assembly-line fashion. Although the play approached many topical issues of the time, it was clearly and most consistently aimed at the insensitive and deadening spirit of the business world. The suffering role of the artist was a convenient contrast which set in vivid relief the opportunistic consequences of the commercial credo.

By contrast O'Neill's surrealistic experiment pits Billy Brown, the unimaginative businessman who would be an artist, against the dissolute but real artist Dion Anthony. In *The Great God Brown* the playwright deliberately moves from the particular story of Brown and Anthony to generalizations about failure of the artistic spirit which reaches hopelessly for the grand but coarse tastes of the multitude which daily reward lack of creativity. Dion sounds like a John Howard Lawson hero as he chants of the dehumanization of the never-ending, commercial parade: "Time to get up! Time to exist! ... Learn to keep step! Join the procession!"[24] The horrors of failed artistry on the part of the talented artist who is victim of his own sensitivity result in destruction, ultimately of both men. As Dion says, "I'll make him look in my mirror yet – and drown in it!"[25] Here we see a businessman who is not content with his easy success which fools the undiscerning public; he recognizes and despises his ineptitude and lack of creativity so vehemently that he reaches for an identity and attempts to assume the personality of another – a personality for which he is in no way suited. The result of course is disaster.

(8) *Spread Eagle* in 1927 verified the reality of business corruption going publicly unpunished. Written by journalists George Brooks and Walter Lister, the drama presented Martin Henderson, a tycoon manipulating international events and public opinion to cause war between the United States and Mexico in order to protect his business interests. Bearing some similarities, at least superficially,

to *The International, Spread Eagle* departs from Lawson's work in its ideology and its relentless realism.

Henderson's business is a coldly efficient conglomerate which performs as strongly in the political arena as in the commercial one. Henderson, who has huge mining investments in Mexico, is so alarmed by threatened Mexican confiscation, that he secretly finances a military coup. "The only kind of Mexican leader that's worth a damn," according to Henderson, "is one so bad he causes American intervention."[26] Henderson hires Charles Parkman, the son of an ex-U.S. president, to be the fall guy in Mexico. When the inevitable coup comes, several Henderson employees are reported executed, Parkman among them. This catastrophe sparks the government which is eager to carry out a police action to protect American lives and property in Mexico – exactly what Henderson counted on. "Although Charlie Parkman had to be martyred to make us realize it," a radio announcer intones, "we're going to make Mexico safe for every American citizen."[27]

In a last-act reversal Parkman emerges wounded but alive. Although he attempts to reveal the corruption of Henderson, the magnate is saved by his calculating assistant Cobb, who demonstrates how he and the newspapers will distort Parkman's story to turn him into a coward. Broken by the threats, Parkman yields to the businessmen, but in the play's only overly-contrived plotting, Henderson's daughter engages herself to Parkman, much to the horror of her father. Henderson must now play out a perpetual charade with a son-in-law he attempted to kill out of greed. Nevertheless, the war goes on. Many men will die erroneously thinking they are protecting honor, the flag and American lives, and the public and government will never know the truth. Although the play is a sensational melodrama, it is also a satirical attack on the dark, selfish forces which maneuver an easily swayed public to underwrite the greed of the powerful in the name of patriotism.

(9) Near the end of the decade socialism was shown on the commercial stage as a positive force. Bearing many similarities to *Give and Take* without Bolshevik jokes or capitalist victory, *Great Scott!* (1929) by Howard Koch opened just a month before the stock market crash. In this comedy Delancy Scott, a recent college graduate, comes home "full of handsome talk about ... industrial economics as they affect the laborer."[28] Inspired to attempt to put

his new ideas to the test, he secures a position in a canning factory where his family works, fires up the other workers with his socialist ideas, effects a strike, and helps to transform the working methods of the industry. He is especially successful in securing profit sharing and improved environmental conditions for the laborers. Although Delancy finds his real calling in teaching and not organized labor, he transforms the local scene while being rewarded with the leading lady as well – an interesting redistribution of the romantic rewards of *Polly Preferred* in 1923.

(10) The end of this period also brought a wave of serious plays depicting big business as a killer. Most of these plays featured leading characters who suffered from Napoleonism. *Wall Street* (1927) by James Rosenberg follows the rise of a stockbroker who climbs to the top but cannot maintain a personal relationship. In his obsession with money and power he remains alone at play's end, the controller of a fortune, but with no one to love, no legacy to bestow. Myron C. Fagan's melodrama *The Great Power* (1928), pits John Power against his children. A twentieth-century Richard III of the business world, Power manipulates the stock market with impunity, ruins the careers of anyone who gets in his way, and corrupts local and national politicians alike. He is so wicked, in fact, that one reviewer quipped "this kind of thing could not go unpunished after 11 o'clock."[29] *Carry On* (1928) by Owen Davis dramatizes the destructive obsession of a textiles manufacturer who for the sake of his business reputation wrecks his family. He even reduces his long-suffering wife "to the status of kitchen drudge,"[30] and fails to rescue his own son from jail. Not surprisingly, his family rebels and overwhelms him.

The most important of these plays, *Meteor* (1929) by S. N. Behrman, follows the early career of Raphael Lord, an energetic but condescending young man who thinks everyone should yield to his vision. True to his word he becomes a multi-millionaire in five years, grows obsessed with accumulating wealth, ignores personal losses including his wife Ann, and ultimately suffers in loneliness. Much of Lord's attention is devoted to oil fields in South America which he is fighting to control. Not unlike Henderson in *Spread Eagle*, Lord's efforts involve political manipulation and military interference. His friend Avery tries to warn him: "The more you stir things up, the greater the chance of bloodshed – bloodshed leads to reprisal. First thing you know, you're identifying dividends with national honor."[31] Lord arrogantly overestimates his mastery of events, however, and jeopardizes his entire fortune. Ann is pleased with his defeat and hopes that he will now abandon his obsessions, but the play ends with Lord's unwillingness to change even as Ann is deserting him. Power is all, and the consequence is a loveless life. As Ann tells him, "you prate of remote Utopias that will pay dividends, but those near you you kill."[32]

"In the late boom in America," Behrman wrote, "the business Napoleon reached his apotheosis ... It is difficult to imagine ... how these colossi swaggered and what willing and sycophantic obeisance the world made to them."[33] Behrman wrote those words during the Depression years. For us in the late twentieth century it is no longer so difficult to imagine.

In reviewing the decade of the 1920s several major trends and shifts are clear as the movement away from the war and toward financial catastrophe demonstrates growing suspicion and alarm with business practice. Examined quantitatively, nineteen of the thirty-nine plays support big business and commercialism, while twenty attack it. Five of the pro-business plays, however, acknowledge corruption but blame it on individuals, not the system or its values. Although the playwrights' tactics may change radically, plays which present big business practices, acquisitive values, and commercialism in a very positive light appear every year from 1919 to 1926, although the number peaks at six plays in 1922. Anti-business plays appear as early as 1921 and continue through 1929 with a peak of six plays in 1928 (see chart below).

Although attacks on individuals appear as early as 1920, the system or its values do not come into question until 1921, and then

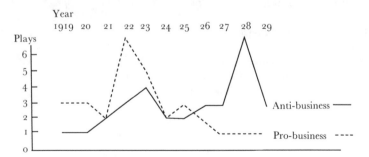

Plays with a business or commercial subject produced professionally in the city of New York (1919–21)

only subtly and exclusively in comedy. The battles over gender issues in business which begin to appear in 1922 never bring the business world to serious task. By 1923, however, some playwrights are unmistakably attacking the core of the business ethic and the damage it was wreaking on the working classes. Most of these plays are linked with strong socialist fervor to a fascination with the expressionistic style. By 1927 most playwrights who bring the system into question are shifting into the arena of political power (demonstrating the relationship of industry and government) and the private lives of industrialists, exposing their foibles, corruption and destructiveness to people close to them, including their own self-destruction. This final shift demonstrates growing alarm, not just among writers with specific ideological messages on their agenda, but playwrights who, while exploring private American character, discovered and felt compelled to reveal the horror of the heart of darkness which apparently permeated so many among the demigods of business.

After the economic crash the dangers of 1920s business practice were obvious to all. The eventual acceptance of socialist values and communist ideology in some quarters led not surprisingly to the great wave of proletarian and crime drama which dominated so much of theatrical activity of the 1930s. During the Great Depression the dramatic world exploded with a plethora of anti-business and commercial, pro-labor and socialist plays which have been so well chronicled by later generations.

## NOTES

1 Lois C. Gottlieb, "The Antibusiness Theme in Late Nineteenth Century American Drama," *The Quarterly Journal of Speech* 64 (1978) 415–26.
2 Guy Bolton, *Polly Preferred* (New York: Samuel French, 1923), 15, 17.
3 Ibid., 44–46.
4 Aaron Hoffman, *Give and Take* (New York: Samuel French, 1926), 72.
5 John J. Martin, "Opportunity," *Dramatic Mirror*, 7 August 1920, 229.
6 "Mill Girl Heroine in New Dance Show," *New York Times*, 20 June 1923, 22.
7 George S. Kaufman and Marc Connelly, *Dulcy* (New York: Samuel French, 1923), 3.
8 Ibid., 38.
9 Philip Barry, *Holiday* in *States of Grace*, ed. Brendan Gill (New York: Harcourt Brace Jovanovich, 1975), 204.

10 Ibid., 241.
11 John Corbin, "Clinging Vine," *New York Times*, 31 December, 1922, Sec. 7, 1.
12 "'Advertising of Kate' Play of Business Girl," *Journal of Commerce and Commercial Bulletin*, 9 May, 1922, 5.
13 It was not in the written play but in the production directed by Philip Moeller and designed by Lee Simpson that Zero was at work on a cosmic-sized adding machine that dwarfed the bookkeeper. See Elmer L. Rice, *The Adding Machine* (Garden City, NY: Doubleday, Page, 1923), 123.
14 Sophie Treadwell, *Machinal* in *Plays by American Women: The Early Years*, ed. Judith E. Barlow (New York: Avon, 1981), 250.
15 John Howard Lawson, *Roger Bloomer* (New York: Thomas Seltzer, 1923), 71.
16 Ibid., 99, 102.
17 Ibid., 103.
18 Ibid., 105.
19 John Howard Lawson, *Processional* in *Contemporary Drama: American Plays I*, ed. E. Bradlee Watson and Benfield Pressey (New York: Charles Scribner's Sons, 1931), 238.
20 John Howard Lawson, *The International* (New York: Macaulay, 1927), 40.
21 Ibid., 179.
22 Eugene O'Neill, *Marco Millions* in *Nine Plays* (New York: Random House, 1932), 286.
23 George S. Kaufman and Marc Connelly, *Beggar on Horseback* (London: Ernest Benn, 1925), 113.
24 Eugene O'Neill, *The Great God Brown*, in *Nine Plays* (New York: Random House, 1932), 318.
25 Ibid., 347.
26 George S. Brooks and Walter B. Lister, *Spread Eagle* (New York: Charles Scribner's Sons, 1927), 40.
27 Ibid., 102.
28 "'Great Scott!' Proves a Baffling Comedy," *New York Times*, 3 September 1929, 25.
29 "The Great Power," *New York Times*, 12 September 1928, 25.
30 J. Brooks Atkinson, "The Play," *New York Times*, 24 January 1928, 26.
31 S. N. Behrman, *Meteor* in *Three Plays* (New York: Farrar & Rinehart, 1934), 175.
32 Ibid., 213.
33 S. N. Behrman, "Napoleonism: 1929" in *Three Plays*, 112.

# CHAPTER 13

# Quicksilver *revisited: a portrait of the American stage in the 1930s*

### *Charles H. Shattuck*

"The pivot of the world is on Forty-fourth Street in New York City at the point where Shubert Alley disgorges from the north side, nearly opposite the Sardi Building on the south side." There, or at the stage door of the Lyric Theatre not far off, Fitzroy Davis set the opening scene of his theatre novel, *Quicksilver*.[1] At eleven in the morning, Monday, 21 September 1935, the acting company of Miss Evelyn Navarre's celebrated *Romeo and Juliet* were gathering there for a first brush-up rehearsal, readying for their second season – a twenty-seven-week road tour of the eastern half of the States.

When *Quicksilver* was published seven years later, George Freedley, director of the Theatre Collection of the New York Public Library, declared it "the truest portrait of the stage today that I know." Unfortunately it has not held up as a theatre classic. Davis wrote with insight, verve, and a flair, but he was not Henry James and *Quicksilver* is not *The Tragic Muse*. Yet if the student of theatre wants to enjoy total immersion in life behind the scenes he must read *Quicksilver*. Here he will find much that neither Henry James nor the Yale Drama School could teach him.

### THE AUTHOR

Davis *had* to write a theatre novel to exploit the vast body of stage lore he had accumulated in his first decade of life in theatre. Born in 1912, he entered Williams College in 1929 and at once launched his busy undergraduate career of acting and directing plays (at least eleven).

Two years after graduation, as we find in his long entry in the biographical dictionary, *Notable Names in the American Theatre*,[2] "*He made his first professional debut as a walk-on in* Romeo and Juliet." That sentence is firmly italicized. Then follows the where and when:

"Grand Opera House, Chicago, Ill., Nov. 25, 1935." Since in the same paragraph he mentions distinguished actors he was associated with in that period (Orson Welles, Lunt and Fontanne) we wonder why he doesn't mention the Juliet of his "first professional debut."

It was Katharine Cornell.

He does not tell us (what we learn elsewhere) that while he "walked on," for Miss Cornell, watching from the wings, he compiled a record of her production, including many line readings, stage business roughly but profusely entered, and sketches of scenes. This document, now in the promptbook collection of the theatre library at Lincoln Center, includes Davis's note to the effect that he used parts of it in writing parts of *Quicksilver*.

Forty years afterwards, in supplying the editor of *Notable Names* with the facts of his career, he omitted Cornell's name from this or any contact with her.

As Malvolio would say, "This is evident to any formal capacity." When *Quicksilver* came out in 1942, a reviewer in *Theatre Arts* prophesied there would be "bitterness out loud" among theatre folk as they "recognize portraits among the company that Miss Evelyn Navarre, 'the first lady of the American theatre' takes on tour in *Romeo and Juliet*."

A friend of mine who knew Davis in later years (he died in 1980) tells me that in the early 1940s everybody assumed that he had written a thinly veiled account of the Cornell tour. It must have been easy, then, for "everybody" to assume that the peculiar, often satiric, even hostile portrait of Evelyn Navarre was based on the person of Miss Cornell. So perhaps, as my friend suggests, it was to avoid a libel suit that Davis spread the word that his portrait of Evelyn Navarre was an amalgam of *several* leading actresses that he had known – Cornell, Fontanne, Le Gallienne, and others. By the time *Notable Names* was published Cornell was dead, the others very old, himself in his middle sixties.

Whatever scandal or bitterness his novel had caused was three decades in the past and largely forgotten. But still, whether out of embarrassment or ill will we do not know, he could not write down Cornell's name anywhere in the last official record of his life.

Undoubtedly the publication of the novel had been an indiscretion (Secrets from the confessional; or, He who tells too much truth from behind the scenes gets blacklisted) – an act which seriously damaged his prospective career in professional theatre. In the year *before* the book appeared he played seven leading roles in good plays in summer theatres. For three years *after the book* he acted not at all. Then from 1945 to 1962 we find him directing or acting in seventeen plays (good ones), but *none* on Broadway or with distinguished company – three in branches of the New York Public Library, five in club theatres in New York, nine in club or community theatres in the Midwest, mostly in the Chicago area. In the 1960s he appeared in one-man song recitals. He wrote theatrical and literary criticism, and lectured widely. But the Theatre passed him by.

## THE TITLE

Any reader will want to know at once the meaning of the title. Davis purposely withholds the word "quicksilver" until well into his text when an event occurs that demands the word and its explanation. It is a metaphor central to Davis's conception of the art of acting. Or rather, I should say, it is Henry Carmichael's conception of that art. Henry, as the reader of the novel discovers early on, is a promising student forced out of college by the Crash of 1929, who by chance, instinct for survival, and a talent for comic acting, slips over from the "real" world into the world of theatre. He becomes the novel's central character and (unobtrusively) spokesman for the author. "Quicksilver" is a metaphor for the thing that distinguishes a real actor's temperament, a magic chemical, a kind of ichor that runs up and down a genuine actor's veins, finger tips to toes, and flashes in the eyes of his audience. In the talented novice quicksilver is uneven, uncontrolled. He must find his technique, must learn how to measure the thing, when to release, when to hold back. Once explained, the word occurs often, its meaning enriched with every repetition.

## THE FRAME STORY

As the reader of *Quicksilver* will soon become aware, it is not one novel but two. The major narrative, of course, is the events of a theatre company's tour, but to add weight and continuity and a perspective from the "real" world, Davis laid over it and wove into it a narrative frame, the persistent but self-destroying love story of Henry Carmichael and Judith Alexander.

These two were son and daughter of two wealthy New York families. In their growing up together, their hand-holding, partying school days, they were "in love." Then came the 1929 Crash. The Carmichaels lost everything.

Henry, who had completed a year at Amherst, had to drop out early in his second year. Thanks to his comical face and his brilliance as a comedian and mimic in college theatricals, he got a small part in a nondescript play that luckily lasted out the season, long enough for him to earn his Equity card and the standard minimum twenty-five a week. The Crash set his life pattern. Theatre was the only work in the world that he was capable of and cared for. Whatever the obstacles, he committed himself irrevocably to theatre.

The Alexanders came through the Crash unharmed, sent their beautiful Judith to the finest finishing school in the City, and lived in contented luxury as if the Crash had never happened. Having always been fond of Henry, they encouraged him to keep up his affectionate relationship with Judith, and continued to expect him, when in town, to brighten their company at Sunday dinners.

This link to better times was Henry's only comfort in his desperate effort to establish a reputation – those dreary days in agents' offices hunting auditions for any kind of part. Here were companionable, interested seniors, and always Judith, more beautiful than ever, to adore. According to family tradition Judith and her mother were direct descendants of a sixteenth-century French beauty of the Després family, whose portrait by Clouet hung in the Alexanders' library. When Henry contemplated Judith's aristocratic profile, her glowing color, he knew the tradition spoke truth, and his love for her deepened. But always when he left her, he confronted the black truth: never in the miserable economy of his profession would he be able to afford her.

As for Judith, her old affection gradually cooled. Of course she was fond of Henry. She sympathized with his troubles. But during his years of erratic engagements and broken road tours she was being courted by bright young men on their way into the professions – law or finance (no *Jews* among them: none of her finishing school set associated with Jews), young men of her own kind, enjoying their youth in fast cars by day and night clubs after dark.

She reviewed Henry's prospects. By quitting Amherst he had lost future contacts with the world of affairs, which might have led to a career like her father's. His first year in the theatre was a lucky stopgap, but now, by *committing* himself to theatre, he had cut himself out of the social class to which she would always belong. She could see no place for an itinerant comedian in the world that was waiting for her.

When the famous Miss Evelyn Navarre took Henry into her *Romeo and Juliet* company to play Peter, and opened it for the season on Broadway, Judith was pleased for Henry's sudden rise in the profession; pleased, too, now that he was regularly accessible, to enjoy his cheerful company again, often at Sunday dinners and sometimes on the town. She was hardly in her element, though, one evening some weeks into the run when Henry insisted on taking her to Ralph's, a smoky, noisy beer and sandwich joint where younger actors congregated every evening to taper off after their work was done. Some of Henry's friends from *Romeo* would be there and he wanted Judith to meet them.

As they entered Ralph's, everyone seemed to know Henry, waving and calling, inviting him to join this table or that. Across the room one of Henry's best friends, Nicky Randall (a Mexican youth whose nickname in the company, because of his lazy ways, was Mañana) was beckoning. He and a couple of girls who played minor parts had saved a table. They and another couple settled in, first names were passed around, and the chatter began – all about the evening's performance, all in a professional jargon that Judith didn't understand. She couldn't join in. No one expected her to. Used to being the center of any conversation, she didn't enjoy being ignored.

But it gave her time to consider her distaste for the theatre crowd. "Most of them have no background," she thought to herself. "They show no interest in talking about anything but theatre – and not *really* theatre, but only grumbles about the parts they were playing or parts they wish they were playing. Furthermore, they live in a slovenly manner, sleep and eat at untidy hours, forget appointments, keep people waiting, and expect to make up for it by pouring out synthetic charm. And these girls across the table! They must have been pretty enough an hour ago, swirling about the stage in the party scene, but out of costume, without makeup, how drab, how dowdy and dull they are."

Something brushed against her leg – the restaurant cat! Henry picked it up and cradled it in his arms, making some silly joke about

Miss Navarre and her lapdog. It meant nothing to Judith, but the whole table roared at Henry's wit. When she made him put the wretched beast down, his jacket was gray with cat hairs. Disgusting! "Just look at yourself," she ordered. Obediently, he brushed his jacket.

"And these are Henry's people," she was thinking. "When he is away from them, when he comes to us at home, he behaves like a gentleman. When he is with them he behaves, as it were, in his shirt sleeves. His real life is here in this crowd. The theatre has ruined him. It will take him out of my world to the end of his days."

From her set silence, Henry knew what she was thinking. He shouldn't have brought her here. For the first time in his five years in the business he was well set in a role he loved to play, in a huge production which looked certain to succeed, with friends to enjoy, with two or three "quicksilver" actors to emulate and half a dozen others worth study. He wanted to share all this with Judith. But it was no use. Ralph's place was no background for the proud descendant of the Clouet lady. He was embarrassed.

And suddenly he was resentful. She despised these people of his, her social inferiors, just as she despised Jews. Could he never break her of this shameless snobbishness? After the glum ride home in the taxi all that she could say to him at the door of her apartment was, "Good night, Henry."

## MISS EVELYN NAVARRE

We are not told when Miss Evelyn Navarre ("Miss Evvy") entered the profession, but certainly she was born to it and to nothing else. She was an instant glamor girl, a natural star number. In whatever popular vehicles her director, Claude Winthrop, and her advance man, Edgar John McLaren, brought her, she could mesmerize fashionable New York audiences. Through the 1920s New York society regarded her as the "First Lady of the American Theatre."

Her beauty was a miracle. A stagehand holding a door for her would catch his breath when her perfumed hair passed close to his face. He would gaze in wonder at her perfect features, at the sparkle in her hazel eyes, at her gorgeous tawny hair. To every man in the audience her velvety caressing voice sent waves of personal affection. Her gliding undulation under Parisian gowns flattered her women adorers, magnetized them into seeming identity with herself. She could wear a sarong, too, and in Oriental romances like *Singapore Belle* she could transport men and women both to a far-off erotic land which the playbill called Malaysia.

This was her public self: the peerless dispenser of concentrated sex appeal. But it was not an invitation to her dressing room. She kept her private self firmly aloof from the public. Three loves she had: her Belgian lapdog, Narcisse Noir; Nicky Randall (Mañana), a Mexican youth she kept in the company to charm her with voluptuous songs to the soft strumming of his guitar; and her secretary, Deborah Blake.

Deborah was one of her supporting actresses. But her ability to keep Evvy's mundane affairs in order had long since won her the official post of secretary. They were always together. On tour they traveled together in Evvy's chauffeured limousine, or shared compartments on trains. They dined together. They shared hotel suites. And Deborah satisfied her employer's emotional needs.

Miss Evvy's devotion to Deborah was so intense that when she had to play an ardent love scene she required Deborah to stand in the wings as near to her as possible in order to stimulate her warmest, lovingest tones of voice. She was terrified, of course, that their relationship would be discovered and made public. Most of the company knew about it, of course, but to protect their own jobs they blanketed it in silence. Fear of Deborah ("Madame Veto") was a factor in controlling gossip. She fired a backstage worker once for making a remark that suggested he "knew too much." "That dyke," Henry Carmichael said, "has too much power."

The financial collapse of 1929 frightened Evvy. As the world moved into the hard times of the 1930s, as she herself was drifting into her forties, she realized she couldn't go on playing ingénues and society belles forever. But what could she do?

She turned to the two men who had long been her mainstays – Winthrop and McLaren. They agreed at once it was time for a bold stroke. She must look beyond costume parades to please women, and beyond bare skin, oeillades, and easy sex-teasing to please men. She must take herself seriously. She must find plays that explore earnest, even tragic relations between men and women. In the long run she must come to Shakespeare. Not yet, for she was not ready. Nor indeed was the public ready. After the successes of Barrymore and Jane Cowl, no actor had yet been able to revive interest in Shakespeare. But the revival was sure to come, and *then* she must be ready.

They offered her exactly what she needed: the role of Elena

Andreyevna in Chekhov's *Uncle Vanya*. That choice, beauty for beauty, passion for passion, was a stroke of genius on Winthrop's part. By countless novelistic glances backward by actors who were in it or spectators who saw it, the author never lets us doubt that it had happened and succeeded.

Miss Evvy founded her own company called Sovereign Productions, Inc., gathered a small cast, including at Winthrop's insistence two actors from England: a famous old Irish actress, Mrs. Johnston-Terry, much loved in London in roles that called for motherly tenderness, to play the Nurse, Marina; and for Astrov, the most complex and difficult character, Frederick Bruce, a forty-year-old "straight man" whose emotional range and control would cover every phase of the Astrov experience. She herself began a course of re-education with Winthrop, to convert all her natural attributes into the melancholy opposite of what her audience had always seen in her.

McLaren, an absolute poet of press-agentry, delighted in the task of teaching the New York audience the appropriateness of Miss Navarre's qualities in a tragic role. He celebrated the triumph of *Uncle Vanya* before the curtain rose on it. The play had a good New York run into the 1933–34 season and then was taken to London, where its even greater success confirmed the New York verdict that Miss Navarre was an authentic tragedienne.

Once *Uncle Vanya* got under way Winthrop decided it was time to turn to Shakespeare. The play would be *Romeo and Juliet*. Miss Navarre studied Juliet while still playing Elena, finding a special pleasure in reverting to the ingénue charms that the audience had always loved, and adding to it the earnestness and suffering she had learned from Elena.

We are told very little about the first New York season of *Romeo and Juliet*. The English visitors were retained. The earthy Irishness of Mrs. Johnston-Terry fully realized the peasant humor of Shakespeare's Nurse as well as her tenderness; and Freddy Bruce laid by his Astrovian depression for Mercutio's joyously bawdy wit. The success was so marked that Sovereign Productions announced a tour for the season to come.

ROMEO: ANTHONY ENGLISH

For the tour Miss Navarre needed a new Romeo, so she sent to London for a golden-haired matinee idol, Anthony English, whose

Romeo, like her Juliet, had lately made great news. Tony declined to come, however, unless he also brought a protégé of his, Roger Winston, whom he depended on as Benvolio. To win Tony she yielded.

During the rehearsals Roger demonstrated, as Henry remarked, that he "can't act for sour spit," and at Providence, their first show on the road, he committed an incredible fluff. Instead of proving Romeo's "swan a crow," he proved his "crow a swan." Some of the cast giggled; some were downright angry that such a bumbler was on hand to spoil their production.

Joel King, the new Tybalt, asked if Roger was Romeo's under-study. During a rehearsal he had noticed him standing just off stage, watching Romeo intensely as if he were memorizing his movements. Henry explained that Tony liked having him stand there because "it lends conviction." What did that mean? "Well," Mañana put it, "you may as well know that Roger's *real* job isn't Benvolio – he's Tony's secretary. Only we pronounce it *Sexretary*."

Joel was outraged. So this golden Romeo was a fag, and Roger was his lover! "He better not make a pass at me," he growled. "I'll beat him to a pulp. If there's anything that makes my stomach turn it's that. How the hell can you guys take it so casually?" Henry explained that they had to put up with it or lose their jobs, so they might as well make a joke of it.

What the audience never knew, what only those veterans of last season's company who knew Miss Evvy's secret ways could know, was that both the lyrical lovers in this production were sexual irregulars.

### TO THE READER

I offer the above pages as a kind of *sampler* of a theatre novel far too long and too loaded to be described or competently analyzed in a brief essay. From my random inquiries it appears that *Quicksilver* has been widely and quite unfairly forgotten. So my sampler is intended as an invitation to neglecters and forgetters to find it and enjoy it. I wish in fact that some risk-daring publisher, having put a knowledgeable editor to work on it, would bring it out again.

It was well reviewed in 1942. In the *New York Times*, for instance, Orville Prescott gave it a warm welcome when it appeared in September, and later praised it highly among his dozen most memorable books of the publishing season. In the *Herald Tribune* Rose Feld praised it for its authentic knowledge of backstage realities, for the author's discriminating portraits of a gallery of highly individual characters, and for creating in prose the magic of theatre. "It will prove more satisfying than a month's free passes to Broadway shows."

The book had two printings and must have been widely read, both for its opening the curtains on what the audience never sees or hears, and for its revelations of what the public habitually suspects about the offstage life of the performers.

For students of acting there are countless discussions of systems and techniques with passages illustrating success or failure. Some of the most rewarding sections are rehearsal scenes showing the interplay between directors and actors.

The book does call for at least minimal editing. Early reviewers wished it cut by a fourth or a third, but that is too much. There *are* longueurs and irrelevancies, as of Henry Carmichael's dying aunt in Buffalo, or the strung-out problem of preventing his mother's marriage to a four-flusher after her divorce; or the introduction of new actors, like the clownish Wilbur Welch for *The Taming of the Shrew*, which never will come off anyway. There are some careless contradictions. The actress of the Nurse, the grand old Mrs. Johnston-Terry, is on top of the world because the world's greatest living playwright, Barney Shore, has written a play especially for her: but is it called *The Empress of the Emerald Isle* or *The Dictatress of the Emerald Isle*? Though the author has a vivid, never pretentious vocabulary, I suspect him here and there, in a rush of enthusiasm, of a pointless neologism. But these and other occasional oddities are fly-specks on his ever-sparkling prose. His dialogue always finds the exactly right tone and rhythm to fit the speaker.

## NOTES

1  Fitzroy Davis, *Quicksilver* (New York: Harcourt, Brace and Company, 1942).
2  *Notable Names in the American Theatre*, ed. Raymond D. McGill (Clifton, NJ: J. T. White, 1976).

# CHAPTER 14

# The economic structure of the Federal Theatre Project

## Barry B. Witham

With the exception of a brief period between 1935 and 1939, most professional theatre in the United States has operated on a box office basis whereby those plays which earn income survive and those that don't, fail. That exception, the Federal Theatre Project, was sponsored by the Works Progress Administration during the Roosevelt presidency under enormous controversy and acclaim, and its accomplishments are still being evaluated by theatre historians. Amidst charges of waste and partisan politics it created hundreds of productions, thousands of jobs and spent over forty million dollars of taxpayer's money. And amidst cries of communism and budget reduction it was eventually eliminated by Congress.

In spite of the fact that the Federal Theatre was designed to function both as a relief and arts program, almost nothing has been written about the economic side of the project.[1] Its accomplishments as a producing agency have been discussed in a number of places, as have its political successes and blunders. But the economic framework which determined nearly everything from play choice to realized production has been left largely unexplored. How much did actors earn, for example? How were productions funded? What were local sponsors and how did they function? How much money did Hallie Flanagan make as National Director? If a "new" theatre history wishes to shed light on the "power" that circulated in the hectic days of the Federal Theatre experiment, there is no better place to start than the complex system of economic welfare which was the foundation of the whole enterprise.

The most significant document for such a study is *Government Operating Procedure Number F-45* "Procedures for Business Manager–Agent Cashier" which outlined the ways monies were encumbered and dispersed by the dozens of individual theatres.[2] Although the document was modified over the years, the basic guidelines for distributing money remained intact. First, there were the federally appropriated funds which came directly to the individual theatres via their state organizations as part of the relief appropriation. This money, which was the largest part of the theatre's budget, was to be used primarily for salaries (labor) with no more than 10 percent allowed for production costs. Second, admissions funds from box office were earmarked to pay production or "other than labor" costs and were ordinarily expended for advertising, materials, travel, rent, taxes and emergency situations. And finally, sponsor's contributions (also treated as admissions) were local donations which might be cash but also might be props, free rent or advertising. Any other incidental income such as concessions or sub-rentals were to be "classed with admissions receipts."

Because productions were limited from the outset to no more than 10 percent for non-labor costs, the technical aspects of most shows were limited. The hope in Washington was that local communities would provide money for production and thus help defray non-labor expenses. Indeed, F-45 addresses the issue this way: "To the extent that such additional costs can be paid for by the communities served through the collection of admissions, such additional costs for equipment, materials, supplies and travel can be afforded."[3] In addition, at the outset of the project it was hoped that local theatres would provide free rent although provisions were made for rentals "either as a fixed amount or as a percentage of admissions."[4] This, too, became a complex issue since some Federal Theatre productions were classified as "non-revenue" (vaudeville, children's shows) while others (Living Newspapers) were conceived as "revenue" earning. And theatre managers were reluctant to provide free rent for a project which earned over a million and a half dollars at its box offices.

The production of plays was further complicated by the restrictions imposed on the participants. Since the Federal Theatre was primarily a welfare endeavor, the companies had to be certified by local WPA offices as genuinely needy. Although there was a special classification for Supervisors – directors, agent cashiers and project coordinators – who could be exempt from relief quotas, each project was allowed to exempt only 10 percent of its workers. Thus, the bulk of the production team not only needed to be certified for welfare, but their salary scale was determined by their WPA classification.

Each actor, for example, had to be placed in one of the follow-

8 Varieties troupe loading for an out-of-town engagement, the Federal Theatre Project, Seattle, 1937

ing categories: Professional, Skilled, Intermediate or Unskilled. Although the scales varied, some depending on cost of living in different areas of the country, the following figures from California in August 1937 are typical. Professional: $93.60 per month (or $23.40 per week); Skilled: $85.44 ($21.36); Intermediate: $64.80 ($16.20) and Unskilled: $55.20 ($13.80).[5] By comparison Supervisors earned $120.00 per month ($30.00 per week); the Field Supervisor $300.00 ($75.00) and Hallie Flanagan as National Director earned $6,400 per year or $533.00 ($133.33).[6]

What is frequently overlooked, however, is the egalitarian nature of the enterprise. Thus, not only actors but every other worker on the production had to be classified by the same system. Designers, shopmen, press agents and poster artists made the same rate as performers if they were classified in the appropriate places. For those projects which had Negro units their Skilled performers made more money than white actors who were classified only as Intermediate. The important point was that the amount of government appropriation was based upon the number and classification of each worker on the project.

And how did those percentages operate in actual practice? Again the figures vary in different parts of the country and in different kinds of productions, but the following breakdown from the 1937 Living Newspaper production of *Power* in Seattle is instructive. The project listed 119 people, 81 of whom were performers.[7] The others were Technicians: 22; Supervisors: 6; and Other (box office, publicity, etc): 10. The 119 are then further broken down by job classification, relief status and sex[8] but not by job description. The largest percentage of the employees were in the Skilled category, 68 of 119 (57 percent). There were 31 listed as Professional; 11 as Intermediate and 3 as Unskilled. The classifications were open to abuse, of course, but in general the guidelines were clear and kept any one group from dominating the highest level. To be a Professional, for example, was extremely controversial because people who had been "certified" by their unions did not want to be re-certified by the WPA. IATSE, in fact, refused to have their members seek WPA certification. Eventually nearly all theatre employees had to satisfy a Federal directive which stated: "a professional is deemed to be one who, for at least fifty weeks in the past ten years, has earned his living in some recognized theatrical activity."[9] Union stagehands, however, never did comply with

Table 1. *Labor analysis of State of Washington Project, December 1938*

*All labor should be listed under appropriate classifications. Monthly earning rates for security wage workers should agree with the schedule of monthly earnings as prescribed by administrative orders.*

| Occupational classification (1) | No. of workers (2) | Status[1] (3) | Man-months (4) | Hours of work (5) | Rate per month (6) | Amount (dollars) (7) |
|---|---|---|---|---|---|---|
| Unskilled:   Office Boy | 1 | C | ½ | 120 | 55.00 | 27.50 |
| Janitors | 2 | C | 12 | 120 | 55.00 | 660.00 |
| Theatre Attendants | 2 | C | 12 | 120 | 55.00 | 660.00 |
| "    " | 1 | C | ½ | 120 | 55.00 | 27.50 |
| | 6 | | 25 | | | 1375.00 |
| Intermediate:   Actors | 4 | C | 24 | 96 | 65.00 | 1560.00 |
| " | 2 | C | 1 | 96 | 65.00 | 65.00 |
| Bus Driver | 1 | C | 6 | 96 | 65.00 | 390.00 |
| Artist | 1 | C | 6 | 96 | 65.00 | 390.00 |
| Clerk | 1 | C | 6 | 96 | 65.00 | 390.00 |
| Fireman | 1 | C | 6 | 96 | 65.00 | 390.00 |
| | 10 | | 49 | | | 3185.00 |
| Skilled:   Actors | 1 | C | ½ | 96 | 85.00 | 42.50 |
| " | 3 | N | 18 | 96 | 85.00 | 1630.00 |
| " | 25 | C | 150 | 96 | 85.00 | 12750.00 |
| Musicians | 5 | C | 30 | 96 | 85.00 | 2550.00 |
| Stage Hands | 3 | C | 18 | 96 | 85.00 | 1530.00 |
| House Manager | 1 | C | 6 | 120 | 85.00 | 410.00 |
| Forewoman | 1 | C | 6 | 120 | 85.00 | 510.00 |
| Wardrobe Sup'r. | 1 | C | 6 | 120 | 85.00 | 510.00 |
| Senior Clerk | 1 | C | 6 | 120 | 85.00 | 510.00 |
| | 41 | | 240½ | | | 20442.50 |
| Professional and technical:   Actors | 14 | C | 84 | 96 | 94.00 | 7896.00 |
| " | 1 | N | 6 | 96 | 94.00 | 564.00 |
| Musicians | 4 | C | 24 | 96 | 94.00 | 2256.00 |
| Scenic Artist | 2 | C | 12 | 96 | 94.00 | 1128.00 |
| Playwright | 1 | C | 6 | 96 | 94.00 | 564.00 |
| Accountant | 1 | C | 6 | 120 | 95.00 | 564.00 |
| Poster Artist | 1 | C | 6 | 96 | 94.00 | 564.00 |
| Secretary Class A | 1 | C | 6 | 120 | 94.00 | 564.00 |
| Theatre Agents | 2 | C | 12 | 120 | 94.00 | 1128.00 |
| Costume Designer | 1 | C | 6 | 120 | 94.00 | 564.00 |
| Technical Artist | 1 | C | 6 | 96 | 94.00 | 564.00 |
| Master Stage Hands | 4 | C | 24 | 96 | 94.00 | 2256.00 |
| | 33 | | 198 | | | 18612.00 |
| Subtotal | 90 | xx | 512½ | xxx | xxx | 43614.50 |

Table 1. *continued*

| Occupational classification (1) | No. of workers (2) | Status[1] (3) | Man-months (4) | Hours of work (5) | Rate per month (6) | Amount (dollars) (7) |
|---|---|---|---|---|---|---|
| Superintendence: | | | | | | |
| State Director | 1 | N | 6 | 140 | 200.00 | 1200.00 |
| Administrative Assistant | 1 | N | 6 | 140 | 150.00 | 900.00 |
| Agent Cashier | 1 | N | 6 | 140 | 150.00 | 900.00 |
| Production Manager | 1 | N | 6 | 140 | 135.00 | 810.00 |
| Supervising Timekeeper | 1 | N | 6 | 140 | 120.00 | 720.00 |
| Subtotal | 5 | xx | 30 | xxx | xxx | 4530.00 |
| Total | 95 | xx | 542 ½ | xxx | xxx | 48144.50 |

[1]Denote thus: C. certified; N. noncertified. Report in item 6 personnel paid from co-sponsors' funds.

WPA certification and were sometimes paid union wages from "other than labor costs." Unskilled were ordinarily janitors, maids and ushers. The percentages for *Power* seem relatively typical. Six months earlier the same project listed 131 total workers with 70 (53 percent) classified as Skilled.

Each state was required to submit an official request for funds (WPA Form 330) every six months and those forms provide further insights into the operation of the classification system. Page three of that form (see table 1) was a Labor Analysis which detailed the pay rate as well as the specific job description for each employee. This page is from the State of Washington as of December 1938 and is part of the request for the first six months of 1939. Of the 95 workers on the project 50 were actors and 15 of those were regarded as "professionals" by the WPA classification system. They were paid at the same rate ($94.00 per month) as other "professionals" such as the playwright, costume designer, agents and musicians. This analysis provides an interesting profile of the job descriptions of a representative Federal Theatre company and reveals a great deal about the nature of the enterprise. Notice, for example, that there was a "forewoman" on the project and that Master Stage Hands were always paid at the highest rate, a result of Hallie Flanagan's failed efforts to bring their union into line with any WPA classification system. The total labor allocation here ($48,144.50) is 90 percent of the entire request which was $53,494.50.

In terms of Relief status, the 1937 company of *Power* listed 104 as being certified for relief and 15 as not. This figure is critical since it was the relationship between relief and non-relief personnel which was one of the most debated aspects of the program. Every project was plagued at some point by the need to employ gifted performers who were not technically eligible for relief. The files of both the national and state offices are filled with pleas to raise the quotas so that the talent level and quality of the productions could be improved. Within the first year pressures became so great that non-relief exemptions were as high as 25 percent, which subsequently raised Congressional questions about the true "relief" nature of the project. Exemptions were reduced to 10 percent again in 1936 and finally in 1939 they were scaled down to only 5 percent as the whole project struggled to survive. As evidenced in table 1, the Washington State unit in their December 1938 request listed 5 superintendent personnel as noncertified as well as four actors for a total percentage of .09.

The individual companies also struggled continuously with production costs and many could not accomplish their technical demands for the acceptable "other than labor" costs. A variety of alternatives and solutions were explored including constant reminders about reducing telephone use, emergency funds and taxi fees. Some appropriated funds (10 percent) could go to materials costs although there was a strict prohibition against any admission funds going towards certified labor expenses or for any appropriated funds to pay for advertising. Table 2 details the non-labor expenses for the Washington State Project in December 1938. While "supplies and materials" represents the largest single category ($1750.00) it is important to put that figure into a working context. For example, the $500.00 for "scenic materials" was for a projected six-month period in which the project planned to present eight new theatrical events including *Spirochete*, *Big White Fog* and *Othello*! Note also the theatre rental fee which was a constant source of discontent for those who wanted the local communities to absorb more non-labor expenses.

Obviously it took strict supervision to budget and maintain a theatrical season when one was routinely limited to 10 percent of labor appropriations. Initially many people in Washington, DC, were opposed to admission charges of any kind but Flanagan was able to convince WPA officials that very few theatres would be able

Table 2. *Non-labor expenses for the State of Washington Project,*
*December 1938*

| | Description (1) | Amount (dollars) (2) |
|---|---|---|
| a. Equipment: | | |
| (1) Purchases: | | |
| (2) Rentals: | | |
| | Electric Equipment | 100.00 |
| | Costumes | 180.00 |
| b. Supplies and materials: | | |
| | Scenic Materials | 500.00 |
| | Costume Materials | 500.00 |
| | Printing and Stationery | 300.00 |
| | Miscellaneous Properties | 200.00 |
| | Photographic Supplies | 250.00 |
| c. Rentals – space: | | |
| (1) Office: | | |
| | Included in Theatre Rental | |
| (2) Other: | Theatre | 1480.00 |
| d. Travel: | | |
| | Travel and Subsistence | 545.50 |
| e. Communications: | | |
| | Long Distance Telephone | 30.00 |
| | Telegraph | 25.00 |
| | Telephone (Local) | 180.00 |
| f. Utilities (light, heat, etc.) | | |
| | Light and Power | 500.00 |
| | Fuel | 300.00 |
| g. Other: (specify) | | |
| | Transportation of Things | 259.50 |
| Total | | 5350.00 |

to operate on the 10 percent formula. Admissions were always a sensitive area because the Federal Government believed that these revenues should be returned to the National Treasury while Flanagan and other officials argued for their use at individual theatres. Eventually a compromise was struck and admissions were allowed to be collected and dispersed locally through the use of an agent cashier who was both treasurer of the company and a Federal officer authorized to spend money for production costs.

The Federal Theatre was not required to make money – indeed 60 percent of their efforts nationwide were free. But the pressure to

compete with the professional theatre in urban areas and the constant need to allocate funds for production costs pushed many of the
projects into a highly competitive and commercial stance. The
following balance sheet from the Blackstone Theatre in Chicago
demonstrates how a project, whose labor was subsidized, could
make money. (See table 3.) By claiming a $15,000 inventory deduc-
tion for the theatre and by earning over $42,000 in box office
receipts the unit was able to show a profit during this eight-month
period of $3,459.43. This amount could then be applied toward
noncertified labor costs or future production costs.

But this was by no means typical. Flanagan worked hard to keep
a 50-cent top on tickets and to insure some free seats at every
performance. Many seats were available at 10 and 25 cents and
more than half of the Federal Theatre productions nationwide had
no admission price at all. In going through the records of the
Chicago project – one of the most successful – it is interesting to note
that during the same period that the Blackstone was turning a profit,
the Civic Theatre (playing *Triple A Plowed Under* and *Chalk Dust*)
had a deficit of $11,020.75 in production expenses versus ticket
income.[10] The certified labor bill was $69,823.98.

Production budgets were always a problem because sponsors just
did not respond to the project in the way that had been anticipated.
Sponsorship was a fundamental part of the whole WPA adventure
and Flanagan hoped that local sponsors would help to defer "other
than labor" expenses as well as allow many of the theatres to become
self-sufficient. In WPA projects other than Federal One (The Arts)
sponsors were required to contract for a certain amount of local
money or support before the government agreed to participate. This
was a safeguard that prevented the funding of projects which had
insufficient backing or no certainty of being accomplished without
massive federal support. But this model did not work in Federal One
because there were no state or local agencies in charge of the Arts.
Thus shortly after Federal One was created, Washington
announced the concept of "co-sponsors" or local groups – public or
private – who would contribute to such items as rent, travel or even
noncertified wages. The guidelines were very informal. Co-sponsors
could be Boys Clubs, Community Groups or local theatres. And
sponsorship could include a host of in-kind services as well as cash
support.

In his study on *Federal Relief Administration and the Arts*, William F.

Table 3. *Analysis of Blackstone Theatre, Chicago, April–December 1936*

| | | | | |
|---|---|---|---|---|
| Admissions: | | | | |
| Three Wise Fools | 4/20 to 6/13 | Incl | 8,225.27 | |
| Broken Dishes | 6/15 to 10/17 | " | 25,656.21 | |
| It Can't Happen Here | 10/27 to 12/12 | " | 8,178.30 | $42,059.78 |
| Cost of Operation Other Than Project Labor: | | | | |
| Expenditures: | | | | |
| Disbursements of Agent Cashier Paid | | | 44,817.99 | |
| "        "        "        "    Unpaid | | | 2,859.57 | |
| | | | 47,677.56 | |
| Inventory deduction | | | 15,000.00 | |
| | | | 32,677.56 | |
| Additional Labor Short Form Payroll | | | | |
| (See Schedule) | | | 1,856.42 | |
| | | | 34,533.98 | 34,533.98 |
| Amount In Excess Of Expenditures Incurred by | | | | |
| Agent Cashier | | | | 7,525.80 |
| Expenditures: | | | | |
| Disbursements of Appropriated Funds | | | | |
| toward Procurement Purchases | | | 4,566.37 | |
| Inventory deduction | | | 500.00 | |
| | | | 4,066.37 | 4,066.37 |
| Admission fees absorbed 100% of Appropriated Funds | | | | |
| Project Allocation for other than labor expenditures | | | | |
| Surplus to be applied toward labor | | | | $ 3,459.43 |

McDonald claims that sponsorship was generally treated as a formality both because it was not lucrative and because Federal One was suspicious of any attempts by local agencies to control or influence the content of the Arts projects.[11] This was probably true of the Writers Project and of the theatres in metropolitan areas like New York and Chicago. But sponsorship was a vital part of many rural theatre ventures and could play a supportive role in a variety of situations, especially in community-based ventures like the Living Newspapers.[12] It is clear from the records that sponsorship was often pursued vigorously by the Federal Theatre Project and documents in the National Archives chronicle both cash and "other" donations. The amounts, however, are not impressive. Figures for July 1937, for example, show only $140 in sponsor's cash for the entire country.[13] For the six-month period from July to December of 1937 over $8,000 is recorded in cash but non-cash sponsorship is estimated as $104,561.89 nationwide.[14] Flanagan's hope that many of the production costs could be covered from co-sponsorship was realized to the extent that "other" often meant props, promotion and group sales, but it certainly did not translate into the kind of local financing that would allow Federal Theatre to survive after 1939 in the manner that it was originally envisioned.

Co-sponsorship sometimes included rent but not often enough and pursuit of rent-free theatres was a continual concern. A review of Federal Theatre leases in 1937 reveals that rates varied enormously but that expenses could be substantial against the "other than labor" costs.[15] The Blackstone Theatre in Chicago, for instance, cost $200.00 per week plus 50 percent of the first $1,000.00 and 30 percent above that. Keiths in Indianapolis took a straight 50 percent of the gross. The Copley in Boston charged $1,200.00 per month and the Metropolitan in Seattle, $425.00 per week. Of course, these were for large-scale "revenue" productions – and still rather inexpensive compared with the Maxine Elliott ($1,833 per month) or the Ritz ($2,500 per month) in New York – but they are indicative of the financial difficulties which confronted the project in spite of its huge labor appropriations.

One area where sponsorship did work effectively was in regional touring, especially in rural areas. In Florida, for example, a unit would contract to go to a high school and play both a matinee and evening performance. The school provided the theatre (auditorium) and would do the advertising. Federal Theatre would specify the ticket prices (10 and 25 cents for matinees and 25 and 35 cents for evenings). The Federal Company then got a guaranteed $50.00 as "first money" and 60 percent of everything after that.[16] It was Flanagan's initial hope that most Federal Theatre could be free and indeed a lot of it was but in many of the tours an arrangement like the Florida example was contracted.

Theatre fare varied, of course, from state to state as did the nature of federal support. In North Carolina, for example, the major emphasis was on providing a few professional personnel for theatres which already existed rather than in creating new producing units. And in spite of Flanagan's reluctance to support "amateur" community theatres, professional advisors were sent for three summers to Manteo, North Carolina, as advisors to support production of *The Lost Colony*. Expense accounts for the summer of 1938 indicate that travel and per diem expenses for Federal Theatre "professionals" exceeded $5,000.00.[17] Revenues went to the local company. In fact the entire state of North Carolina had returned only $130.50 in box office income to the Federal Theatre Project by the end of that summer.

By comparison, however, many communities believed that the federal funds could rejuvenate the stock system and bring professional theatre back to smaller cities. San Antonio, Texas, devised an elaborate system of bookkeeping so that a four-play season could be done successfully using the 90 percent formula and others invested heavily in vaudeville, children's theatre or religious presentations. Flanagan encouraged units to focus on problems and issues that were peculiar to their region such as the Living Newspaper *Timber* which was in rehearsal in Seattle when the project was finally discontinued in 1939.

But several projects did not survive and by 1938 had been cancelled in Alabama, Iowa, Nebraska, Texas and Indiana. Those that were deemed most successful were in New York, Chicago and Los Angeles. In fact nearly 50 percent of the total expenditures of the entire enterprise were in New York City. McDonald points out that if Massachusetts, Illinois and California were added to the list, these four states accounted for 81 percent of national expenditures.[18]

This predicament was a constant threat to the integrity of the project. Theatre people were not allowed to cross state lines to obtain certification but the public tended to support theatres that were in the major cities. Flanagan responded by emphasizing the importance of touring in rural areas and by seeking other creative outlets such as building theatres, and encouraging programs in marionettes and dance. But by 1937 the pattern of successful metropolitan theatres had emerged and Flanagan met with Harry Hopkins to seek solutions. The next day she wrote to George Kondolf, the Director of the Chicago project, and summarized that meeting.

Mr. Hopkins feels that we are very weak if we abandon the national aspect of our program at this time; he urges us to keep what ground we have gained in various states; he questions specifically whether we should give up any small projects in rural districts ... He also insisted that we get people into the field both in settlements and in touring companies. When we spoke of the difficulties attendant on this we were told that those were our problems to solve, that he wanted a national program and not two or three big metropolitan shows.[19]

The task was formidable because producing successful theatre required, among other things, publicity and advertising. But the

projects were limited by statute to non-labor funds and thus admissions were critical for these costs. An examination of how box office
funds were actually dispersed is instructive. For the three-month
period January–March 1937, for example, the New York City
Project spent nearly $11,000 for advertising out of their admissions
receipts.[20] In California they spent $6,730.19 and in Massachusetts,
$4,562.37. These amounts were substantially more than the total
box office income of projects in Nebraska, Texas, Iowa, New Hampshire and others. Moreover, box office could aid in other categories.
During this same three-month period the Illinois unit spent a little
over $10,000 in Emergency Employment, a category that was
intended for noncertified hiring in the event of "sudden illness or
unavoidable absence." But it was also used for extras and chorus
"fill-ins" as well as a dodge to get around certification in a variety of
"emergency" situations. (Washington was adamant, however,
about not using this category for overtime for regular employees.)
Still the pattern which had emerged by 1937 of the rich getting
richer plagued the project until its demise. The theatres that had
access to audience, advertising and admission funds were not limited
to the 10 percent requirement for production costs and had a
chance, at least, of succeeding. Those forced to survive on their labor
allotment, no matter how ambitions or imaginative, often withered.

Flanagan wrestled with this dilemma constantly and in a poig-
nant and angry letter written on board the Great Northern
Yellowstone Special train from Seattle to Portland in 1937 she
explained to Ellen Woodward:

If any further cuts are ordered, all of these projects outside the big cities will
have to close. We must arrange to send better directors and better equipment . . . Why should W.P.A. be spending $20,000 in labor to build a Show
Boat Theatre for the University of Washington when our own company,
after struggling valiantly for two years, has no money to lease a theatre? We
have had to move into a little old movie house which needs everything done
in the way of repainting and remodelling . . .

You know how I believe in Bonneville Dam. But it struck me as pretty
pathetic, thinking of a million dollars being spent there for a ladder for
salmon to run up and spawn, that here, in a shabby, bare old room, with a
gigantic picture of President Roosevelt smiling down on them, were the
actors we are trying to save. After two years of good work and good press,
they still have no place to act – to say nothing of spawn![21]

The financial structure of the Federal Theatre Project was
extremely complex and any attempt to evaluate its accomplishments

without a consideration of economic demands is obviously limited. Every production was a series of artistic compromises, but those compromises were reflections of deeper tensions – between relief and non-relief personnel; between labor and non-labor costs and between sponsor and non-sponsor funds. In such an environment – further complicated by the unique character of dozens of local projects – the history of the Federal Theatre has only begun to be written.

## NOTES

An earlier version of this paper was presented at the xi World Congress of the International Federation for Theatre Research in Stockholm, June 1989.

1 William F. McDonald's excellent *Federal Relief Administration and the Arts* (Ohio State, 1969) is an exception although he does not include local records or have access to a number of documents which have been made available in the last two decades.
2 "Procedures for Business Manager–Agent Cashier," National Archives, Record Group 69, Federal Theatre Project, Entry 1, National Office Correspondence With States, Box 78, File: Washington, DC, Office.
3 Ibid., 1.
4 Ibid., 23.
5 "California Statistics for 1937," National Archives, Record Group 69, Federal Theatre Project, Entry 14, Reports Containing Statistics, Box 79.
6 "Central Office–Federal Theatre Project," National Archives, Record Group 69, Federal Theatre Project, Records of the Central Office. McDonald claims that Flanagan eventually earned $7,200 but I have been unable to verify that. The figure here ($6,400) is accurate to 1 July 1939 – only a few weeks short of the project's demise – and reflects her government classification as P 6.
7 "Semi-Monthly Activity Reports, Project #7028," National Archives, Record Group 69, Federal Theatre Project, Entry: Oregon and Wa., Box 94.
8 There were twenty-nine women in the company: one supervisor, eight professionals, sixteen skilled and four intermediate.
9 "Correspondence of the Talent Bureau," National Archives, Record Group 69, Federal Theatre Project, Box 248, Folder: Basis for Employment in FTP.
10 "Analysis of Operation of Civic Theatre – Chicago, Illinois," National Archives, Record Group 69, Federal Theatre Project, Entry Statistical Reports, Box 82, Folder: Costs of a few FTP Productions.

11 McDonald, *Federal Relief*, 269.
12 See, for example, the relationship between *Power* and the public utility, City Light in Barry B. Witham, "The Living Newspaper's *Power* in Seattle," *Theatre History Studies* 9 (1989), 22–35.
13 "Semi-Monthly Activity Reports," Box 94.
14 Ibid.
15 "Federal Theatre Leases," National Archives, Record Group 69, Federal Theatre Project, Entry 1, National Office General Correspondence, Box 13.
16 "Sponsoring Contracts," National Archives, Record Group 69, Federal Theatre Project, Entry 1, National Office General Correspondence, Box 33.
17 "Expense Account from *The Lost Colony* Receipts," 3 July–5 September 1938, National Archives, Record Group 69, Federal Theatre Project, Entry Statistical Reports, Box 82, Folder: Costs of a Few FTP Productions.
18 McDonald, *Federal Relief*, 282.
19 Letter from Flanagan to George Kondolf, 17 June 1937. National Archives, Record Group 69, Federal Theatre Project, National Office General Correspondence.
20 "Expenditures-Admissions Funds Account," National Archives, Record Group 69, Federal Theatre Project, Entry 14, Reports Containing Statistics.
21 Letter from Hallie Flanagan to Ellen Woodward, 4 November 1937, National Archives, Record Group 69, Federal Theatre Project, Central Files: State of Washington, Box 2740.

# CHAPTER 15

# The American Repertory Theatre (1946–1947) and the repertory ideal, a case study

## Daniel J. Watermeier

The history of the ART – as it came to be called – is brief, encompassing a mere two years, including the months of planning and preparation and a single Broadway season. It is, moreover, the history of a failure. Failures, however, can sometimes be more instructive than successes. How and why the ART failed illustrates the difficulties of organizing a commercially viable, classical repertory company under the conditions prevalent in the post-war New York theatre. It also reveals how in the arena of theatre organization high ideals, skill, talent, even careful planning and hard work, are inextricably entangled with and often compromised by various business and economic exigencies, by the pressures of competition, by audience tastes and interests, and by other factors which, for lack of a more concrete term, can only be labeled human. Lastly, it suggests why in New York a classical repertory theatre, along the lines of the Comédie Française or the Royal Shakespeare Company, will continue to be an "impossible dream."

The ART was conceived during the summer of 1945, when Eva Le Gallienne, Cheryl Crawford, and Margaret Webster were collaborating on a production of *The Tempest* as "unofficial" designer, producer, and director, respectively. During the weeks of production preparation, they discovered that they shared an interest in starting a repertory theatre. In fact, according to Webster, she and Le Gallienne – they had been friends for years – were "forever planning schemes for repertory theatres."[1] Each, of course, had a background in repertory theatre. Le Gallienne had successfully directed the Civic Repertory Theatre from 1926 until the Depression closed its doors in 1934. Webster had been raised in the tradition of English repertory. Crawford had cut her theatrical teeth with the Theatre Guild and, in addition, was a founding member of the Group Theatre. Repertory was for each the "ideal" theatrical organization. It was also a solution to their dissatisfactions with the then current state of the American theatre. In Crawford's words "only a repertory organization could take the theatre and actors out of mere 'show biz' and put them into the cultural haven they deserved." Repertory would be the "salvation" of the American theatre.[2]

Their ambitions were by no means unique at this particular time. With the end of the war, there seemed to be a renewed interest in developing a national theatre. The October 1945 issue of *Theatre Arts*, for example, carried a scheme for a Public Theatre Foundation and editorialized:

We need a National Theatre for many reasons, not least of them for the service it can render in the battle for better understanding. Already the process has started in Europe, the weaving of the healing warp and woof of intellectual as well as material exchange. England has sent its Old Vic company to play in the hallowed precincts of the Comédie Française, the Comédie has played London. But the United States has no method of inviting these artists to its shores, nor of sending a similarly high-calibre repertory, reflecting the best in our theatre, to the capitals of our Allies. Let us wait no longer. Surely, during the war, the individuals who make up the American Theatre have come of age. Surely they can now get together and launch a constructive National Theatre program.

As if in direct answer to this challenge, the next issue of *Theatre Arts* announced the formation of the American Repertory Theatre. Originally Webster and Le Gallienne wanted a theatre "away from the narrow, constrictive and appallingly expensive confines of Manhattan." Their grand scheme, influenced perhaps by the Federal Theatre Project, was "to establish a circuit of three (or more) repertory theatres, each having a different home base ... Washington or Baltimore, St. Louis or Milwaukee, San Francisco or Los Angeles; after a given number of weeks in their home city they would rotate to each other's theatres; thus giving the company year-round employment and the citizens year-round entertainment, with a variation of actors, plays, and production styles." They approached a number of actors with their idea and visited several cities to explore potential civic backing. But the response ranged from lukewarm to hostile.[3] Crawford, on the other hand, gravitated towards a repertory theatre in New York. Crawford's influence, coupled with lack of interest outside of New York, perhaps persuaded Le Gallienne and Webster to drop their original plan.

After *The Tempest* opened in November the trio set about in earnest to organize and finance their theatre. Crawford, by her own account, "did some quick figuring and came up with three hundred thousand dollars to mount six productions." In retrospect, she admitted that "a lot of guesswork went into this sum" and that it was predicated on winning certain concessions from the various theatrical unions who, if offered the promise of a full season's engagement, might be disposed to negotiate contracts favorable to the ART.[4]

The forming of the ART was given a considerable boost in November 1945 by a contribution of $100,000 from producer Joseph Verner Reed who had been associated with Webster's successful productions of *Richard II* (1937) and *Hamlet* (1938) starring Maurice Evans. The remaining required capital was raised, however, by direct solicitation. On the advice of various "financial wizards" they set up a "profit-making" corporation capitalized at $300,000. They printed a handsome prospectus describing their plans in detail and offering stock at $500 per share.[5] Webster wrote: "We worked like dogs. We wrote, we talked, we appealed."[6] In dribs and drabs the money trickled into the ART's coffers. Eventually they would raise $291,000 from 142 sponsors ranging from William Paley to a college fraternity. An additional $30,000 was raised from over 5,000 "patrons" who for a $6.00 contribution were to be given access to tickets in advance of the public and an invitation to a projected series of staged readings.[7] In July 1946, about four months before their opening, Crawford wrote Webster: "I find that I am tired, not physically, but my spiritual bin is empty from money-raising, money-cutting, glad-handing and the grinding repetitions of our aims." But she still had high hopes: "I'm looking forward to our work with such happy anticipation. I haven't felt this way since I started in the theatre when everything was glittering."[8]

Another major problem the organizers faced was recruiting actors. Several dozen leading American actors and actresses – "stars" – were proselytized for the company. Among those asked to join were Marlon Brando, José Ferrer, Maurice Evans, Barbara Bel Geddes, Hume Cronyn and Jessica Tandy, Judith Anderson, Vincent Price, Ida Lupino, Greer Garson, Tyrone Power, Susan Hayward, and Charles Laughton. According to Le Gallienne, Webster talked to Greer Garson about roles in *Antony and Cleopatra* and *School for Scandal*, although Webster herself seems to recall that it was Katharine Hepburn. Mary Martin was approached with *Caesar and Cleopatra*, and Lee J. Cobb with *The Merchant of Venice*.[9] All those solicited were interested in the idea of an American repertory theatre, but when told that the top salary was only five hundred dollars a week – half of what name performers could command in the theatre – and everyone was to sign for two seasons which would have prohibited lucrative film work, enthusiasm quickly waned.[10]

While many "stars" refused them, several accomplished theatre veterans and many rising young talents were eager to join the enterprise. Eventually, a permanent company of thirty-one members was assembled. Walter Hampden, Victor Jory, Ernest Truex, Richard Waring, Philip Bourneuf, and Le Gallienne headed the group. June Duprez, a young film actress, was recruited to play romantic leads.[11] Among the supporting players hired were Eli Wallach, Ann Jackson, William Windom and Efrem Zimbalist, Jr. all of whom would later achieve prominence in film, television, and theatre.

The ART faced still a third problem – finding a theatre. The number of Broadway theatres had been declining steadily since the beginning of the Depression. In 1945–46, for example, there were reportedly only thirty-six theatres. Yet in the latter years of the war the total number of New York productions had increased slightly and, perhaps more importantly, the average run for a show, musicals in particular, had increased significantly. Finding any theatre, much less one suitable to the objectives of the ART, was no simple task.[12]

They finally leased the International Theatre at 5 Columbus Circle, the present site of the New York Coliseum, fifteen blocks north of Broadway. The International was not ideal. Its seating capacity of about 1,100 was considered too small for a "popular theatre." Various producers had tried to reclaim it for the legitimate theatre, including the Shuberts and Ziegfeld, but it seemed simply too remote to attract audiences. In fact, performers sometimes called the International "The Artic Circle."[13] The International, however, had been renovated and handsomely redecorated in 1944 by its owner, the Marquis de Cuevas, to host a season of his International Company. Most importantly, the Marquis asked for a rental of only $2,200 a week, about one-third the average theatre rental at the time.[14]

The plan was to present six plays during the first season. The first three of these were to be rehearsed prior to opening and the others added by mid-season. But what plays? The directors thought that part of their purpose was to present the "neglected classics" which were unlikely to receive commercial productions. They also wanted plays which would allow each important actor in the company at least one worthwhile part suitable to their individual talents and abilities. Some prospective plays were rejected for social or political reasons. Webster and Le Gallienne, for example, pushed *The Merchant of Venice*, but Crawford rejected it because she feared it would antagonize the ART's prospective Jewish patrons. The directors finally compromised on Shakespeare's *Henry VIII*, Ibsen's *John Gabriel Borkman*, Barrie's *What Every Woman Knows*, and Shaw's *Androcles and the Lion*. A new play, preferably American, would be selected as the season progressed.[15]

In a March 1946 essay in *Theatre Arts* entitled "We Believe ...," the directors joined by Victor Jory formally announced a fall opening for the ART and enthusiastically summarized their goal: to create a model repertory theatre like the Comédie Française, the Moscow Art Theatre, or the Old Vic. Only in a repertory of this kind, they asserted, could artists and audiences grow and create a vital, dynamic theatre which cherished the dramatic heritage. They felt that the American actor, director, scene designer, critic, playwright, and spectator, wanted repertory theatre and would favorably respond to their project. Crawford even believed that if properly managed a repertory company could be financially profitable, independent of state or federal subsidy.[16]

In May the Old Vic company headed by Laurence Olivier, Ralph Richardson, Margaret Leighton, and Joyce Redman played a six-week engagement in New York, presenting 1 and 2 *Henry IV*, *Uncle Vanya*, and, on a double bill, *Oedipus the King* and Sheridan's *The Critic*. Critical reception was generally warm, often enthusiastic, although George Jean Nathan described *Henry IV* as "second-rate" and *Uncle Vanya* "sorely lacking." On balance, he thought that the Old Vic was "an only fairish troupe headed by the competent and commendable Olivier and at times competent and commendable Richardson, along with a few serviceable supporting players, and on the whole nothing to set the Thames or the Hudson on fire."[17] The tour, however, had been carefully promoted and managed, so that every performance played to capacity despite Nathan's lukewarm response. In fact, the engagement returned a modest unanticipated

9   Scene from *Henry VIII*, design by David Ffolkes, with Victor Jory as Henry.
International Theatre, New York, 1946

profit to both the Old Vic and their American sponsors.[18] Later the
principals of the ART were apprised in detail of "the appalling
expense, the union demands, and other problems which could have
turned the Old Vic's visit into a disaster." At the time, however,
ignorant of these problems they were greatly encouraged by the Old
Vic's reception. As Webster remembers, "the outlook for classical
repertory seemed good."[19]

In August rehearsals began and on 20 September the ART
previewed *Henry VIII* in Princeton. The company then played for
two weeks in Philadelphia where *What Every Woman Knows* was
added to the repertory. *John Gabriel Borkman* was added during a
three-week preview in Boston. Finally after a year of planning and
preparation on 6 November the ART opened in New York with
*Henry VIII*; *What Every Woman Knows* was added on 8 November; and
*John Gabriel Borkman* was added on 12 November. Each play was
then rotated in repertory for three or four consecutive performances
at a time.

Perhaps because of pre-opening encouragement from many critics, or because of the reception accorded the Old Vic, or because of an inflated assessment of their own achievement, the directors expected an enthusiastic, or at least a sympathetic, critical reception. They were clearly disappointed. Crawford described the notices as "discouraging." The critics, she wrote, who had been "wild" about the Old Vic seemed to have "no understanding or appreciation of the repertory idea."[20] Le Gallienne labeled the notices as "lukewarm." She complained also that "the company was judged each time on the basis of its work in the particular play under review, with no relation to its work in general."[21] This assessment was echoed by Webster, who, rereading the reviews twenty-five years after the fact, still thought that the critics viewed each production "as if it had been done by quite different actors in quite distinct theatres."[22]

Perceptions, however, are often shaped by expectations and personal biases. An objective examination of the reviews does not support the view that they were always "lukewarm," or "discouraging" nor were the critics particularly neglectful of the "repertory angle." The reviews were not all good, but neither were they all bad. On the whole, they were judicious assessments of the merits and shortcomings of the ART's productions.[23]

Some critics were, with some justification, critical of the plays. For example, John Mason Brown thought *Henry* "a tedious work, unresolved, spotty, meagre even in its poetry ... hardly more than a procession of woes and reports of court political knavery." Brooks Atkinson of the *New York Times* also complained about the sentimentality and "pawky humor" of *What Every Woman Knows*, and disliked *Borkman* for its "oppressive zombie-like atmosphere."

These negative views were balanced, however, by many notices of high praise for the productions as a whole, even some critics who had reservations about the worth of the plays. Stark Young, for example, praised *Henry* as "generous and fresh, full of energy, competence and sincerity, and supported by able acting and able directing."[24] Atkinson concluded ultimately that the production of *What Every Woman Knows* was "as good as reading an urbane novel by the fireside on a cold night with a scuttle of bourbon near by." He also wrote that *Borkman* was "a vibrant production with the rhythm of a dance of death and tone of a song of doom. With the parts beautifully modulated and the pace swift and biting, the performance is a work in black magic ... Only reckless playgoers will want to miss it."[25]

The critics universally admired the sumptuous beauty and atmospheric effectiveness of the settings and costumes. David Ffolkes's Holbeinesque, gold encrusted decor for *Henry*, for which he would later receive a "Tony Award," received frequent commendation. Nathan, who disliked almost everything about all three productions, conceded his admiration for Paul Morrison's gloomy setting for *Borkman* and his charming interior for *What Every Woman Knows*.

Waring, Bourneuf, Hampden and Truex were often praised for their various performances. Jory and Le Gallienne received occasional drubbings, but also many positive notices. In his most vituperative style, Nathan attacked Jory's Henry as a "mere recitational exercise punctuated alternately with corporeal wobbles and stern stances." Le Gallienne's Katherine, he wrote, "suggested less Henry's queen than an ambitious and hard-working ingenue handicapped by an emotional equipment that stops and is dried up between the tongue and the trachea."[26] But Howard Barnes of the *New York Herald Tribune* thought Le Gallienne's Katherine "sensitive and splendid" and "masterly," while Jory was "regally ominous" as Henry. Atkinson complained that Le Gallienne was "overacting" as the Comtesse de la Brière in *What Every Woman Knows*, but Arthur Pollock of the *Brooklyn Eagle* thought that she had "never played with so light a spirit or provided an audience more pleasure." Louis Kronenberger of *P.M.* compared Jory's *Borkman* to "some embittered old school tragedian," but many agreed with Atkinson who thought that it would establish Jory "as a stage actor of first-rate quality." In fact, for the most part, Jory, Le Gallienne, and Webster were acclaimed for their performances in *Borkman*.

Le Gallienne writes that the critics were "unnecessarily hard" on Duprez's Maggie in *What Every Woman Knows*, particularly so in comparing it to the notable portrayals of Maude Adams in 1908 and Helen Hayes in 1926.[27] Many critics were clearly unimpressed with her performance. Nathan, probably the only critic to have seen on stage both Maude Adams and Helen Hayes, observed that Duprez was "nowhere even within hailing distance" of either. Several other critics alluded to the Hayes and Adams portrayals, but only Nathan made a direct comparison. Le Gallienne's contention that the "reviews consisted almost entirely of panegyrics in praise of Maude Adams and Helen Hayes" is inaccurate.[28] In fact, several critics liked Duprez's Maggie. Robert Garland, writing in the *Journal American*, thought Duprez was "outstanding," while Barnes called her an "ingratiating, glowing, human Maggie." Atkinson praised her "excellent performance, well-balanced between personal modesty and guile."

There is no evidence to support, moreover, the contention that the critics neglected the "repertory idea." Many critics related the productions and performances to each other. For example, Atkinson concluded in his review of *What Every Woman Knows*:

After the panoply of *Henry VIII* the performance of the Barrie play begins to give us some notion about the capacity of this repertory company. Let it be said at once that it is going to be all right.

Richard Cooke of *The Wall Street Journal* in his review of *What Every Woman Knows* noted that in his estimation "repertory advanced Duprez and Truex and slowed down Le Gallienne." Robert Coleman, of *The Daily Mirror* who had criticized Le Gallienne for her "fidgety tricks" as the Comtesse de la Brière, noted their absence in her "admirably economical" portrayal of Ella Rentheim. Richard Watts, Jr., of *The Post* who had complained that in *Henry VIII* the ART "did not get off to the most exhilarating of starts" thought that with *Borkman* the company proved "worthy of the hopes that had been placed in it." Nathan's reviews were consistently censorious, but they also reveal his acute awareness of the "repertory idea." His first review of the ART simultaneously treated, for example, both *Henry VIII* and *What Every Woman Knows*. His review of *Borkman* – albeit negative – concluded: "On the whole a misguided interpretation and one that arouses increased qualms as to the repertory competencies of the company." Brown, Young and Joseph Wood Krutch also tended to review the ART's productions in the context of "repertory."[29]

On 19 December *Androcles and the Lion* with Sean O'Casey's one-act comedy *Pound on Demand* as a "curtain raiser," were introduced into the repertory. Wolfgang Roth's striking, colorful expressionistic settings captured the jaunty humor of *Androcles* and the company headed by Truex as Androcles, Duprez as Lavinia, Jory as Ferrovius, and Bourneuf as Caesar, delighted both audiences and critics. Krutch, echoing his colleagues, wrote that the performance was "very nearly perfect, a sheer delight." Only Nathan was condemnatory, writing that *Androcles* was like watching "amateurs at a first rehearsal."

10   Scene from *Androcles and the Lion*, design by Wolfgang Roth, with Ernest Truex
as Androcles. International Theatre, New York, 1946

Le Gallienne also attributed the ART's eventual failure to lack of
union cooperation. The directors had begun negotiations with Local
No. 1 of IATSE in April asking them to base the permanent crew of
stagehands on the minimum required for any production as had
been the case at Le Gallienne's essentially "off-Broadway" Civic
Repertory Theatre. The union, however, had no guidelines for a
Broadway repertory operation. According to Webster the union
officials "listened and gave no answer." In fact, they did not give the
ART a final decision until three weeks before the New York
opening. Although the union conceded a one-hour rather than a
three-hour additional crew call every time the show changed, they
ruled that the ART had to employ the maximum number of men in
each department in every show, whether they were needed or not:

It happened that *Henry* needed more "grips" than the other two shows,
*What Every Woman Knows* more prop men and *Borkman* an additional

electrician. So we had to employ the *Henry* grips, *What Every Woman Knows* props and *Borkman* electrics for every production. When it came to *Androcles*, we were paying eight unnecessary men at every performance.[30]

Similarly Local 802 of the AFM imposed more musicians than was necessary for *Androcles*. *Henry*, for example, was classified a "drama with music" with eight required musicians. ART's directors had planned for this, but they had not anticipated that *Androcles* also would be classified as a "drama with music" because of a waltz played for the dance of Androcles and the Lion and a few trumpet calls and required to carry eight musicians as well.[31]

In all, by the time *Androcles* opened, union requirements had added about $1,275.00 more to the weekly operating costs than Crawford had originally projected.[32] As Webster noted this was not "an astronomical figure, but just about equal to the combined salaries of Crawford, Le Gallienne, Webster, and Hampden." In the interests of the ART, the directors and some of the featured per-formers were working for about $300 a week, far below their actual earning power. Under these circumstances, that union workers were unwilling, or unable, to make similar sacrifices was particularly galling to them.[33]

Le Gallienne also blamed the unions for the excessive costs of the productions, including an exorbitant $40,000 for the lavish costumes for *Henry VIII*. Items such as simple, soft black velvet caps worn by the judges during the trial scene cost $25 apiece simply because, according to Le Gallienne, they had to go through the hands of three different unions before completion. In any place but New York, she wrote, the costumes "could have been made with equal excellence for one-third the cost."[34] The ART, however, was a New York company, operating under New York conditions. The union requirements and labor costs were not imposed inequitably on the ART. One union official, undoubtedly reflecting the view of the various theatrical unions as a whole, defended their demands as "reasonable."[35]

According to an itemization in the Webster Papers, the first four productions cost a total of $165,000. *Androcles* reportedly cost $25,000. The exact costs for the other productions are not given, but dividing the balance would indicate an average cost of about $46,300 each, comparatively high for the period considering the types of plays being presented. Added to the production costs was an expenditure of $70,780 for repairs to the theatre, the purchase of lighting equipment and a Hammond organ, presumably for *Henry VIII*, and insurance for personnel and the theatre, bringing the total pre-opening costs to almost $236,000. The operating loss for the out-of-town tryouts, moreover, was $30,765. Crawford maintained that since certain physical items could be used in subsequent productions, amortization would eventually reduce overall costs, but over a quarter of a million dollars was a sizeable initial outlay, far greater than the average for the most complicated, lavish productions of the era.[36]

Crawford originally estimated the weekly operating costs at about $16,000. A note in the Webster Papers reveals that the first three weeks of performances grossed almost $54,000 or an average of slightly more than $2,500 a performance. This would indicate a weekly "profit" of only about $2,000. At that rate it would have taken over two years to recoup the investment. With the introduction of *Androcles* in the repertory, however, as noted above, operating costs rose to almost $18,000 a week, mainly because of the unanticipated union requirements. Moreover, although attendance records are unknown, the demand for tickets, after the opening weeks, clearly dwindled. By 11 January the operating loss in New York was reportedly $45,332 with a projected operating loss for the current week. The ART had spent or encumbered all of its capitalization and continued operating losses were certain.[37]

There was little that could be done to significantly reduce operating expenditures, so the directors explored increasing income by (1) raising ticket prices, (2) increasing audience attendance, and (3) soliciting contributions. Instead of increasing prices, Le Gallienne, however, who had always thought they were too high, argued with Crawford that they should be reduced to attract a larger "popular" audience. The ART's ticket prices, ranging from $4.80 to $1.20 on weekends and from $4.20 to $1.20 on weekdays (except on opening nights when the range was from $7.50 to $2.40), were, however, about average for a Broadway attraction and less than the $6.65 top ticket price for straight shows on Broadway in the 1946–47 season. Le Gallienne and Crawford finally reached a compromise. They offered a reduced price for a series of tickets to all four productions.[38] It did not, however, significantly increase attendance or revenues. As Jack Poggi has pointed out the demand for theatre tickets tends to remain "inelastic" – e.g., attendance does not generally go up when prices are lowered or go down when they are raised.[39] In an effort to attract larger audiences, the ART abandoned repertory and presented *Androcles*, their most popular production, for a run. They also solicited contributions and eventually received over $26,000 from private and organizational donors, including $5,000 from Equity.

With part of this money, on 27 February, they made a feeble effort to recapture their original plan by mounting not a new play but a revival of Sidney Howard's *Yellow Jack*. It was generally well received by the critics, but the public still did not come in sufficient numbers to warrant its continuance. It closed after twenty performances.

Why wasn't the ART attracting larger audiences? It is unlikely that the so-called remoteness of the International Theatre was a factor. Three subway lines and numerous buses stopped literally at the theatre's door. The Century Theatre, moreover, located only a few blocks away on Seventh Avenue between Fifty-eighth and Fifty-ninth Streets, was a commercially successful house which had hosted several repertory companies, including the Old Vic.[40] Ticket prices may have been too high, but as Webster observed, there did not appear to be a demand for their cheap seats.[41] Other productions were successful with ticket prices equal to or greater than the ART's prices. Repertory scheduling may have been viewed as an inconvenience to prospective ticket buyers, especially buyers accustomed to the established Broadway single-production, long-run system. Repertory instead of promoting audience development, actually worked against it. Almost thirty years later, Walter Kerr, tracing the demise of both the A.P.A. and the Lincoln Center Repertory Company observed that in New York "repertory kills repertory."[42] The choice of plays, moreover, was crucial. Krutch, rightly I think, called them "worthy second-best," and asked for more plays of "brilliance, passion, and power." Barnes called them "an odd assortment of wares" and asked for plays to warrant public enthusiasm, "plays of enchantment." Atkinson in a special essay in the Sunday *New York Times* (3 March 1947) called them insufficiently popular for an institution dependent on public support. In the context of the times, an audience that had gone through a traumatic economic depression, followed by World War II, was not in the mood for the vapid regal panoply of *Henry VIII* or the philosophical gloom of *Borkman*. The "heroism" of physicians battling malaria was faint, in comparison, to the countless heroes of the war. "Rosie the

Riveter" may have found *What Every Woman Knows* hopelessly old-fashioned if not anti-feminist. *Androcles*, on the other hand, with its charming, witty, clever, but intellectually unpretentious plot and humor was closer to post-war euphoria.

Le Gallienne, Truex, Jory, Waring, and Hampden were talented, and capable performers, but they did not generate the kind of "star" quality that motivated audiences to flock to see Laurence Olivier or the many stars then appearing on Broadway or in the movies. Atkinson, for example, wrote (in the 3 March article cited above) that the ART company "overshadowed by middle aged actors" was competent in "an academic style," but unexciting. Moreover, they had been unable to demonstrate "that repertory acting results in performances superior to the old huckstering method that has created the brilliant performances for *The Iceman Cometh, Joan of Lorraine, Another Part of the Forest, All My Sons*, and *John Loves Mary* to cite some of the best group performances on Broadway."

One also must consider that the large "popular" audience which the ART hoped to attract did not in reality exist, at least not for "classical theatre." As early as 2 January 1947 Webster realized that their audience was "a cheap-price public, not a public of ... 'carriages'" and that "their number is no longer great enough to make the kind of shows they like pay off."[43] Both Moore and Poggi have suggested that a major restraint on play going, however, is not a limited audience with limited money, but rather the quality of the productions. Poggi has argued that historically audiences demand "the very best" actors, authors, directors, and productions. "The very best" is limited, not the audiences. Shows of "high quality," regardless of the ticket price, find a public.[44] Historically, for example, "classic" plays have never fared well on the modern Broadway stage except when given "high quality" productions with "star" actors.

The ART did not provide the "very best" plays or actors then available. This becomes strikingly evident, I believe, when the ART's program is viewed in comparison to their competition in the season of 1946–47. It was a season of superb revivals on Broadway including *Cyrano de Bergerac* with José Ferrer (193 performances); *Lady Windermere's Fan* with Cornelia Otis Skinner (228 performances); and *The Playboy of the Western World* with Burgess Meredith (81 performances). As noted above, there were also a number of outstanding productions of new plays, including O'Neill's *The*

*Iceman Cometh* (136 performances); Coward's *Present Laughter* with Clifton Webb (158 performances); Anderson's *Joan of Lorraine* with Ingrid Bergman (199 performances); Hellman's *Another Part of the Forest* (182 performances) and Miller's *All My Sons* (142 performances). *Annie Get Your Gun, Carousel, Show Boat, Lute Song, Brigadoon, Finian's Rainbow*, and *Street Scene* led a notable list of new musicals and musical revivals. The Lunts were in *O'Mistress Mine*, Helen Hayes in *Happy Birthday*, Judy Holliday in *Born Yesterday* and Frank Fay in *Harvey*. In March, John Gielgud successfully revived *The Importance of Being Earnest* for the Theatre Guild with a stellar English company. Lastly, on Broadway at the Golden Theatre, Olivier's film version of *Henry V* played throughout the winter. With such competition, the ART must have seemed, and to a large extent was, second-rate by comparison.

The ART also may have lacked from the start a clearly defined purpose or mission. Le Gallienne, for example, seems to have wanted "a popular theatre at popular prices" like her Civic Repertory Theatre. She and Webster, as noted above, wanted to locate outside of New York altogether. Crawford, on the other hand, wanted a commercial, Broadway theatre. She wanted to compete with, in fact to best, Broadway on its own terms. Webster even reports that she often served as a buffer between the conflicting objectives of Le Gallienne and Crawford.[45] Among the three, there was mutual respect, cooperation and compromise, but no genuine consensus as to the aims and objectives of the ART. Cooperation and compromise is not vision.

A confusion of purpose can be seen in the choice of "neglected" classics which, nevertheless, were mounted in a lavish, Broadway fashion. The ART was to be an "alternative theatre," but, at least initially, with a company of "stars." Webster even admits that they wanted "stars" mainly to impress the critics.[46] This goal was no different from any other commercial Broadway producer. Generally, the history of the modern stage has demonstrated that successful theatre companies have been led by forceful, single managers or sometimes by a harmonious partnership of an actor or actress and a director. The ART's managerial structure diffused authority, weakening the potential for strong leadership and the ability to effectively respond to crises. It was not a management for an artistically and economically risky enterprise.[47]

Following the closing of *Yellow Jack*, Le Gallienne's popular Civic

Repertory production of *Alice in Wonderland* was revived in a last ditch effort to keep the ART alive. It opened on 5 April and was deemed an unqualified popular and critical success. On 15 May *Alice* was moved to the Majestic Theatre where it ran for almost 100 performances closing on 28 June. But despite this fairly long run, it did not pay back its production costs of over $80,000. On 10 June Crawford resigned from the ART. After the closing of *Alice*, Webster and Le Gallienne struggled on for almost a year trying to "resuscitate the enterprise in some form or other" but finally they too admitted defeat and dissolved the ART in May 1948.[48]

In retrospect, the ART's directors simply attempted too much, too quickly, in the wrong venue. Blinded by their own idealism, the directors underestimated the problems and misjudged the initial enthusiasm of their colleagues and the public which in turn prompted the commission of several serious and irreversible artistic, organizational, and financial errors. Others – notably the A.P.A. and the Lincoln Center Repertory Theatre – would try and fail for very much the same reasons. Le Gallienne observed that "given time and a chance to grow," the ART may have succeeded in contributing something of lasting value to the American theatre.[49] In the crucible of the commercial Broadway theatre with its high economic risks and competitive pressures, however, there was far too little time, and very few opportunities to grow.

A generation later, of course, Webster and Le Gallienne's original dream of a circuit of repertory theatres located in various cities outside of New York began to be realized to a certain extent with the establishment of a collection of nonprofit regional resident theatres. With the exception, however, of a few "festival" theatres or occasions – the Oregon Shakespeare Festival or the Actors Theatre of Louisville's Humana Festival of New American Plays – not even these regional theatres have been able to sustain, principally for economic reasons, resident companies or a true rotating repertory schedule. Repertory theatre remains an artistic ideal, but without substantial subsidization from governmental, private, or corporate sources, it remains economically unrealistic.[50]

## NOTES

1 Margaret Webster, *Don't Put Your Daughter On the Stage* (New York: Alfred A. Knopf, 1972), 108.
2 Cheryl Crawford, *One Naked Individual* (New York: Bobbs-Merrill Co., 1977), 150.

3 Webster, *Don't Put*, 150–51.

4 Crawford, *One Naked Individual*, 150–52.

5 A copy of the prospectus is in the Webster Papers at the Library of Congress in Washington, DC.

6 Webster, *Don't Put*, 154.

7 A partial list of contributors is included in the Webster Papers. Crawford reported the total contributions in the *New York Times*, 3 November 1946, 1–2. See also Crawford, *One Naked Individual*, 152–53; Eva La Gallienne, *With a Quiet Heart* (New York: The Viking Press, 1953), 249; and Webster, *Don't Put*, 154.

8 Crawford, *One Naked Individual*, 152. Crawford's typescript letter is in the Webster Papers, Library of Congress.

9 In a letter in the Webster Papers to Brooks Atkinson, dated 3 March [1946], Webster listed the names of thirty-seven prominent actors and actresses taken at random from her files. She noted that "a hell of a lot more" were solicited. See also Webster, *Don't Put*, 157; Le Gallienne, *With a Quiet Heart*, 252–54.

10 Crawford, *One Naked Individual*, 151–52.

11 Duprez, the daughter of the American comedian Fred Duprez (1884–1938), had been a featured player in several Korda brothers films in the late 1930s and early 1940s, including *The Four Feathers* (1939) and *The Thief of Bagdad* (1941). In 1944 she had appeared with distinction in Clifford Odets's film *None But the Lonely Heart* which starred Cary Grant and Ethel Barrymore. Her stage experience, however, was limited to a few appearances in minor roles when she was a teenager. But her talent had been touted by Odets, so the directors took a chance and offered her a contract. See Le Gallienne, *With a Quiet Heart*, 257–58.

12 See Thomas Gale Moore, *The Economics of the American Theatre* (Durham, NC: Duke University Press, 1968), 147–48, 152–54. An editorial in *Theatre Arts* (September 1946), 500, complained about the shortage of Broadway theatres.

13 Mary C. Henderson, *The City and The Theatre* (Clifton, NJ: James T. White and Company, 1973), 175.

14 Le Gallienne (*With a Quiet Heart*, 251–52) wrote that the rental was $70,000 a year. According to Moore (*Economics*, 58 and 155) the average weekly theatre share at this time was about $7,000 in 1966 dollars, while the average total seasonal theatre income was about $90,000 in 1966 dollars. The figure of $2,200 a week was taken from a schedule of running costs in the Webster Papers.

15 Webster, *Don't Put*, 157; Le Gallienne, *With a Quiet Heart*, 258–59.

16 Cheryl Crawford and Victor Jory, Eva Le Gallienne and Margaret Webster, "We Believe ..." *Theatre Arts* (March 1946), 176–78.

17 George Gene Nathan, *Theatre Book of the Year: 1946–1947* (New York: Alfred A. Knopf, 1947), 3–12.

18 Edward Choate and John F. Matthews, "The Old Vic: The Statistics," *Theatre Arts* (November 1946), 643–45.

19 Webster, *Don't Put*, 152. In her memoirs Crawford (*One Naked Indi-vidual*, 150, 153–54) erroneously places the Old Vic visit in 1944 rather than 1946. She infers, moreover, that this visit was a major impetus for initiating plans for the ART when in actuality the plans preceded the Old Vic visit by at least a year. Her error suggests, however, that the Old Vic's successes significantly influenced her projections for the ART's success.

20 Crawford, *One Naked Individual*, 153–54.

21 Le Gallienne, *With a Quiet Heart*, 269–73.

22 Webster, *Don't Put*, 161–63.

23 Reviews of ART productions from New York daily newspapers are collected in *The New York Theatre Critics' Reviews* (1946), 217–70. Reviewers for weekly journals are cited separately. Nathan's reviews for the *Journal American* are collected in the *Theatre Book of the Year: 1946–1947*, 156–58, 169, 232.

24 Stark Young, *New Republic* (25 November 1946), 694–95.

25 See *The New York Theatre Critics' Reviews* (1946), 217–70.

26 Nathan, *Theatre Book*, 156–58.

27 Le Gallienne, *With a Quiet Heart*, 269.

28 Ibid.

29 See John Mason Brown, "That Magic Word," *Saturday Review of Literature*, 30 November 1946, 28–29; Joseph Wood Krutch, *The Nation*, 15 March 1947, 313. See also Robert Porterfield and Robert Breen, "Towards a National Theatre," *Theatre Arts* (October 1945), 599–602, and Robert Brustein, "Where Are the Repertory Critics" in *Critical Moments: Reflections on Theatre and Society, 1973–1979* (New York: Random House, 1980).

30 Webster, *Don't Put*, 165.

31 Ibid.; Le Gallienne, *With a Quiet Heart*, 273–74.

32 A report in the Webster Papers from John Yorke, business manager of the ART, lists the unnecessary weekly labor costs as Local #1 of IATSE, $720; APTAM, $115; and Local 802 of the AFM, $391. Taxes added another $49 a week.

33 The figure of $300 a week is taken from an "Outline of Financial Position" in the Webster Papers. The prospectus for the ART noted that Crawford and Webster "had been receiving average monies of around $50,000 a year" while Le Gallienne's "usual acting salary is $1,000 against 10 percent of the total gross receipts" – per week one assumes. Choate and Matthews reported that Olivier and Richardson received $400 a week, plus $75 a week for expenses during the Old Vic's New York engagement, which was more than their London guarantee, but did not include any percentage of the gross as did their London arrangements.

34 Le Gallienne, *With a Quiet Heart*, 263.

35 In an article in the *New York Times*, Charles R. Iucci, secretary of Local

No. 802 AFM, defended the hiring of one additional, if unnecessary, musician for *Androcles and the Lion*. It was not, he wrote, "the result of some caprice of whim" but "an honest effort to protect the rights of musicians without injury to the employer or the stage." Clipping in the Webster Papers.

36 See Tino Balio and Robert G. McLaughlin, "The Economic Dilemma of the Broadway Theatre," *Educational Theatre Journal* (March 1969), 81–100. Using Balio and McLaughlin's tables, a production like *Borkman* probably cost about $21,000 in the period 1941–45, while a production like *Henry VIII* probably cost about $45,000. In the period 1946–55, a very complex fullscale musical cost about $167,000. Moore (*Economics*, 48) has estimated that the average production costs for the period 1939–42 in 1966 dollars was $62,192. Notes in the Webster Papers report that the Theatre Guild's 1944 production of *Othello*, directed by Webster, cost $50,057.94, while Webster's production of *The Tempest* in 1945 cost $47,235.37. *Carousel* which opened on 19 April 1945 reportedly cost about $180,000 while *South Pacific* (1949) cost about $225,000. See Abe Laufe, *Broadway's Greatest Musicals*, rev. ed. (New York: Funk and Wagnalls, 1977).

37 See Crawford, *One Naked Individual*, 154; Webster, *Don't Put*, 164; Webster Papers.

38 Le Gallienne, *With a Quiet Heart*, 267; Webster, *Don't Put*, 166.

39 Jack Poggi, *Theatre in America: The Impact of Economic Forces, 1870–1967* (Ithaca, NY: Cornell University Press, 1968), 93–94.

40 Henderson, *City*, 175, 223.

41 Webster, *Don't Put*, 166.

42 Walter Kerr, "Repertory was the Impossible Dream," *New York Times Magazine*, 25 February 1973, 36–37, 39, 41, 43.

43 Webster, *Don't Put*, 171–72.

44 Moore, *Economics*, 13–16, 90–93, 165–75; Poggi, *Theatre*, 86–88.

45 Webster, *Don't Put*, 166.

46 Ibid., 154

47 In her letter of resignation now in the Webster Papers and quoted in part by Webster (*Don't Put*, 169), Crawford wrote that she was leaving the ART because she was both "artistically and managerially" dissatisfied: "My position on both sides is that of advisor, suggestor, consultant, but in no way final in any decision. And that is very unsatisfying to me. If I have to be responsible for a result, I want to feel responsible for what caused that result, good or bad. This is in no way a criticism of you. You have both earned the right to pick the plays you wish to do, to cast them and produce them according to your own conceptions. In fact, I see no other way in which you could work satisfactorily, but I have very little part in this and don't even believe that a person in my position should have. Only I don't want that person to be me. In the purely business end, which is not my sole interest, I feel

a similar lack of authority. My profound admiration and respect for both of you may keep me from asserting myself even to a degree that you could accept but I never could be a fighter against you because I feel your own artistic integrity and knowledge too strongly and besides, I am never sure that I am solely right. It occurs to me that I am not *strong* enough to work with partners, that I can only be decisive and properly executive when I have to make up my mind alone and stand or fall by that decision. And I don't see how the greatest good will or best intentions can overcome this."

48  Webster, *Don't Put*, 170.
49  Le Gallienne, *With a Quiet Heart*, 277.
50  To the best of my knowledge, the Missouri Repertory Theatre was the last major regional theatre to attempt to maintain a resident company and rotating repertory schedule. The MRT abandoned these practices, however, in 1984.

# CHAPTER 16

# Sojourning in Never Never Land: the idea of Hollywood in recent theatre autobiographies

*Thomas Postlewait*

## THE THEATRE OF INTEGRITY

Over the last two decades, a number of the major figures who shaped American drama and theatre between 1930 and 1970 have published their autobiographies and personal manifestos: Tennessee Williams, Arthur Miller, Lillian Hellman, Lee Strasberg, Harold Clurman, Cheryl Crawford, John Houseman, Robert Lewis, and Elia Kazan. Although these narratives vary greatly in method and purpose – and sometimes contradict one another on key issues – they still provide vital testimony on modern American theatre. When read collectively, they offer us a sense of an era, a record of some of the most important accomplishments and most persistent values in the period.

Perhaps, in attempting to define this era, the most obvious place to begin is with the familiar topic of realism, especially since a number of these people argued over how best to implement and achieve a realistic theatre. To be expected, this realistic agenda receives a certain amount of attention in these autobiographies (e.g., the Group Theatre's endeavors, Strasberg's method acting, Hellman's justifications for her dramatic style and content).[1] But overall most of these key figures (e.g., Lewis, Houseman, Williams, and even Kazan and Miller), looking back at their careers, do not make much of this heritage.[2] If anything, they attempt to distance themselves from realism and naturalism. Yet they do not spell out a clear alternative to realism, except to praise style, imagination, mood, and spirit – vague concepts that suggest a rather unsystematic aesthetic philosophy. In practice, these various artists took an eclectic or pragmatic approach to theatre, modifying and enhancing realism with borrowings from the various styles and ideas of the modernist movements of Europe. But no single idea of the American theatre emerges in these autobiographies.

If we wish to identify a more substantial cultural tradition that these theatre artists shared, we need to turn from aesthetics to social beliefs and programs. Though different from one another in many ways, the group of them were loosely joined by a set of shared progressive values. Sometimes this progressivism was little more than a sentiment, expressed as sympathy for the suffering of others. But at their best, these artists showed a heartfelt allegiance to principles of social justice and individual dignity. In various ways, for each of them, a sense of personal integrity depended upon this allegiance. Consequently, in theatre organizations, plays, productions, essays, and comments, they struggled to find and maintain a balance between reformist and civil-libertarian values. For example, even Williams, perhaps the least political-minded of the group (or, we should say, the one most focused on the civil-libertarian issues), could announce in his memoir that he sought a change in the human spirit, "an enlightened form of socialism, I would suppose."[3] For some of the others, including Hellman, Miller, and Kazan, the leftist politics of the 1930s contributed to their progressive outlook. Yet we should note that Marxism and communism were usually less definitive than the American traditions of liberal democracy and social reform.

In general terms, then, these theatre people shared a set of progressive values that took shape during the Depression and World War II, then were applied and modified during the Cold War. Yet despite this condition of being part of a social, political, and artistic community, each of these figures came to see himself or herself not simply as an individual but as an outsider. More specifically, each of them grew up with a spirit of rebellion or a sense of isolation that often took the form of an acute awareness of gender, racial, ethnic, or sexual identity (e.g., homosexuality for Williams, female identity for Hellman, Jewish identity for Miller, Greek heritage for Kazan, polygot national confusion for Houseman). Not so surprisingly, while some of them are quite explicit about these issues (e.g., Williams, Kazan), others are strikingly silent, thus inviting our conjectures (e.g., Lewis, Crawford). And some use their autobiographies to evade or mask certain aspects of these issues (e.g., Strasberg, Clurman, Hellman).

What the autobiographies do reveal, both explicitly and impli-

citly, is a dilemma that develops out of these personal and progressive values. That is, each person, while attempting to honor a
commitment to progressive and communal values, discovered that
demands of personal integrity often made commitment impossible.
This dilemma is a recurring theme in the autobiographies. Often, as
we know, group loyalties fractured when set against the personal
code of independence. Even Crawford, the one most given to
accommodation and mediation, thought of herself as "One Naked
Individual," the title of her autobiography.[4] Fittingly, her favorite
writers were Thoreau and Whitman – the perfect American heritage
for the double bind of the spirit of individualism and the romance of
community.

Out of the dynamic relation between progressive values and a
personal sense of revolt or alienation, there emerges for each of them
an abiding attitude or mindset: an almost compulsive need to
declare and defend one's personal integrity. Given this imperative,
all of them feel obliged (to greater and lesser degrees) to spell out the
occasions and conditions when they not only maintained their own
integrity (sometimes identified exclusively with selfhood, sometimes
extended to the group) but also achieved honor (often confused with
fame). Even when John Houseman, calling himself a "chameleon,"
denies this concern (suggesting that fame and fortune served as the
motivating factors in his behavior), the denial becomes a record of
the issue's importance:

No one who has read this or my earlier book [*Run-Through*] can fairly
accuse me of altruism. For close to fifty years my personal and professional
lives have been inseparable: in neither have moral considerations played a
dominant part. Most of my choices in life have been motivated by expedi-
ency or by instinctive impulses stimulated by fear; the rest have been
determined by accidents and conjunctions in which I have been usually
fortunate. If I seem to have devoted more time than most people in my
profession to public service (such as the Federal Theatre of the W.P.A. and
the Voice of America), it was not out of patriotism or from a sense of duty
but because those were, at the time, the best and the most stimulating jobs
available.[5]

Of course, when Houseman makes the argument that the achievements of the Mercury Theatre were as significant as those of the
Group Theatre, he shows that he is quite concerned with maintaining his honor, based upon service to the principle of repertory
theatre production. This principle carries forward, rather consist-

ently for him, through the American Shakespeare Festival Theatre to the Juilliard Music School Drama Division and the Juilliard Acting Company.

On those occasions when these figures are not reporting on their own integrity (or lamenting the lack thereof), they are often commenting on the suspect integrity of others. The best of people, at key moments, are often found wanting. For example, Elia Kazan's famous testimony before the House Un-American Activities Committee (HUAC) is a crucial test case not only for Kazan himself but for almost everyone else. The HUAC hearings, which Hellman calls "scoundrel time," become a morality play, the essential test of character for most of these people. Sooner or later in the struggle for integrity, the issue of betrayal of either self or others must be faced.

In a collective way, therefore, these autobiographies delineate a social mentality and rhetoric that we might call "Integrity and Its Discontents" or, perhaps, "Integrity under Siege." A period in American theatre culture can be identified by this attitude, which manifests itself in various conditions: the attempts at repertory theatre, the confrontations with HUAC, the struggles with Broadway commercialism, the temptations of Hollywood. In order to focus this essay, I want to look at this last condition: the lure of Hollywood. I am interested less in the specific details of each individual's experiences in Hollywood than in the way the idea of the place functions in these personal narratives. This "never never land," as Crawford calls it, was always more than a mere job opportunity, always more than just a location. Like the show trials of HUAC, Hollywood was a testing place for character, a measure of one's integrity. It was a way-station in an American mystery play.

## THE TEMPTATIONS OF FAME AND SEX

Theatre autobiographies are commodities in the culture of fame. They are also, each in its own way, testimonials of personal achievement. In the period under examination, the achievement is usually charted as a struggle of art against commercialization, of personal integrity against the betrayal of one's talent (a threat that comes from within or without). This recurring conflict can be described as a series of dualistic choices: group commitment versus personal ambition, artistic achievement versus commercial success, noble poverty versus greed, the stage versus film, New York versus Hollywood, nonprofit theatre versus Broadway, acknowledging one's heritage versus denying one's roots, anti-fascism versus pro-communism, freedom of conscience versus conformity to the group.

These individual choices may seem to set up a neat, uncompli-cated opposition between right and wrong, but when more than one pair comes into play they can also create a dilemma, a counter-balance between two positive or two negative choices. Thus, we should note that the list begins with *group commitment*, surely a worthy value, versus *personal ambition*, potentially a fault. The list ends with *freedom of conscience*, without doubt something good, versus *conformity to the group*, something bad. How can a person square these differ-ences when in some cases commitment to the group is a sign of artistic integrity (e.g., the Group Theatre, repertory theatre) and in other cases a sign of artistic betrayal (e.g., featherbedding by theatre unions, the Hollywood studio system)? Likewise, commitment to individual principles is usually something positive for an artist (e.g., personal honor, vision, and independence), yet at other times it is a negative attribute (e.g., selfishness, disloyalty, and greed). These choices, which have their origin in the American struggle between the principles of individualism and those of democracy, are augmen-ted in the American theatre by a kind of idealism that dreams of absolutes.

This kind of struggle repeatedly turns upon the consequential meanings of five concepts: *commitment, cooperation, compromise, collabor-ation*, and *corruption*. For example, one can begin to take the measure of Bobby Lewis by tracing his use of the terms *commitment* and *collaboration* in *Slings and Arrows*.[6] These concepts strike at the essen-tial nature of theatre work, in both its positive and negative attri-butes. Lewis repeatedly presents an anecdote that illustrates his commitment to art, a high standard that he opposes to the corrupt-ing collaborative nature of commercialism. And for politically minded theatre people, such as Lillian Hellman, Arthur Miller, and Elia Kazan, the meanings multiply, especially given the nature of the social struggles in the era, from the Depression through the McCarthy witch hunts. Not surprisingly, then, the collaborative nature of film work becomes an especially troubling problem for these people. But as I wish to show, Hollywood only intensifies certain situations and conditions that operate in the theatre.

At a primary level, the struggle between individual and group values takes a rather melodramatic or allegorical form, as good fights evil in the capitalist world of success and failure. The condition is a familiar one, for it is dramatized, with varying degrees of sophistication, in many American plays and productions of this era (e.g., *Golden Boy*, *The Little Foxes*, *All My Sons*). The standard temptations and vices that pull one into unwanted compromise and corruption include money, sex, drugs, alcohol, fame, and power.

As much as any American playwright, Tennessee Williams has presented characters who struggle with these temptations, which are often felt and understood by the characters in the most excruciatingly personal ways. But the psychological intimacy of their pain suggests, to us if not them, the larger conditioning forces of social, political and moral culture. In the plays of the 1940s and 1950s, one Broadway hit after another, Williams shows just how dangerous the various temptations can be, elaborating them – sometimes sensationally –with an astute sense of their threatening powers and agonizing consequences. Yet his own seductive fame and success during this period seemed to have escaped the dangers that often consumed his characters. Then in the 1960s disaster struck, fulfilling Williams's dark premonitions of a "collapse" in his career.[7] Unable, after fifteen years of hits, to meet the changing artistic and economic demands for success and fame on Broadway, Williams almost destroyed himself.

In his memoirs, Williams reports that drugs and alcohol took their devastating toll on him during his "Stoned Age." The "subterranean fault" in his mind cracked open, and in 1969 he ended up in a mental ward.[8] Filled with anger, frustration, and self-doubt, he seemed no longer able to balance the drives for recognition and sex, which were necessarily yoked in his private and professional lives. His autobiography, consistent with his plays, makes the case for the mysterious power and dignity of his sexual needs. Williams thus presents the details of his homosexual life in order to assert his integrity – first, to demonstrate the quality he praises in Tallulah Bankhead, honesty without shame, and, second, to show that the Bacchantic impulse is manifested equally in his many loves and plays. Writing his memoir is apparently part of the cure, the struggle back to self-identity and truth, a truth enhanced by his honesty about his homosexuality. He wants no pity from us, just understanding – and perhaps the acknowledgement that he has remained committed to his art, no matter what the pain. The ideal reader, by the end of the memoir, might even be prepared to grant that integrity is redeemed.

Arthur Miller also represents himself as struggling with the problems of fame in the early 1950s, following upon the success of *Death of a Salesman*. Would his artistic role as an outsider be compromised by the popular acceptance of his work? In *Timebends*, his carefully wrought autobiography, Miller reports that he confronted this concern by battling nobly against the base world of Hollywood. Refusing to modify his screenplay called *The Hook*, a waterfront story of organized crime and corruption, he avoided contaminating it with an anti-communist bias that the studio wanted. Thus he shows that he would rather walk away from Hollywood than compromise his artistic principles.[9]

But Miller proved less successful in resisting the lure of Hollywood sex when Kazan introduced him to Marilyn Monroe. She quickly became for Miller an allegorical figure, a personification of Glamour: "her perfection seeming to invite the inevitable wound that would make her more like others. It was a perfection that aroused a wish to defend it ..."[10] For Kazan, however, she aroused less ethical considerations. In fact, at the time that Miller was courting Monroe (though Miller did not know this), Kazan was sleeping with her.[11] Miller, lacking the cynic's (or even the journeyman's) attitude toward sex and Hollywood, was soon willing to sacrifice his secure first marriage for Marilyn's charms and vulnerabilities. He would even, he hoped, save her from herself and Hollywood.

Miller's description of his affair with and marriage to Monroe, despite his earnestness and his justifications, reads as a case of honor confused, if not compromised. In his own way, Miller admits as much when he castigates his own "naivety" and "self-absorption" during this period. Consequently, despite the many details he provides on their relationship, Marilyn remains a symbol rather than a person: "I could not understand how she had come to symbolize a kind of authenticity; perhaps it was simply that ... her very body was a white beam of truth."[12] As Miller discovers, and points out, Monroe's personal confusion and suffering could be traced back to early childhood abandonment, but he also wishes to see her painful insecurities as the quintessential emblem of the horrible contradictions of fame in the film world. Hollywood is, he feels, a perversion of the American Dream. It is the world of artificiality, "a desert that had to be watered before it would green up, a fake to start with ... Did anyone ever feel he belonged in this place?"[13]

Yet in order to save Marilyn and the marriage, Miller decides to go forward with a screenplay, *The Misfits*. His logic, precious but familiar, is based upon a principle of integrity.

That I had always looked down on screenwriting and had refused offer after offer to write pictures helped persuade me that something of import-ance was being sacrificed in this venture, and sacrifice is the essence of commitment. Thus *The Misfits* was loaded with a freight that needed a very strong vessel to bear; nothing else was possible, since I longed for her as much as for peace. She still blanked out the sun.[14]

By the time of the filming of *The Misfits*, however, Marilyn had become a sad, self-destructive person. So, Miller, despite his good intentions, became a spectator at the death of his marriage, with Marilyn struggling painfully to play out the sacrificial role he had written for her in *The Misfits*. And in *Timebends* he gives her one last role: the victim of stardom. Possessed by Hollywood – that is to say, by Miller's idea of Hollywood – she could love and respect herself only as a star, not a real person. For Marilyn, her stardom was her condition of being, as Miller, belatedly, came to recognize: "The simple fact, terrible and lethal, was that no space whatever existed between herself and this star. *She was 'Marilyn Monroe' and that was what was killing her.*"[15] Well, yes and no.

It is true, of course, that Hollywood contributed to her self-destruction, yet her suffering had additional causes. Miller no doubt understood much about the specific nature of Monroe's vulner-abilities and about the personal qualities of her life that distin-guished her problems from those of a thousand other beautiful actresses. But in his memoirs he seems determined to turn her into a symbol of Hollywood, which he represents as the condition of all that is wrong in American culture. He reads the landscape and everything that inhabits it as an environment of threatening moral signs. Everything signifies. *Timebends*, often very astute in its judg-ments, has too many moments when the symbolic flights, instead of lifting off, sink under the weight of the moral indictment. Miller thus leaves the impression of moral arrogance, if not pomposity. Accord-ingly, despite its realistic texture of history and language, the memoirs take on, like his play *After the Fall*, the quality of a sermon, sanctioned by a liberal ethic that does not always sustain him against confusion and the threats of corruption (as he perceives them). His earnestness, however admirable in principle, can be a burden for him and us.

### TRICKSTERS IN THE DEN OF THE BEAST

Miller is hardly alone in seeing Hollywood as the avatar of fame, glamour, sex, and money. In the various autobiographies, Hollywood is the most familiar – and most overworked – emblem of temptation and evil. In one sense, this view of show business is to be expected, for the studio bosses, driven by crass capitalism, often seem to be ready-made villains right out of central casting. The litany against Hollywood thus flows quite easily. As Arthur Miller states: "The whole make-believe business seemed detestable now, a destroyer of people, especially those actors unable to settle for an ounce less than the full measure of truthfulness."[16]

The only defense apparently is never to go west. Hence, Cheryl Crawford, after the breakup of the Group Theatre, proudly resists a job offer from Hollywood, which is seducing her colleagues. With Odets and many others in mind, she writes: "It's curious about Hollywood: nearly every writer blasted it but most of them liked the cash."[17] Elia Kazan makes the same point about Odets: "I look back at Clifford Odets – no one I've known was more talented. He couldn't resist the money, the flattery, the apparent safety and security in the movie community. And he lost himself."[18] Hollywood demands hyperbole, it would seem. Bobby Lewis also notes that money, success, and the "need to sin" drew people like Odets to Hollywood. In *Golden Boy* Odets wrote about this temptation, but as Lewis points out Odets "himself became a Golden Boy who went 'off his line' to achieve 'success and fame.' This hunger for success plagued Clifford even as he was writing his play on the subject."[19] Odets's fall becomes an obligatory theme, and opportunity for everyone to feel superior.

Of course, Bobby Lewis went to Hollywood too, but as he says, "I made a vow I would not let California become my artistic graveyard."[20] So the story he wants to tell is the self-enhancing one of going into the den of the beast and coming out with his integrity intact (and with his pockets full of booty from the "gold coast"). Hardly an exclusive story, for it is basically the same one that Clurman, Houseman, Kazan, Williams, Hellman, Miller, and almost everyone else wishes to tell about themselves. Although certain poor, weak souls like Odets may be corrupted there, these sojourners in tinseltown survive and even flourish as they chart a self-protective track through the entertainment jungle.

To illustrate this point, they tell heroic stories of themselves as they either revolt against or outwit the studios. Miller and Hellman, in defense of art, bravely speak their minds to studio heads. Houseman and Kazan refuse to produce trash (or, if obliged to do so, they turn trash into art). Williams and Clurman use their time on the payroll to write their own work and to enjoy the sun. And they all take the money and run – without conscience, of course, because the studios are corrupt anyway.

As Lillian Hellman declared to the novelist Peter Feibleman, when he was considering a screenwriting job in Hollywood:

The only excuse for this place is a job and you'd better leave the day the job's done – I can't take the temptations of Hollywood and I have more character than you do. It's no place for a serious writer, you'll wind up with a swimming pool if you stay ... Writing for movies is a sucker's game these days, it's not worth giving up your life no matter how much it pays. Just take the money and get out.[21]

Hellman did well at that, once she became famous. But for her first job in Hollywood during the early 1930s, she was hired as a mere manuscript reader, a boring, simpleminded job that paid little. She thus spent her time, as she reports, fighting "torpor" and "learning to drink hard." "I was out of place and the drinking made uninteresting people matter less and, late at night, matter not at all."[22] However, with the success of *The Children's Hour* in New York, she gained the right to adapt her own play. And when the film version, *These Three* (1936), was a success, she was free to set the terms for her film work. "By that time I ... was able to write a clause in a contract with Samuel Goldwyn that allowed me a choice of scripts and did not require me, except for short periods, to go to Hollywood."[23] Then during the 1940s and 1950s, when the studios wanted her to renounce or deny her leftist values, she did no film work, refusing of course to compromise her principles. Still, off and on she had a substantial and lucrative career as a screen writer, adapting a number of her own plays and working on other screenplays, including *Dead End* (1937) and *The Chase* (1966). And of course *Julia* (1977), based upon her imaginative portrait in *Pentimento*, turned her into a celebrity, in the person of Jane Fonda.

The most heroic act that an artistic rebel can make in Hollywood, short of controlling every aspect of production, is to stand up to the studio bosses, but that usually cuts off funds, production and career. Apparently, few brave souls told the studio heads to go to hell. Few can match Hellman's stories of noble resolve. Or her good fortune. Still, in the art of anecdotes there are many ways to demonstrate one's fine judgment and convictions. For example, if you can't always praise yourself, praise the integrity of others, especially those in Hollywood who determinedly accomplish their artistic aims. By praising another's integrity, one partakes in it.

Bobby Lewis, for instance, selects as heroes Fred Astaire and Charlie Chaplin. Chaplin, who gets a whole chapter in *Slings and Arrows*, is the quintessential artist, someone who refuses to compromise his genius. The crucial point is the same one that Lewis makes, with pride, in his description of his own first major success in New York as a director of Saroyan's *My Heart's in the Highlands*. It was a "pure" production, committed to style, "uncontaminated by the crazy collaborative nature of the Broadway theatrical process." Chaplin's film of *Monsieur Verdoux*, in which Lewis plays a small role, is the same kind of pure art because Chaplin "was everything – writer, star, director, producer, and casting director, as well as supervisor of all other departments: costume, scenery, makeup, lighting, shooting schedules, camera setups, and the musical score."[24] Lewis lets us know that he was capable of assessing Chaplin's achievements, unlike many Hollywood people who were jealous of Chaplin and hated him for his independence. He thus was able to identify with Chaplin's talent, his politics, and his essential role as an outsider.

Short of being Chaplin, one usually had to compromise. So, the strategy that these cunning outsiders commonly followed, as they explain, was to rely judiciously on acts of duplicity and hypocrisy (in other words, when in Rome . . .). By becoming a trickster, one can benefit from Hollywood without sacrificing one's true, inner self. For instance, Harold Clurman proudly claims: "Hollywood never touched me. I wrote *The Fervent Years* there and had time to read *War and Peace*. I was also at last able to repay many of the debts I had accumulated on behalf of the Group Theatre."[25] Of course, the reader, familiar with the corrupt nature of Hollywood, is supposed to admire not only Clurman's cultural superiority (what studio head would read Tolstoy?) but his ability to produce such an important work as *The Fervent Years* – the record of vital theatre accomplishments, back east in the true world of entertainment. New York outsmarts Hollywood. And what better revenge can there be: Hollywood, after the fact, pays for the debts of the Group Theatre.

Similarly, Tennessee Williams turns his six-month contract in Hollywood to his advantage. Working for MGM in 1943, he was supposed to prepare a script for Lana Turner called *Marriage is a Private Affair*.

I was set to work writing a screenplay based on a dreadful novel to be transmogrified into a starring vehicle for a young lady who couldn't act her way out of her form-fitting cashmeres but was an intimate friend of the producer who had engaged me and I was soon told that my dialogue was beyond the young lady's comprehension although I had avoided any language that was at all eclectic or multisyllabic.[26]

We of course are supposed to share his disgust and appreciate his disdainful wit.

Unwilling or unable to write trash, he soon figures out that he should "throw in the sponge." Indeed, he claims that he spent the remaining months of his contract drawing his salary of $250 per week while enjoying the California beaches. The standard moral of this narrative, for both Williams and his biographer Donald Spoto, is that personal cunning and talent triumphed over stupidity and decadence in Hollywood. But there is something that Williams does not tell us. He actually spent a substantial part of his time there transforming his short story "Portrait of a Girl in Glass" and his play called "The Gentleman Caller" into a screenplay for MGM to consider. To be expected, the studio rejected it, so one year later his career was launched in the good world of theatre with *The Glass Menagerie*. Fine and good, Williams escaped Hollywood, but we should note that the filmic qualities of *The Glass Menagerie* derive directly from the fact that it was first a screenplay.[27] So, against conventional wisdom, we might well draw a different moral: Hollywood was a major and positive factor in launching Williams's theatre career.

## HOLLYWOOD, CAPITAL OF THE AMERICAN THEATRE

Could it be possible that Hollywood served others as well? Might we not benefit from a less demonizing version of the film world? Although these autobiographers tend to represent Hollywood as a waste land, we should probably doubt some aspects of their reports. Indeed, their easy dismissal of Hollywood is surprising, or misleading, for almost all of them wanted to participate in films, and not just to make money quickly. We might keep in mind that film techniques and aesthetics (e.g., scenic plot construction, musical theme, time-jumps, dissolves, montage – as in simultaneous design and action) have contributed substantially to not only Williams's plays but those of many other playwrights in the modern era. Especially when sound came in, film and theatre professionals were bound together, whether desiring one another or not. For example, almost every major and minor playwright of the 1930s and 1940s worked in film, at one time or another: Robert Sherwood, Clifford Odets, George S. Kaufman, S. J. Perelman, Maxwell Anderson, Sidney Howard, Elmer Rice, John Howard Lawson, Albert Maltz, John Wesley, Garson Kanin, Charles MacArthur, Ben Hecht, Sam and Bella Spewack, Zoë Akins, and Thornton Wilder. As Harold Clurman noted of Hollywood, "everyone seems to have touched down at one time or another."[28]

With unintended irony, Cheryl Crawford makes the same point when she brags about all of the famous actors who studied at the Actors Studio in New York since its founding in 1947: "Altogether they have received ninety-eight Academy Award nominations and twenty-one Oscars."[29] Notice that she says Oscars, not Tony Awards, even though the initial aim of Actors Studio, when founded by Kazan, Lewis, and Crawford (and later taken over by Lee Strasberg), was supposedly to train actors for the live stage. But Crawford's list – which includes Paul Newman, Walter Matthau, Rod Steiger, James Dean, Al Pacino, Robert De Niro, Dustin Hoffman, Shelley Winters, Eva Marie Saint, Joanne Woodward, Kim Stanley, Ellen Burstyn, and Jane Fonda – is just one more piece of evidence that points toward the yoking of theatre and film.

Even those playwrights who attacked Hollywood had their works turned into films quite often. In the process, the playwrights received large payments and, just as importantly, found a much larger audience. Admittedly, some of the films proved to be a disservice to the plays they were derived from. But sometimes the film was a fine accomplishment, as good in its own way as the play. And sometimes better. The list of plays turned into film is substantial: the majority of Hellman's plays, the majority of Williams's plays (and his novel, *The Roman Spring of Mrs. Stone*), many of Inge's plays. Even Miller has had some of his plays adapted to film or television. This partnership, surely a major aspect of the history of modern theatre, suggests that Hollywood served these theatre people rather well, all things considered.

Perhaps someone like John Houseman is a better guide to the territory. Of course, like the others, he is prepared to write about the place in the prose of doom:

I have lived in Southern California for thirty years, on and off. (I have owned houses there, made friends, had love affairs, married, raised children and enjoyed some satisfying professional successes.) But this does not protect me from the wave of sickening anxiety that sweeps over me each time I face the sprawling, hideous approaches to the City of the Angels. There is something in that air – that hazy, sundrenched, polluted, subtropical, earthquake-threatened atmosphere that fills me with loathing and gloom. I become used to it after a while; I even get to like it – especially the beach on which I live. But that first devastating impression persists.[30]

Hollywood is the perfect environment for the imagination of decadence.

Yet Houseman also understood the fascination of the place, for he felt it himself. Like Miller, he fell in love with a star, but more lightheartedly. "For many years of my life I found wealth and celebrity an infallible aphrodisiac. To be known from coast to coast as the lover of one of the brightest young stars in the Hollywood firmament gave me a satisfaction and a self-assurance for which I was sincerely grateful."[31] We are grateful too, in our vicarious way, for his report on his love affair with Joan Fontaine. And when the affair ends, he accepts it in a matter-of-fact way, moving on to the next affair. How refreshing, after Miller's allegory of love.

Is Houseman merely the exception that proves the rule about Hollywood? Should we see his detachment as a sign of moral strength or weakness? During his career he not only moved back and forth between theatre and film, New York and Hollywood, but actively produced theatre in Los Angeles, including works by Saroyan, Wilder, and Brecht (Laughton's *Galileo*). At the same time, he produced films, including *The Blue Dahlia*, the film noir classic written by Raymond Chandler. And his other films included Nicholas Ray's *They Live By Night*, Joseph Mankiewicz's *Julius Caesar*, Vincent Minnelli's *The Bad and the Beautiful*, Minnelli's *Lust for Life*, and of course Orson Welles's *Citizen Kane*, for which he helped write the screenplay, with Herman Mankiewicz (though Welles claimed the credit).

The case of Kazan is even more compelling in this matter. His career, equally successful in theatre and film, is a crucial place to look if we want to attempt to take the measure of Hollywood for theatre professionals. Kazan is a difficult, sometimes evasive individual, and the autobiography does little to make him lovable. But the work is one of the *key* documents of the era – inviting us to struggle with him, to enter into the heart of the debate over the integrity of the theatre artist in Hollywood. His strengths and weaknesses, his successes and failures, are far better emblems of Hollywood and the times than Monroe's life, far better than perhaps any other life in the theatre. Or in film. Whatever the case, Kazan – and, in turn, Houseman – offers us a radical departure from the scapegoating of Hollywood. Their lives provide the essential evidence that theatre and film became joined during this era.

Quite simply, then, the history of theatre since the 1930s cannot be separated from the history of Hollywood. The dynamic relation between theatre and film, Hollywood and New York, shapes the development and significance of theatre – aesthetically, socially, and economically. In other words, much of the history of Broadway occurred in Hollywood. And continues to do so. It's time we attend to this history in our study of American theatre.

## NOTES

1 Harold Clurman, *All People Are Famous* (New York: Harcourt Brace Jovanovich, 1974); Clurman, *The Fervent Years: The Story of the Group Theatre and the Thirties* (New York: Hill and Wang, 1957); Lee Strasberg, *A Dream of Passion: The Development of the Method* (Boston: Little, Brown, 1987); Lillian Hellman, *Maybe, A Story* (Boston: Little, Brown, 1980); Hellman, *Pentimento* (Boston: Little, Brown, 1973); Hellman, *Scoundrel Time* (Boston: Little, Brown, 1976); Hellman, *Unfinished Woman* (Boston: Little, Brown, 1969).

2 Robert Lewis, *Slings and Arrows: Theater in My Life* (New York: Stein and Day, 1984); John Houseman, *Final Dress* (New York: Simon and Schuster, 1983); Houseman, *Front and Center* (New York: Simon and Schuster, 1979); Houseman, *Run-Through* (New York: Simon and Schuster, 1972); Elia Kazan, *A Life* (New York: A. Knopf, 1988); Arthur Miller, *Timebends, A Life* (New York: Grove Press, 1987).

3 Tennessee Williams, *Memoirs* (Garden City, NY: Doubleday, 1975), 93–94.

4 Cheryl Crawford, *One Naked Individual: My Fifty Years in the Theatre* (Indianapolis: Bobbs-Merrill, 1977).

5 John Houseman, *Front and Center* (New York: Simon and Schuster, 1979), 316.

6 Lewis, *Slings and Arrows*.

7 Williams, *Memoirs*, 92.
8 Ibid., 216.
9 Arthur Miller, *Timebends, A Life* (New York: Grove Press, 1987), 300–8. For a somewhat different, and perhaps revealing, version of the negotiations on *The Hook* in 1950, see Elia Kazan's autobiography *A Life* (New York: A. Knopf, 1988), 401–14, 426. Kazan and Miller remember the sequence of events and the shaping motives in different ways. And of course, Kazan's and Budd Schulberg's *On the Waterfront*, made four years later, tells a story of personal honor quite at odds with Miller's *The Hook*. By then both Kazan and Schulberg had "named names" before HUAC. Their views on the nature of informing were at odds with those of Miller. He, in turn, created his subsequent version of waterfront integrity and betrayal in *A View from the Bridge*.
10 Miller, *Timebends*, 302–03.
11 Both Kazan and Miller lament, in great detail, their betrayal of their first wives, but Kazan endlessly rationalizes his behavior and stays married, with difficulty he acknowledges, while Miller turns his betrayal into a morality play culminating in divorce, which he attained by living in the empty spaces of Nevada (occasionally talking to Marilyn on the phone). He presents his struggle as emblematic of American confusion and destiny. Miller seems to make a better case in his moral justification than Kazan on a number of occasions (including their appearances before the HUAC), but also with a tone of self-importance. Kazan, often appearing to be cunning in his dealings with people, especially women, is nonetheless a complex figure who will not stay contained within a morality play, even one written by an accomplished writer like Miller. And Kazan's autobiography proves to be equally complex and fascinating – in its own way an achievement every bit the measure of Miller's more stylish work. Both autobiographies are major works (as are the four memoirs of Hellman and the three of Houseman).
12 Miller, *Timebends*, 370.
13 Ibid., 488–89.
14 Ibid., 461.
15 Ibid., 483.
16 Ibid., 483.
17 Crawford, *One Naked Individual*, 98–99.
18 Kazan, *A Life*, 273.
19 Lewis, *Slings*, 99.
20 Ibid., 135.
21 Peter Feibleman, *Lilly, Reminiscences of Lillian Hellman* (New York: William Morrow, 1988), 53.
22 Lillian Hellman, *Unfinished Woman* (Boston: Little, Brown, 1969), 56.
23 Ibid., 66.
24 Lewis, *Slings*, 159.

25 Clurman, *All People*, 119–20. Kazan offers a somewhat different perspective on Clurman in Hollywood: "Harold Clurman, one of the men
   I've most admired, was lucky: The people who ran the studios did not
   want him, and he had to come east again; that saved him, for he seemed
   lost in southern California. But I'm not praising the East over the
   West." Kazan, *A Life*, 273.
26 Williams, *Memoirs*, 76.
27 Donald Spoto, in his biography, *The Kindness of Strangers: The Life of
   Tennessee Williams* (Boston: Little, Brown, and Co., 1987), accurately
   describes the qualities of the play: "With its indication of dissolves and
   image-overlays, its insertion of musical motifs and its plastic, dreamlike
   construction, it was conceived as a film of memory" (95). But he refuses
   to grant the world of Hollywood any place in this achievement; instead,
   he accepts the dismissive tone and attitude that Williams presents in his
   memoirs and letters. And why not, since this is the perceived truth
   about Hollywood that everyone is prepared to accept.
28 Clurman, *All People*, 225.
29 Crawford, *One Naked Individual*, 221.
30 Houseman, *Front and Center*, 107.
31 Ibid., 159.

# CHAPTER 17

# Consuming the past: commercial American theatre in the Reagan era

## Alan Woods

The eight years of Ronald Reagan's presidency (1981–89) were marked by unprecedented defense spending, an international trade deficit of $500 billion by 1989, and an absolute increase in the concentration of wealth among the already richest members of American society.[1] At the same time, national pride was restored after the malaise of the late 1970s by successful international policies, both military and diplomatic, which would culminate in the collapse of the Soviet bloc shortly after Reagan ended his term of office. The Reagan era has been characterized as the culmination of a conservative revolution, and as a period in which Americans questioned, if not rejected, the liberal social agenda of the preceding four decades.

In such a period of shift and change, the commercial theatre of the United States also changed decisively, as did its noncommercial counterpart, regional nonprofit theatre throughout the country. If the theatre is a reflective medium, as is generally assumed, the nature of the theatre should reflect in some way the political and social changes the Reagan presidency represents.

The commercial theatre reflected the apparent national prosperity during the Reagan years, rising steadily in terms of box office income. The gross receipts of the Broadway stage rose from $194,481,091 for the 1980–81 season to $263,364,442 for 1988–89.[2] The touring theatre was equally prosperous, with figures for the same two seasons increasing from $218,921,935 to $367,109, 232. As with the national economy, however, the figures hid an industry in some crisis: the total number of productions presented on the Broadway stage dropped from sixty-seven in 1980–81 to twenty-nine eight years later.[3] Equally worrying were other indicators: the number of new musicals – which dominate the commercial theatre through their long runs and normally account for over two-thirds of the total box office – dropped from nineteen in 1980–81 to seven at the end of the period. Attendance for all Broadway productions also dropped, from 10,822,324 to 7,968,273.

The Broadway theatre's prosperity was financial only, when other aspects of the industry are surveyed. The figures are themselves misleading, since the gross increases are due not to increased attendance or production, but rather to higher ticket prices. Tickets had averaged $17.97 in 1980–81; by 1988–89, the average had almost doubled to $32.88. The rate of increase was well beyond the 25 percent increase in the cost of living during the same period.[4] The decade also saw a continuation of the trend toward exceedingly long runs, which suggested an increasing reliance upon tourist patronage in selling tickets and a corresponding drop in regular local theatregoers. The commercial theatre was, therefore, almost exactly reflective of economic factors nationally during the Reagan years: an absolute increase in income was offset by sagging production figures, while enormous increases in ticket prices provided an illusion of economic health. On the national level, business investment between 1983 and 1986 ran well behind average figures for the preceding three decades, despite a well-publicized business boom.[5]

Broadway productions are intended, of course, to make a profit, although only about one in six returns money to its investors. The plays and musicals which open on Broadway represent their producers' best guesses as to what the audience will accept. Successful shows presumably are profitable because large numbers of people find them worth the price of admission. Successful productions should, therefore, either reflect concerns shared by their audiences, present views audiences find at least acceptable, or present no views at all.[6] A number of trends are visible in the Broadway theatre's production records for the 1980s. All are interesting reflections of audience concerns in the Reagan era.

The public "obsession with the beauty and power of money," with "displays of opulence," were among the most notable social trends of the Reagan years.[7] The theatrical equivalent of the conspicuous consumption exemplified by real estate magnate Donald Trump could well be the work of British composer Andrew Lloyd Webber, which has dominated the American commercial theatre since the phenomenal success of *Evita* in 1978. Lloyd Webber's *Cats* opened in New York in 1982, while his *The Phantom of the Opera* premiered in 1988. Both were still running at the end of the 1990–91 season, with no signs of closing; *Cats* had become the third longest-running production in the history of the Broadway theatre.[8]

Both musicals are visual spectaculars. For *Cats*, the stage of the Winter Garden Theater was torn out to put in an elaborate junk yard setting, and for the effect of flying a giant tire at the show's end. *The Phantom of the Opera* required the installation of new flooring at the Majestic Theater for the complicated and heavy equipment needed to obtain a "lake of fire" effect. Equally spectacular effects were demanded by Lloyd Webber's *Starlight Express* (1987), with its cast on rollerskates zooming throughout the Gershwin Theater, and by the astoundingly successful Anglo-French musical, *Les Misérables*, dominated by rotating barricades.

The spectacle of these elaborate musicals appears to be their chief attraction, not their plots or dramatic action. Only *Les Misérables*, based as it is on Victor Hugo's classic nineteenth-century novel, has a strong narrative element, although it is subsumed in the musical's spectacular visual effects. As a consequence, the content has become negligible or safely familiar. Lloyd Webber has been accused of writing derivative music which is strongly reminiscent of earlier composers,[9] while the books for these hugely successful musicals are based on well-known sources. Instead of challenging an audience, these musicals have provided flashy and (obviously) expensive entertainment. Part of the appeal of attending the opening of *The Phantom of the Opera*, for instance, was knowing that at an investment cost of $8 million, it was the most expensive musical ever produced, and that its advance ticket sale of $18 million was the greatest ever recorded.[10]

Just as the conspicuous consumption and ostentatiously public display of wealth of the Reagan years found theatrical expression in elaborate musicals, their simplified story lines also reflect an aspect of the Reagan era. Much of the rhetoric emerging from the Reagan White House had a similar effect: issues were simplified to slogans, essentially devoid of content.[11]

There is, of course, nothing new in elaborate visual displays; nor is there anything strikingly new about an emphasis on cost. The commercial theatre has stressed how expensive major productions are since the appearance of the quantification ethic in the 1890s.[12] In the past, however, visual spectacles were a relatively small portion of the entertainment mix; in the 1980s, they dominated the commercial theatre, financially, in terms of attendance, and in their high visibility.

The musicals mentioned above are all in the operatic style popularized by Lloyd Webber, containing virtually no spoken dialogue and almost entirely sung. The traditional American book musical, although greatly reduced in numbers from the golden years of the 1940s and 1950s, was represented during the 1980s by such successful shows as *Dreamgirls* (1981), *La Cage aux Folles* (1983) and *Big River* (1985), and by a number of ambitious failures, notably *Rags* (1986) and Peter Allen's *Legs Diamond* (1988). The highly regarded Stephen Sondheim began the period with the failure of *Merrily We Roll Along* (1981), but then provided the Pulitzer Prize-winning *Sunday in the Park with George* (1984) and *Into the Woods* (1987). Although each of these productions relied on spectacle, each also commented, in varying degrees, upon social conditions. For example, Tom Eyen's book for *Dreamgirls* used the traditional (if not stereotyped) notion that striving for success alone leaves the star lonely at the top. Perhaps significantly, *Dreamgirls* was a success at the beginning of the Reagan period; a 1987 revival failed.

*La Cage aux Folles*, with its celebration of the right to one's individuality in the face of a restrictive society, was certainly well within the commercial theatre's traditions; a leading character defiantly asserting a right to individuality has been a mainstay of the musical theatre, whether in Cohan's *George Washington, Jr.* (1906), Rodgers and Hart's *Pal Joey* (1941), or Styne, Laurents and Sondheim's *Gypsy* (1959). But *La Cage aux Folles* was unique in another way; together with Harvey Fierstein's *Torch Song Trilogy* (1982), it marked the open acceptance of male homosexuals as sympathetic dramatic characters by Broadway's mainstream audiences. That acceptance was apparently short-lived, however. Homosexuality virtually disappears as subject matter on the Broadway stage after the success of the first (and to date, only commercially successful) AIDS drama, *As Is*, in 1985. Emily Mann's *Execution of Justice*, with its vivid depiction of the San Francisco gay community was highly successful in regional theatres, but failed when produced in New York in 1986. The homosexuality of the lead character in the moderately successful *Breaking the Code* (1987) is directly responsible for his destruction; homosexuality and AIDS figure in only one additional production during the period, the failed *Eastern Standard*

(1988). The AIDS epidemic itself may have as much to do as the growing conservatism of the country with the relative paucity of homosexual characters on Broadway stages after 1985, although AIDS has become a far more familiar topic on American television than in the commercial theatre.

Sondheim and Lapine's *Sunday in the Park with George* explores the nature of artistic creativity; its second act effectively satirizes the contemporary art market, and the drive for celebrity status regardless of accomplishment. The same writers produced *Into the Woods* in 1987, with its warning that life is far more complex than fiction, and that reductive simplifications can be dangerously misleading. While successful, neither of the Sondheim–Lapine musicals enjoyed the long-run popularity of musicals which offered lavish displays of scenery and far simpler visions of life much more consonant with the political oversimplifications offered the American people nationally.[13]

An emphasis on nostalgia permeated the theatre of the 1980s. Early in the decade, a number of major musicals of the past were revived with their original stars: Angela Lansbury as *Mame* (1983), Stephanie Mills in *The Wiz* (1984), Yul Brynner in his final performances in *The King and I* (1985). While this was hardly unique to the 1980s – Carol Channing had reappeared in *Hello, Dolly!* with regularity throughout the 1970s – the nostalgia element did add a few fillips, as when the musical *Zorba* was revived in 1984, not with its original stars (Herschel Bernardi and Maria Karnilova), but with Anthony Quinn and Lila Kedrova, stars of the (nonmusical) film source for the musical.

Nostalgia was also a factor in the success of *Foxfire* (1982), which created a mythologized Appalachia populated by the theatre's senior acting couple, Hume Cronyn and Jessica Tandy; and in the revivals of *You Can't Take It With You* (1983) and Thornton Wilder's classic *Our Town* (1988). All three plays celebrated individuality, a not uncommon theatrical theme, but without the need to defy either a restrictive society or governmental authority.

Neil Simon's autobiographical trilogy of plays, beginning with *Brighton Beach Memoirs* (1983), continuing with *Biloxi Blues* (1985) and concluding with *Broadway Bound* (1986) also had their share of nostalgic appeal. *Brighton Beach Memoirs* depicted a relatively painless Great Depression, while *Biloxi Blues* used basic training as its comic situation. Although both *Biloxi Blues* and *Broadway Bound* had darker moments – the latter with its unflattering look at marriage – all three of Simon's works harked back to a simpler past, simpler for having been simplified and a little sentimentalized in the process.

Also notable during the decade was the appearance of what can only be called "ersatz nostalgia": productions which intended to evoke a simpler (and safer) past for their audiences, but did so without reviving work which might be uncooperatingly complex. *My One and Only* (1983), for example, put Gershwin songs in an entirely new book which attempted to resemble a show from the 1930s. *Seven Brides for Seven Brothers* (1983) adapted the 1954 movie for an unsuccessful musical which looked like a revival, but wasn't. *Singin' in the Rain* (1985) provided Twyla Tharp's highly contemporary reworking of another film musical. Lincoln Center's revival of *Anything Goes* (1987) did succeed, using most of Cole Porter's score from the 1934 original, but interpolating familiar songs from other Porter musicals. The original book was extensively revised as well. While more authentic than *My One and Only*, the Lincoln Center *Anything Goes* was an adaptation, not, strictly speaking, a revival of the original work.

These "ersatz nostalgia" productions essentially remade the past, revising it to meet the interests and concerns of contemporary audiences while suggesting that they were actual recreations of the past.

The casual appropriation and falsification of the past for contemporary consumption was another hallmark of the Reagan period seen in the comparison between Reagan's first term and that of Franklin Roosevelt's in the 1930s. This practice reached a peak of sorts in the misinformation which surrounded the Iran/Contra affairs of the last part of the decade.[14]

Major revivals of American drama, while less nostalgic, served as a reminder of the achievements of the theatre's past.[15] Eugene O'Neill's *A Moon for the Misbegotten* was revived by the American Repertory Theatre on Broadway (1984) as a vehicle for Kate Nelligan. The National Theatre of Great Britain revived *Strange Interlude* (1985) around the talents of Glenda Jackson. *The Iceman Cometh* reunited its original star and director, Jason Robards and José Quintero, in a 1985 production originating at the American National Theatre in Washington, DC. Jonathan Miller's production of *Long Day's Journey Into Night* played on Broadway in the spring of 1986 with actor Jack Lemmon playing the leading role.

And the Yale Repertory Theatre's productions of *Long Day's Journey Into Night* and *Ah, Wilderness!* were performed in rotating repertory to open the first New York International Festival of the Arts in June 1988. Jason Robards and Colleen Dewhurst starred in both productions.

Significantly, all but one of the O'Neill revivals originated in nonprofit theatres, reflecting the increased reliance of the commercial theatre on the nonprofit sector for development of projects. Supported by both public and private monies, the nonprofit theatres were able to nurture the serious work which increasing costs and other factors made increasingly unattractive to Broadway producers. The Miller–Lemmon *Long Day's Journey Into Night* was created for both Broadway and London's commercial West End theatres, relying upon Lemmon's drawing power to make a profit on a limited engagement.

The O'Neill revivals present somewhat complex cases. They were all conceived, on one level, as star vehicles: Robards and Dewhurst had long histories of appearing in major productions of O'Neill's plays; Nelligan had scored a major success in David Hare's *Plenty* the previous season. The Miller *Long Day's Journey Into Night* was made possible only by Lemmon's appearance. Jackson's star status was enhanced by her numerous appearances in American films during the 1970s. All of the O'Neill productions were presented for limited engagements.

The plays had a nostalgic appeal, functioning, at least in part, to celebrate the stage's past achievements. Three of the productions attempted to 'modernize' O'Neill, to provide new interpretations of texts which had been problematic in the past. Critics noted that *A Moon for the Misbegotten* seemed very English, and that Kate Nelligan was a bit miscast; that *Strange Interlude* appeared clipped; and that Miller's *Long Day's Journey Into Night* appeared forced and raced in tempo – as one noted, "What's missing is the tragedy."[16]

The more traditional O'Neill productions fared better critically; reviewers hailed Robards and Dewhurst in both plays. Audiences were not as responsive, however, and the productions had far shorter runs (twenty-eight performances for *Long Day's Journey Into Night*, twelve for *Ah, Wilderness!*) than had been forecast. In the 1980s these plays proved too complex and too disturbing for a period seeking simple, easily grasped truths.

The two other widely recognized major playwrights of the recent past, Arthur Miller and Tennessee Williams, were less produced; with the exception of a major revival of *Death of a Salesman*, starring Dustin Hoffman, Kate Reid, and John Malkovich (1984), these playwrights received little or no attention.[17]

The few new plays which succeeded in the 1980s were, predictably, a very mixed group. Virtually none of the Broadway productions were in any way political. Only Jane Wagner's one-person script, *The Search for Signs of Intelligent Life in the Universe* (1985), a vehicle for Lily Tomlin, brought any satire on social or political institutions before the Broadway audiences. While the success of the piece must be attributed to Tomlin's popularity, the play itself contained satirical commentary decidedly atypical for Broadway (i.e., bag ladies and the homeless). Jackie Mason's 1986 run in *The World According to Me* (with a revival in 1988) also included jokes aimed squarely at political and social targets, but his show was adapted from his night-club act and varied nightly.

Many of the social issues facing the United States were conspicuous by their absence from Broadway stages. There was, for example, no mention of abortion at all in the commercial theatre's plays (and precious little of pregnancy, apart from the 1983 musical, *Baby*). The problem of the homeless figured in the 1988 failure, *Eastern Standard*, while the stock market and high finance were central to Caryl Churchill's *Serious Money*, another 1988 failure. Drugs were central to the action of only two successes, the 1984 *Hurlyburly* and *Cuba and His Teddy Bear*, a 1986 limited run production with Robert De Niro and Ralph Macchio in the leads, transferred from the New York Public Theatre.

David Rabe's *Hurlyburly* and David Mamet's *Speed-the-Plow* (1988) contained sharp critiques of the self-centered materialism of the 1980s, but both productions relied upon Hollywood stars to fill the seats. The rapidity with which Mamet's play closed after Madonna left the cast implied that audiences were drawn more by the performers than by the desire to contemplate social criticism.

The Broadway stage was equally silent on international politics. How the Nazis appealed to middle-class Germans figured in the British import *Good* (1982), but the production ran only a few months. The plight of South Africa was noticed through the six-month run of Athol Fugard's *Master Harold ... and the Boys* (1982), and the year-and-a-half success of *Sarafina!* (1988).

Of the plays which did achieve long runs and high profits, two from the beginning of Reagan's presidency, *Fifth of July* and *Crimes of the Heart*, and two from the final year of his second term, *Burn This* and *M. Butterfly*, may serve as exemplars to further demonstrate the ways the social and political positions espoused by the president were reinforced by the commercial stage.

Lanford Wilson's *Fifth of July*[18] opened on 5 November 1980 (coincidentally, the day after Ronald Reagan's election) with Christopher Reeve and Swoosie Kurtz as its stars. It closed on 24 January 1982, after 511 performances, Reeve having been replaced by Richard Thomas, Timothy Bottoms, and Joseph Bottoms, among others. *Crimes of the Heart* was Beth Henley's Broadway debut as a playwright a year later, on 4 November 1981. Transferred from off-Broadway, where it had won the Pulitzer Prize for drama, it played for 535 performances, closing on 13 February 1983.

At the end of Reagan's presidency, Lanford Wilson was represented on Broadway by *Burn This*, which opened on Broadway on 14 October 1987, after preliminary productions at the Circle Repertory Company off-Broadway, the Steppenwolf Theatre in Chicago, and the Mark Taper Forum in Los Angeles. It played for 437 performances, closing 29 October 1988; Joan Allen and John Malkovich were the leading performers. Quite apart from its content and themes, *Burn This* represents what had become the standard mode of production by the end of the decade, with its lengthy pre-Broadway history at nonprofit regional theatres. By contrast, David Henry Hwang's *M. Butterfly* opened in New York on 20 March 1988, after a pre-Broadway tryout engagement in Washington, DC. It was the only production which opened on Broadway during the 1987–88 season which had not been produced elsewhere, other than works by the two nonprofit Broadway theatres, the Circle in the Square and the Lincoln Center Repertory Theatre.[19] An immediate success, *M. Butterfly* ran for 777 performances.

*Fifth of July* was written in the pre-Reagan theatre, and first produced in 1978. The play, with its treatment of Vietnam-era radicals a decade after the war, uses the social turmoil of the late 1960s as background for the crisis of conscience and will facing its central character, the double amputee Kenneth Talley. Past activism has shaped all of the characters; all have been scarred by the events of the past and their political involvement. Ken Talley's triumph in the play, and the hope the play suggests for the future, is in his ability to once again become engaged socially and politically, after a lengthy period of detachment in which he retreated from the world. The garden his lover Jed is creating on the Talley farm will take five years to show any results. Jed's nurturing of the plants, fertilized literally by the ashes of Sally's dead husband, parallels his nurturing of Ken, and Ken's rebirth at the play's end.

In sharp contrast to Jed is the cynical figure of John, constantly ministering to Gwen in order to control her wealth. Gwen's rebirth is spontaneous, in spite of John; burnt out by the late 1960s, her experiences then provide the catalyst for her emergence as a singer. Again, the activism of the past, treated by the characters as a childish phase, has created the possibility for continued growth and development. *Fifth of July* looks forward, accepting and incorporating the past but, as the play's title suggests, wanting to move beyond the parades and fireworks.

*Crimes of the Heart* was also written before the Reagan era, having first been produced at the Actors Theatre of Louisville in 1979, then off-Broadway in 1980. Henley's play is well within a familiar commercial theatre genre: the southern familial comedy, with slightly bizarre characters seeking to restore family solidarity and secure personal fulfillment at the same time. With the stroke-prone Old Granddaddy in a coma, conformity-seeking cousin Chick safely driven away in the last act, the three sisters who form the nuclear family unit appear to have found at least a moment of togetherness by the end of the play – even if the problems besetting them have by no means been solved. Babe still faces court action for having shot her husband; Meg is no closer to a singing career, while Lenny may or may not find happiness with Charlie in Memphis.

While not resolving the sisters' problems, Henley's comedy instead transcends them. The problems simply become irrelevant to the sense of unity embodied by the play's final scene. While this is often the case with successful comedies on the commercial stage, *Crimes of the Heart* can easily stand for the growing sense of empowerment and national pride that the Reagan presidency represented, regardless of facts.[20] The play also reinforces the traditional theatrical celebration of the power of the individual against a repressive society; the voice of the conforming majority, Chick, is presented as a caricature, while husband-shooting Babe and loosely-moraled Meg are clearly attractive and sympathetic. This message is hardly unique to the Reagan period, but, as mentioned above, one of the mainstays of President Reagan's rhetoric privileged precisely this image of the strong individual defying restrictive governmental policies. Henley's play thus embodies one of the central themes of the Reagan campaign.

At the end of the Reagan era, there are major changes in the successful plays.[21] Lanford Wilson's *Burn This* has virtually no political reverberation and only a little social commentary, unlike both *Fifth of July* and his other (less successful) Broadway play of the 1980s, *Angels Fall* (1983), with its background of nuclear accident providing social and political context. The passion of Anna and Pale in *Burn This* is unexplained, a natural force driving both characters despite their rational realization of the stark, if not insurmountable distance between them.

Anna and Pale inhabit different worlds. Anna's world of art, devastated by the offstage deaths of Rob and Dom before the play begins, is as sterile as the empty loft. Her choreographic success at play's end comes from transforming her relationship with Pale into art; his sexual passion liberates her artistry. Pale, foulmouthed and violent, spews forth lengthy diatribes which employ epithets and stereotypical expressions reminiscent of the resurgence of such slurs in the general society – often blamed on the Republican president's attack on affirmative action programs and less than enthusiastic record on civil rights.

Robbie and Dom's homosexuality offends Pale, who suggests it might have been responsible for their deaths in a boating accident. Anna's description of Robbie's funeral, with a family either unaware of his homosexuality or unwilling to admit their knowledge, closely resembles many reports of families responding to AIDS deaths, and more than one reviewer saw the shadow of AIDS in the play. But the single gay character in the play, Larry, is a wisecracking, campy, and ultimately stereotyped homosexual familiar in commercial theatre from the period when homsexuality could not be mentioned openly. In suggesting, however indirectly, that homosexuality is a source of anguish, *Burn This* returns to a traditionally acceptable moral universe which *Fifth of July*, with its casual presentation of Ken and Jed's partnership, had explicitly rejected. When coupled with the play's suggestion that passion-driven physical sex liberates Anna, and that Pale loses all control when in sexual need, it becomes apparent that *Burn This* supports a highly conservative set of values, underneath its contemporary surface.

*M. Butterfly* also evokes traditional values. The play's power results from its exploration of the Eurocentric perception of Asia in general, and the European male's stereotyping of Asian women in particular. It suggests vividly that the "feminine" is learned behavior, conforming to a role defined by, and created for, men. The stereotype is so strongly enculturated that Gallimard refuses to accept Song's masculinity until the penultimate scene, preferring to live in fantasy. Indeed, Gallimard dies in the fantasy, becoming Butterfly and so fusing with the culturally-imposed stereotype, seeking validation in death.

On at least the surface level, *M. Butterfly* exposes the stereotypes it explores, thus apparently challenging them and pushing its audience to examine their own perceptions, their own complicity in permitting the stereotypes to exist. Yet Hwang's play, for all its exploitation of social stereotyping, allows its audience a safe distance from the issues. The challenge is never confrontational. Instead of forcing the audience to accept its perpetuation of the stereotypes, the play distances the events in several ways. Although the parallels with the American characters from Puccini's *Madama Butterfly* are made explicit in the play's opening scenes, Gallimard and his colleagues are French – and the play uses, without apparent irony, the stereotype of the sexy French, contrasting Gallimard's ineptness with his friend, Marc.

The French characters are not only distanced from their American audiences by their ethnicity. The French diplomats in China are xenophobic and narrow-minded, and are linked with the loss of Indochina. The exotic qualities of Song Liling and the Beijing Opera are, it can be argued, as exploited by *M. Butterfly* as by the crass Europeans presented in the play.[22] Further, the character of Comrade Chin directly reinforces a stereotypical view of Chinese communists as humorless and sexless functionaries. And by committing *seppuku* at the end of the play, Gallimard reinscribes the stereotype, empowering it once again.

Commercial theatre, traditionally, reinforces the views of its paying customers, rather than challenging them. The views presented during the Reagan era were not dissimiliar to those presented by Ronald Reagan himself. The American theatre retreated from the social and political activism of the late 1960s and 1970s as firmly as the general population, reflecting at least an attempt to invalidate a simpler view of society than had been present at the beginning of the decade. With its emphasis on sentimental reworkings of the past, the presentation of ersatz nostalgia and spectacles virtually devoid of meaning, the commercial American theatre reinforced many of the themes central to the Reagan Revolution.

## NOTES

1  Kevin Phillips, *The Politics of Rich and Poor: Wealth and the American Electorate in the Reagan Aftermath* (New York: Random House, 1990), 122, *et passim*.

2  Box office figures, and the production figures to be cited below, are taken from *Variety*, 6 June 1990. Box office figures are on pages 56, 60, while production figures are on page 65.

3  It should be noted that the 1980–81 production level of 67 productions, identical to that of the previous season, was a bit of an anomaly; productions on Broadway ranged from a low of forty-six in 1970–71 to the high of sixty-seven at decade's end. The average for the decade of the 1970s was fifty-six. For the following decade, by contrast, the average was forty.

4  The total inflation rate between 1981 and 1989 was 25.2 percent; *The World Almanac and Book of Facts 1991* (New York: World Almanac, 1991), 115.

5  Benjamin Friedman, *Day of Reckoning* (New York: Random House, 1988), 198–201.

6  In a pioneering study, J. S. R. Goodlad determined that the subject matter of popular drama on radio and television revealed topics the general audience was prepared to discuss, although not necessarily ready to reach consensus. Goodlad, *The Sociology of Popular Drama* (London: Heinemann, 1971).

7  The phrases are those of Lewis H. Lapham, in *Money and Class in America: Notes and Observations on our Civil Religion* (New York: Weidenfeld & Nicolson, 1988), 40.

8  Information regarding Broadway productions, including opening dates, lengths of run, and other data, are drawn from the annual compilations edited by John Willis (*Theatre World*) and Otis L. Guernsey, Jr. (*The Burns Mantle Theater Yearbook: The Best Plays of 19xx–19xx*, with the dates changing annually). The Willis yearbook is published in New York by Crown. Guernsey's volume was published in New York by Dodd, Mead & Company through the 1986–1987 volume; starting with the 1987–1988 volume, the publisher was Applause Theatre Book Publishers in New York. Jeffrey Sweet joined Guernsey as co-editor, beginning with the 1985–1986 volume.

9  See, for example, Howard Kissel, "Cats," *Women's Wear Daily*, 8 October 1982, reprinted in *New York Theatre Critics Reviews* 43 (1982), 195.

10 Jack Kroll, "The 'Phantom' Hits Broadway," *Newsweek*, 8 February 1988, rpt. *New York Theatre Critics Reviews* 49 (1988), 396.
11 Haynes Johnson, *Sleepwalking Through History: America in the Reagan Years* (New York & London: W. W. Norton and Company, 1991), 139–40.
12 George Santayana, "Materialism and Idealism in America," *The Landmark* 1 (January 1919); rpt. Santayana, *The Genteel Tradition*, ed. Douglas L. Wilson (Cambridge, MA: Harvard University Press, 1967), 127–28.
13 See, for example, Martin Schram's discussion of television's oversimplification of issues, in *The Great American Video Game: Presidential Politics in the Television Age* (New York: William Morrow, 1987), 26. In a more general context, see James Schlesinger, *America at Century's End* (New York: Columbia University Press, 1989), 81ff.
14 Such distortions were frequent in Regan's career; see Garry Wills, *Reagan's America: Innocents at Home* (Garden City, NY: Doubleday, 1987), 162–70, 375–77.
15 Most of the revivals presented in the Broadway district were the work of the Circle in the Square Theater or the Lincoln Center Repertory Theatre, both nonprofit theatres included as part of the Broadway theatre by *Variety*, and the yearbooks edited by Willis, Guernsey and Sweet. Their revivals are not considered here. The Circle in the Square, for example, presented revivals of Williams's *A Streetcar Named Desire* and *The Night of the Iguana* (both in 1988), but neither was extended or transferred for a commercial run.
16 Joel Siegel, "Long Day's Journey Into Night," WABC-TV, 28 April 1986, *New York Theatre Critics Reviews* 47 (1986), 308.
17 The productions included Miller's *A View From the Bridge* (1983) and *All My Sons* (1987), both productions originating at the Long Wharf Theatre in Connecticut, and Williams's *The Glass Menagerie* (1983).
18 The title of the play is given as "*Fifth of July*" in programs for the Broadway engagement, in newspaper advertisements, and in the various yearbooks listed above. Programs and advertisements for its off-Broadway run in 1978 at the Circle Repertory Company, and the published script (New York: Hill and Wang, 1979), print the title as "*5th of July*." The Broadway spelling is used here.
19 The Lincoln Center Repertory Theatre did produce David Mamet's *Speed-the-Plow* directly in a Broadway theatre on 3 May 1988, but the circumstances were extraordinary: the play was originally set for the Vivian Beaumont Theater at Lincoln Center, but the great success of *Anything Goes* made the space unavailable. *Speed-the-Plow* was then scheduled for the smaller Mitzi E. Newhouse Theater, but demand for tickets and interest aroused by casting Madonna in the play necessitated opening the production in the larger Royale Theater on Broadway.
20 See, for example, Robert Schmuhl, *Statecraft and Stagecraft: American*

*Political Life in the Age of Personality* (Notre Dame and London: University of Notre Dame Press, 1990), 28.

21 It should be noted that *Burn This* and *M. Butterfly* were, along with *Speed-the-Plow*, the only successful non-musical plays produced during the 1987–88 Broadway season.

22 The production's insistence upon billing actor B. D. Wong by his initials was an attempt to maintain the illusion of Song's femininity; presumably, the audience was to be surprised when Wong stripped at the end of the play. Without any further contextualizing, this appears to be as fully exploitative as the stereotyping presented in the play.

# CHAPTER 18

# Narrative strategies in selected studies of American theatre economics

### Margaret M. Knapp

> Oh ... The theatre is dying,/The theatre is dying,/The theatre
> is practically dead!
>
> Oscar Hammerstein II, "Intermission Talk" (1953)[1]

For much of the twentieth century, observers of theatre in America have been predicting its imminent dissolution. Even a cursory review of the literature of theatre economics turns up such items as Alfred L. Bernheim's February 1929 article, "The Theater: A Depressed Industry," which appeared during a season when 225 productions opened on Broadway, over sixty companies were on tour, and local amateur and professional theatrical activity could be found in hundreds of towns and cities across the country.[2] Since the 1930s, when the Great Depression precipitated a sharp decrease in the amount of both amateur and professional theatrical production, dozens of writers have assessed the American theatre and found it in a perilous state. Some have directed dire warnings at the New York theatre; others have included the rest of the country in their prophecies of disaster. A few have concentrated on what they perceived as the artistic shortcomings of the American stage, while many more have written of its financial deficiencies. Statistics have been gathered, causes have been identified, solutions proposed, adjustments made. And yet, year after year both the theatre and the prophecies continue. In March 1991 *Atlantic Monthly* published an essay entitled "The Death of Broadway,"[3] and a few months later *New York Times* drama critic Frank Rich cheered the theatrical community with "The Great Dark Way: Slowly, the Lights Are Dimming on Broadway," which appeared on 2 June 1991, the day of the Tony Awards.[4]

One can only wonder how the American theatre continues to exist in the face of so many carefully reasoned arguments that its non-existence is inevitable, if not long overdue. I propose to explore this

gap between the theatre's continued existence and the many pre-
dictions that its end is in sight by examining a few of the assumptions, methodologies, and rhetorical strategies employed in studies
of American theatre economics.

Full-length studies of theatre finance, such as Alfred L. Bernheim's *The Business of the Theatre* and Morton Eustis's *B'way Inc.! The
Theatre as a Business*, had appeared sporadically before World War
II,[5] but the economics of the arts received its most widespread and
thorough scrutiny in the 1960s, a decade when the Kennedy administration made high culture fashionable, when economic prosperity
fueled greater interest in such "frills" as the arts, when major
corporate foundations offered significant financial support to arts
institutions, and when government at all levels began to subsidize
the arts through the National Endowment for the Arts and state and
local arts councils.

Six months before the National Endowment for the Arts (NEA)
was established in September 1965, the Rockefeller Brothers Fund
published *The Performing Arts: Problems and Prospects*.[6] The result of
an investigation by a special panel made up largely of corporate
executives with an interest in the arts, the Rockefeller Report, as it
came to be known, examined the role of arts in American society,
discussed each of the performing arts individually, and then surveyed the various forms of private, public, and corporate funding
available to arts organizations. A year later, the Twentieth Century
Fund sponsored an exhaustive study called *The Performing Arts – The
Economic Dilemma*,[7] authored by William J. Baumol and William G.
Bowen, two Princeton University economists who had also been
consultants to the Rockefeller Report. The study attempted to
provide what the authors felt was a sorely needed economic investigation resting on solid statistical data. Two years later, Jack Poggi
offered *Theater in America: The Impact of Economic Forces, 1870–1967*, in
which he thanked Baumol and Bowen for sharing their insights and
the results of their research with him (vii). Poggi's examination
focused exclusively on theatre, and took a longer historical view
than the Rockefeller or Baumol and Bowen studies, which tended to
concentrate on contemporary conditions. The fourth major
economic study of this period, Thomas Gale Moore's *The Economics
of the American Theater*, also appeared in 1968.[8] In his acknowledgements Moore expressed his gratitude to the Rockefeller Foundation
for its financial support (vi). Unlike Poggi, Moore followed the

pattern set forth by the Rockefeller and Baumol and Bowen studies in concentrating on current financial conditions.

It is obvious that these four studies shared more than a similarity of subject matter.[9] Two were directly funded by foundations with corporate connections (the Twentieth Century Fund had been established by Edward A. Filene, a Boston department store magnate); Moore's study benefitted from Rockefeller Foundation funding; and Poggi was mentored by Baumol and Bowen. Moreover, all four studies were predictive and prescriptive as well as descriptive. The authors of the Rockefeller Report included numerous recommendations for improving the arts in America. Baumol and Bowen hoped "to explain the financial problems of the performing groups and to explore the implications of these problems for the future of the arts in the United States" (4). In his final chapter, Poggi provided answers to the question, "what solutions – if any – will work?" (285). Moore's book ended with a chapter devoted to "Remedies and Suggestions" (131–43).[10] The four studies were thus meant to have an influence on future directions in the arts as well as to survey and analyze the arts in their own day.

In addition to subject matter and a penchant for prescribing and predicting, the four studies also shared two basic assumptions: that the theatre was in trouble, and that its problems could be revealed, and ultimately solved, through a positivist methodology that identified the difficulty, gathered evidence, interpreted the evidence, and reported the results. The authors expended surprisingly little effort on establishing whether in fact a significant problem existed. Baumol and Bowen began their Introduction with the sentence, "In the performing arts, crisis is apparently a way of life" (3), and the other three studies agreed that the theatre was in a bad state. The evidence produced for this shared concern was sketchy, tending either to be anecdotal or to rely on statistical comparisons with the "good old days" of the 1920s when over 250 productions a year opened on Broadway, or the even older "good old days" of the turn of the century when over 400 shows a year toured across the country.

The cursory treatment which these authors gave to the existence of a problem suggests they were confident that their readers would readily acknowledge that such a problem existed. But why were they able to assume such complicity? The answer may lie in the field of discourse within which theatre economics has traditionally been discussed, and particularly in two narrative strategies commonly employed in analyses of the financial status of the arts. In the four post-1960s studies (noted above), as well as in most other writing about theatre economics, the search for economic data as well as interpretation and reporting of that data have been controlled by two powerful metaphors. The first is an organic metaphor, in which theatre is equated with a living organism, one that is born, grows, flourishes, reaches maturity, declines, dies, and may be miraculously reborn. Examples abound: Baumol and Bowen examined "the rates of growth in these various compartments of the arts" (35); Moore wrote of the "death, metamorphosis, and rebirth of resident companies" (97), and a 1975 report of the National Committee for Cultural Resources announced that at the grass-roots level the performing arts were "burgeoning."[11] The metaphor linking the theatre with an organism proved most useful in explaining long-term trends and changes of a gradual nature. Poggi, for example, wrote of a "decline" in Broadway production activity that encompassed several decades (chapter 3).

Where the growth/decline metaphor was inadequate for describing the sporadic, often unpredictable increase and decrease in theatre activity, it was transmogrified into a related metaphor, that of health/sickness. In this narrative, the patient (theatre) has usually started out in a state of health at some putative earlier time, but then exhibits symptoms of illness, becomes critical, undergoes a crisis, and finally recovers, dies, or lingers in a moribund state. Typically, the illness is traced to some specific "disease," as when Moore quoted a playwright as saying that critics were the most dangerous (to the health and future of the theatre) element of all (38). The best-known example of this metaphor is the oft-repeated trope which refers to Broadway as "the Fabulous Invalid," after the title of a 1938 comedy by Kaufman and Hart.

The sickness/health metaphor permeated the economic studies of the 1960s. The Rockefeller Report referred to "the basic health of the professional arts organizations" (15), Baumol and Bowen mentioned that in some quarters off-Broadway was "mourned for dead" (3), and denied that they were looking for "a panacea which would promise to cure the arts of their financial ills" (4). Poggi quoted Chekhov as writing, "If many remedies are prescribed for an illness, you may know the illness is incurable" (xx), while Moore asked "What is the best criterion for evaluating the health of the theater?" (7). And more recently Thomas M. Disch predicted in his article "The Death of Broadway" that "in the nineties the Fabulous Invalid is destined to become the Inglorious Corpse" (92). The health/sickness metaphor has thus been invoked either to explain sudden upswings or downswings in theatrical activity, or to characterize long-term positive or negative trends.

Like the metaphor of theatre as organism, the sickness/health metaphor requires an unthinking acceptance of the assumption that the health of the theatre is tied to the amount of professional theatrical activity, either on Broadway alone, or in New York and in major regional theatres. Although the *quality* of theatrical productions is alluded to in all of the studies, the widespread use of statistics in all four books forced the authors to adopt *quantity* (number of tickets sold, number of productions opening, number of theatres in use, etc.) as the measure of health or sickness. The organic and sickness/health metaphors also imply that the problems of the theatre are either endemic and therefore can be solved by forces within the theatre, (better plays, lower union scales, a return to repertory), or are susceptible to treatment by one or more "quick fixes" from outside (foundation or government funding, contracts with film studios or cable television companies, more efficient fundraising procedures). Fundamental changes in the economic system within which theatre operates are rarely if ever proposed.

A second powerful metaphor in studies of theatre economics is that of the "theatre industry," or, in its earlier formulation, "show business." Since the commercial theatre does function directly as a profit-making endeavor, and since even nonprofit theatres compete for audiences within a market economy, "theatre as an industry" seems to be part metaphor and part descriptor. In the early part of the century the phrases "show business" and "theatre industry" identified the rapidly expanding commercial theatre of New York and the road. As the financing of commercial theatre activity grew more complex, the business aspects of "show business" grew in importance, until it was difficult to distinguish between theatre and other types of financial speculation. By 1914, Walter Prichard Eaton was equating the downturn in theatre activity with similar vagaries in the stock market when he wrote of "The Slump in the Theatrical Business," and in 1929 Howard Barnes dissected "The Broadway Real Estate Racket."[12] In the 1960s economic analyses of the theatre invited their readers to view theatre as coextensive with industry, thereby minimizing the metaphorical dimensions of "show business." The notion of a theatre industry was expanded to include nonprofit as well as commercial theatre. Phrases that would have been more at home in a corporate annual report began to appear in studies of the arts. Baumol and Bowen, for example, devoted several pages to demonstrating that while major gains in productivity had been made across the board in American industry, "in the live performing arts there is as little room for productivity increases through the accumulation of capital as there is for new technology" (165), and elsewhere bemoaned the large percentage of costs devoted to salaries and wages (209ff.) which made theatre a "labor intensive" industry, as later economists were to describe it. Though all of the studies acknowledged that its aesthetic component set theatre apart from industry, the temptation to conflate art and commerce often proved irresistible. The Rockefeller Report claimed that "there is no reason why the business operations of a nonprofit organization should not be as expertly managed as those of any profit-seeking organization" (55), and recommended that in order to increase corporate donations, "arts organizations practice good budgeting procedures and strict accounting methods under the guidance of independent budget committees representing the community at large [i.e., businessmen and women]" (78–79). The Report urged arts organizations seeking corporate and foundation support to reconfigure their financial operations to resemble those of corporations.

The power of the theatre-as-industry metaphor was especially felt in the 1960s, when the Ford and Rockefeller Foundations provided massive funding for the arts, and when the National Endowment for the Arts was established. In general, the foundations favored non-profit arts institutions that adhered to corporate practices in their financial operations, as the recommendations of the Rockefeller Report quoted above demonstrate. The NEA, whose structure was modeled on the New York State Council on the Arts, which in turn derived its operating procedures from the Rockefeller Foundation,[13] was mandated to support "productions which have substantial artistic and cultural significance, giving emphasis to American creativity and the maintenance and encouragement of *professional* excellence ... "[14] The complexity of NEA grant application procedures, coupled with the emphasis on professionalism, followed the foundations' lead in favoring established, professional arts organizations whose financial stability could be judged according to corporate standards. It is not surprising, then, that the economic studies of the mid-1960s, with their connections to the world of corporate foundations, should choose to limit their research on nonprofit theatre to established and professional arts institutions, rather than fledgling arts groups or individual artists.

Under the twin influences of corporate and governmental funding, many arts organizations accepted the theatre-as-industry metaphor and presented themselves as quasi-industrial entities. NEA guidelines and research reports were peppered with recommendations that arts organizations "identify constituencies," "perform internal policy analyses," and "learn more about their operations and markets," processes that would no doubt soothe corporation, foundation, and NEA grants officers.[15]

Meanwhile, the commercial Broadway theatre, which had always been comfortable with the appellation "show business," came under the scrutiny of New York State for shady financing practices, with the result that after 1964, Broadway investors had to follow the pattern established in other business fields by organizing into limited risk partnerships, what Baumol and Bowen called "a new business firm organized expressly for the production of that play" (20). More recently, supporters of the commercial theatre couched their arguments in the latest economic terminology when they blamed increased costs on the fact that theatre was a "labor intensive" industry, and argued for greater city and state support on the grounds that "the arts in the New York–New Jersey metropolitan area are a perfect illustration of the agglomeration principle, where a critical mass of related economic functions established in a narrow geographic area acts as an engine of sustained activity and growth."[16]

The theatre-as-industry metaphor has thus become pervasive in studies of theatre economics. Its power as a narrative strategy lies in the difference between metaphors and similes. Most economic narratives do not contend that the theatre is in some ways *like* a living organism, or *like* an industry. Rather, they invite us to accept the equivalence that the metaphors so insistently assert. The result is that important distinctions between the theatre on the one hand, and living organisms or capitalist industries on the other hand, are erased. In particular, the marginality, the danger, the dissonance that theatre can offer are minimized, controlled, and recuperated by these narratives.

The theatre-as-industry metaphor has been especially powerful in controlling the discourse of theatre economics, with some far-reaching consequences. More and more, the very existence of theatre is defended in terms of its profitability. Advocates seeking special government treatment of the arts often point to the amount of total revenue produced by the arts in a specific area, e.g., the $480 million that the Broadway and off-Broadway theatres were said to have generated in 1983.[17] The NEA, while warning that "to substitute the economic value of the arts for their human, spiritual, and aesthetic value could be dangerous," nevertheless disseminated information on the economic impact of nonprofit arts groups on selected cities and explained how local organizations could make effective use of such information in fundraising.[18] Thus, even nonprofit theatres have been encouraged to sell themselves on the basis of an indirect financial profitability for their communities.

The insistence on profitability led inevitably to a search for ways to increase earnings. Baumol and Bowen, taking a pessimistic view, equated the financial problems of performing groups to those of other low technology service trades (405) and predicted little if any increase in income. Two decades later, Harold L. Vogel, a vice president at Merrill Lynch Capital Markets, blamed the performing arts' financial problems on the "ineluctable element" that "productivity cannot be raised significantly in the performance of performing arts."[19] Using the yardstick of direct profitability, the arts, other than in a few select areas, could well seem to be "in decline."

On the other hand, the profitability argument was expanded to include other significant, though indirect, benefits. The Rockefeller Report argued that "the arts can be a major source of strength for the business community. They provide cultural resources increasingly recognized as essential to a suitable environment for business enterprise" (81). According to the Report, one of the important contributions that the arts could make to that "suitable environment" was to occupy the increased leisure of American workers which might be "both an individual and a community problem if it is not channeled into constructive and satisfying ranges of activity" (7). In this instance, the arts were to increase business profitability by providing what business could not, control over their employees during their leisure time.

Although the economic studies of the 1960s defined what constituted profitability in the arts and suggested ways in which that

profitability could be increased, they rarely tackled the more fundamental question of why the arts needed to be profitable at all. Even
some studies that offered non-economic justifications still located
their value outside of the arts themselves, as when the Rockefeller
Report called the arts "the culmination of other achievements – the
attainment that in the end gives a society its hope for a lasting place
in history … " (4), thereby making its case for the arts on the basis
of national prestige. One way or another, the arts could be made to
"pay."

The theatre-as-industry metaphor is so integral to our thinking
about theatre economics that it is sometimes difficult to recognize its
effects. Over the past few years the NEA has been under fire from
groups and individuals who wish to see more direct government
control over the kinds of arts projects that get funded. Although it
has brought forth cries of "censorship" from many quarters, the
threat to regulate the NEA is understandable in the context of
government regulation of business. For more than a quarter century
arts organizations have been characterized as businesses by the NEA
and corporate foundations, and have learned to justify themselves
on the basis of profitability. The uniqueness of the arts as a form of
expression has been minimized or ignored in attempts to conform to
the industrial model. It should therefore come as no surprise that
some members of Congress and the Bush administration saw nothing
wrong with permanent government regulation of the arts industry
on the pattern of the Food and Drug Administration or the Federal
Trade Commission.

If it has accomplished nothing else, the NEA controversy has
forced those concerned about the arts to seek greater control over
public discourse. But it may be a case of too little, too late. So
widespread has been the acceptance of the organic and industrial
metaphors and their implications, that it is virtually impossible to
imagine a discourse about theatre economics, whether commercial
or nonprofit, that does not employ them. Through them, we are
seduced into viewing theatre as a capitalist enterprise which must
perforce function within a capitalist marketplace. Growth and
decline, health and sickness are defined through increases and
decreases in the quantity of professional theatre productions at the
major commercial and nonprofit institutions. Any reduction in
quantity at these venues is traced to one or more internal "diseases"
that have interfered with the theatre's production of surplus capital.

And the "theatre industry" becomes more than a metaphor when theatre companies take their places alongside other American businesses, conforming to the rules of the capitalist marketplace in order to receive corporate and government funding. Until the discursive practices of theatre economists are opened up to include other narrative strategies, the two metaphors, however bankrupt, will continue to channel our thinking about the financial structure of theatre.

Is the theatre dying? It depends on how you ask.

## NOTES

1 Richard Rodgers and Oscar Hammerstein, II, *Me and Juliet, Six Plays by Rodgers and Hammerstein* (New York: Random House, n.d.), 510.
2 Alfred L. Bernheim, "The Theater: A Depressed Industry," *New Republic* 57 (13 February 1929), 341–43. Statistics on the 1928–29 season are taken from Jack Poggi, *Theater in America: The Impact of Economic Forces, 1870–1967* (Ithaca: Cornell University Press, 1968), 47, 30. Subsequent references to the Poggi book appear as page numbers in the text.
3 Thomas M. Disch, "The Death of Broadway," *Atlantic Monthly* 267 (March 1991), 92–96, 98–99, 102, 104. Subsequent references appear as page numbers in the text.
4 Frank Rich, "The Great Dark Way: Slowly, the Lights are Dimming on Broadway," *New York Times* (2 June 1991), Section 2: 1, 28.
5 Alfred L. Bernheim, *The Business of the Theatre* (New York: Actors' Equity Assn., 1932; repr. New York: Benjamin Blom, 1964); Morton Eustis, *B'way Inc.!: The Theatre as a Business* (New York: Dodd, Mead, 1934).
6 Rockefeller Panel, *The Performing Arts: Problems and Prospects* (New York: McGraw-Hill, 1965). Subsequent references appear as page numbers in the text.
7 William J. Baumol and William G. Bowen, *Performing Arts – The Economic Dilemma* (New York: Twentieth Century Fund, 1966). Subsequent references appear as page numbers in the text.
8 Thomas Gale Moore, *The Economics of the American Theater* (Durham, NC: Duke University Press, 1968). Subsequent references appear as page numbers in the text.
9 Although the Rockefeller Report and the Baumol and Bowen study both encompass all of the performing arts, my analysis is confined to the sections on theatre except where otherwise noted.
10 A detailed analysis of the solutions offered, the extent to which they have been adopted in the past quarter century, or the results obtained, is beyond the scope of this essay. It should be noted, however, that

although many of the suggestions offered in the economic studies have been put into practice by theatre organizations, the perception that the American theatre is in serious trouble persists.

11 National Committee for Cultural Resources, *National Report on the Arts* (New York: National Committee for Cultural Resources, 1975), 11.

12 Walter Prichard Eaton, "The Slump in the Theatrical Business," *American Magazine* 77 (April 1914), 46–50; Howard Barnes, "The Broadway Real Estate Racket," *Theatre* 50 (November 1929), 15–16, 76.

13 Wallace Dace, "The Economics of Inspiration," *Performing Arts Journal* 4(1979), 170.

14 *United States Statutes at Large* 79 (Washington, DC: U.S. Government Printing Office, 1966), 846. My italics.

15 National Endowment for the Arts, *Economic Impact of Arts and Cultural Institutions* (Washington, DC: Research Division of NEA, 1981), 10–11.

16 *The Arts as Industry: Their Economic Importance to the New York–New Jersey Metropolitan Region* (New York: Cultural Assistance Center, 1983), 6.

17 Ibid., 3.

18 *Impact of Arts*, 10ff.

19 Harold L. Vogel, *Entertainment Industry Economics: A Guide for Financial Analysis* (Cambridge: Cambridge University Press, 1986), 333.

# CHAPTER 19

# Multiculturalism versus technoculturalism: its challenge to American theatre and the functions of arts management

*Stephen Langley*

Two of the most far-reaching issues to emerge as America approaches the twenty-first century are those of multiculturalism and what might be termed technoculturalism. How the nation deals with the growing diversity of its population, in which no single radical or cultural group now constitutes a majority in many areas, will greatly determine its future. And how the so-called global village uses and responds to the technology of communication systems will greatly determine its future. What is multiculturalism? What is technoculturalism? How are they challenging the American theatre and what role can management play in helping the performing arts keep pace with rapidly changing social and technological developments?

## THE ISSUES

For nearly three hundred years American life was dominated by European culture as imported and promulgated by the White Anglo-Saxon Protestant establishment which attempted to impose it on all Americans regardless of their heritage. This was not monoculturalism, such as that found in Japan or Scandinavia where there is basically one cultural family, but rather, unicentric culturalism, such as that also found in a class-dominated Great Britain and a Russian-dominated Soviet Union. It might also be called cultural imperialism. Cultural democracy, on the other hand, is still an ideal, a model concept for a new kind of social order yet to be achieved. But as increasing numbers of Americans demand cultural equity and as diverse groups achieve empowerment, cultural democracy moves closer to becoming a reality.

During the 1980s multiculturalism became a prevalent issue in North America due to a declining dollar that attracted a large influx of foreign tourists, businesses and investments simultaneously with huge numbers of arriving emigrants and illegal aliens, especially from Latino and Asian countries. National population shifts caused by economic upheavals changed the profile of many communities seemingly over night. And these factors coincided with increasingly effective civil rights advocacy to demand that attention be paid. When America woke up to the 1990s and looked in the mirror, it saw a face of many colors with character lines it could no longer hide with the blush of youth or the white of face powder, and it heard a voice of many tongues and inflections. Thus, cultural and racial equity were at last placed on the national agenda – especially in the areas of labor, education, business and the arts – not because of any moral imperative, but simply because the numbers had changed.

Multiculturalism in its current usage asserts that there are a variety of equally valid though considerably different lifestyles within the human family and demands that a democratic society with a diverse population give a representative voice to its constituent groups and equal opportunity to all. In its broadest definition, multiculturalism has also come to embrace certain interest groups that choose to identify themselves not primarily with a linguistic, political, religious or ethnic bond, but rather with some physical, gender or preference bond, such as those who are physically challenged, women or gay. As with traditional cultural groups, the agenda for these typically include social acceptance, economic security, parity in the workplace and political empowerment at least proportionate to their numbers.

Inevitably, there has been resistance to the multiculturalism movement. This has found expression within conservative groups in general and on the American campus in particular among those who identify themselves with "political correctness" (PC).

The great irony about America's belated attention to its multicultural makeup is that it occurred just when the electronic media and technology are perfecting our ability to obliterate diversity. Historically, cultural assimilation has been accelerated by mass migrations, crusades, wars, colonization and, more recently, by emigration, air travel and the increasing economic interdependence of nations. Yet, these have all had only moderate influence on the global psyche compared with the growing impact of telecommunications. How many cultures will be able to maintain their identities once they are fully "wired?" If cultural Darwinism is part of the dynamic, then cultures that cannot adapt and evolve will not survive. People who would promote a multicultural society should perhaps focus their attention less on each other and more on the phenomenon that threatens to absorb all traditional cultures into a synthetic marketplace of consumers. Consider how quickly the movies made theatre elitist, how quickly TV made movies elitist and then how quickly cable and VCRs put the networks in jeopardy. Mass media is by definition irreconcilable with individualism and diversity. Not only must it appeal to the mainstream, this monster species keeps enlarging the mainstream as it feeds it, thereby enlarging itself. The process has already begun to erode countless traditional habits, social units, diets, dialects, morals, religions and languages. This may not be altogether regrettable. But the unbridled growth of consumerism as stimulated by media technology is also on its way to eroding the planet itself, which simply cannot sustain unlimited industrial development.

Technoculturalism, then, is the distribution of information and entertainment products designed for wide multicultural and international consumption on a commercial basis using technological delivery systems and thereby accelerating the completion of a global village with a unicultural society. The term does not condemn technology as such or the advent of mass media; rather it questions how technology is being used, by whom and to what ends. It identifies one of the two adversaries in the present socio-economic–political contest between cultural conformity and cultural diversity. It suggests that objections to our "Eurocentric" society merely obscure the fact that our real cultural base is now capitalist–technological America – or, at least, what we still own of it. Given this almost universally admired model, the continued growth of media technology seems to point in only one direction. Indeed, if a vote were taken worldwide, how many people would opt for their own cultural heritage, much less multiculturalism, over technocentric cultural consumerism?

## THE CHALLENGE

Multiculturalism, it might be argued, is the last gasp of tribalism, the last significant opportunity for the human race to celebrate its diversity beyond the comparatively superficial differences imposed by skin color, national boundaries and cultural imperialism. Because cultures are most clearly and powerfully defined by the art they produce, it should be obvious that the arts are of central importance in the reinforcement of cultural diversity. This will remain the case at least until the popular uses of technology are made to enhance and enlighten the human condition rather than dilute and diminish it.

Several recent events on the performing arts front have helped to nourish appreciation for multiculturalism. These include the growth of international festivals during the 1980s from New York to Charlestown and from Chicago to the 1984 Olympics in Los Angeles. And a fund was established (financed by private foundations and administered by Arts International) to support appearances by American artists and ensembles at European festivals, where they have often been among the few not sponsored by their government. Also, there was an increase in cultural exchange between the Soviet Union and the United States due to perestroika, and between Japan and the United States due to new sponsorship deals fueled by a booming Japanese economy. By bringing more live performances by foreign artists to American audiences, a new awareness was lent to the value of our own artistic resources. And there was considerable discussion in arts circles (as well as some in the popular press) about the intercultural theatre productions of such major directors as Peter Brook, Lee Breuer and Pina Bausch. Their work has suggested the rich possibilities waiting to be mined from a culturally diverse terrain.

By the 1990s, however, American arts companies and institutions were ready for more than international exchange and intercultural exploration, though these would obviously continue. Many had actively begun to address the multicultural issue in relation to their own communities and institutions. This on-going process of evaluation has made it increasingly clear that established programming, staffing and support in the performing arts has usually been culturally exclusive, that many cultural groups have been under-served by arts activities and that the management systems used to deliver works of art to the public need to be reexamined and in many cases restructured.

## THE ROLE OF MANAGEMENT FUNCTIONS IN MEETING THE CHALLENGE

Given that management is concerned with long-range planning and policy implementation as well as the administration of day-to-day operations, its fundamental role is that of facilitator. The most basic functions that management employs to achieve results are: planning, organizing, staffing, supervising and controlling. The same functions are used both in arts management and media management, but with different results because of different goals.

For present purposes, we will focus on nonprofit theatre companies and examine how such companies might utilize basic management functions to implement a policy of multiculturalism as a competitive advantage in this era of growing technoculturalism.

### Planning

Planning in theatre begins when some artistic concept of vision is articulated, perhaps in the form of a mission statement, and accompanied by concrete policies and programs that define the objectives of the project. Good management helps the artistic leaders and, where they exist, the trustees to express their goals so these can be understood by everyone who gets involved – artists and staff, audience and press, donors and funders.

When a multicultural policy is adopted, it requires careful definition so that no potentially valuable resources, participants or supporters are excluded. For example, terms such as Latino and Hispanic, Caribbean and West Indian have different connotations for different people, as do feminist and women, deaf and hearing impaired. A theatre dedicated to producing plays by African-American writers will have a more limited repertory than one that produces plays about the African-American experience. And it is important not to confuse race or color with culture. Too, while a theatre of, by and for its own community alone is monocultural, a company may be dedicated to the works of a single culture and yet be multicultural by virtue of its staffing, marketing and outreach policies. Multiculturalism seeks neither to segregate nor assimilate, but it does seek to relate and to include.

In contrast to media policy, multicultural arts planning seeks programming that speaks to the human condition by illuminating its peculiarities rather than its commonalities. It opens the doors to different cultural homesteads and also builds roadways so that neighbors can visit each other. This requires financial planning that reflects the goals of multiculturalism. Among other things, the sources of income will be as important as the income itself. Do ticket prices, for instance, exclude the very audience the programming is designed to attract? Does corporate funding come from companies that also support politicians or causes that are diametrically opposed to those of the theatre company? Is it better to tap sources of funding and services from within the company's own cultural family – limited and difficult as this may be – or from unrelated sources? Theatre companies are like small Mom and Pop businesses in today's world, not like multinational corporations. Their success depends heavily on loyalty and support within their own communities. As a case in point, the late Joseph Papp, producer of the New York Shakespeare Festival, one of the nation's largest and oldest multicultural theatres, turned down a substantial NEA grant rather than sign an anti-obscenity pledge that he found in violation of rights to artistic freedom. This gesture threatened the fiscal health of the institution, though it strengthened its integrity in the minds of its artistic community and its audience.

Successful marketing policy for a theatre company is also formulated early; selecting the artistic home and creating an internal environment that is user-friendly for performers and staff as well as audiences, researching the external environment and developing target strategies, developing projects that permit the company to extend its reach into the community – such as touring, artists-in-schools, benefits for local causes and internship programs for traditionally excluded participants. Attracting new audiences to live theatre may require new types of venues and performance spaces, as well as theatregoing habits and etiquette, and increased cultural sensitivity at all staff levels. Planning in the nonprofit sector, unlike the commercial sector, aims at accommodating different types of behavior, not at promoting just one.

## Organizing

Once the leadership of a theatre company – usually the artistic head and a volunteer board of trustees or advisors – has agreed on its mission and long-term objectives, effective management decides how to organize the venture. How will the company be structured, legalized and financed? How will the performance material be selected, rehearsed and performed? When, where and how often? For whom, for how many and for how much? How will the staff be selected and organized and what will the salaries be?

In a multicultural setting each of these matters serves double duty, because decision-making is based on a policy of inclusion as well as the need for expedience. While management of commercial media companies is driven by the profit motive, the nonprofit theatre company is driven by its mission and its human resources.

Familiarity with incipient theatre groups around the country brings realization that many have no traditional organization at all: no board of trustees, no 501 (c)(3), no management. This situation cannot be ignored. Dozens of black theatre groups that thrived during the 1960s and 1970s but then disappeared suffered from inadequate internal management and/or external audience and funding support. Sometimes this stemmed from lack of know-how and support agencies, other times from pride and not wanting to "buy into the system." Artists, whose lifestyles may be as non-traditional as their art, are sometimes resistant if not hostile when asked to conform to traditional methodologies – which is perfectly correct behavior in the rationale of multiculturalism, not to mention the rationale of artistic exploration. The challenge to arts management is in helping such artists and groups gain legitimacy without compromising their principles or forcing them into the mainstream. Meeting this challenge could well lead to the discovery of new and more effective models of operation quite different from the nonprofit structure currently in vogue.

While there are now numerous training programs for arts managers, from day-long workshops to graduate degree programs, only a few actively recruit minority students or deal with non-traditional management alternatives. There is only one national organization, the Association of American Cultures (TAAC) in Washington, DC, devoted exclusively to the protection of cultural diversity in the arts. However, the funding of ethnic artists and multicultural companies has become a clearly stated priority at the National Endowment for the Arts as well as at most regional, state and city arts agencies. So, arguably, there is somewhat less likelihood today that a struggling ethnic artist or multicultural arts company of promise will fall through the cracks than was the case in the recent past.

## Staffing

The question of who is placed in positions of authority is a matter of empowerment, a key element of the multicultural issue. Government agencies in the arts field led the way in multicultural staffing. And some of the private funders, like the Ford Foundation and the Rockefeller Foundation, have long had well-balanced boards and staffs. Furthermore, most government arts agencies as well as many foundation and corporate funders now evaluate grant requests with an eye to how well the board and staff of the arts group in question reflects its community.

Some theatres were originated as multicultural ventures, such as the AMAS Musical Theatre in New York, the Mixed Blood Theatre Company in Minneapolis and the Detroit Repertory. Others are only now adopting a policy that reflects the demographics of their community, such as the Arena Stage in Washington, DC, which recently began the transition by hiring an African-American associate artistic director.

One of the most frequent yet insidious comments one hears from people charged with appointing new employees is "I'll hire the person best qualified for the job." This easily translates into "Because I'm so qualified, the candidate I select will obviously look and think like me!"

A search for job applicants reflects the channels through which the search is conducted. Not all qualified candidates, for instance, read the want ads in the Los Angeles *Times* or the Washington *Post* or, for that matter, the *Hellenic Times*, the *Korea Herald* or *El Diario*; not all belong to a particular union or club; not all are known to the same employment agency or search firm. A truly multicultural search requires that personal contacts and information networks be expanded until token comments and candidates are out of the picture and a diversity of highly qualified applicants is found.

Casting for the theatre is a type of staffing and brings up the question of union affiliation for artistic employees at multicultural companies. This is important because union affiliation – particularly with Actors' Equity Association – is sometimes a qualification for grants, for critical attention in the press, for the participation of guest artists, for the rights to perform recently established hits and for the opportunity to perform new works by major or promising writers. In short, the union status of a theatre company, like its fiscal/legal status, is widely equated with professionalism. This may seem unreasonable to a company of Pacific Islanders, Latino-Americans or physically challenged veterans. But here again, management is charged with labor organizations – for gaining fair compensation and professional status for all artists of accomplishment. It is unlikely that such solutions will be found, however, unless the management staff is as multicultural as the policies it advocates.

Due to pioneering efforts in nontraditional casting from coast to coast and the largely positive attention this has received in the press, many audiences have come to accept it if not expect it. Supporting this policy is the Non-Traditional Casting Project, a national organization based in New York and dedicated to "the casting of ethnic, female or disabled actors in roles where race, ethnicity, gender or physical capability are not necessary to the characters' or play's development." Having established a national data bank of resumés for such performers, the Project's goal is to offer casting options to every producer or director who says something like, "I'd love to cast a person of color, but I don't know where to find one." Similar services are needed to assist in the multicultural recruitment of trustees and managers.

The most publicized example of nontraditional casting in recent years was a convoluted one involving the Broadway production of *Miss Saigon*, which had been a hit in London with a white British actor in the lead role of a Eurasian character. When the show's producer announced his desire to let the same talented actor re-create his role on Broadway, several leading Asian-American theatre artists strongly protested on the grounds that the role should be played by someone of Asian descent. This despite the fact that the character was half Caucasian. Nonetheless, Actors' Equity agreed with the Asian viewpoint and thereby stirred up a much-publicized controversy that challenges the nontraditional casting issue by asking, "If it's all right to use black and Asian actors in roles conceived for white actors, why isn't it all right to use white actors in roles conceived for black and Asian actors?" Equity eventually revised its thinking and ruled in favor of talent rather than race, so the British actor opened on Broadway.

More germane examples of nontraditional casting can readily be found in the annals of a company like the New York Shakespeare Festival, where Morgan Freeman and Tracey Ullman recently played the lead roles in *The Taming of the Shrew*, Denzel Washington played *Richard III* with a culturally mixed cast and Raul Julia and James Earl Jones played Shakespearean roles early in their careers. The fact is, of course, that nontraditional casting is every actor's dream.

Both in casting and staffing, multicultural theatre projects have a moral obligation not only to avoid stereotyping but to eliminate it. Only through this policy might it be possible to educate mainstream attitudes and thereby influence the media, which is largely responsible for creating those attitudes in the first place. It does this by treating cultural differences superficially in the form of stereotypical characters and situations: the lazy Puerto Rican janitor, the solicitous Asian houseboy, the bossy Jewish mother-in-law, the sinister black drug pusher and so forth. Theatre committed to multicultural policy does not concern itself with types, it concerns itself with human beings.

### Supervising

After the major goals have been set, the organizational structure put into place and the personnel hired, the function of management is to make it all work as planned. This entails coordinating various activities, correcting misjudgments and mistakes, and always keeping the focus on the stated mission of the company. It may also entail multicultural job orientation to break down preconditioned attitudes. For example, perhaps a black employee is having difficulty taking orders from an Asian supervisor or the white ushers are being less than courteous to the black audiences. This latter situation arose when the Lincoln Center Theatre production of *Sarafina* transferred to a Broadway house staffed by union ushers who were mainly white, middle-aged women. Some personnel may need to be shifted into different positions or, better still, helped to dispense with their old perceptions through individual counselling or group sensitivity training.

In the commercial sector, labor management aims at gaining the greatest productivity for the lowest wages. Personnel management in the nonprofit sector aims at bringing out the best in people – employees and volunteers alike – so the organization can best fulfill its mission.

### Controlling

The most common strategies used by management to control an operation include bookkeeping and accounting systems for budget control; audits and reconciliations for cash (and ticket) control; requisition and purchase systems to control expenditures; inventory control mechanisms; time sheets, work reviews and job evaluations for personnel control and, in the theatre, artistic surveillance to control the product. Artists in general and people who have always functioned outside the mainstream of society in particular, to emphasize an earlier point, are understandably suspicious of anything or anyone who interferes with their own carefully and perhaps painfully constructed methods of protecting and nurturing their creativity, which may well equate with their survival. So the introduction of standard management techniques in a multicultural environment often requires more than a business school mentality, and never more so than when management must explain how control mechanisms can facilitate artistic freedom and creativity.

The ultimate test of a theatre production is judged by the appropriateness and quality of the experience it provides for an audience. The ultimate test of a media product is the size of the audience it reaches – bigger being better. In other words success in the arts is qualitative whereas in the media business it is quantitative. Furthermore, with regard to a multicultural theatre the composition of the audience may be more important than its size. Theatre is people oriented, media is numbers oriented. The one reinforces diversity, the other conformity.

## CONCLUSION

To preserve America's diversity it is necessary to value and encourage the artistic expression that flows from and illuminates the soul of each culture whose torchbearers inhabit its landscape. This entails, first, preserving past works while encouraging the creation of new ones. Second, to qualify as valuable, works must be appreciated within the cultural family that fosters them and then, if the framework is to become truly multicultural, also by members of other cultural families. Finally, multiculturalism honors a laissez faire attitude and is open to new influences, even seeking them out. Without challenge there is unlikely to be much creative response or vitality, to borrow from Toynbee's view of history. A culture that has ceased to evolve is a dead culture, which may also be said of a language or an art form.

The arts have been challenged for some years now by film and media but have not responded very much or very well. This is especially true of the theatre. Yet, the media is responding and improving its reach every day. It does this in part by pulling together the common threads it discovers in diverse fabrics. A logical response from the arts community would be to strengthen those fabrics by giving expression to the diversity of each. This is, after all, inherent in the artistic process – the revelation of truth through an idiosyncratic medium. Conversely, the highest function of the media is the revelation of information through electronic formulae. Diversity, then, is the stuff of artistic creation, the antithesis of the media message. American theatre, like American society, would do well to ask if our sometimes misguided use of media technology – which intentionally promotes consumerism as well as, perhaps unintentionally, violence and illiteracy – is not deculturalizing our civilization, just as industrialization is destabilizing our planet.

The arts may provide an antidote to technoculturalism and help buy the time needed to foster cultural democracy and to make media technology serve rather than manipulate the mind of humanity.

Multiculturalism in America provides the arts with their closest allies, audiences and sources of inspiration – and their best opportunity to extend their reach.

Arts management can strengthen multiculturalism by protecting and facilitating its artistic production and thereby helping to counter the formidable challenge of technoculturalism.

# CHAPTER 20

# Checklist of selected books on American theatre, 1960–90

## Compiled by Don B. Wilmeth

The following sources are intended to serve as a complement and supplement to those authorities included in Barnard Hewitt's *Theatre U.S.A. 1668 to 1957* (New York, 1959). Limitation of space requires the exclusion of sources other than published books, although in consulting this checklist one should be aware that many authoritative efforts are to be found in theses and dissertations as well as journal/serial essays. Of the latter, the following current serials most often contain research or criticism on American theatre and drama: *American Theatre, Journal of American Drama and Theatre, Theatre History Studies, Nineteenth Century Theatre, The Theatre Journal, Performance Arts Resources, Studies in American Drama 1945–Present, The Drama Review, Theatre Three,* and *Performance Art Journal*. Although American theatre is now defined broadly, including many variant forms of performance and venues, the following, again by necessity of space, concentrates on so-called legitimate theatre, and then only selectively. Necessary exclusions include critical studies of individual playwrights (some biographies do appear), sources on musical theatre, and editions of plays, though the user will note a number of exceptions cited because of a useful overview or bibliography. Sources on popular entertainments, which have proliferated in the last twenty years, could easily dominate this list. Only representative and important studies have been cited, however; the circus and most outdoor amusements have been excluded altogether. For those interested in more extensive bibliographies on popular entertainments, including the circus, various outdoor amusements, and musical theatre and the revue, my three bibliographical essays in *Handbook of American Popular Culture*, 2nd edition, edited by M. Thomas Inge (Westport, CT, 1989) might prove helpful.

Abramson, Doris E. *Negro Playwrights in the American Theatre 1925–1959*. New York: Columbia University Press, 1969

Adams, Cindy. *Lee Strasberg: The Imperfect Genius of the Actors Studio*. Garden City, NY: Doubleday & Co., 1980

Adler, Thomas P. *Mirror on the Stage: The Pulitzer Plays as an Approach to American Drama*. West Lafayette, IN: Purdue University Press, 1987

Alpert, Hollis, *The Barrymores*. New York: The Dial Press, 1964

Appelbaum, Stanley, ed. *The New York Stage: Famous Productions in Photographs (1883–1939)*. New York: Dover, 1976
  *Great Actors and Actresses of the American Stage in Historic Photographs (1850–1950)*. New York: Dover, 1983
Archer, Stephen M. *American Actors and Actresses: A Guide to Information Sources*. Detroit: Gale Research, 1983
Aronson, Arnold. *American Set Design*. New York: Theatre Communications Group, 1985
Ashby, Clifford and Suzanne DePauw May. *Trouping Through Texas: Harley Sadler and His Tent Show*. Bowling Green, OH: Bowling Green University Popular Press, 1982
Atkinson, Brooks. *Broadway*. Rev. ed. New York: Macmillan, 1974
Auster, Albert. *Actresses and Suffragists: Women in the American Theater 1890–1920*. New York: Praeger, 1984
Avery, Laurence G. *Dramatist in America: Letters of Maxwell Anderson, 1912–1958*. Chapel Hill: University of North Carolina Press, 1977
Backalenick, Irene. *East Side Story: Ten Years with the Jewish Repertory Theatre*. Lanham, MD: University Press of America, 1988
Baine, Rodney M. *Robert Munford: America's First Comic Dramatist*. Athens: University of Georgia Press, 1967
Banks, Ann, ed. *First-Person America*. New York: Alfred A. Knopf, 1980
Barker, Barbara M. *Ballet or Ballyhoo: The American Careers of Maria Bonfanti, Rita Sangalli, and Giuseppini Morlacchi*. New York: Dance Horizons, 1984
  ed. *Bolossy Kiralfy: Creator of Great Musical Spectacles*. Ann Arbor: UMI Research Press, 1988
Barrow, Kenneth. *Helen Hayes: First Lady of the American Theatre*. Garden City, NY: Doubleday, 1985
Barstow, Arthur. *The Director's Voice: Twenty-One Interviews*. New York: Theatre Communications Group, 1988
Bartholomeusz, Dennis. *The Winter's Tale in Performance in England and America 1611–1976*. Cambridge: Cambridge University Press, 1982
Bassham, Ben L. *The Theatrical Photographs of Napoleon Sarony*. Kent: Kent State University Press, 1978
Bauland, Peter. *The Hooded Eagle: Modern German Drama on the New York Stage*. Syracuse: Syracuse University Press, 1968
Baumol, William J. and William G. Bowen. *Performing Arts: The Economic Dilemma*. New York: The Twentieth Century Fund, 1966
Becker, Ralph E. *Miracle on the Potomac: The Kennedy Center from the Beginning*. Silver Spring, MD: Bertleby Press, 1989
Beckerman, Bernard and Howard Siegman, eds. *On Stage: Selected Theater Reviews from The New York Times 1920–1970*. New York: Arno Press, 1973
Bedard, Roger L. and C. John Tolch, eds. *Spotlight on the Child: Studies in the History of American Children's Theatre*. Westport, CT: Greenwood Press, 1989

Benston, Kimberly. *Baraka: The Renegade and the Mask*. New Haven: Yale University Press, 1976

Bentley, Joanne. *Hallie Flanagan: A Life in the American Theatre*. New York: Alfred A. Knopf, 1988

Berkowitz, Gerald M. *New Broadways: Theatre Across America 1950–1980*. Totowa, NJ: Rowman and Littlefield, 1982

Bigsby, C. W. E. *A Critical Introduction to Twentieth-Century American Drama*. 3 vols. Cambridge; Cambridge University Press. Volume 1: *1900–1940*, 1982; Volume 2: *Williams/Miller/Albee*, 1984; Volume 3: *Beyond Broadway*, 1985

Biner, Pierre. *The Living Theatre*. New York: Horizon Press, 1972

Bishop, Mary, ed. *The Ohio Theatre 1928–1979*. Columbus: Columbus Association for the Performing Arts, 1978

Blau, Herbert. *Take Up the Bodies: Theater at the Vanishing Point*. Urbana: University of Illinois, 1982

Blum, Daniel. *A Pictorial History of the American Theatre: 100 Years, 1860–1960*. New York: Bonanza Books, 1960; 4th edition, ed. John Willis (1860–1976). New York: Crown, 1977

Blumenthal, Eileen. *Joseph Chaikin*. Cambridge: Cambridge University Press, 1984

Bogard, Travis and Jackson R. Bryer, eds. *Selected Letters of Eugene O'Neill*. New Haven: Yale University Press, 1988

Bogard, Travis, Richard Moody and Walter J. Meserve. *The Revels History of Drama in English. Volume VIII: American Drama*. London: Methuen, 1977

Bogdan, Robert. *Freak Show: Presenting Human Oddities for Amusement and Profit*. Chicago: University of Chicago Press, 1988

Bordman, Gerald. *The Oxford Companion to American Theatre*. New York: Oxford University Press, 1984

Boskin, Joseph. *Sambo: The Rise & Demise of an American Jester*. New York: Oxford University Press, 1985

Bost, James S. *Monarchs of the Mimic World or The American Theatre of the Eighteenth Century Through the Managers – The Men Who Made It*. Orono: University of Maine, 1977

Botto, Louis. *At This Theatre; Playbill Magazine's Informal History of Broadway Theatres*. New York: Dodd, Mead, 1984

Brecht, Stefan. *The Bread and Puppet Theatre*. 2 vols. London: Methuen, 1988

Brennan-Gibson, Margaret. *Clifford Odets, American Playwright: The Years from 1906 to 1940*. New York: Atheneum, 1981

Brett, Roger. *Temples of Illusion* [The Providence, RI, stage]. Providence: Brett Theatrical, 1976

Brockman, C. Lance, curator. *The Twin City Scenic Collection: Popular Entertainment 1895–1929*. Minneapolis: University Art Museum, 1987

Bronner, Edwin J. *The Encyclopedia of the American Theatre 1900–1975*. San Diego/New York: A. S. Barnes, 1980

Brown, Jared. *The Fabulous Lunts*. New York: Atheneum, 1986
*Zero Mostel*. New York: Atheneum, 1989

Brown, John Mason. *Dramatis Personae*. New York: Viking Press, 1963
*The Worlds of Robert E. Sherwood: Mirror to His Times*. New York: Harper & Row, 1965

Brown, John Russell and Bernard Harris, eds. *American Theatre*. London: Edward Arnold, 1967

Brown-Guillory, Elizabeth. *Their Place on the Stage: Black Women Playwrights in America*. Westport, CT: Greenwood Press, 1988

Brustein, Robert. *Seasons of Discontent: Dramatic Opinion 1959–1965*. New York: Simon and Schuster, 1965
*Who Needs Theatre: Dramatic Opinions*. New York: The Atlantic Monthly Press, 1987

Burdick, Elizabeth B., Peggy C. Hansen, and Brenda Zanger, eds. *Contemporary Stage Design U.S.A.* New York: International Theatre Institute of the US (dist. by Wesleyan University Press), 1974

Burge, James C. *Lines of Business: Casting Practice and Policy in the American Theatre 1752–1899*. New York; Peter Lang, 1986

Burns, Morris U. *The Dramatic Criticism of Alexander Woollcott*. Metuchen, NJ: Scarecrow Press, 1980

Buttitta, Tony and Barry Witham. *Uncle Sam Presents: A Memoir of the Federal Theatre 1935–1939*. Philadelphia: University of Pennsylvania Press, 1982

Callow, Simon. *Charles Laughton: A Difficult Actor*. New York: Grove Press, 1987

Carlson, Marvin. *The Italian Shakespeareans: Performances by Ristori, Salvini, and Rossi in England and America*. Washington: Folger Shakespeare Library, 1985

Chinoy, Helen Krich and Linda Walsh Jenkins. *Women in American Theatre*. Rev. ed. New York: Theatre Communications Group, 1987

Christopher, Milbourne. *The Illustrated History of Magic*. New York: Thomas Y. Crowell, 1973

Churchill, Allen, *The Great White Way: A Re-Creation of Broadway's Golden Era of Theatrical Entertainment*. New York: E. P. Dutton, 1962
*The Theatrical 20s*. New York: McGraw-Hill, 1975

Clarke, Norman. *The Mighty Hippodrome*. South Brunswick and New York: A. S. Barnes, 1968

Clurman, Harold. *The Divine Pastime: Theatre Essays*. New York: Macmillan, 1974
*All People Are Famous*. New York: Harcourt Brace Jovanovich, 1974

Cohn, Ruby, *Dialogue in American Drama*. Bloomington: Indiana University Press, 1971

Coigney, Martha Wadsworth, ed. *Theatre 2: The American Theatre 1868–*

*1968*. New York: International Theatre Institute of US, 1970; *Theatre 3: 1969–70*. New York: Charles Scribner's Sons, 1970; *Theatre 4: 1970–71*. Scribner's, 1972: *Theatre 5: 1971–72*. Scribner's, 1973. See also Gilder below

Coleman, Marion Moore. *Fair Rosalind: The American Career of Helena Modjeska*. Cheshire, CT: Cherry Hill Books, 1969

Comtois, M. E. and Lynn F. Miller. *Contemporary American Theater Critics: A Directory and Anthology of Their Works*. Metuchen, NJ: Scarecrow Press, 1977

Conolly, L. W., ed. *Theatrical Touring and Founding in North America*. Westport, CT: Greenwood Press, 1982

Cook, Doris E. *Sherlock Holmes and Much More, or Some of the Facts About William Gillette*. Hartford, CT: Connecticut Historical Society, 1970

Cooper, Roberta Krensky. *The American Shakespeare Theatre, Stratford, 1955–1985*. Washington, DC: Folger Shakespeare Library, 1986

Crawford, Cheryl. *One Naked Individual: My Fifty Years in the Theatre*. Indianapolis/New York: Bobbs-Merrill, 1977

Cruise, Boyd and Merle Harton. *Signor Faranta's Iron Theatre* [New Orleans]. New Orleans: The Historic New Orleans Collection, 1982

Csida, Joseph and June Bundy Csida. *American Entertainment: A Unique History of Popular Show Business*. New York: Billboard/Watson Tuptill, 1978

Curtin, Kaier. *"We Can Always Call Them Bulgarian": The Emergence of Lesbians and Gay Men on the American Stage*. Boston: Alyson Publications, 1987

Dalrymple, Jean. *From the Last Row*. Clifton, NJ: James T. White, 1975

Daniel, Walter C. *"De Lawd": Richard B. Harrison and "The Green Pastures."* Westport, CT: Greenwood Press, 1986

Davis, R. G. *The San Francisco Mime Troupe: The First Ten Years*. Palo Alto, CA: Ramparts Press, 1975

Davis, Susan G. *Parades and Power: Street Theatre in Nineteenth Century Philadelphia*. Philadelphia: Temple University Press, 1986

Dawes, Edwin A. *The Great Illusionists*. Secaucus, NJ: Chartwell Books, 1979

Demastes, William W. *Beyond Naturalism: A New Realism in American Theatre*. Westport, CT: Greenwood Press, 1988

Dent, Thomas C. and Richard Schechner, eds. *The Free Southern Theater by the Free Southern Theater*. Indianapolis: Bobbs-Merrill, 1969

Dimeglio, John E. *Vaudeville U.S.A.* Bowling Green, OH: Bowling Green University Popular Press, 1973

Donohue, Joseph W., Jr., ed. *The Theatrical Manager in England and America*. Princeton, NJ: Princeton University Press, 1971

Dormon, James H., Jr. *Theater in the Ante Bellum South 1815–1861*. Chapel Hill: University of North Carolina, 1967

Doty, Gresdna Ann. *The Career of Mrs. Anne Brunton Merry in the American Theatre*. Baton Rouge: Louisiana University Press, 1971

Douglas, Jane, ed. *Trustable and Preshus Friends* [Elsie Leslie]. New York: Harcourt Brace Jovanovich, 1977

Downer, Alan S. *American Drama and its Critics*. Chicago: University of Chicago Press, 1965

*American Drama*. New York: Thomas Y. Cowell, 1960

ed. *The Memoir of John Durang: American Actor, 1785–1816*. Pittsburgh: University of Pittsburgh Press, 1966

ed. *The American Theater Today*. New York: Basic Books, 1967

Duberman, Martin Bauml. *Paul Robeson*. New York: Alfred A. Knopf, 1989

Dukore, Bernard F. *American Dramatists 1918–1945*. New York: Grove Press, 1984

Durham, Weldon B., ed. *American Theatre Companies*. 3 vols. Westport, CT: Greenwood Press, *1749–1887*, 1986; *1888–1930*, 1987; *1931–1986*, 1989

Eckey, Lorelei F., Maxine Allen Schoyer, William T. Schoyer. *1,001 Broadways: Hometown Talent on Stage*. Ames: The Iowa State University Press, 1982

Eddleman, Floyd Eugene. *American Drama Criticism. Supplement II*. Hamden, CT: The Shoe String Press, 1976

Edwards, Anne, *The De Milles, An American Family*. New York: Harry N. Abrams, 1988

Engle, Lehman. *The Critics*. New York: Macmillan, 1976

Erenberg, Lewis A. *Steppin' Out: New York Nightlife and the Transformation of American Culture, 1890–1930*. Westport, CT: Greenwood Press, 1981

Ernst, Alice Henson. *Trouping in the Oregon Country: A History of Frontier Theatre*. 1961, Reprint. Westport, CT: Greenwood Press, 1974

Evans, Maurice. *All This ... And Evans Too! A Memoir*. Columbia, SC: University of South Carolina Press, 1987

Fabre, Geneviève. *Drumbeats, Masks, and Metaphor: Contemporary Afro-American Theatre*. Cambridge, MA: Harvard University Press, 1983

*Federal Theatre Project: A Catalog-Calendar of Productions*. Compiled by staff of the Fenwick Library, George Mason University. Westport, CT: Greenwood Press, 1986

*Federal Theatre Project Collection*. Washington, DC: Library of Congress, 1987

Fehl, Fred; text by William Stott with Jane Stott. *On Broadway: Performance Photographs by Fred Fehl*. Austin: University of Texas Press, 1978

Fehl, Fred. *Stars of the Broadway Stage 1940–1967*. New York: Dover, 1983

Fiedler, Leslie. *Freaks: Myths & Images of the Secret Self*. New York: Simon & Schuster, 1978

Fisher, Judith L. and Stephen Watt, eds. *When They Weren't Doing Shakespeare: Essays on Nineteenth-Century British & American Theatre*. Athens: University of Georgia Press, 1989

Fox, Ted. *Show Time at the Apollo*. New York: Holt, Rinehart and Winston, 1983

France, Rachel. *A Century of Plays by American Women*. New York: Richards Rosen, 1979

France, Richard. *The Theatre of Orson Welles.* Lewisburg: Bucknell University Press, 1977

Free, William and Charles Lower. *History Into Drama: A Source Book on Symphonic Drama.* New York: Odyssey, 1963

Frenz, Horst, ed. *American Playwrights on Drama.* New York: Hill and Wang, 1965

Frick, John W. *New York's First Theatrical Center. The Rialto at Union Square.* Ann Arbor: UMI Research Press, 1985

Friedl, Bettina, ed. *On to Victory: Propaganda Plays of the Woman Suffrage Movement.* Boston: Northeastern University Press, 1987

Furman, Evelyn E. Livingston. *The Tabor Opera House: A Captivating History.* Leadville, Colorado: n.p., 1972

Furnas, J. C. *Fanny Kemble: Leading Lady of the Nineteenth-Century Stage.* New York: The Dial Press, 1982

Gardner, R. H. *The Splintered Stage: The Decline of the American Theater.* New York: Macmillan, 1965

Garfield, David. *A Player's Place: The Story of The Actors Studio.* New York: Macmillan, 1980

Gassner, John. *Theatre at the Crossroads.* New York: Holt, Rinehart and Winston, 1960

Gentile, John S. *Cast of One: One-Person Shows from the Chautauqua Platform to the Broadway Stage.* Champaign: University of Illinois Press, 1989

Gilder, Rosamond, ed. *Theatre 1.* New York: ITI of US and DBS Publications, 1969. See also Coigney above

Gill, Brendan. *Tallulah* [Bankhead]. New York: Holt, Rinehart & Winston, 1972

Gill, Glenda. *White Grease on Black Performers.* New York: Peter Lang, 1989

Gohdes, Clarence. *Literature and Theater of the States and Regions of the USA. An Historical Bibliography.* Durham, NC: Duke University Press, 1967

Golden, Joseph. *The Death of Tinker Bell: The American Theatre in the 20th Century.* Syracuse: Syracuse University Press, 1967

Goldman, William. *The Season: A Candid Look at Broadway.* New York: Harcourt, Brace & World, 1969

Goldstein, Malcolm. *The Political Stage: American Drama and Theater of the Great Depression.* New York: Oxford University Press, 1974

*George S. Kaufman: His Life, His Theater.* New York: Oxford University Press, 1979

Gordon, Max, with Lewis Funke. *Max Gordon Presents.* New York: Bernard Geis Associates, 1963

Gordon, Ruth. *Ruth Gordon: An Open Book.* Garden City, NY: Doubleday, 1980

Gossett, Thomas F. *"Uncle Tom's Cabin" and American Culture.* Dallas: Southern Methodist University Press, 1985

Gottfried, Martin. *Opening Nights: Theater Criticism of the Sixties.* New York: Putnam's, 1969

*Jed Harris: The Curse of Genius.* Boston: Little, Brown, 1984

Green, Stanley. *The Great Clowns of Broadway.* New York: Oxford University Press, 1984

Greenfield, Thomas A. *Work and Work Ethic in American Drama, 1920–1970.* Columbia: University of Missouri Press, 1982

Grimsted, David. *Melodrama Unveiled: American Theater and Culture 1800–1850.* Chicago: University of Chicago Press, 1968

Guernsey, Otis L., Jr. *Curtain Time: The New York Theater 1965–1987.* New York: Applause Books, 1987

*Playwrights, Lyricists, Composers on Theater.* New York: Dodd, Mead, 1974

Hagen, Uta. *Sources: A Memoir.* New York: PAJ Publications, 1983

Haring-Smith, Tori. *From Farce to Metadrama: A Stage History of "The Taming of the Shrew," 1594–1983.* Westport, CT: Greenwood Press, 1985

Harris, Richard H. *Modern Drama in America and England, 1950–1970.* Detroit: Gale Research, 1982

Harrison, Gilbert A. *The Enthusiast: A Life of Thornton Wilder.* New Haven and New York: Ticknor & Fields, 1983

Hart, Lynda, ed. *Making A Spectacle: Feminist Essays on Contemporary Women's Theatre.* Ann Arbor: University of Michigan Press, 1989

Haskins, Jim. *The Cotton Club: A Pictorial and Social History of the Most Famous Symbol of the Jazz Era.* New York: Random House, 1977

Henderson, Kathy. *First Stage: Profiles of the New American Actors.* New York: Quill, 1985

Henderson, Mary C. *The City & the Theatre: New York Playhouses from Bowling Green to Times Square.* Clifton, NJ: James T. White, 1973

*Theater in America: 200 Years of Plays, Players, and Productions.* New York: Harry N. Abrams, 1986

*Broadway Ballyhoo: The American Theater Seen in Posters, Photographs, Magazines, Caricatures, and Programs.* New York: Abrams, 1989

Herron, Ima Honaker. *The Small Town in American Drama.* Dallas: Southern Methodist University Press, 1969

Hill, Errol. *The Theatre of Black Americans.* 2 vols. Englewood Cliffs, NJ: Prentice-Hall, 1980

*Shakespeare in Sable: A History of Black Shakespearean Actors.* Amherst: University of Massachusetts Press, 1984

Hill, West T., Jr. *The Theatre in Early Kentucky 1790–1820.* Lexington: University of Kentucky Press, 1971

Himmelstein, Morgan Y. *Drama Was a Weapon: The Left-Wing Theatre in New York 1929–1941.* New Brunswick, NJ: Rutgers University Press, 1963

Hirsch, Foster. *A Method to Their Madness: The History of the Actors Studio.* New York: W. W. Norton, 1984

Hirschfeld, Albert. *Hirschfeld by Hirschfeld.* New York: Dodd, Mead, & Co., 1979

Hodge, Francis. *Yankee Theatre: The Image of America on the Stage, 1825–1850.* Austin: University of Texas Press, 1964

Houseman, John. *Run-Through*. New York: Simon & Schuster, 1972
*Unfinished Business. Memoirs, 1902–1988*. New York: Applause Books, 1989
Hughes, Langston and Milton Meltzer. *Black Magic: A Pictorial History of Black Entertainers in America*. New York: Bonanza Books, 1967
Jacobs, Susan. *On Stage: The Making of a Broadway Play*. New York: Alfred A. Knopf, 1967
Jay, Ricky. *Learned Pigs & Fireproof Women: Unique, Eccentric and Amazing Entertainers*. New York: Villard Books, 1987
Jenkins, Ron. *Acrobats of the Soul: Comedy & Virtuosity in Contemporary American Theatre*. New York: Theatre Communications Group, 1988
Jewell, James C. with Thomas E. Howard. *Broadway and the Tony Awards: The First Three Decades 1947–1977*. Washington, DC: University Press of America, 1977
Johnson, Claudia D. *American Actress: Perspective on the Nineteenth Century*. Chicago: Nelson-Hall, 1984
Johnson, Stephen Burge. *The Roof Gardens of Broadway Theatres, 1883–1942*. Ann Arbor: UMI Research Press, 1985
Jones, Eugene H. *Native Americans as Shown on the Stage 1753–1916*. Metuchen, NJ: Scarecrow Press, 1988
Kaminsky, Laura J., ed. *Nonprofit Repertory Theatre in North America, 1958–1975*. Westport, CT: Greenwood Press, 1977
Kazan, Elia. *Elia Kazan: A Life*. New York: Alfred A. Knopf, 1988
Kennedy, Adrienne. *People Who Led to My Plays*. New York: Alfred A. Knopf, 1987
Kennedy, Harold J. *No Pickle, No Performance*. Garden City, NY: Doubleday, 1978
Kerr, Walter. *God on the Gymnasium Floor and Other Theatrical Adventures*. New York: Simon and Schuster, 1970
King, Christine E. and Brenda Coven. *Joseph Papp and the New York Shakespeare Festival: An Annotated Bibliography*. New York: Garland, 1988
Klein, Carole. *Aline* [Bernstein]. New York: Harper & Row, 1979
Kobler, John. *Damned in Paradise: The Life of John Barrymore*. New York: Atheneum, 1977
Koenig, Linda Lee. *The Vagabonds: America's Oldest Little Theater* [Baltimore, Maryland]. Rutherford: Fairleigh Dickinson University Press, 1983
Kolin, Philip C., ed. *American Playwrights Since 1945: A Guide to Scholarship, Criticism, and Performance*. Westport, CT: Greenwood Press, 1989
Koon, Helen Wickham. *How Shakespeare Won the West: Players and Performances in America's Gold Rush, 1849–1865*. Jefferson, NC: McFarland & Co., 1989
Kotsilibas-Davis, James. *The Barrymores: The Royal Family in Hollywood*. New York: Crown, 1981
*Great Times Good Times: The Odyssey of Maurice Barrymore*. Garden City, NY: Doubleday, 1977

Lahr, John. *Notes on a Cowardly Lion* [Bert Lahr]. New York: Alfred A. Knopf, 1969
  *Up Against the Fourth Wall.* New York: Grove Press, 1970
Larson, Carl F. W. *American Regional Theatre History to 1900: A Bibliography.* Metuchen, NJ: Scarecrow Press, 1979
Larson, Gary O. *The Reluctant Patron: The United States Government and the Arts, 1943–1965.* Philadelphia: University of Pennsylvania Press, 1983
Larson, Orville K. *Scene Design in the American Theatre.* Fayetteville: University of Arkansas Press, 1989
Laufe, Abe. *Anatomy of a Hit: Long-Run Plays on Broadway from 1900 to the Present Day.* New York: Hawthorn, 1966
  *The Wicked Stage: A History of Theater Censorship and Harassment in the United States.* New York: Frederick Ungar, 1978
Lawrence, Jerome. *Actor: The Life and Times of Paul Muni.* New York: Putnam's Sons, 1974
Leach, Joseph. *Bright Particular Star: The Life and Times of Charlotte Cushman.* New Haven: Yale University Press, 1970
Lee, Douglas Bennett, Roger L. Meersman, Donn B. Murphy. *Stage for a Nation: The National Theatre, 150 Years.* Lanham, Maryland: University Press of America, 1985
Leiter, Samuel L. *Ten Seasons: New York Theatre in the Seventies.* Westport, CT: Greenwood Press, 1986
  ed. *The Encyclopedia of the New York Stage* 2 vols. Westport, CT: Greenwood Press, *1920–1930,* 1985; *1930–1940,* 1989
Leonard, William Torbert. *Broadway Bound: A Guide to Shows That Died Aborning.* Metuchen, NJ: Scarecrow Press, 1983
  *Masquerade in Black.* Metuchen: Scarecrow, 1986
  *Once Was Enough.* Metuchen: Scarecrow, 1986
Levine, Ira A. *Left-Wing Dramatic Theory in the American Theatre.* Ann Arbor: UMI Research Press, 1985
Levine, Lawrence W. *Highbrow Lowbrow: The Emergence of Cultural Hierarchy in America.* Cambridge, MA: Harvard University Press, 1988
Lewis, Allan. *American Plays and Playwrights of the Contemporary Theatre.* New York: Crown, 1965
  *The Contemporary Theatre.* Rev. ed. New York: Crown, 1971
Lewis, Emory. *Stages: The Fifty-Year Childhood of the American Theatre.* Englewood Cliffs, NJ: Prentice-Hall, 1969
Lewis, Philip C. *Trouping: How the Show Came to Town.* New York: Harper & Row, 1973
Lewis, Robert. *Slings and Arrows: Theater in My Life.* New York: Stein & Day, 1984
Little, Stuart W. *Off-Broadway: The Prophetic Theater.* New York: Coward, McCann & Geoghegan, 1972
  *Enter Joseph Papp: In Search of a New American Theater.* New York: Coward, McCann & Geoghegan, 1974

*After the Fact: Conflict and Consensus. A Report on the First American Congress of Theatre.* New York: Arno, 1975

and Arthur Cantor. *The Playmakers.* New York: W. W. Norton, 1970

Long, E. Hudson. *American Drama From Its Beginning to the Present* [Bibliography]. New York: Appleton–Century–Crofts, 1970

Lovell, John, Jr. *Digests of Great American Plays.* New York: Crowell, 1961

Lowry, W. McNeil, ed. *The Performing Arts and American Society.* Englewood Cliffs, NJ: Prentice-Hall, 1978

Lynes, Russell. *The Lively Audience: A Social History of the Visual and Performing Arts in America 1890–1950.* New York: Harper & Row, 1985

Lyon, James K. *Bertolt Brecht in America.* Princeton, NJ: Princeton University Press, 1980

Malina, Judith. *The Diaries of Judith Malina, 1947–1957.* New York: Grove Press, 1984

Malpede, Karen, ed. *Women in Theatre: Compassion & Hope.* New York: Limelight, 1983

Mankowitz, Wolf. *Mazeppa: The Lives, Loves, and Legends of Adah Isaacs Menken.* New York: Stein & Day, 1982

Mapp, Edward. *Directory of Blacks in the Performing Arts.* Metuchen, NJ: Scarecrow, 1978

Marker, Lise-Lone. *David Belasco; Naturalism in the American Theatre.* Princeton, NJ: Princeton University Press, 1975

Marranca, Bonnie. *Theatrewritings.* New York: PAJ Publications, 1984

Marshall, Herbert and Mildred Stock. *Ira Aldridge: The Negro Tragedian.* Carbondale: Southern Illinois University Press, 1968

Martin, Jerry L. *Henry L. Brunk and Brunk's Comedians: Tent Repertoire Empire of the Southwest.* Bowling Green, OH: Bowling Green University Popular Press, 1984

Martin, Linda and Kerry Segrave. *Women in Comedy: The Funny Ladies from the Turn of the Century to the Present.* Secaucus, NJ: Citadel Press, 1986

Mathews, Jane De Hart. *The Federal Theatre, 1935–1939: Plays, Relief, and Politics.* Princeton, NJ: Princeton University Press, 1967

Matlaw, Myron, ed. *The Black Crook and Other Nineteenth-Century American Plays.* New York: Dutton, 1967. Useful historical introduction

ed. *American Popular Entertainment.* Westport, CT: Greenwood Press, 1979

McArthur, Benjamin. *Actors and American Culture, 1880–1920.* Philadelphia: Temple University Press, 1984

McCabe, John. *George M. Cohan: The Man Who Owned Broadway.* Garden City, NY: Doubleday, 1973

McCarthy, Mary. *Mary McCarthy's Theatre Chronicles 1937–1962.* New York: Farrar, Straus, and Co., 1963

McCaslin, Nellie. *Historical Guide to Children's Theatre in America.* Westport, CT: Greenwood Press, 1987

McConachie, Bruce A. and Daniel Friedman, eds. *Theatre for Working-Class Audiences in the United States, 1830–1980.* Westport, CT: Greenwood Press, 1985

McCullough, Jack W. *Living Pictures on the New York Stage*. Ann Arbor: UMI Research Press, 1983

McLean, Albert F. *American Vaudeville as Ritual*. Lexington: University of Kentucky Press, 1965

McNamara, Brooks. *The American Playhouse in the Eighteenth Century*. Cambridge, MA: Harvard University Press, 1969

   *Step Right Up: An Illustrated History of the American Medicine Show*. Garden City, NY: Doubleday, 1976

   ed. *American Popular Entertainments: A Collection of Jokes, Monologues & Comedy Routines*. New York: PAJ Publications, 1983

McNamara, Brooks, Jerry Rojo and Richard Schechner. *Theatres, Spaces, Environments: Eighteen Projects*. New York: Drama Book Specialists, 1975

Meserve, Walter J. *An Outline History of American Drama*. Totowa, NJ: Littlefield, Adams & Co., 1965

   ed. *Discussions of Modern American Drama*. Boston: D. C. Heath, 1965

   *American Drama to 1900: A Guide to Information Sources*. Detroit: Gale Research, 1980

   *An Emerging Entertainment: The Drama of the American People to 1828*. Bloomington: Indiana University Press, 1977

   *Heralds of Promise: The Drama of the American People in the Age of Jackson, 1829–1849*. Westport, CT: Greenwood Press, 1986

Mickel, Jere C. *Footlights on the Prairie: The Story of the Repertory Tent Players in the Midwest*. St. Cloud, MN: North Star Press, 1980 (c. 1974)

Mielziner, Jo. *Designing for the Theatre: A Memoir and a Portfolio*. New York: Bramhall House, 1965

Miller, Arthur. *The Theater Essays of Arthur Miller*. Ed. Robert A. Martin. New York: Viking Press, 1978

   *Timebends. A Life*. New York: Grove Press, 1987

Miller, James. *The Detroit Yiddish Theater, 1920 to 1937*. Detroit: Wayne State University Press, 1967

Miller, Jordan Y., ed. *American Dramatic Literature: Ten Modern Plays in Historical Perspective*. New York: McGraw-Hill, 1961. Useful historical introduction

Miller, Tice L. *Bohemians and Critics: American Theatre Criticism in the Nineteenth Century*. Metuchen, NJ: Scarecrow, 1981

Mills, John. *Hamlet on Stage: The Great Tradition*. Westport, CT: Greenwood Press, 1985

Minsky, Morton and Milt Machlin. *Minsky's Burlesque: A Fast and Funny Look at America's Bawdiest Era*. New York: Arbor House, 1986

Mitchell, Loften. *Black Drama: The Story of the American Negro in the Theatre*. New York: Hawthorn, 1967

   *Voices of the Black Theatre*. Clifton, NJ: James T. White, 1975

Moody, Richard. *Edwin Forrest. First Star of the American Stage*. New York: Alfred A. Knopf, 1960

   ed. *Dramas from the American Theatre 1762–1909*. Cleveland: World Publishing Co., 1966. Excellent introductions and bibliographies

*Ned Harrigan: From Corlear's Hook to Herald Square.* Chicago: Nelson Hall, 1980

Moore, Lester L. *Outside Broadway: A History of the Professional Theater in Newark, New Jersey, from the beginning to 1867.* Metuchen, NJ: Scarecrow, 1970

Mordden, Ethan. *The American Theatre.* New York: Oxford University Press, 1981

Morrison, Theodore. *Chautauqua.* Chicago: University of Chicago Press, 1974

Morrow, Lee Alan. *The Tony Award Book: Four Decades of Great American Theater.* New York: Abbeville Press, 1987

Mosedale, John. *The Men Who Invented Broadway: Damon Runyon, Walter Winchell & Their World.* New York: Richard Marek, 1981

Mosel, Tad, with Gertrude Macy. *Leading Lady: The World and Theatre of Katharine Cornell.* Boston: Little, Brown, 1978

Moskow, Michael H. *Labor Relations in the Performing Arts.* New York: Associated Council of the Arts, 1969

Moyer, Ronald L. *American Actors, 1861–1910: An Annotated Bibliography.* Troy, NY: The Whitston Publishing Co., 1979

Mullin, Donald C. *Victorian Actors and Actresses in Review: A Dictionary of Contemporary Views of Representative British and American Actors and Actresses, 1837–1901.* Westport, CT: Greenwood Press, 1983

Murphy, Brenda. *American Realism and American Drama, 1880–1940.* Cambridge and New York: Cambridge University Press, 1987

Nannes, Caspar. *Politics in the American Drama.* Washington, DC: Catholic University of America Press, 1960

Nathan, George Jean. *The Magic Mirror: Selected Writings on the Theatre.* New York: Alfred A. Knopf, 1960

Nathan, Hans. *Dan Emmett and the Rise of Early Negro Minstrelsy.* Norman: University of Oklahoma Press, 1962

Nelson, Stephen. *"Only a Paper Moon": The Theatre of Billy Rose.* Ann Arbor: UMI Research Press, 1987

Netzer, Dick. *The Subsidized Muse: Public Support for the Arts in the United States.* Cambridge and New York: Cambridge University Press, 1978

*New York Times Directory of the Theatre.* Introd. by Clive Barnes. New York: Arno Press, 1973

Newton, Esther. *Mother Camp: Female Impersonators in America.* Chicago: University of Chicago Press, 1979

Nightingale, Benedict. *Fifth Row Center: A Critic's Year On and Off Broadway.* New York: Times Books, 1986

Novick, Julius. *Beyond Broadway: The Quest for Permanent Theatres.* New York: Hill & Wang, 1968

Nye, Russel Blaine. *Society and Culture in America 1830–1860.* New York: Harper & Row, 1974

O'Connor, John and Lorraine Brown, eds. *Free, Adult, Uncensored: The*

*Living History of the Federal Theatre Project.* Washington, DC; New Republic Books, 1978

Oenslager, Donald M. *The Theatre of Donald Oenslager.* Middleton, CT: Wesleyan University Press, 1978

Ohringer, Frederic. *A Portrait of the Theatre.* Toronto: Merritt, 1979

Olney, Julian. *Beyond Broadway* [Charles Laughton–Paul Gregory]. Ardmore, PA: Dorrance & Co., 1979

Olszewski, George J. *Restoration of Ford's Theatre.* Washington, DC: US Dept. of the Interior, 1963

Owen, Bobbi. *Costume Design on Broadway: Designers and Their Credits, 1915–1985,* Westport, CT: Greenwood Press, 1987

Paolucci, Anne. *From Tension to Tonic: The Plays of Edward Albee.* Carbondale: Southern Illinois University Press, 1972

Parker, Dorothy, ed. *Essays on Modern American Drama: Williams, Miller, Albee, and Shepard.* Toronto: University of Toronto Press, 1987

*Performing Arts: Problems and Prospects* (Rockefeller Panel Report). New York: McGraw-Hill, 1965

Perry, John. *James A. Herne, The American Ibsen.* Chicago: Nelson Hall, 1978

Pilkington, John, ed. *Stark Young: A Life in the Arts. Letters, 1900–1962.* 2 vols. Baton Rouge: Louisiana State University Press, 1975

Poggi, Jack. *Theater in America: The Impact of Economic Forces, 1870–1967.* Ithaca: Cornell University Press, 1968

*Portraits of the American Stage, 1771–1971.* Washington: Smithsonian Institute Press, 1971

Postlewait, Thomas and Bruce A. McConachie, eds. *Interpreting the Theatrical Past: Essays in the Historiography of Performance.* Iowa City: University of Iowa Press, 1989

Pottlitzer, Joanne. *Hispanic Theater in the United States and Puerto Rico.* New York: Ford Foundation, 1988

Quintero, José. *If You Don't Dance They Beat You.* Boston: Little, Brown, 1974

Rampersad, Arnold. *The Life of Langston Hughes.* 2 vols. New York: Oxford University Press, 1986 and 1988

Ranald, Margaret Loftus. *The Eugene O'Neill Companion.* Westport, CT: Greenwood Press, 1984. Contains useful bibliographies and overviews

Rankin, Hugh F. *The Theater in Colonial America.* Chapel Hill: The University of North Carolina Press, 1965

Redfield, William. *Letters from an Actor.* New York: The Viking Press, 1967

Reynolds, R. C. *Stage Left: The Development of the American Social Drama in the Thirties.* Troy, NY: Whitston, 1986

Rice, Elmer. *Minority Report: An Autobiography.* New York: Simon & Schuster, 1963

Rich, Frank and Lisa Aronson. *The Theatre Art of Boris Aronson.* New York: Alfred A. Knopf, 1987

Rinear, David L. *The Temple of Momus: Mitchell's Olympic Theatre*. Metuchen, NJ: Scarecrow, 1987

Ripley, John. *Julius Caesar on Stage in England and America 1599–1973*. New York and Cambridge: Cambridge University Press, 1980

Ritchey, David, compiler. *A Guide to the Baltimore Stage in the Eighteenth Century: A History and Day Book Calendar*. Westport, CT: Greenwood Press, 1982

Robinson, Alice M., Vera Mowry Roberts and Milly S. Barranger. *Notable Women in the American Theatre*. Westport, CT: Greenwood Press, 1989

Rogoff, Gordon. *Theatre Is Not Safe: Theatre Criticism 1962–1986*. Evanston: Northwestern University Press, 1987

Rosenfeld, Lulla. *Bright Star of Exile: Jacob Adler and the Yiddish Theatre*. New York: Crowell, 1977

Rosenthal, Jean and Lael Wertenbakker. *The Magic of Light: The Craft and Career of Jean Rosenthal, Pioneer in Lighting for the Modern Stage*. Boston: Little, Brown, 1972

Rydell, Robert W. *All the World's a Fair: Visions of Empire at American International Expositions, 1876–1916*. Chicago: University of Chicago Press, 1984

Ryzuk, Mary S. *The Circle Repertory Company: The First Fifteen Years*. Ames: Iowa State University Press, 1989

Sampson, Henry T. *The Ghost Walks: A Chronological History of Blacks in Show Business, 1865–1910*. Metuchen, NJ: Scarecrow, 1988

Samuel, Raphael, Ewan MacColl, and Stuart Cosgrove. *Theatres of the Left 1880–1935: Workers' Theatre Movements in Britain and America*. London and Boston: Routledge & Kegan Paul, 1985

Sanders, Leslie Catherine. *The Development of Black Theater in America: From Shadows to Selves*. Baton Rouge: Louisiana State University Press, 1988

Sandrow, Nahma. *Vagabond Stars: A World History of Yiddish Theater*. New York: Harper & Row, 1977

Sarlos, Robert Karoly. *Jig Cook and the Provincetown Players: Theatre in Ferment*. Amherst: University of Massachusetts Press, 1982

Savran, David. *In Their Own Words. Contemporary American Playwrights*. New York: Theatre Communications Group, 1988

  *The Wooster Group, 1975–1985*: Breaking the Rules. Ann Arbor: UMI Research Press, 1986

Saxon, A. H. *P. T. Barnum: The Legend and the Man*. New York: Columbia University Press, 1989

Sayre, Henry M. *The Object of Performance: The American Avant-Garde Since 1970*. Chicago: University of Chicago Press, 1989

Schanke, Robert A. *Ibsen in America: A Century of Change*. Metuchen, NJ: Scarecrow, 1988

Schechter, Joel, *Durov's Pig: Clowns, Politics and Theatre*. New York: Theatre Communications Group, 1985

Schevill, James. *Break Out: In Search of New Theatrical Environments.* Chicago: Swallo Press, 1973

Schroeder, Patricia R. *The Presence of the Past in Modern American Drama.* Rutherford: Fairleigh Dickinson University Press, 1989

Seldes, Marian. *The Bright Lights. A Theatre Life.* Boston: Houghton Mifflin, 1978

Seller, Maxine Schwartz. *Ethnic Theatre in the United States.* Westport, CT: Greenwood Press, 1983

Senelick, Laurence. *The Age and Stage of George L. Fox, 1825–1877.* Hanover, NH: University Press of New England, 1988

Shacter, Susan and Don Shewey. *Caught in the Act: New York Actors Face to Face.* New York: New American Library, 1986

Shank, Theodore. *American Alternative Theater.* New York: Grove Press, 1982

Shattuck, Charles H. *The Hamlet of Edwin Booth.* Urbana: University of Illinois Press, 1969

*Shakespeare on the American Stage: From the Hallams to Edwin Booth.* Washington, DC: Folger Shakespeare Library, 1976

*Shakespeare on the American Stage: From Booth and Barrett to Sothern and Marlowe.* Washington: Folger and Cranbury, NJ: Associated University Presses, 1987

Shaw, Dale. *Titans of the American Stage: Edwin Forrest, the Booths, the O'Neills.* Philadelphia: The Westminster Press, 1971

Sheaffer, Louis. *O'Neill: Son and Playwright.* Boston: Little Brown, 1968; *Son and Artist.* Little Brown, 1973

Sheehy, Helen. *Margo: The Life and Theatre of Margo Jones.* Dallas: Southern Methodist University Press, 1989

Shivers, Alfred S. *The Life of Maxwell Anderson.* New York: Stein & Day, 1983

Shockley, Martin Staples. *The Richmond Stage 1784–1812.* Charlottesville: University Press of Virginia, 1977

Shyer, Laurence. *Robert Wilson and His Collaborators.* New York: Theatre Communications Group, 1989

Simon, John. *Uneasy Stages: A Chronicle of the New York Theater, 1963–1973.* New York: Random House, 1975

*Singularities: Essays on the Theater 1964–1974.* New York: Random House, 1975

Simon, Louis M. *A History of The Actor's Fund of America.* New York: Theatre Arts Books, 1972

Slide, Anthony. *The Vaudevillians: A Dictionary of Vaudeville Performers.* Westport, CT: Arlington House, 1981

Slout, William L. *Theatre in a Tent: The Development of a Provincial Entertainment.* Bowling Green, OH: Bowling Green University Popular Press, 1972

Smiley, Sam. *The Drama of Attack; Didactic Plays of the American Depression.* Columbia: University of Missouri Press, 1972

Smith, Geddeth. *The Brief Career of Eliza Poe*. Rutherford: Fairleigh Dickinson University Press, 1988

Smith, Michael. *Theatre Journal: Winter 1967*. Columbia: University of Missouri Press, 1968

Spitzer, Marian. *The Palace*. New York: Atheneum, 1969

Spoto, Donald. *The Kindness of Strangers: The Life of Tennessee Williams*. Boston: Little, Brown, 1985

Spritz, Kenneth. *Theatrical Evolution: 1776–1976*. Yonkers, NY: The Hudson River Museum, 1976

Stagg, Jerry. *The Brothers Shubert*. New York: Random House, 1968

Stanley, William T. *Broadway in the West End. An Index of Reviews of American Theatre in London, 1950–1975*. Westport, CT: Greenwood Press, 1978

Staples, Shirley. *Male-Female Comedy Teams in American Vaudeville, 1865–1932*. Ann Arbor: UMI Research Press, 1984

Stein, Charles W., ed. *American Vaudeville As Seen by Its Contemporaries*. New York: Alfred A. Knopf, 1984

Sterne, Richard L. *John Gielgud Directs Richard Burton in Hamlet*. New York: Random House, 1967

Stratman, Carl J. *American Theatrical Periodicals, 1798–1967. A Bibliographical Guide*. Durham, NC: Duke University Press, 1970

*Bibliography of the American Theatre Excluding New York City*. Chicago: Loyola University Press, 1970

Sweet, Jeffrey, ed. *Something Wonderful Right Away: An Oral History of The Second City & The Compass Players*. New York: Avon/Discus, 1978

Szilassy, Zoltán. *American Theater of the 1960s*. Carbondale: Southern Illinois University Press, 1986

Tanselle, G. Thomas. *Royall Tyler*. Cambridge, MA: Harvard University Press, 1967

Taubman, Howard. *The Making of the American Theatre*. New York: Coward McCann, 1965

Taylor, Dwight. *Blood-and-Thunder* [on Charles A. Taylor]. New York: Atheneum, 1962

Toll, Robert C. *Blacking Up: The Minstrel Show in Nineteenth-Century America*. New York: Oxford University Press, 1974

*On With The Show: The First Century of Show Business in America*. New York: Oxford University Press, 1976

*The Entertainment Machine: American Show Business in the Twentieth Century*. New York: Oxford University Press, 1982

Toohey, John L. *A History of the Pulitzer Prize Plays*. New York: The Citadel Press, 1967

Vaughan, Stuart. *A Possible Theatre*. New York: McGraw-Hill, 1969

Vaughn, Jack A. *Early American Dramatists From the Beginning to 1900*. New York: Frederick Ungar, 1981

Voss, Ralph F. *A Life of William Inge: The Strains of Triumph*. Lawrence: University Press of Kansas, 1989

Wainscott, Ronald H. *Staging O'Neill: The Experimental Years, 1920–1934.* New Haven: Yale University Press, 1988

Waldau, Roy S. *Vintage Years of the Theatre Guild 1928–1939.* Cleveland: Case Western Reserve University Press, 1972

Waldman, Max. *Waldman on Theater.* Garden City, NY: Doubleday, 1971

Warren, Neilla, ed. *The Letters of Ruth Draper. A Self-Portrait of a Great Actress.* New York: Charles Scribner's Sons, 1979

Watermeier, Daniel J., ed. *Between Actor and Critic; Selected Letters of Edwin Booth and William Winter.* Princeton, NJ: Princeton University Press, 1971

    ed. *Edwin Booth's Performances: The Mary Isabella Stone Commentaries.* Ann Arbor: UMI Research Press, 1989

Watson, Margaret G. *Silver Theatre: Amusements of Nevada's Mining Frontier, 1850 to 1864.* Glendale, CA: The Arthur H. Clark Co., 1964

Wearing, J. P. *American and British Theatrical Biography: A Directory.* Metuchen, NJ: Scarecrow, 1979

Webster, Margaret. *The Same Only Different.* New York: Alfred A. Knopf, 1969

Wharton, John F. *Life Among the Playwrights.* New York: Quadrangle, 1974

Whiting, Frank M. *Minnesota Theatre: From Old Fort Snelling to the Guthrie.* Minneapolis: Pogo Press, 1988

Wilk, John R. *The Creation of an Ensemble: The First Years of the American Conservatory Theatre.* Carbondale: Southern Illinois University Press, 1986

Williams, Henry B., ed. *The American Theatre: A Sum of Its Parts.* New York: Samuel French, 1971

Williams, Jay. *Stage Left.* New York: Scribner's, 1974

Williams, Mance. *Black Theatre in the 1960s and 1970s: A Historical-Critical Analysis of the Movement.* Westport, CT: Greenwood Press, 1985

Wilmeth, Don B. *The American Stage to World War I: A Guide to Information Sources.* Detroit: Gale Research, 1978

    *American and English Popular Entertainment: A Guide to Information Sources.* Detroit: Gale Research, 1980

    *George Frederick Cooke: Machiavel of the Stage.* Westport, CT: Greenwood Press, 1980

    *The Language of American Popular Entertainment: A Glossary of Argot, Slang, and Terminology.* Westport, CT: Greenwood Press, 1981

    *Variety Entertainment and Outdoor Amusements: A Reference Guide.* Westport, CT: Greenwood Press, 1982

    and Rosemary Cullen, eds. *Plays by Augustin Daly.* Cambridge: Cambridge University Press, 1984. Contains useful historical essay

    and Rosemary Cullen, eds. *Plays by William Gillette.* Cambridge: Cambridge University Press, 1983. Contains essay on Gillette's career

Wilson, Garff B. *A History of American Acting.* Bloomington: Indiana University Press, 1966

*Three Hundred Years of American Drama and Theatre.* Englewood Cliffs, NJ: Prentice-Hall, 1973

Wright, William. *Lillian Hellman: The Image, The Woman.* New York: Simon & Schuster, 1986

Young, William C. *American Theatrical Arts: A Guide to Manuscripts and Special Collections in the United States and Canada.* Chicago: American Library Associations, 1971

*Famous Actors and Actresses on the American Stage: Documents of American Theater History.* 2 vols. New York: R. R. Bowker, 1975

*Famous American Playhouses: Documents of American Theater History.* 2 vols. Chicago: American Library Association, 1973

Zeidman, Irving. *The American Burlesque Show.* New York: Hawthorn, 1967

Zellers, Parker. *Tony Pastor: Dean of the Vaudeville Stage.* Ypsilanti: Eastern Michigan University Press, 1971

Ziegler, Joseph Wesley. *Regional Theatre: The Revolutionary Stage.* Minneapolis: University of Minnesota, 1973

Zivanovic, Judith K., ed. *Opera Houses of the Midwest.* n.p.: The Mid-America Theatre Conference, 1988

# Index